Chris Wilkins

Managerial Marketing:
The Ultimate Advantage

Managerial Marketing:
The Ultimate Advantage

B. CHARLES AMES
Chairman and CEO, ACME-Cleveland Corp.

JAMES D. HLAVACEK
Weatherhead School of Management
Case Western Reserve University,
and Principal, Managerial Marketing, Inc.

MANAGERIAL MARKETING, INC.
P.O. BOX 1177
MOUNTAINSIDE, N.J. 07092

This book is dedicated to our understanding and supportive partners,
Jay Ames and Ursula Hlavacek.

First Edition

Library of Congress Cataloging in Publication Data

Ames, B. Charles.
Managerial marketing

Bibliography: p.
Includes index.
1. Marketing—Management. I. Hlavacek, James D.
II. Title.
HF5415.13.A45 1984 658.8 84-15423
ISBN 0-930239-00-8

Manufactured in the United States of America

Acknowledgments

While we are entirely responsible for writing this book, many people made some very helpful contributions.

First we owe a thank you to Ted Alfred, Dean of the Weatherhead School of Management at Case Western Reserve University, who served as a matchmaker in bringing us together. We are also very indebted to the hundreds of managers, from a wide range of industries, who influenced our thinking. These managers and their corporations served as our laboratories to observe good and bad marketing management practice.

There were a number of people who provided us with specific examples, materials, approaches, and constructive comments. They were: Igor Ansoff, Ray Corey, Bob Garda, Dick Grimm, George Havens, Dick Hill, Phil Hofmann, Hugh Luke, Don Manning, Mike Marvin, Tommy McCuistion, Jim Narus, Emory Orahood, Andy Pearson, Mohan Reddy, Sara Roche, Paul Ruckman, Milt Shapiro, Don Sommers, and Tim Wilson.

The writing and rewriting of chapters created an enormous typing task. We are grateful to Cheryl Guizzotti, Adrienne Koppenhaver, Anita Nuibe, and Debbie White for wading through our notations and deciphering our handwriting.

Foreword

This is a book that has been waiting to be written. Its timing is brilliant; if anything, it is a bit overdue.

In an era when competition has become intense in countless industrial businesses, when the nature of competition has become global, and when the pace of technological change has cut the life cycles of many products from years to months, Chuck Ames and Jim Hlavacek have written a book that is at once conceptually insightful and practically useful.

Readers, from the chief executives of major industrial organizations to the sales managers of small single-product divisions, will find this book immensely helpful. Starting with the simple proposition that "gearing the business to be responsive to customer or user needs . . . is what marketing is all about," the authors present early in their book an excellent summary of how customers make buying decisions and then describe some helpful ways to build understanding of both your customers and your competitors.

The chapter on segmenting markets should be valuable to every industrial marketing executive.

Building on the notion of market segmentation, which has been a hallmark of consumer-goods marketing for decades, Ames and Hlavacek illustrate a variety of approaches for delineating markets and customer groups in the industrial world.

And so it goes. The book is unprecedented in its coverage of industrial marketing topics. It ranges from product development to the implementation of sales programs, from pricing to broad matters of organization structure.

Recently two of my partners collaborated on a book that became an extraordinary bestseller, *In Search of Excellence.** In this book Peters and Waterman identify eight attributes of management that they found were common to a sample of high performing companies. One of those eight attributes is "being close to the customer," and the point is illustrated by examples from corporations like IBM, Boeing, Caterpillar, Hewlett Packard, and Proctor and Gamble.

In *Managerial Marketing: The Ultimate Advantage* Ames and Hlavacek take the idea of being "close to the customer" and develop it into a readable and important handbook for executives. It is a book that should be widely read . . . and studied.

D. Ronald Daniel
Managing Director
McKinsey & Company

**In Search of Excellence,* Thomas J. Peters, Robert H. Waterman, Harper & Row, 1982.

Contents in Brief

Detailed Contents

II EVALUATING THE MARKET ENVIRONMENT 65

III MANAGING THE MARKETING MIX 139

Introduction

During the past few years, markets the world over, as well as the businesses that serve these markets, have undergone a period of dramatic and, for many, painful change. Demand eroded sharply in many markets that represent the industrial backbone of our country (e.g., chemicals, steel, machine tools, automotive, farm, and construction equipment) and many question when or even whether former demand levels will be achieved. At the same time, a wave of foreign competition and a host of new materials, products and technologies crowded their way into the marketplace and captured share position from producers that failed to recognize or respond to the rapid technological and structural changes that have occurred. Many companies and even industries have been seriously weakened and in some cases destroyed by the magnitude and velocity of these changes.

Some of the market and competitive dislocations that have occurred will correct themselves as the world recovers from the oil shock, several years of extraordinary inflation, and the most severe recession since the 1930s. Many markets that have been in a free-fall condition will stabilize and demand patterns will improve. However, the high growth rates of the 1960s and 1970s are unlikely to be achieved again. In fact, many markets will show flat or declining growth trends. The head-start quality and manufacturing cost advantages achieved by the Japanese will diminish as other industrial powers respond by upgrading their manufacturing capabilities. Also, the labor cost advantages enjoyed by many lesser developed countries will diminish as the more advanced industrial nations build more automation into their manufacturing base.

As business confidence is restored and companies the world over seek to rebuild and strengthen their competitive positions, billions will be invested in new products, new technologies, and factory automation. While the prospect of this scenario is encouraging, it does not signal the end of problems for many companies that now must contend with smaller or slower-growing markets and an already eroded business base. Certainly, it is doubtful that these firms will be able to grow and prosper by merely riding industry growth curves as they have in the past. Some will drain their uncommitted capital or go deeper into debt to develop new technologies and products and lower-cost manufacturing capabilities but still fail to regain lost ground. Others will enter new fields that appear promising to improve their sales and market position but fail to generate necessary profit returns. Superior performance will only be consistently achieved by those companies blessed with management that ensures all major spending and investment decisions for new products, technologies, and manufacturing capabilities are driven by market-based considerations. This is the underlying theme of our book, which is based on our firm belief that management in almost any business can achieve an "ultimate advantage" if it ensures the firm is driven by marketing decisions.

Our reasoning is underscored by the following comments taken from a talk given by Jack Welch, Chairman and CEO of the General Electric Company. Mr. Welch's talk, titled "Where Is Marketing Now That We Really Need It?"[1] clearly indicates that

[1]"Where Is Marketing Now That We Really Need It?" The Conference Board's 1981 Marketing Conference, October 28, 1981.

marketing or lack of it is high on the list of causes for our industrial decline.

> "The edge has been dulled, and the effects . . . the losses . . . are there: loss of productivity growth—loss of quality—loss of world share—loss of entire markets—and what's worse, loss of jobs. Today, Germany—not the U.S.—is the number one exporter of manufactured goods. And Japan—not the U.S.—is selling the most automobiles. As to causes? Lots of contradictory explanations.
>
> "Old equipment in aging factories: Do we lack the will, the capital, the machinery, or don't we have the way? . . . R & D: Some say too little 'R,' others, not enough 'D' . . . Work management? . . . Bureaucracy: Too much government intervention, or, not enough government support? And there's the cultural explanation—Americans . . . and their differences from both the Germans and Japanese.
>
> "There are lots of reasons for why we are out of condition. And I can subscribe to all of them as elements of the picture. But that's all they are—pieces of the picture—piecemeal causes—they don't frame the issue. By themselves, they don't account for the decline of our competitiveness in so many industries.
>
> "Yet I suggest a case can be made—a case closer to the interests of this audience today—that there's another cause . . . perhaps even a more comprehensive one—on which I haven't seen much public debate. I believe one could argue that our most significant miss has been in marketing—something we in America pioneered as a management concept nearly thirty years ago, but of late haven't practiced too well. . . . Something, I'd like to suggest, that the imperatives of the Eighties will force us to rediscover."

WHY IT IS DIFFICULT TO ACHIEVE

Mr. Welch's question, "Where Is Marketing Now That We Really Need It?" is clearly on target. The answer is less clear because in this day and age, no one really quarrels with the importance of marketing. In fact, it would be hard to get anyone to argue against the idea that gearing the business to be responsive to customer or user needs—which is a simple but meaningful description of what marketing is all about—is not only sensible, but the only way to run the business. Executives and managers all around the world agree that increased marketing effectiveness is the key to being more competitive and accelerating profit growth. Despite their agreement on this point, many of these executives are disappointed with their company's marketing capabilities. To quote one company president:

> "I can't really say that our marketing group is doing the job it should and I don't know what to do about it. Our sales and administrative costs are up because of staff additions and higher salaries in the marketing department, but we are not getting the marketing leadership we need. We are about to invest 25 million dollars for new plant and equipment and I am uneasy about the whole project. Frankly, I don't feel comfortable about our ability to retain our competitive position against foreign competition with our current product lines and this big manufacturing investment will lock us into these products for the next ten years."

And, in the words of another president:

> "Our marketing effort or focus is simply too narrow. We concentrate way too much on selling more of today's product, and we think far too little about what our customers and competitors are doing or where new technology could lead us. Our engineering and manufacturing operations do not look to marketing for leadership and I know a lot of the things they do would be done differently if we were a stronger marketing company. There is no doubt in my mind that marketing is important, but how do we make it work the way it should?"

These executives are clearly concerned and perplexed about what they should do to achieve the improvement they want. The examples illustrate an all too common problem. Too many executives tend to regard marketing solely as an isolated function and reason that if they pay enough money or hire enough people the company's marketing should improve. Unfortunately, it doesn't work this way. Obviously, marketing is a function, but simply pouring more money or people into this function does not in any sense ensure a stronger marketing company. To be a significant force in a company, marketing must start at the top. Top management must provide the leadership and direction to ensure that marketing considerations are woven into the very fabric of every function or discipline involved in the business. Every business plan and decision must be based on an awareness and understanding of customer requirements and competitor positions in each market. Thinking this way is the only sound basis for the intelligent allocation of the company's resources, which is management's most important responsibility. Failure to think this way will likely lead to results that parallel those in the examples. The marketing function is expanded and costs are increased but the company's true marketing capabilities do not improve and top management is increasingly concerned about their company's ability to compete.

PURPOSE AND FOCUS

This book is not simply another book about marketing concepts or theories. It is a "how to" management book that describes what management at all levels and in all disciplines must do to make marketing a more powerful force in any company. Its focus is on the understanding management must have of marketing fundamentals and the role management must play to make a company operate effectively around the marketing concept.

The book should be of interest and practical value to several groups. In the broadest sense, it should be of interest to anyone working in or responsible for a business that is concerned about the competitive challenges ahead. More specifically, it should be of paramount importance to any CEO or senior manager who wants to ensure that marketing is the powerful force it should be in his or her company. Finally, it should be of interest to any ambitious employee in any discipline who aspires to a management position and wants to learn more about the requirements for effective marketing.

HOW THE BOOK SHOULD BE READ

While this is a serious book that deals with practical business concepts and proven principles, it has been written in a lively, conversational style designed to hold the reader's interest. The one-page vignettes or mini-cases that precede each chapter are unique and worth emphasizing. They are all taken from real-life situations and are designed to illustrate quickly the kinds of problems that prevent effective marketing. They provide a preview of the chapter content that follows, which in turn explains how to deal with the situations described in the vignette. Be sure to read all of the vignettes. They are fun, provocative, and interesting examples of what goes on in the business world and will strike a responsive chord among readers who have experienced similar situations.

There is logic to the sequence of chapters; however, each chapter is a freestanding module of "how to" information. This adds a great deal of flexibility to the way the book may be read and used. For the reader who is new to the marketing scene, it is probably better to stay close to the chapter sequence since the early chapters provide an essential foundation for the chapters that follow. For readers with substantial marketing experience, the book may be regarded as a reference source, and chapters may be selected according to particular interests or current needs.

I

ESTABLISHING THE FOUNDATIONS

1

The Substance of Managerial Marketing

Ambex was a successful $25 million manufacturer of telecommunications equipment located on the West Coast, which had grown rapidly around a narrow line of technologically superior transmission devices. The company's president, who invented the products and founded the business in 1972, was convinced he had to do a better job of marketing to be competitive. He had personally recruited and hired Charles Bruce to do the job. Charles had majored in marketing and worked as a sales engineer and an area sales manager for a competing manufacturer for five years before returning to school for an MBA. He was pleased with his new assignment: The position of marketing manager was new to the company, and he wanted a chance to show how a strong marketing effort could pay off.

His enthusiasm, however, was short-lived. A week after he arrived on the job, the company's senior vice president of manufacturing made it clear what he and the other operations managers thought of the idea of marketing. He pointed out that his department had worked well with the company sales manager over the years, and it was hard for him to see what Charles was going to "bring to the ball game." But he did invite Charles to attend his next weekly staff meeting to explain to the manufacturing group what marketing was and how it could help the company.

Charles, anxious to have the opportunity to explain why marketing was so important to the future of Ambex, agreed. That night he sat down to plan his presentation. Charles was no fool; he knew full well how important this meeting was to his success at Ambex and ultimately to his career as a marketing executive.

Why did Charles get such a cold reception?

Why does he have to prove the value of marketing?

What are some things he should do to prepare for the meeting?

Only in a very few industrial companies can executives honestly say they are happy with what marketing has done for them. More important, in even fewer can they support this belief with concrete evidence of improved results. The majority of executives in the industrial world talk about the concept, but it's hard to find examples where strong marketing has actually produced positive results. And in many companies, executives are downright discouraged with the results of their efforts. Very few of these executives have written the concept off; it is fundamentally too sound. But many of them are perplexed about what they need to do to get the results they want.

This chapter is designed to shed some light on the roadblocks that have prevented industrial companies from getting the payoff they should from marketing, as well as to present some ideas on how to clear these obstacles out of the way. It should serve as a useful introduction to later chapters, which will cover the key points made here in greater detail.

WHERE MARKETING FAILS

Marketing in the industrial world has not measured up to expectations in many companies because management has concentrated on the trappings rather than the substance. When most executives talk about what their companies have done to become more marketing-oriented, they usually point to such things as:

Declarations of support from top management in the form of speeches, annual reports, or talks to the investment community.

Creation of a marketing organization, including appointment of a marketing head and product or market managers, transfer to marketing of the product development and service functions, establishment of a market research function, salespeople reassigned around markets, advertising function strengthened.

Adoption of new administrative mechanisms, such as formal marketing planning approaches, more and better sales information, and revised information systems structured around markets rather than products.

Increased marketing expenditures for staffing, training and development, advertising, marketing, research.

Our point is not that these moves are useless, but that by themselves they are no guarantee of marketing success. Effective industrial or business-to-business marketing requires a fundamental shift in attitude throughout the company so that everyone in every functional area places paramount importance on being responsive to market needs. This is why the steps taken in most companies are nothing but trappings: They fail to accomplish this shift in attitude. And without this shift in attitude, the most highly developed marketing operation cannot produce any real results.

Why have so few companies gone beyond the trappings and achieved the change in attitude that ensures substantive marketing? Experience suggests that frequently one or more of these situations exist:

In a surprising number of cases, management does not fully understand the marketing concept as it applies to industrial companies.

In many other cases, management understands the implications of the marketing concept but has not committed itself to the actions and decisions needed to reinforce it.

In almost every case, management has failed to install the administrative mechanisms necessary for effective implementation of the concept.

We'll discuss each of these situations in turn, illustrating the kinds of problems they can cause and pointing out the major steps required to build substance into the industrial or business-to-business marketing effort.

UNDERSTANDING THE CONCEPT: KEY DIMENSIONS

When we say that in many cases management does not understand how the marketing concept applies to industrial companies, you may wonder how highly paid, presumably intelligent executives can fail to understand a concept that has been talked about and written about so extensively. But time and time again, we have found evidence that although most executives are quick to say that they understand and believe in the marketing concept, many of their actions and decisions show otherwise.

To prove our point, we need to define what marketing in the industrial world is not. It is not simply a departmental operation set up to handle advertising, promotion, merchandising, and selling, as might be the case in a consumer goods company. Nor does it necessarily mean striving for the greatest short-term profit contribution, going all out for volume, or seeking to serve everyone in the market. Rather, marketing in the industrial world is a total business philosophy aimed at improving profit performance by identifying the needs of each key customer group and then designing and producing a product or service package that will enable the company to serve selected customer groups or segments more effectively than its competition.

Marketing in the industrial world is much more a general management responsibility than it is in the consumer products field. In a consumer goods company, major changes in marketing strategy can be made and carried out within the marketing department through changes in advertising emphasis or weight, promotion emphasis or type, package design, and the like. In an industrial company, changes in marketing strategy are more likely to involve commitments for new equipment, shifts in product development activities, or departures from traditional engineering and manufacturing approaches, any one of which would have companywide implications. Marketing may identify the need for such departures, but general management must make the decision on the course the company will take to respond to the market. More important, it must see that this course is pursued in every functional area.

This definition reveals four key dimensions of business marketing: (1) aiming for improved profit performance; (2) identifying customer requirements; (3) selecting customer groups for which the company can develop a competitive edge; and (4) designing and producing the right product or service package or packages. Let's enlarge on each point.

1. *Aiming for improved profit performance.* Too many industrial companies talk a lot about a marketing and profit orientation, but a close look at how they make decisions reveals that volume is still the main consideration. Many of these companies would actually have a better profit picture if they gave a lower priority to volume, even if it meant scaling back the business.
2. *Identifying customer requirements.* There are still many equipment manufacturers who know all there is to know about their own technology and virtually nothing about how their customers really operate and make money. Many of these manufacturers spend millions developing labor-saving machinery for the least costly parts of their customers' production processes, or they design costly features without considering the value of such features to their customers. Then they wonder why their sales personnel are not able to sell the products.
3. *Selecting customer groups for emphasis.* We all know companies that strive to be all things to all customers. Companies that take a shotgun approach to the market inevitably end up with a warehouse of marginal product items and a long list of unproductive customers who generate a small fraction of sales and an even smaller fraction of profits. It is not surprising that more selective companies earn better profits, for they concentrate their limited resources on filling specialized product needs for customers who will pay for value.
4. *Designing the product or service package.* We have all heard horror stories about companies that failed in the marketplace because they tried to sell a Cadillac when the trade wanted a Model A Ford. Actually, a company does not have to be this far off the mark with its product or service package to be a marketing flop. The buying decision hinges on minor differences, and a company is in trouble whenever the competition has a package that matches the customer's needs just a little better.

Now that industrial or business marketing has been defined as a total business philosophy, it should be easy to distinguish those executives who understand the concept from those who do not. The president or general manager who consciously frames a total business strategy in response to market needs shows that he or she understands the marketing concept. The president or general manager who merely enlarges the marketing department, who continually spurs salespeople on to find new customers of any sort, or who indiscriminately adds more products to the line does not understand the concept in the industrial context.

COMMITMENT TO ACTION

Understanding the marketing concept is one thing; following through with the commitment to make tough decisions is quite another. Many companies stumble badly here.

Companies with a superior marketing effort, on the other hand, repeatedly demonstrate their commitment to follow the marketing concept by their willingness to require cooperation from all functions, to invest for long-term goals, and to face up to deficiencies in product, price, or service.

Functional Cooperation

A willingness to require—and force, if necessary—all functions to make the changes needed to be responsive to market needs is the first commitment top management must make. In many cases, doing this is more difficult than one might think. (See the box for an example that shows how hard it can be.)

Management often has had to overcome a long-standing preoccupation with objectives that cripple the marketing effort—objectives such as "get maximum engineering content into the units," "keep the plant loaded," "increase the value added," or "move maximum tonnage." Why these attitudes are so hard to overcome is understandable when you consider that in many industrial companies the product is the origin and chief reason for the past success of the enterprise. So people are naturally reluctant to abandon a concept that has proved itself superior. Remember too that marketing recommendations lack the precision of technical data. Typically, top management is confronted with hard numbers from manufacturing and engineering—material costs, production costs, installation costs, and so on. Marketing must make its case on the basis of forecasts and judgments. Of course these forecasts are quantified, but they can never be stated with as much precision as the performance data submitted by manufacturing and engineering. Finally, many general management executives have a technical background themselves and frequently tend to assess their products from a technical rather than a user point of view.

THE RUGGED ENGINEERING TRAP

In a capital goods company, management had historically focused on selling the largest, highest-powered, most maintenance-free units possible, with the thought that this approach favored its manufacturing economics. However, user needs had shifted toward smaller, less costly units without the rugged engineering characteristics required for maintenance-free operation. Since this trend was clear, and the company was losing its market position, marketing had recommended a major redesign of the product line. The company's manufacturing and engineering executives, who were acknowledged industry experts, argued convincingly that the current product design was still superior to any competitor's, and all that was needed was a better selling effort.

Faced with these conflicting points of view, top management decided to stick with the original product and put pressure on the marketing group for a more aggressive selling effort. It was not until the company lost substantial market share and its entire profit structure was threatened that the president could bring himself to put aside the expert opinion of his engineering and manufacturing executives and force the redesign.

An article about Sperry dramatically illustrates this point.[1] The company obviously has a large and presumably sophisticated marketing department. It spends millions of dollars each year on advertising and promotion programs, product development, and marketing planning. Yet the perception among financial analysts is clearly that it is not in any sense a marketing-oriented company:

> Sperry's mainframe mentality has locked them into solving problems with big computers, while the market is now moving to small micro processors. Sperry's technically oriented executives continue to focus on building bigger computers when the trend is in the other direction.
>
> Along the way, Sperry has also acquired a reputation for lacking sensitivity to customers and marketing. Says McClellen of Salomon Brothers, "They have never been marketing-oriented, and office automation is a tough marketing game." Explains a former Sperry executive, "The problem there is that their big computers were more than competitively necessary; they were at the leading technology edge, but there is a lack of marketing. I don't think the executives at Sperry realize the need and reason for marketing. Marketing, of course, encompasses not only selling, but also the packaging of products and systems to meet the current marketplace demand. A perfect example is Sperry's failure to have the new smaller micro computer products [which] has severely hurt the company."
>
> Wall Street analysts also note that IBM, Burroughs, NCR and Control Data have elected to buy state of the art technology and equipment from small specialty manufacturers like Convergent Technologies and Altos Computer. Sperry, by contrast, has opted to design and assemble new systems on its own. Many analysts are leery of what they call Sperry's "not invented here" philosophy and attitude on the company's part that no one but its own engineers can design a good product. However, the technology is moving too fast for them to rely on their own capabilities for everything.

In short, the task of shifting a company that has been dominated by engineering and manufacturing considerations to one that is truly marketing-oriented is enormous. It takes a lot of effort on the part of marketing executives to ensure that their proposals are carefully thought through, solidly documented with market and economic facts, and show an understanding of their impact on operating functions. And it also requires top management's understanding, as well as active support with both actions and words, to make the transition successfully.

Investing for the Long Term

Another commitment management must make is a willingness to invest to achieve long-term goals. The idea of investing to strengthen one's marketing position is accepted and practiced every day in consumer goods companies, even though these investments commonly have a relatively long payback period. For some reason, this idea does not seem to be acceptable or even considered in most industrial companies. Yet one could argue that an investment point of view is more critical in industrial companies than in consumer

[1] "Sperry's Mainframe Mentality," *Financial World*, March 15, 1983.

package goods companies because of the long time frame attached to the design, manufacture, and selling cycle for any new product. Designing performance or cost improvements for an already established product is a long, hard job. Developing the test or performance data to prove these advantages takes even more time. Finally, it is understandably difficult to get an industrial customer to even try a new or different piece of equipment that may cost thousands or even hundreds of thousands of dollars and, more important, affect an entire product process. So it can take years to gain full customer acceptance and build a solid market base for a product or service innovation in the industrial world.

Despite these considerations, management in many industrial companies is reluctant to look at increased expense for product development, testing, or launching as an investment, or to take any actions to build a stronger market position if those actions cut into short-term profits. One company, for example, had committed over a million dollars to the development of several new products to make its line more competitive. It had also invested heavily in manufacturing equipment to get the new products ready for the market. When plans for market introduction were being made, the marketing director requested a budget increase to set up a special sales group to work on these new products. He pointed out that although the added costs of a special sales group would not be recovered during the first year or so, by the end of two years the added volume would more than cover the cost of this group. The division manager at first balked at the budget increase, claiming it would cut too deeply into short-term profits. It took a lot of effort, but the marketing director finally convinced him this was shortsighted by saying: "If we don't get these products established this year, we will lose the slim lead time we have in the market—and the $2 million we sank into development and equipment will be down the drain."

Unhappily, only rarely does marketing succeed in getting the breathing room it needs to make a substantive contribution, as it did in this case. Usually, the overriding emphasis on the short term prevents new products from being developed or effectively launched when they are clearly needed. Division managers generally are reluctant to weed out marginal products or customers so the mix can be upgraded, even when this is clearly the right move. In all these cases, it is clear that the actions needed to respond to the market were blocked, without regard for the long-term impact, because they would have led to a temporary drop in profits.

Too few industrial executives are sympathetic to the idea of investing marketing dollars for a longer-term payoff, though they are perfectly willing to think in these terms when it comes to a capital proposal for new plant or equipment. There are executives who can be convinced that this approach can pay off. But until more of them start to think naturally in these terms, the marketing effort operates under a serious constraint.

Facing Up to Deficiencies

Management must also demonstrate its commitment to the marketing concept with a willingness to face up to critical deficiencies in product, costs, price, or service. A critical deficiency is anything the customer or user perceives that causes a negative reaction. These disadvantages are tough to overcome in any business, but they are impossible to ignore in the industrial world. Deficiencies cannot be glossed over when some steely-

THE TOP QUALITY PRODUCT THAT FAILED

A company that makes electronic test equipment was losing considerable business because management would not face up to the fact that its product was inferior to its competitors' in terms of both price and performance characteristics. This was the situation:

The company had been losing its share of market in one of its major product lines for several years. During this period, three different product managers had made the point that competitor changes in product and price had made it impossible to compete with this line as currently designed and priced. They recommended a redesign program to take cost out of the line and to add certain product features. At the same time, they proposed a lower price structure to make the line more competitive.

Top executives, including the vice president of marketing, reacted negatively. They simply could not accept the fact that their product line, which had traditionally been the top quality product, was that far out of position. Instead, they blamed the product managers for not having a good grasp of the business and for not being imaginative in their recommendations to rebuild market share.

It was not until a new division general manager came on the scene that this position was reversed. He took a fresh, unprejudiced look at his company's product as compared with the competition. The conclusion that he reached was that the product managers had been right, and that no amount of "more aggressive selling," "creative merchandising," or any other so-called marketing activity could overcome the basic competitive disadvantages of this product.

eyed engineer or purchasing agent typically makes or controls the buying decision. Unlike the consumer, the industrial buyer is largely unaffected by the emotional appeals of advertising, packaging, and merchandising.

Many industrial managers have a natural tendency to view their products through rose-colored glasses and to conclude that any advantages claimed for competitors' products are exaggerated or insignificant, that the competition is "giving the business away," or that it has a "cheaply engineered" or "shoddily manufactured" line, which explains its lower price (see the box). Admittedly, facing up to critical deficiencies is difficult, but we are not suggesting that a company must always do things differently or always suffer a short-term profit loss in order to follow the marketing concept successfully. It is clear, however, that critical deficiencies must be acknowledged if that is what it takes to be responsive to the market. Management cannot allow emotional ties to what has been done in the past to overrule market considerations. Otherwise, as a marketing manager in one company said: "Management does a lot of talking about following the marketing concept, but in reality it's a joke."

IMPLEMENTING THE CONCEPT

The third reason companies have not succeeded in getting positive results from marketing is ineffective implementation. The three key ingredients essential to proper implementation are (1) qualified people, (2) reliable market and economic information, and (3) planning to ensure the right strategic focus for the business. Many executives who are vitally interested in making marketing the cutting edge of the business are often frustrated in this attempt because of deficiencies in these areas. Let's examine each one individually to see where the difficulty lies.

Qualified People

It takes superior knowledge of the market competition and the economics of the business, along with a healthy dose of good business judgment, to be an effective marketing executive in the industrial world. Without these characteristics, the marketing executive cannot command the respect of the other executives and get them to follow marketing's lead. Yet many companies have staffed key marketing positions (marketing director, product manager, market manager) with people who clearly do not have any of these qualities.

Where does management go wrong? In some cases, the problem stems from a tendency to equate marketing with aggressive selling and thus to look only to the sales department for people to move into these positions. Many sales people simply are not able to develop a total company perspective, and their sales or volume orientation tends to dominate their marketing recommendations and decisions. As you would expect, with this point of view, they quickly lose the respect of other functional and top management executives, and they have no chance to influence major decisions. In other cases, management turns to the outside in a search for candidates with skills that will make the company marketing-oriented overnight. But except in rare cases, these people perform well below expectations, for they typically come equipped with skills that are not really applicable. There is no accepted bag of skills in business marketing that is readily transferable from one situation to another as there is in consumer goods marketing, where basic advertising and promotion skills are applicable to a wide range of product and market situations.

The experience of an equipment supplier to the telecommunications field illustrates this point. Top management had decided that the company needed a stronger marketing effort and recruited a successful sales manager from an electrical products company. His background included three years as a product line marketing manager, so he appeared to be very well qualified. His performance, however, was dismal. He did not understand the underlying technology and was unable to shepherd the company's new product program against very stiff competition, particularly from abroad. He also failed to understand the intricacies of designing and selling complex communication systems and was frequently caught off base with proposals that did not meet customer requirements. After six months, both top management and the individual recognized that he had a great deal of learning to do before he could really contribute to the company's marketing effort, and there was a real question in everyone's mind as to whether or not he should remain in the job.

Success in business-to-business marketing depends on skills related to a specific situation. It requires a comprehensive understanding of the particular market and of the economic and operating characteristics of the customers or users that make up that market. It also requires mature business judgment to achieve a balance among functional considerations (product design, manufacturing cost, selling price alternatives) and between long- and short-term interests, and then to come up with sound recommendations for achieving maximum profit growth.

In effect, the industrial marketing executive must be an embryo general manager, and this is what the most successful companies look for in staffing their key marketing positions. There is no magic in the way they get these people. They have no special recruiting sources, no extraordinary training or development programs; they do not pay excessive salaries, though they make sure salaries are fully competitive. What these companies do is very basic. They are aware that marketing people are attracted to a company in which the marketing function receives top priority. They therefore make certain that marketing is set up in the organization as the lead function, and they see to it that everyone understands its role. This means the marketing department has the responsibility for identifying the changing needs of the market and the opportunities these represent for the company. It means also that the marketing department is expected to translate market requirements into the actions that must be taken by the other principal functions of the company (R&D, engineering, manufacturing, finance) to capitalize on these opportunities. When we refer to marketing as the lead function of the company, we do not mean that marketing is organizationally superior to the other functions. Its role is to show the way to the marketplace, and the role of the other functions is to follow this lead and get the company firmly established.

Successful companies are also careful not to overlook sources that might provide good candidates. They seek able people who have the necessary qualities—or the potential to develop them—without regard for their functional background. In many cases, people from the financial, engineering, or manufacturing ends of the business have developed into marketing executives fully as effective as those who came via the sales route. Finally, these companies recognize that there is no shortcut to developing marketing executives. Whether they are home-grown or imported, they must be given both the time and the opportunity to learn about the business. The importance of this broad understanding of the business cannot be overemphasized; it is the foundation that permits the good marketing executive to make the kind of balanced decisions and recommendations that will ensure for marketing its rightful role as the lead function of the business.

Reliable Information

Even marketing people with the highest qualifications cannot operate effectively without reliable information. Yet many marketing executives complain that they simply do not have access to the kind of information necessary to make intelligent plans and decisions. Their complaints, which relate to both market data (market share, sales to end user segments) and cost and profit information, could be overcome with relative ease, for the raw data are almost always available somewhere in the company. The trouble is that information typically is not organized in a way that is useful to marketing executives. In the case of cost and profit data, accountants usually design the information for external reporting and for manufacturing and cost control. It is not geared to nailing down the profit consequences of selling individual items or various mixes to different customer groups or through different channels. And all too often, market data are fragmented and incomplete. For this marketing executives must shoulder most of the blame, for they simply have not defined the information they need and shown how it should be drawn together.

An example can show how important it is to have reliable market and economic data.

In one broad-line industrial products company, marketing management wanted to weed out some of the marginal items in the line to reduce inventory costs and free sales time for more profitable items. Exhibit 1-1 shows the picture the managers developed using the profit information available to them—gross margin. On the basis of this analysis, they decided to cut out several low-margin items, such as fiber B. Fortunately, before any items were dropped, a plant controller made a special analysis to determine the variable contribution per machine-hour that each item generated—that is, the profit each product contributed for the amount of plant capacity it used. His analysis, shown in Exhibit 1-1, revealed a different picture from the gross margin comparisons and caused everyone to wonder if they were on the right track. Then the division controller decided to look even deeper and made another special analysis to factor in the selling costs. As Exhibit 1-1 shows, once selling costs were considered, what initially were thought to be the low-profit items were actually the most profitable. Complete information resulted in a conclusion just the reverse of the original one. Now the company has completely recast its information structure so its marketing executives get this kind of information as a matter of course.

Many companies with successful marketing records have made similar revisions in their information structure. This does not mean they have stopped collecting the information necessary for external reporting or effective manufacturing control. Rather, they have added to their information structure data that enable their marketing executives to make fact-based decisions on products, channels, markets, and customers.

Strategic Planning

Most industrial companies regard planning as a key ingredient in their marketing effort. Many of them are quick to admit, however, that their efforts to do a good job of planning are not nearly as effective as they should be, and they cite this shortcoming as one of the chief reasons the marketing concept has not really taken hold. In a high percentage of cases, they are right. Soundly conceived market-oriented plans are the framework that keeps all the company functions operating around the marketing concept.

Planning, of course, is a broad and complicated subject in itself, and we cover it in more detail in later chapters. It is clear, however, that the reason many companies have difficulty with planning is that they pattern their efforts after companies in the consumer goods field. They tend to regard marketing as a separate function, and they develop separate marketing plans. This approach makes sense in the consumer products field, where the key volume and profit-making activities are within the marketing department (advertising, merchandising, promotion). It does not make sense in an industrial company, where activities outside the marketing function (manufacturing, engineering, technical service) typically control success or failure in the marketplace.

Companies that do a superior job of marketing concentrate their planning efforts on making sure they have the right strategic focus for the business. Reviewing the strategic focus is time well spent in an industrial company. For one thing, it is all too easy to develop "marketing myopia"[2] and allow the need to "load the plant" or "increase engineering

[2] See Theodore Levitt, "Marketing Myopia," *Harvard Business Review*, July–August 1960, p. 45.

EXHIBIT 1-1

THE CASE FOR GOOD INFORMATION

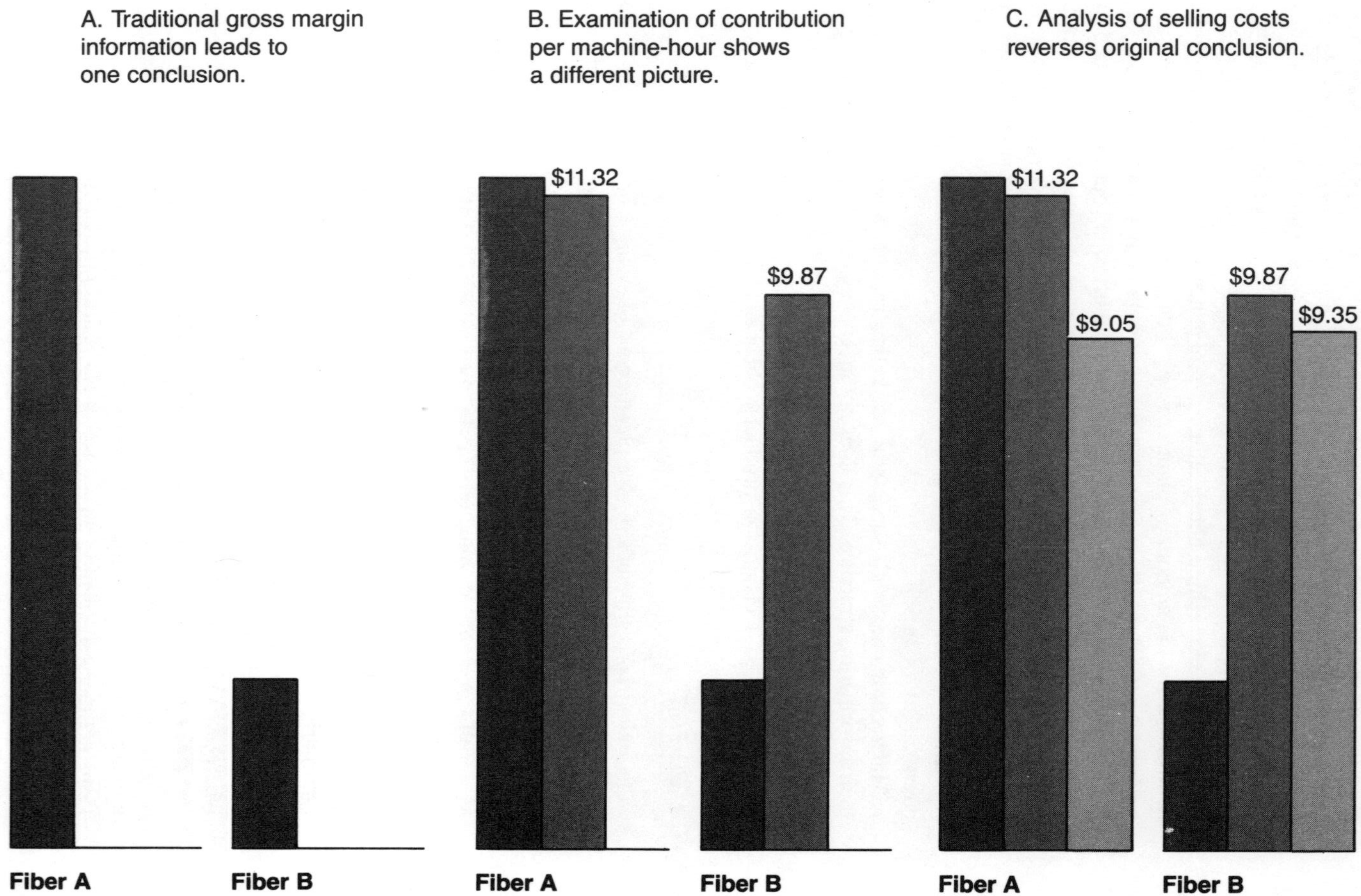

content" to override indications that customer needs are changing or that additional needs exist. Because of this pitfall, in many companies the thinking of management is constrained by existing products and technology; opportunities to gain a competitive edge in present markets, develop new markets, or enter related markets go unnoticed. Moreover, the velocity of technological change and the consequent impact of this change on the competitive structure, on customer acceptance of existing products, and on new market opportunities can easily make obsolete a strategic focus that was once highly successful (see the box).

In companies that take the strategic approach to planning, the marketing department, of course, plays the lead role in defining needs and opportunities, as well as in determining what it takes to serve various markets or segments. From this point on, however, planning becomes a collaborative effort, with all the key functions contributing their points of view in a series of face-to-face discussions. These companies place much less emphasis on the planning system—that is, on such components as format, techniques, and lengthy memos. Naturally, the recommended plan gets the inputs and final stamp of approval from top management before it becomes an operating blueprint for the business. This approach—based on a continuous dialogue between key managers rather than on the completion of forms by function heads working in isolation—ensures the kind of balancing among functions, and between long- and short-term interests, that is required to make the marketing concept work.

SHIFTING THE STRATEGIC FOCUS

The experience of a motor manufacturer shows how a shift in strategic focus can create vast differences in market potential and ultimately change the entire character of the business. Here is the picture:

> The company had traditionally held a 25 percent to 30 percent share of a market that was worth about $400 million and was growing at about 5 percent a year. Recognizing that it would probably have to cut into its margins to capture a larger share from competitors, management took a hard look at how the market might be defined differently to expand the opportunity.
>
> The first step was to include the drive linkage and systems that were powered directly from their motors. This more than doubled the potential market for this company and opened up a whole range of new product opportunities. Management then shifted its view of the market to include the whole field of automation. As management defined automation, this shift in focus gave the company a market of some $2 billion—eight to ten times the size of its original market opportunity. More important, the automation market is growing over 10 percent a year, or twice as fast as the motor market alone.
>
> In recent months, the president of the company has said repeatedly: "It took us a long time to define our market in the right way, but once we did, the door was open for a whole stream of new product businesses that we wouldn't even consider before. Getting the right product and market focus has contributed to our accelerated growth and profits more than anything else."

SUMMARY

There is nothing particularly sophisticated about the marketing concept as it applies to the industrial world. Nor is there anything conceptually difficult about what it takes to build substance into business-to-business marketing as opposed to simply having the trappings. What it takes is total company involvement—from top management to the shop floor—in the marketing effort, and management willingness to depart from traditional practices if this is what is required to be responsive to the market.

There are four key dimensions of the business marketing concept: (1) aiming for improved profit performance, (2) identifying customer requirements, (3) selecting customer groups, and (4) designing and producing the right product or services packages.

However, understanding the marketing concept is not enough. The marketing concept will not succeed without a strong commitment that involves functional cooperation, an investment in long-term goals, and facing up to company deficiencies.

In addition to commitment, successful implementation of the marketing concept is dependent on qualified people, reliable market and economic information, and planning to ensure the right strategic focus for the business.

Saying there is nothing particularly sophisticated about the marketing concept does not in any sense minimize the task of making an operations-oriented company into one that is market-oriented. It is a tough job. It takes time, probably several years, and a lot of training and development effort. Proof of the difficulty lies in the fact that only a few companies have done the job well. For those few that have been successful, however, the time and effort involved have been well spent. Their responsiveness to the market will give them a competitive advantage that is certain to accelerate their profit growth in the years ahead.

2

Industrial and Consumer Markets

The chairman and CEO of a *Fortune* 100 diversified manufacturing corporation, who had spent parts of his career in both the consumer and the industrial sectors of the company, was concerned that the industrial sector did not have as much of a marketing emphasis as the consumer sector. The consumer goods sector of the corporation was known for its strong advertising and promotion support. So the CEO appointed a marketing executive from one of the consumer goods units to a new position as corporate vice president of marketing, with the primary responsibility of developing more marketing emphasis in the industrial units. The CEO told the new corporate vice president of marketing: "I would like to see a marketing renaissance in our industrial business units!"

After three months in the job, the new corporate vice president of marketing had come to four conclusions about what he saw as the trouble in the industrial business units. First, marketing in the industrial units was a self-contained operation, whereas in the consumer divisions marketing teams were also located at the group level. Second, advertising and promotion activities appeared to have relatively low priority. Third, the industrial marketing executives appeared to be more concerned about customer needs and their operations than about psychological appeals or the esthetics of their products. Finally, industrial marketing tended to address worldwide customer needs and downplayed cultural differences among countries.

Before making recommendations to the CEO to correct these problems, the corporate vice president discussed his observations with some industrial sector executives. To his surprise, they disagreed sharply—and they told him why: "There is a world of difference between consumer and industrial marketing. What works in their world usually doesn't work in ours. You should spend some time in our plants and with our customers to learn how and why we go to market as we do. Once you have a chance to do this, we'll all feel more comfortable about how you might be of help to us."

Was the CEO wrong? Was the VP wrong? Were the industrial executives just being defensive?

How are industrial customers different from household buyers?

Why would psychological appeals and media hype fail to sell an industrial product?

The characteristics of the industrial marketplace are very different from those of the consumer goods marketplace. It is the failure to recognize and understand these differences that is the root of so many misconceptions about marketing in so many industrial firms. Industrial or business markets exist at all steps in the production chain from the extraction of raw materials up to, but not including, wholesale and retail transactions, which are consumer activities. Sometimes, industrial distributors or facilitators operate between five value-added stages. Table 2.1 shows the value-added stages in the chain.

TABLE 2.1

STAGES IN THE PRODUCTION CHAIN

First Stage	*Second Stage*	*Third Stage*	*Fourth Stage*	*Fifth Stage*	➡	*Consumption*
Raw materials extraction	Material processing	Manufacturing of parts and subassembly	Final assembly	Distribution and after-market		Wholesale and retail sale to household consumers

At each stage, actions add value to the product. Generally, the greater the value added at each step, the larger the profit margin or spread between purchase costs and selling price. Many industrial firms provide products or services at more than one stage in the chain. The more stages an industrial firm participates in, the more linked or integrated the firm is. For example, in stage 1, a firm extracts a metal ore from open pit mines. In stage 2, manufacturing or processing, it separates the foreign material from the metal ore and in a chemical process produces nearly pure concentrate pellets. Also in stage 2, metal ingots are produced and then transformed into strips, coils, and bars. In stage 3, the material is made into electronic chip components that are sold to stage 4 manufacturers of computers and numerous electronic products.

Of the six stages in the production chain, industrial marketing dominates the first five stages. While it is difficult to be precise on this point, it is clear that the dollar value of industrial or business-to-business transactions is far greater than the value of transactions in the final stage—wholesale-retail household consumption. There are also many more people employed in the five industrial stages than there are in the manufacturing and marketing of household products. This is why one can argue persuasively that activities in our industrial markets impact our whole economy to a far greater extent than the manufacturing and retailing of consumer products.

One way to appreciate the stages, and the interrelationship of stages, in the production chain in the business marketplace is to examine the dynamics involved in the manufacture of a major industrial product. The Electromotive Division of General Motors produces diesel locomotives. Every working day, their main production facility completes 5.5 diesel locomotives that cost between $550,000 and $750,000 each. The only other American producer is General Electric. The domestic customer base consists of about eight railroads. Internationally, the customers are government-owned railroads that often have different track gauge specifications. The life cycle of industrial products is usually long; for locomotives, it is 30 years or longer. As a consequence, the maintenance and overhaul or replacement parts demand is great. Rebuilding and supplying replacement parts business exceeds the 900 new units per year purchased by the industry. As more locomotives are produced and put into service, the maintenance market demand increases geometrically. In 1980, GM had 27,000 locomotives in place that needed parts.

The General Motors division assembles the locomotive units at the third stage in the value-added chain. Thousands of industrial firms supply General Motors with crank cases, controls, wheels, components, and subassemblies for the horsepower specifications of each railroad in each country. This same complex supplier process takes on a different set of dynamics when General Motors tailors its basic diesel engine to fit specific end-user requirements for oil rigs or mobile power units or tugboat engines. Note the breadth and levels of business activity derived from the demand for the original product.

DERIVED DEMAND

The demand for all industrial products can be traced to and is derived from consumption at the individual or household level, even though that demand may be very remote from the specific industrial product supplied. This is why changes in consumer spending patterns have such major repercussions for the entire economy. For example, when consumers started conserving electricity in response to the high electric bills that accompanied the energy crisis, demand for electricity slackened. As a consequence, utilities cut back orders for new generating equipment from suppliers of gas turbines. These suppliers in turn reduced their orders to component and subassembly manufacturers. And these firms reduced their orders for steel and specialty metals produced by companies that extract raw materials from the earth. Less extraction, in turn, reduced the need for heavy mining machinery, and so another web of suppliers saw their business reduced.

Some industrial or business markets depend on demand that is derived from both private and public sector spending, or a combination of both. Take construction equipment as an example. Private sector spending includes the building of private roads, private industrial and commercial buildings, and residential housing. Public sector spending includes the construction of roads, waterways, or projects such as bridges, public office buildings, or government housing. Both private and public sectors are important markets for products such as excavating machines, cranes, and other kinds of heavy construction equipment.

Since all industrial product demand is derived from consumer spending patterns, it is important for the industrial manufacturer to watch for major population trends and shifts in social patterns (such as later marriages, fewer household formations, lower birth rates) that will ultimately affect industries the company supplies now or might supply in the future. A major population trend in the United States and in other developed countries is that people are having fewer children and having them later. The implications of this trend are quite severe for many industrial manufacturers in the production chain. For example, the supplier of glass containers to the baby food industry most likely will be faced with a declining market. Conversely, related trends toward increased leisure time and activity and toward discretionary spending can favorably impact other manufacturers—such as the manufacturer of aircraft required to meet the increased demand for transportation and the manufacturer of restaurant equipment required to accommodate the increased demand for dining outside the home. The astute marketer identifies these trends and serves the industries that have a favorable derived demand for the long term, shifting the focus away from declining markets. Because the concept of derived demand is so fundamental, the industrial marketer should always look beyond immediate customers to analyze the causal factors of demand.

NARROWER CUSTOMER BASE

Most consumer goods products are purchased by thousands or even millions of customers every day, month, or year. An industrial product has a much narrower customer base. An active base of 4,000 to 5,000 customers is considered very large for an industrial product. It is not unusual for 100 to 250 key or major customers from that base to account for well over half the sales volume. In some situations, a handful of customers represent 100 percent of a firm's customer base, and one or two other suppliers may be vying to serve this same small group of customers. The narrow industrial customer base is especially common when original equipment manufacturers (OEMs) supply a large customer like General Motors or Caterpillar with a component or subassembly. A manufacturer of large aircraft landing gear, for example, has a domestic customer base limited to Boeing, Lockheed, and McDonnell-Douglas. Similarly, the three jet engine marketers —United Technologies, General Electric, and Rolls Royce—have only a handful of commercial and military aircraft buyers.

The narrower the industrial customer base, the more control or influence the customer has over suppliers. This narrow customer base leads to a much closer relationship between buyer and seller than exists in consumer markets. No one household customer can exert this kind of purchasing power. As an industrial customer's quantity requirements grow, it can exert added pressure for concessions (lower prices, extended terms, consigned stocks, and so on). Industrial firms with a very narrow base of, say, two to four customers for a product line will often attempt to reduce their vulnerability to swings in their customers' business by broadening the base so no one customer is more than 10 percent of the demand for one product line.

There are many approaches to broadening a customer base. One involves marketing the same product to customers in new countries. Another approach is to seek new applications or new market uses for the same product. A third approach is to focus more on the maintenance and replacement aftermarket, which nearly always has a broader customer base than the original market for the product. If it is difficult to have a broader base of customer prospects, it is desirable to concentrate on the more rapid growth customers who are growing or maintaining a strong competitive position.

MORE RATIONAL BUYING DECISIONS

Industrial products are not sold because someone really wants to buy them. Industrial or business customers have economic requirements, not wants. Unlike consumer products, industrial products do not make anyone look or feel better, and they generally do not have any significant esthetic value. Industrial products are bought only to help the user manufacture, distribute, or sell more effectively so that it can improve its economic and competitive position. This means industrial buyers require much more specific cost and performance information about the products they purchase. This information is essential so the buying organization can determine the economic value of the item to its operations or its customers. The industrial supplier has the burden of providing documented test data to support any cost or performance claims. This means there is no place for exaggeration or puffery in industrial advertising and promotional activities. Many industrial customers routinely check actual cost and performance against suppliers' claims and demand restitution in the event unfavorable variances occur.

Industrial firms emphasize price and quality checks and balances in procurement that are often nonexistent in household purchase situations. In addition, most industrial customers are well aware of their needs. As a consequence, customers often provide parameters and specification requirements that help guide product development or determine whether a product will function within their system. In contrast, household customers' needs and wants are often much less specific or even latent. Household customers' less defined needs often result in purchases they later realize they really do not need or want. In the industrial world there is personal and career risk for wrong purchase decisions. When an industrial item is purchased but never used, the purchaser has failed in its responsibility to employ the capital that has been invested in the business prudently. For example, a maintenance manager for a major oil producer came under fire from top management when, to save money, he replaced the original pump on an oil field gathering system with a much lower-priced one. The pumping application required a high pressure pump that could move high viscosity crude oil. The lower-priced pump was not designed to meet the rigorous requirements of this application and soon developed leaks and broke down completely on several occasions. Management's criticism of the maintenance manager's decision was understandable. The savings on the pump was a few hundred dollars; the downtime cost of each oil rig was $50,000 an hour.

MORE BUYING INFLUENCES AND LOCATIONS

Nearly all household consumer decisions involve only one or two influences or decision makers—wife and husband or child. The industrial procurement decision typically revolves around engineering, manufacturing, and even sales considerations for the end product. This means that all these departments, in addition to the purchasing agent, have a voice in the buying decision. Engineers usually set the technical performance parameters or standards that a supplier's product must meet. The engineering and production personnel evaluate the quality of the supplier's shipped product. Purchasing personnel compare competitive prices and on-time shipment performance. To complicate matters, the engineer, production manager, and purchasing manager may be influencing the purchase decision from two or three different locations.

The industrial decision is even more complex when the product is formally purchased centrally but requirements are determined and ordered in multiple locations. The decentralized units may exert considerable influence on decision makers in the central purchasing location.

DIFFERENT BASIS FOR SEGMENTATION

Household or individual customers are often segmented by psychological and sociological factors. For example, in addition to standard demographic data, a manufacturer of health and beauty aids or designer jeans might be very interested in life styles, dress codes, hair styles, and so on. Industrial firms and industrial customers are more likely to be concerned about industry characteristics, four-digit SICs, technical and functional requirements, applications, annual purchase quantities, cost and benefits, and any physical alteration to the product. (In Chapter 5 we will discuss the whole subject of market segmentation in the industrial world in much greater detail.)

GREATER IMPORTANCE OF TECHNOLOGY

The products marketed by most industrial producers often have a significant impact on their customers' production processes. This means the manufacturer of industrial products must consider the tasks and functions that the customer needs to have performed. The industrial marketer must consider the capabilities of its products, components, or materials and the customer's or user's system. There is a much greater focus on a customer's production system and alternative technological solutions in the industrial buying and selling situation than in the household buying and selling situation. In consumer goods companies, a large amount of the marketing expenditure or budget is allocated to advertising, promotion, and merchandising, which form the central core of consumer goods marketing. In industrial firms, there is usually a heavy investment in technical field selling, technical support services, and engineering considerations. Marketing such products often means interaction between company technical and engineering personnel and customers.

Spending levels for technology and the risks of failure are generally much greater in the industrial world. It is not unusual for industrial success or failure to hinge on advances in either product, process, or materials technology. While product, process, and materials technology are important considerations in the consumer world, disadvantages can often be offset by creative advertising and/or strong brand loyalty.

MULTINATIONAL MARKETS

Industrial firms, largely because of the uniqueness and benefits of their technology or products, tend to be more export-focused than consumer goods firms. Different preferences and social norms are less likely to affect the purchase and use of industrial products than consumer products because accepted worldwide standards ensure product specifications are met. For this reason, technological or performance advantages of superior industrial products generally override geographic or cultural differences. As a result, the major exporters of finished products in industrialized countries tend to be industrial firms rather than consumer goods firms. In a *Fortune* magazine listing of the 100 leading U.S. exporters, industrial firms dominated the list. The major firms included aircraft and aircraft component manufacturers. The exports of this group of aerospace companies amounted to more than a third of the total export sales of the top 50 U.S. exporters in 1979. These high-technology companies in turn are fed by parts and components suppliers in the United States and from foreign-based operations. Other large industrial exporters with major international businesses include DuPont, Union Carbide, and Monsanto in chemicals; and John Deere and GMC in industrial and farm equipment. Table 2.2 shows the top 25 U.S. exporters and their main product lines.

Another view of the worldwide marketplace for industrial products can be seen in an analysis of the machine tool industry. As shown in Table 2.3, the machine tool industry is truly international, with significant import and export trade among all the producing countries. For example, the United States is a major manufacturer or producer of machine cutting tools; however, in 1977 it imported or bought nearly as much as it produced. Exhibit 2-1 shows the world electronics market in 1980 and projected market shares for 1990. Table 2.4 shows market shares in Europe for integrated circuit supplies and the supplier's country of origin.

GREATER INTERDEPARTMENTAL DEPENDENCE

Securing and maintaining a better market position for an industrial product is not simply a matter of changing the advertising campaign, changing the advertising agency, changing the package design, or changing the name of the product. Success with industrial products depends on being able to show performance advantages that result from engineering, production, or technological developments. The fact that these developments originate outside the marketing department creates an interdependence among marketing, R&D, engineering, and technology in the industrial firm. Industrial marketing and success depend largely on the activities of functions like engineering, manufacturing, and technical services (see the box, page 28). The closer the linkage, and the better the communication between marketing and R&D, the shorter the lead time to the marketplace and the more successfully customer requirements can be met. The process can make or break the company. One company, for example, took almost three years to develop an aircraft industry alloy product. By the time it was developed according to users' specifications, they no longer needed it in that type of aircraft.

Because of the functional interdependence in an industrial goods company, the role of an industrial product manager or marketing planner is significantly different from that of his or her counterpart in consumer goods firms. The industrial product manager cannot develop self-contained marketing plans and strategies, but must work closely with all operating functions.

TABLE 2.2

THE LEADING EXPORTERS

Rank 1979	Company	Products	Exports ($000)	Fortune 500 Sales ($000)	Fortune 500 Rank	Exports as percent of sales %	Exports as percent of sales Rank
1	Boeing (Seattle)	Aircraft	$3,967,900	$ 8,131,000	29	48.80%	1
2	General Electric (Fairfield, Conn.)	Generating equipment, aircraft engines	2,772,100	22,460,600	9	12.34	26
3	Caterpillar Tractor (Peoria, Ill.)	Construction equipment, engines	2,499,900	7,613,200	33	32.84	4
4	McDonnell Douglas (St. Louis)	Aircraft	1,788,425	5,278,531	54	33.88	3
5	E.I. du Pont de Nemours (Wilmington, Del.)	Chemicals, fibers, plastics	1,764,000	12,571,800	16	14.03	20
6	United Technologies (Hartford)	Aircraft engines, helicopters	1,417,257	9,053,358	26	15.65	17
7	Weyerhaeuser (Tacoma, Wash.)	Pulp, logs, lumber, wood products	978,000	4,422,653	26	22.11	10
8	Lockheed (Burbank, Calif.)	Aircraft and related support services	956,000	4,069,800	82	23.49	9
9	Westinghouse Electric (Pittsburgh)	Generating equipment, defense systems	879,840	7,332,000	37	12.00	27
10	Raytheon (Lexington, Mass.)	Electronic equipment	734,000	3,727,930	92	19.69	12
11	Northrop (Los Angeles)	Aircraft and related support services	701,577	1,582,477	204	44.33	2
12	Union Carbide (New York)	Chemicals, plastics	602,000	9,176,500	25	6.56	44
13	Archer-Daniels-Midland (Decatur, Ill.)	Soybean meal and oil, wheat, corn	564,808	2,297,838	153	24.58	8
14	Signal Companies (Beverly Hills, Calif.)	Trucks, engines, chemicals	544,700	4,241,200	75	12.84	24
15	Rockwell International (Pittsburgh)	Electronic, automotive, and industrial equipment	536,000	6,466,100	45	8.29	40
16	Philip Morris (New York)	Tobacco products	521,235	6,144,091	49	8.48	38
17	Occidental Petroleum (Los Angeles)	Agricultural and chemical products, coal	499,000	9,554,795	21	5.22	50
18	Kaiser Aluminum & Chemical (Oakland, Calif.)	Aluminum	496,800	2,926,500	113	16.98	14
19	Textron (Providence)	Helicopters, chain saws, metal products	489,000	3,392,974	100	14.41	19
20	Deere (Moline, Ill.)	Farm equipment	480,000	4,933,104	60	9.73	33
21	R.J. Reynolds Industries (Winston-Salem, N.C.)	Tobacco products	476,000	7,133,100	39	6.67	42
22	FMC (Chicago)	Industrial and farm equipment	462,398	3,307,484	102	13.98	21
23	International Harvester (Chicago)	Farm equipment, trucks	447,000	8,392,042	27	5.33	49
24	Dresser Industries (Dallas)	Oil-field and industrial equipment	435,500	3,457,400	98	12.60	25
25	Monsanto (St. Louis)	Herbicides, textile fibers, specialty chemicals	406,400	6,192,600	48	6.56	43

Source: Fortune, September 22, 1980, p. 115.

TABLE 2.3

WORLD MACHINE-TOOL PRODUCTION AND TRADE
(Millions of U.S. dollars)

	1981				
	Production			*Trade*	
Country	*Total*	*Cutting*	*Forming*	*Export*	*Import*
1. Japan	$4798.1	$3861.3	$936.8	$1692.9	$215.8
2. United States	5111.2	4046.9	1064.3	972.1	1437.0
3. FRG (West Germany)	3953.5	2774.3	1179.2	2584.9	616.4
4. Soviet Union*	2932.3	2268.5	663.8	242.4	951.9
5. Italy	1513.0	1029.2	483.8	795.2	300.0
6. GDR (East Germany)*	827.7	632.8	194.9	673.6	214.6
7. Switzerland	845.7	803.4	42.3	740.3	188.9
8. United Kingdom	932.9	797.0	135.9	537.4	432.0
9. France	809.6	625.8	183.8	390.5	566.6
10. Rumania*	624.9	578.7	46.2	133.1	311.5
11. PRC (China)*	440.0[u]	330.0[u]	110.0[u]	30.0[u]	125.0[u]
12. Czechoslovakia*	357.8	311.5	46.3	310.4	168.2
13. Yugoslavia	276.7	188.0	88.7	55.1	131.0
14. Spain	319.6	219.3	100.3	206.8	141.9
15. Poland*	310.0[u]	270.0[u]	40.0[u]	170.0[u]	200.0[u]
16. Canada	269.2	208.0	61.2	99.8	557.4
17. Sweden	204.8	127.4	77.4	164.3	191.4
18. India	209.0	173.2	35.8	23.1	103.9
19. Bulgaria*	201.5	182.0[c]	19.5[c]	200.9	267.8
20. Brazil	305.0	231.7	73.3	73.9	123.6
21. Korea*	178.1	115.8	62.3	32.0	324.5
22. Taiwan	249.4	237.2	12.2	182.6	99.2
23. Hungary*	127.7	111.2	16.5	95.7	127.3
24. Austria	107.8	74.1	33.7	107.8	290.2
25. Belgium	103.3	33.1	70.2	119.2	139.5
26. Israel	70.0[c]	55.0[c]	15.0[c]	33.8	71.5
27. Australia	68.9[cj]	43.6[cj]	25.3[cj]	7.3[j]	195.6[j]
28. Netherlands	60.5	31.7	28.8	74.2	110.6
29. Denmark	41.6	16.9	24.7	31.9	28.2
30. Singapore	43.5	38.8	4.7	27.0	114.4
31. Argentina	35.3[u]	18.8[u]	16.5[u]	19.5[u]	70.0[u]
32. South Africa	36.8	14.7[c]	22.0[c]	5.0[c]	250.0[c]
33. Mexico*	24.0[u]	12.0[u]	12.0[u]	4.0[u]	450.0[u]
34. Portugal	16.3[u]	7.3[u]	9.0[u]	4.1	53.9
35. Hong Kong	12.5[c]	3.1[c]	9.4[c]	4.1	4.0
Total	$26418.1	$20472.3	$5945.8	$10844.9	$9573.8

Source: *American Machinist*
Notes: Whenever possible, data include machine tools only; they do not include parts and attachments.
[c]Rough estimate from fragmentary data.
[j]Year ended June 30.
[u]Unrevised.
*Country with controlled currency whose official rate may not represent real value.
Exchange rates: Controlled currencies have been converted as follows: Soviet Union at 80% of the official rate; GDR at 65% of the FRG rate; Czechoslovakia at the official rate; Bulgaria at 65% of the official rate. Poland and PRC (China) are based on estimates of the amount of production so no exchange rate is involved. Hungary, Korea, Mexico, and Rumania are all members of the IMF and though conversion is currently restricted were converted at IMF rates.

EXHIBIT 2-1

THE WORLD ELECTRONICS MARKET (Billions of 1979 U.S. dollars)

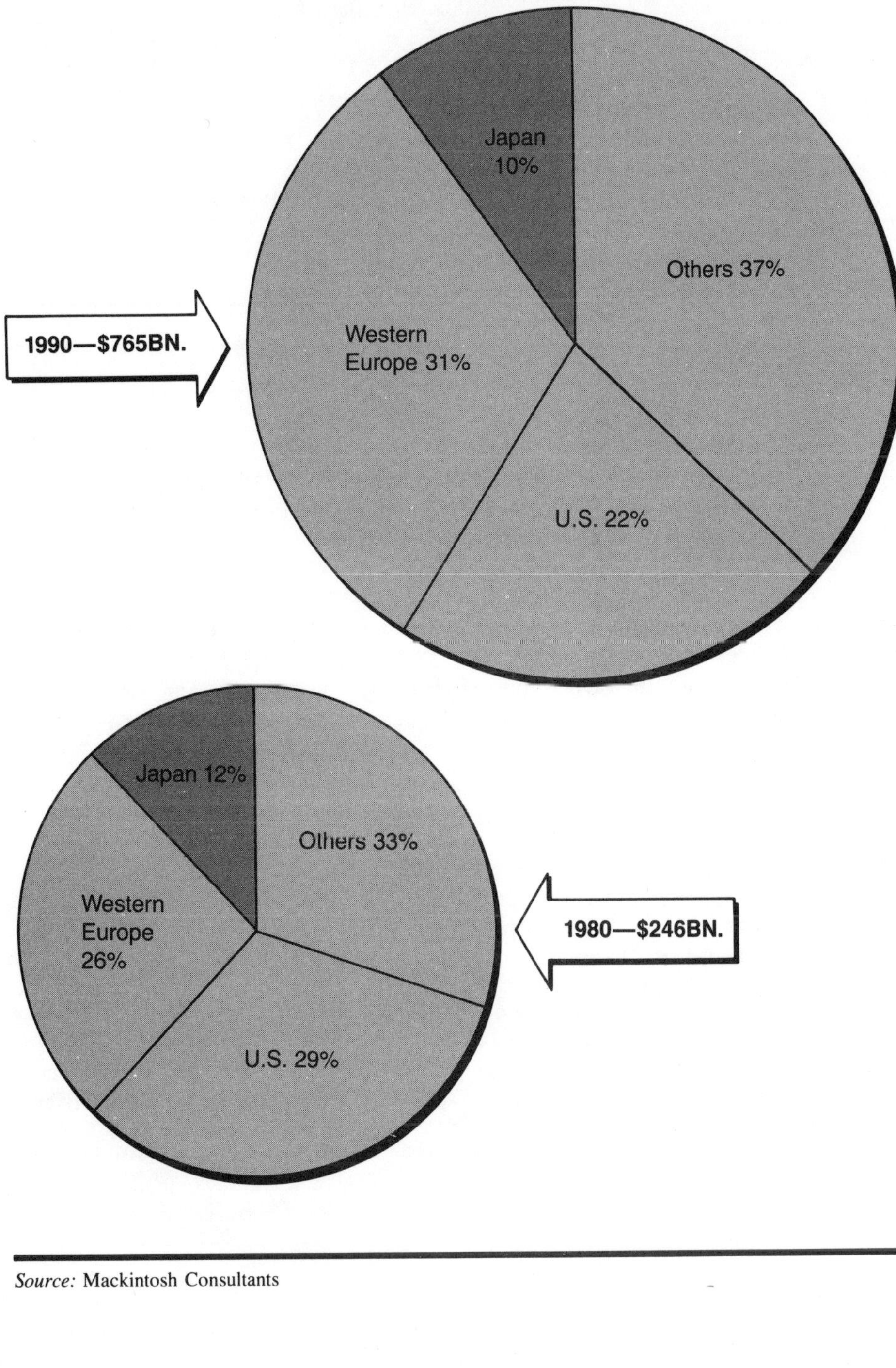

Source: Mackintosh Consultants

TABLE 2.4 ***INTEGRATED CIRCUITS: EUROPEAN MARKET SHARES, 1979***

1. Texas Instruments (U.S.)	15.9%
2. Phillips (Netherlands)	14.7
3. Intel (U.S.)	8.0
4. Motorola (U.S.)	8.0
5. Siemens (Germany)	7.5
6. National (U.S.)	7.0
7. Fairchild (U.S.)	4.7
8. ITT (U.S.)	4.2
9. SGS-ATES (France)	3.7
10. NEC (Japan)	3.1
Others	23.2

CUSTOMER CONTACT

In a typical consumer goods company, product managers spend about 75 percent of their time on packaging, advertising, and couponing, since these factors, more than any others, control the growth and profitability of the business. In a large, broad-based industrial electronics company, in contrast, product managers spend much of their time working with their counterparts in engineering to evaluate bid opportunities to determine the focus of product development, and to coordinate and participate in technical discussions with major customer groups or user segments. These activities are what make a product a success.

Since most industrial products are bought during or after face-to-face technical selling, experience in the field with engineering, production, and purchasing personnel provides

INTERDEPENDENCE IN A CHEMICAL COMPANY

A field salesman for a chemical company perceived a need for a liquid that could be used in a customer's cooling system. He communicated this need through the organization to the R&D people. After some research, R&D determined that mercury was the best liquid for the application. However, marketing soon discovered that mercury could not be used, as the application required a low-cost fluid of low toxicity. Marketing then provided R&D with better technical parameters and more specific customer requirements.

An application engineering team went to work developing a liquid that fit the customer's technical performance requirements. After six months of work and meetings between the supplier's and the buyer's technical personnel, a satisfactory product was developed. Manufacturing and cost personnel then determined the feasibility and economics of manufacturing in various quantities. Finally an agreement was negotiated with the customer that led to a firm purchase order.

a valuable base for developing business marketing programs and making product and market decisions. Top executives of the more successful industrial goods companies spend considerable amounts of time with ultimate customers in the marketplace, unlike their counterparts in consumer goods firms whose contacts in the marketplace are limited to wholesalers and retailers that distribute their products. Top managers at IBM and Digital Equipment, for example, spend approximately 30 days a year meeting with key customers. Such firms believe there is no substitute for meeting periodically with customers to keep abreast of the market.

MULTIPLICITY OF MARKETS AND CHANNELS

Another major distinguishing characteristic between consumer and business markets is the multiplicity of markets and channels with which the industrial firm must deal. A consumer goods company typically markets its brands through one or two channels; a multiproduct industrial firm is likely to sell in many different markets through a variety of channels. One equipment company promotes *one* of its product lines to 20 distinct markets that are reached through different distribution channels. No company can market to such a complex combination of markets and channels with a single marketing strategy or plan; what is needed is a number of different marketing plans. Although essentially the same product is sold to all markets, different customer applications result in different ways of purchasing the product. The delivery systems (distribution channels) must be selected to meet each distinct purchase and user situation. The implication for the industrial product manager is that he or she must understand how the product is made and used, and what happens when design or manufacturing changes are introduced. For example, the Parker Hannifin Corporation is the world's largest manufacturer of O-Rings, which are used in fluid and air connections to seal against leaks. Various sizes and forms of O-Rings are used in literally hundreds of applications ranging from aircraft landing gear to cigarette lighters. Different sales and distribution channels are obviously required to effectively serve each identified market segment. Some of these products are standard catalog items; others are custom designed. Some are sold direct to OEMs and end users; others are sold through different types of distributors. Some markets buy primarily on price and delivery; others place a premium on application engineering and technical superiority. To meet the unique requirements of these different markets, Parker Hannifin has set up a number of full-fledged divisions that operate almost as totally separate businesses. They may share technical and selling information, but the responsibility for serving assigned markets has been clearly designated to different division managers.

LESS END-USER INFORMATION

Consumer goods producers can readily purchase bi-monthly market data (based on a valid sample of retail outlets) that show inventory movement, relative market share, out of stock occurrences, and competitive prices. The A. C. Nielsen Company and the Market Research Corporation of America regularly provide consumer goods companies with this vital set of market facts. No industrial firm we know has access to anything close to this kind of data. At best they get annual aggregate shipment data from a trade association from which they might be able to determine their relative market share position. Often, however, this information is outdated by the time they get it, or it is unreliable, as many industrial firms refuse to participate in trade association surveys or will report inaccurate information. Since many industrial customers sell products to other industrial firms, an item often becomes a component of another firm's finished product, which creates a major information problem for the original producer of the item; it is very difficult for the industrial producer to know where and in what final applications its product is being used. Many industrial customers and distributors are reluctant or unwilling to keep track of information that will tell their suppliers who their customers are. As a result, many industrial firms do not know where and how major portions of their output are being used, and they must go to extraordinary lengths to develop meaningful information about the ultimate users of their products.

PRODUCT MANAGEMENT

The differences between business marketing and consumer goods marketing can also be seen in their product manager systems. In business marketing, product managers are typically older and have spent some time in the business. Many industrial product managers have a technical background and generally remain within the industry or in a closely allied group of industries. The need to understand how the product is made and used, and what happens when design or manufacturing changes are introduced, is crucial to the successful industrial product manager.

It is rare indeed for an industrial product manager to have spent a major part of his or her career in an advertising agency as an account executive. In the consumer goods industry, however, it is common for product managers to move between advertising agencies and manufacturing firms. The reason is that the advertising agency's role and activities are a major part of the consumer goods marketing and product management responsibility.

The need for industrial firms to be in close face-to-face contact with their customers causes many industrial firms to be more sales-oriented. A sales orientation, rather than a market focus, can result in shorter-range goals and a lack of concentrated efforts. This shorter time horizon often fails to group customers with like problem needs together for later sales emphasis. Some of the factors that distinguish an industrial marketing focus from an industrial sales focus are shown below:

Marketing-Focused Industrial Company	*Sales-Focused Industrial Company*
Long-term planning to serve markets	Short-range planning to achieve sales goals
Define and segment total market and identify specific requirements	Profile the market by account potential
Select segments and customers to serve	Sell products to anyone who will buy
Products and technology vary with market needs	Products and technology are fixed

KEY PART OF LONG-TERM CORPORATE STRATEGY

Business-to-business marketing strategy is often indistinguishable from corporate strategy. Business market strategy involves general management in making the decision on which course the company will take as it responds to market needs, and it requires top management or division general management involvement to provide the follow-up to ensure that the strategy is pursued in every functional area of the business unit.

Ideally, industrial product organizations should view all strategic marketing decisions as long-term investments because of the long time frames needed to design, make, and ultimately market and sell an industrial product. In consumer goods, product "changes" are usually quicker to perform and often involve only packaging, promotion, or advertising campaign changes. An industrial product improvement, such as designing performance or cost improvements into an already proven product, can take months and typically years and considerable capital expense before test and performance data are generated to prove the advantages over competitive or substitute products. It may take just as long for an industrial customer to try a new component or piece of equipment that may cost thousands of dollars or ultimately affect its entire production plan. In many cases, it takes three to six years for an industry to openly purchase and use a product improvement.

SUMMARY

Because business and consumer markets are very different, the marketing effort for each needs to reflect and take into account these differences.

The demand for industrial products is derived, not direct; there are often several levels of customer between the industrial producer and the ultimate consumer. Industrial products are bought rationally and primarily for economic reasons; many people participate in the buying decision, not just the members of a household. And careers can depend on the quality of the decisions.

An industrial producer may have a large segment of the total market and still have only three or four customers because the customer base is generally very narrow. And in industrial products, technology is not just a gimmick, it is vital. Technology makes the marketing of industrial products a worldwide operation, since these products carry no cultural "freight" and are needed for the development of industry. Technology also means a close working relationship between producer and buyer; products must be matched to the changing requirements of the user, and often a sale is made only after in-depth, face-to-face consultations and visits to manufacturing or producing sites. All this is far different from repackaging a household product, mounting a new advertising campaign, and conveniently purchasing bi-monthly reports containing market data that reflect the success or failure of the new packaging and advertising campaign.

3

How Buying Decisions Are Made

Jim Rodgers, a recent college graduate, had been recruited by Worldwide Electric to join its sales training program. Worldwide was known for having one of the finest training programs in the industry. The in-house phase of the program took six months and covered the company's products, markets, and selling requirements. It emphasized the increasingly more sophisticated customer evaluations of competitive offerings and supplier capabilities.

The second phase of the program consisted of on-the-job training with senior salespeople. Every new salesperson was required to work with two to three senior staff over a three-month period. The trainee worked with the senior salespeople to prepare and make sales calls and was expected to work out the strategy and purpose of each call.

Jim was impressed with the in-house training program, which emphasized analytical and comprehensive account evaluations to determine how and why each company buys from a given supplier. When he began phase two of his training, he set out to analyze each account to determine his company's past history and competitive position with the account, to learn who made or influenced the buying decision, and to find out what caused the account to buy from the company. On the second day in the field, the first senior salesman he traveled with said: "You'll only get paralysis from all that analysis. Let's go and call on the accounts in this town, where I'm close friends with the buying people."

Why does the senior salesman place so much emphasis on personal relationships?

Is the senior salesman being practical or is he living in the past?

Should Jim follow his advice?

Why did the company program stress analysis and planning?

Sound procurement practices can favorably affect a firm's profitability. For the long term, they result in securing the better suppliers. In the shorter term, a 2 percent procurement savings will favorably affect the profit and loss statement or provide the firm with a competitive cost advantage that could be passed on to customers. The high cost of inventories and the many longer-term negative effects of poor quality put a great deal of pressure on procurement. Furthermore, when a company faces limited market growth prospects with mature products, there is certainly more pressure for internal efficiencies to improve earnings.

Materials planning and procurement have received more time and attention in recent years as enlightened management has become aware of the importance these activities can have on the ability to serve the marketplace. A quote from Reliance Electric's procurement policy statement brings this point into sharp focus.

> Suppliers play a vital role in Reliance's commitments to provide our customers with maximum total value to help them achieve superior financial results. Reliance, in turn, seeks to buy from suppliers who provide us with maximum total value.
>
> The elements of total value include more than quality, delivery, and price. Technological innovations, assured supply during shortages, cost reduction aid, and engineering, managerial, or process assistance are some of the vendor contributions Reliance considers in determining total value.
>
> Reliance believes the best way to achieve maximum total value received from its purchases is to establish business partnerships with suppliers. In a supplier/customer partnership both parties coordinate and combine their actions to produce mutually profitable, superior results.

With more and more industrial firms thinking this way about procurement, it is critically important for industrial marketers and sales personnel to thoroughly understand the industrial buying process and the major considerations that impact the buying decision. This understanding is fundamental to the development of sound product-market and account strategies, as well as to the actual sales implementation.

Today's industrial buyers often know more about the value of a supplier's product and the competitive substitutes than the supplier knows. Armed with product performance information and driven by economic-based buying, the progressive industrial buying organization identifies, evaluates, selects, and switches to the supplier(s) providing the greatest value. The same buyers are evaluating more worldwide sources of supply. When NCR needed a new 5,000-line telephone system for its headquarters, it rejected American and Canadian manufacturers in favor of Japan's Nippon Electric Company. An NCR company spokesman stated:

> In the past we always did business with the local telephone company, but this time we looked around and found the Japanese had the best equipment for the money. It really wasn't much of a contest.[1]

[1]"Japanese Now Target Communications Gear as a Growth Industry," *The Wall Street Journal,* January 13, 1983, p. 1.

Business-to-business marketing is not merely attracting more customers. It always involves serving and maintaining the customers after they agree to buy. The relationship, in many respects, begins only after the formal sale is made. The customer determines the long-term requirements and service level necessary to maintain and keep its business. When a large customer has its own competitive problems, it nearly always seeks help from existing or new suppliers. For example, the Xerox Corporation realized in 1980 that it was not cost- or quality-competitive in the small copier market, the fastest growing market segment. In order to reposition itself more competitively in that segment, Xerox examined its supplier situation. First, it had many parts redesigned so that assembly would be less labor-intensive. It standardized more parts across many machine models and decided to buy more items rather than continue to make them. Xerox reduced its parts inventory to one month from the previous three months. It awarded more business to suppliers that had lower rejection rates and could also meet the new "just-in-time" delivery requirement. The move to make Xerox more competitive from 1980 to 1982 resulted in reducing the number of its suppliers from 2,200 to 1,400.

A thorough understanding of industrial procurement practices is necessary for a firm to be and remain a successful supplier. Industrial salespeople who are not tuned into sound organizational buying practices will serve fewer accounts and enjoy less of each customer's business. Many industrial salespeople do not appreciate the need to understand the buying process for each of their products and market segments. The following comments are often heard from unresponsive sales executives:

"There are too many people involved."

"It varies greatly by each company."

"The right price is all that counts."

These comments are often nothing more than an excuse for superficial thinking. The people speaking probably do not know their customers' procurement requirements. A lack of awareness of competitive suppliers' practices may also exist. These comments are most often heard from salespeople who achieved some success by riding an industry growth curve when procurement was not very sophisticated and when social visits and friendships generated many purchase orders. Today, things have changed. With the increased use of sophisticated buying methods like value analysis, supplier rating systems, formal buying committees, and worldwide competition, only the astute suppliers will succeed. (Since government buying is somewhat different from the process and relationship between for-profit suppliers and buyers, it has been placed in an appendix to this chapter.)

MULTIPLE BUYING INFLUENCES

It is rare, except in very small organizations,[2] for one person to be solely responsible for the industrial buying decision. In industrial organizations, the buying decision for most items is usually shared by several people. These multiple influencers have been called

[2]Hugh P. Buckner, *How Industry Buys* (London: Hutchinson, 1966); and John H. Platten, Jr., *How Industry Buys* (New York: Scientific American, 1955).

"the buying center" or the decision-making unit.[3] Whatever terms are used to identify the decision makers, it is the task of the industrial marketer to determine who initiates, who specifies, who ultimately controls, and who can reject the decision to purchase a particular product or service. Locating the decision makers is not as quick and easy as interviewing the members of an identifiable household or conducting random interviews at a shopping center. Organizational titles are often misleading in terms of a person's buying responsibility or influence role. The people involved in an industrial buying decision are often at different geographic locations. Specifications may be written at one location, annual volume requirements determined at another. Still another centralized location may make the final choice of supplier. Therefore, phrases like "buying center" or "decision-making unit" may be interesting academic terms, but operationally they are often not very helpful in analyzing the actual decision that the industrial salesperson must effectively influence on an account-by-account basis.

The Purchasing Manager

The multiple purchase influences in industrial buying typically involve engineers, production people, purchasing agents, middle management, and sometimes top management. The professional industrial salesperson needs to know the buying role influence and the procedure or process firms use to purchase a product. The salesperson usually enters the organizational buying network through the purchasing department, even if that department does not actually make the purchase decision for the item. The protocol is first to register with the purchasing department before identifying and seeing other people in the organization. As a consequence, purchasing personnel can open many doors to the actual network or they can hinder the salesperson in seeing the other appropriate influencers in the organization.

The purchasing function has gained significant status since the mid-1970s. When material shortages and price fluctuations were as great as they were in the 1974–75 energy crisis, the procurement function suddenly was seen as vital. Today purchasing managers are using more analytical tools and techniques, including economic order quantity (EOQ), value analysis, and supplier rating systems. Many purchasing departments are making greater use of their internal engineering capability to evaluate supplier products. It is not unusual for purchased materials to account for as much as 50 percent of total manufacturing costs. So a 1 or 2 percent improvement on the procurement side of the operation can immediately and dramatically affect the economics and profit of the business. Firms are realizing that it would take a considerable amount of additional sales revenue to equal the incremental profit increase obtained from more prudent procurement. In times of limited economic growth, the internal efficiencies provided by better procurement practices can help sustain the attractiveness of the business (see the box).

Industrial procurement managers are increasingly involved in decisions beyond the traditional purchasing of inventory and negotiating supplier contracts. The purchasing manager has more knowledge of price trends for purchasing products and materials than any

[3]See Patrick J. Robinson, Charles W. Faris, and Yoram Wind, *Industrial Buying and Creative Marketing* (Boston: Allyn and Bacon, 1967); Frederick E. Webster and Yoram Wind, *Organizational Buying Behavior* (Englewood Cliffs, N.J.: Prentice-Hall, 1972); and Jagdish Sheth and Arch Woodside, *Consumer and Industrial Buying Behavior* (New York: Elsevier North-Holland, 1978).

MODERN PROCUREMENT PRACTICE

An increasingly sophisticated approach to procurement is seen in the changing buyer-seller relationships between U.S. automakers and their steel suppliers.

According to an ARMCO salesman, "GM's steel buying had become automatic process. At the beginning of each year a supplier would be awarded a fixed percentage of GM's needs for specific types of steels at each plant. We did the same thing the same way every year in Detroit, and we'd get our share of the pie."

In the past, an automaker who wanted steel made to certain specifications was apt to be told that he would have to accept the standards and tolerances of the American Iron and Steel Institute. As *Fortune* magazine states, "Neither buyers nor suppliers paid much attention to quality. Thousands of tons of rejected steel piled up at many auto plants. Banking on the consumer's willingness to absorb price increases, the suppliers and buyers chose to pass costs on rather than disrupt the comforts of doing business as usual."

Because of declining sales over the last several years, automakers have had to introduce new procurement practices in order to increase efficiency and reduce costs. GM cut the number of mills supplying its plants from 341 to 272. Ford now offers larger orders and longer-term contracts to suppliers who meet higher standards. Suppliers now receive a detailed list of over 5,000 parts made at 53 plants on which they can quote. More important, GM suppliers are now given advance notice of GM's production plans to help their own planning–something suppliers never got before. GM is gaining lower rejection rates, lower inventories, and manufacturing efficiencies from the greater reliability of material from suppliers.

The changes in steel buying practices have made things more difficult for suppliers. Suppliers have been forced to rationalize their operations, sharpen their marketing and selling skills, and look at their own production costs. Most important, suppliers have had to reconsider the mix of products they sell. Bethlehem invested $60 million in a continuous heat treating line, and Jones and Laughlin is building a $160 million slab caster mainly dedicated to auto steel.

With the changes in procurement practices has come increased cooperation between buyers and suppliers. ARMCO presented GM with a study showing that GM could reduce the number of steel sizes it orders by 50 percent by combining different sizes of products whose gauges (thicknesses) are within .05 millimeters of each other or whose widths were within a range of 2 percent. Such standardization benefits both buyers and suppliers by improving quality, lowering material costs, and reducing inventories. ARMCO also showed GM how it could substitute lower priced steel for some it was already buying from ARMCO, saving about $10 per ton on steel averaging $500 per ton without compromising quality.

Source: Steven Flax, "How Detroit Is Reforming the Steelmakers," *Fortune,* May 16, 1983.

other executive. In firms where 50 percent of all costs of manufacturing is accounted for by material purchases, the purchasing manager's predictions on material costs have a major impact on marketing and overall business strategy. And research, development, and engineering staffs are now realizing that purchasing can facilitate their new product programs by identifying qualified vendors with special product, process, or some other know-how that supports their efforts.

Engineering and Production

After the purchasing agent, the other two major influences in most industrial manufacturing purchases involve engineering and production. Engineering and sometimes production are involved in setting specifications and quality standards. With multiplant locations and the repurchase of standardized items in quantity, there is more and more centralized procurement. This has implications for the marketer, who in many cases must exert influence and market to both the decentralized locations and the centralized formal purchasing points. In large corporations, more procurement is being done at the corporate level for the more uniform or standardized products used across many operating divisions. For example, the B. F. Goodrich Company found 60 separate orders being placed each year with six different producers for 120 lift trucks. Each lift truck costs about $18,000, and many of Goodrich's orders were placed with local distributors. Now all such orders are placed through Goodrich's corporate purchasing department. The saving to Goodrich on this item was about $400,000 a year,[4] after it was bid and placed directly with two suppliers. Furthermore, 62 percent of the sales dollars at Goodrich is spent for supplies and services; as one of their executives stated: "No one area touches as much of the corporation's money as purchasing." Centralized buying of 350,000 items at Goodrich saved the company about $18.2 million in 1980, nearly one-third of its 1980 earnings of $61.8 million.[5] The trend of more organizational buyers to place more orders centrally has forced some suppliers to realign their pricing and sales force activities.

The Buying Committee

Central purchases are usually reviewed and approved by a buying committee. These committees are typically composed of an engineer and representatives from various technical groups, production supervisors, buyers, and often specialists such as methods people or internal auditors. As an example, one equipment manufacturer has an electrical components committee that includes electrical engineers, the production supervisor of the electrical assembly section, a specialist, and a buyer. The committee meets once every two weeks. The members discuss changes, design specifications, order quantities, particular components or materials, and price-quantity stability for key items. Such buying committees are often very slow in evaluating alternatives and making a decision. In response to the increase in buying committees, one large supply division general manager stated: "When the customer's dust settles in choosing a supplier(s) for an item, it is still the design engineer who is responsible for quality, the shop or production foreman who is responsible for output, and the buyer who is responsible for contract negotiations and the fulfillment of that contract." Yet, many believe that committee procurement activities will grow in importance as the materials management concept increases and greater cooperation, coordination, and cost savings are sought between departments.

Setting product specifications and placing the actual purchase orders with a specific supplier can create authority and power conflicts.[6] The supplier can be caught between

[4] "New Status for Purchasing," *The New York Times*, June 2, 1981, p. 25.
[5] *The New York Times*, ibid.
[6] George Strauss, "Work/Flow Frictions, Interfunctional Rivalry, and Professionalism: A Case Study of Purchasing Agents," *Human Organization*, 23, 2 (1964), 137–49.

the desires of purchasing agents and the engineers who have control over specifications. Purchasing agents tend to stress price; engineers generally stress quality. It is much easier for engineers to specify by brand rather than develop precise technical specifications. Purchasing managers dislike brand specification because it biases the purchase to the supplier of the named brand. If a brand is specified, the purchasing department may attempt to have technical specifications written or have the engineers add the words "or equivalent." These changes allow the purchasing agent more influence and negotiating leverage in making the buy. In most confrontations between engineers and purchasing in selecting suppliers, the engineers usually prevail. As one production engineering manager stated: "Some engineers become purchasing agents, but no purchasing agents become engineers." Due to the close working relationships and interdependence between production and procurement activities, some companies have regrouped or combined the production scheduling function with procurement and called the combined function "materials requirement planning." This is also an attempt to gain greater coordination and cooperation between suppliers and users.

PLANNING MATERIAL NEEDS

The materials requirement planning (MRP) concept brings together production, engineering, scheduling, and value analysis. It is a focused organizational unit that analyzes and manages industrial buying practices—specifications, design, annual requirements, sources, quality, and price. A materials management staff is a unit as important as a financial or market analysis staff. The existence of a multidisciplinary materials management operation can be an advantage to the astute supplier salesperson for two reasons. First, it is easier to identify the buying influencers when such an organization exists. Second, it is easier to get a sympathetic ear for the idea of developing long-range material plans.

Materials requirements planning is a technique of working backward from the scheduled quantities and need dates for end items specified in a master production schedule.[7] An MRP computer program is run periodically, usually once a week, to incorporate new production plans and information about the scheduled receipt of components and materials. The inventory status file is updated each time the MRP program is run to reflect the scheduled usage, the balance on hand, the quantities on order, and when they are scheduled to be received.[8]

In a company where the performance and cost of materials are a major part of its success, there should be greater emphasis on the materials management function. A materials management program can help a producer achieve a lower-cost position in the marketplace. The materials management unit in some organizations has installed computers to order and keep track of suppliers. When a unit's inventory is down to a programmed reorder point, the computer returns a card that shows who the existing vendor(s) is (are), and an automatic reorder occurs. As a consequence, new firms marketing

[7]James B. Dilworth, *Production and Operations Management*, 2d ed. (New York: Random House, 1983), p. 239.
[8]Ibid., p. 240.

to such a firm will have difficulty if they are not programmed on the computer. But once the supplier manages to get a product onto the computer reorder system, it is equally difficult for a competitor to remove it.

For MRP to work effectively, buyers must inform suppliers well in advance of their production schedules and supply requirements. In return, the buyer can carry less inventory. To better link directly into a customer's production needs, some producers and suppliers have linked computers to exchange supply and delivery information. Dana supplies drive shafts to Ford with such a computer linkage. Dana delivers to Ford daily, and it knows four days in advance exactly what each Ford factory needs. It is not a system to push inventory back up the pipeline; it is a system that keeps both producer and buyer happy and inventory down. Weak suppliers are rapidly weeded out. Too many irregularities and defective items will disrupt the entire system.

This approach is very similar to the Japanese "just-in-time" (JIT) or *kanban* system. The Japanese system is characterized by more frequent deliveries in smaller quantities, longer-term supply contracts, fewer suppliers, and a very close relationship between suppliers' and buyers' people. Some of the benefits of the JIT system are lower inventory carrying costs, quicker detection of defects, less need for inspection, and a faster response to engineering changes. The benefits of JIT buying are greatest in the case of materials used every production day.[9]

ECONOMIC-BASED BUYING

An understanding of organizational buying and subsequent marketing strategy development must focus on the economic need underlying industrial purchases. Industrial firms buy a product or service for only one purpose: to fulfill an economic need. The economic function is basic; the type of product or service that performs the function is secondary. Industrial firms are very much influenced in their purchasing behavior by the same profit-making motive that influences the sellers or suppliers who market to them. The profit-making motive of the industrial buyer creates a strong desire for cost-benefit value. Key needs motivating industrial buyers to purchase a certain product include energy consumption, energy costs, productivity, material costs, capacity utilization, OSHA, and on-time delivery. These are also economic needs. As the vice president of marketing at IBM states: "Every proposal should be overwhelmingly cost-justifiable from the customer's standpoint."[10] An ex-IBMer states: "An IBM salesman always sells the cheapest product that will get the job done," adding that he wishes the same could be said of his present company.[11] IBM has also stated that it is in the business of solving customer information problems rather than merely selling computers.[12] The economic basis of industrial buying can be seen in the cost-benefit value of purchasing an industrial robot (see the box).

Problem recognition does not always originate with the industrial buyer. The industrial

[9]Richard J. Schonberger, *Japanese Manufacturing Techniques* (New York: Free Press, 1982), p. 163.
[10]Thomas J. Peters and Robert H. Waterman, *In Search of Excellence: Lessons from America's Best Run Companies* (New York: Harper & Row, 1982), p. 161.
[11]Ibid.
[12]J. W. Cannon, *Business Strategy and Policy* (New York: Harcourt Brace Jovanovich, 1968), p. 15.

INDUSTRIAL ROBOTS

Industrial robots are typically used to perform the more routine, unskilled, or semi-skilled tasks. The more advanced robots are able to sense, touch, grasp, hold, and place items. Specific applications now include spot and arc welding, spray painting, machine tool loading, press loading and unloading, heat treating, metal part deburring, and assembly. The increasing reliability and cost-benefit value of robots provide high potential for improved manufacturing productivity.

The most obvious benefits of introducing robots are in terms of reducing labor costs. Up to 1981, 45 percent of all robots were installed to cut the expense of labor. As wages and fringe benefits increase each year, robots become more attractive. In 1983, each factory robot typically costs $50,000. Each robot has a six- to seven-year life and replaces one worker per shift whose average annual wage-benefit cost is about $21,000. When the robot is operated in two shifts daily, it pays for itself in just over a year. If there are three shifts, the payback is less than one year. The use of robots in continuous shifts favorably affects breakeven points and offers significant improvements in productivity. Robots are also more flexible than less automated machines. This feature allows for shorter production runs. In some applications, a robot is more efficient than humans. A robot used for painting uses 20 to 30 percent less paint than the worker it replaces. Robots do not require air conditioning, lighting, or special protection. By taking humans out of hot, dirty, or dangerous situations, the organization can improve industrial safety without increasing costs. Robots also offer a benefit or insurance against a shortage of skilled labor, especially in rural areas where plants are often located. In larger industrial cities, an aging and smaller skilled manufacturing work force can be supplemented with robots.

supplier with a new and better product must often show the problem area to the customer and explain the resulting cost and benefits of the new solution. Plant managers and manufacturing executives had to be shown in detail the significant cost-benefits of robots before trial machines were allowed in their plants. Due to the new technology of many new industrial products, the supplier must often take the initiative and educate users as to how new products will better solve a problem or need.

VALUE ANALYSIS

Value analysis is a key analytical tool used systematically to study the cost-benefits of a material, component, or machine. There are many names for this procedure, including value engineering, purchasing research, and product research. Some companies make a distinction between value analysis and value engineering. In those firms, value analysis is directed toward existing products and is primarily concerned with cost reduction. Value engineering focuses more on products and proposals that are in the development stages. In the following discussion, we use the term value analysis in the inclusive sense, for both proposed and existing products.[13]

[13]Gary J. Zenz, *Purchasing and the Management of Materials* (New York: Wiley, 1981), p. 389.

How Value Analysis Works

Value analysis begins by asking the question: "What function does the item perform?" For example, the function of a fastener is to join two or more parts. Every item has a primary function and may also have a secondary function. In defining a function, it is best to be as brief as possible: "It measures temperature," or "It connects two pieces." Value analysis then examines the value of the function performed by the material, part, or machine. It also examines the value of the identified function in terms of alternative methods such as welding, taping, stapling, or glueing in a specific application. The best product to purchase is the one that will satisfactorily perform the identified function(s) at the lowest costs without degradation of quality.[14] The lowest cost for the function performed involves the use of cost and price analysis for the alternative solutions or products. Maximum value is achieved when the essential function(s) are achieved for minimum costs, as shown in the following equation:

$$\frac{\text{Function desired}}{\text{Minimum cost}} = \text{Maximum value}$$

Value analysis causes organizations to pay greater attention to substitutability, consolidating, eliminating, simplification, and standardization. A value analysis buying orientation results in a continuous search for new materials, processes, and products to perform a function better and/or at a lower cost. The value analysis approach often includes a checklist that asks questions about the item or component.

Value analysis personnel of a major farm equipment manufacturer assist suppliers with specifications and with finding substitute parts or materials by providing present and potential suppliers with the value analysis checklist shown in Exhibit 3-1.

Analyzing Prices and Costs

When procurement managers receive price increases for major or critical items, the search intensifies for functional alternatives, alternative suppliers, or cost reductions by suppliers. If the price is too high, or even if it isn't, the buyer will frequently go over the prices in detail. One of the buyer's objectives is to see where the highest costs and profits are for the supplier. The buyer may even bend the minimal specifications in such a way as to reduce the supplier's cost and price. Many buying organizations conduct an intensive price-cost analysis as a separate part of the value analysis procedure. The buyer's question is essentially: "What is the cost to the supplier for the item we purchase, and how much should we pay for the item?" Supplier costs are questioned in relation to efficiency, age of equipment, and reasonable return on investment. Buyers often visit existing and competitive suppliers' facilities to help answer these questions.

If the conclusion is that all the suppliers' prices are too high for the item, the customer may decide to make the item rather than buy it. In many situations, the customer will make specific recommendations to the supplier on how to reduce or contain costs. The search for alternative, multiple, or new suppliers is often fueled by the customer's desire

[14]Fred Asbudnick, "Value Engineering—A Form of Industrial Engineering," *Journal of Industrial Engineering*, 15 (July–August 1964), p. 184.

EXHIBIT 3-1

SUPPLIER VALUE ANALYSIS CHECKLIST

Name and number ____________________

Buyer ____________________

In order to assure the functional usefulness of the above part, we solicit your help through answers to the following questions:

QUESTIONS	CHECK Yes	CHECK No	SUGGESTIONS
1. Do you understand part function?			
2. Could costs be reduced by relaxing requirements:			
Tolerances?			
Finishes?			
Testing?			
By how much? ________			
3. Could costs be reduced thru changes in:			
Material?			
Ordering quantities?			
The use of castings, forgings, stampings, etc.?			
By how much? ________			
4. Can you suggest any other changes that would:			
Reduce weight?			
Simplify the part?			
Reduce overall costs?			
By how much? ________			
5. Do you feel that any of the specifications are too stringent?			
6. How can we help alleviate your greatest element of cost in supplying this part?			
7. Do you have a standard item that could be substituted for this part?			What is it? ________ What does it cost? ________
8. Other suggestions?			

SUPPLIER: ADDRESS:

SIGNATURE TITLE DATE

*If "No," functional information can be obtained from Buyer involved.

to reduce prices on certain items. Exhibit 3-2 gives examples of how a customer value analysis study reduced costs for three items. The value analysis approach can result in the substitution of lower-priced materials or components without a reduction of quality. The total costs of an air shutoff valve disk used in sewage aeration tanks was reduced by 88 percent by switching from cast bronze to molded plastic.[15] The molded parts cost 97 cents each, as compared to a unit cost of $5.66 for the cast bronze parts. In addition, the eliminated machining cost per unit on the part was $2.30. A yearly savings of approximately $14,000 was obtained by applying value analysis to this small part.[16] The molded plastic supplier was not the same firm that supplied the cast bronze valve disk.

Guiding Product Development

The functional approach to value analysis helps product development and manufacturing engineering objectively assess each product and its relation to components. A value analysis team composed of engineering, marketing, and accounting personnel would examine each of the subassemblies in relation to each other and to the total end product. The result could be a new material, possible elimination of the item, or a different method of manufacturing.

The Xerox Corporation involves vendors in value analysis in the predesign stage. Their early supplier involvement program is staffed by 11 senior buyers who do no actual buying. Instead, they work with the best of Xerox's vendors, taken from a list of approximately 100 "consulting suppliers," who may be called in for advice at the concept stage or during the predesign idea stage. These suppliers can be called in by the value analysis team to brainstorm new approaches. Together they work on new ideas before drawings are produced or use sketches in order to get production started prior to a bill-of-material release. As a result of supplier involvement at an early stage, a machine frame that had previously been roll-formed with secondary piercing is now press-formed and pierced in progressive dies. Cost per machine has been reduced from $36 to $14. And Xerox projects manufacturing savings of $60 million since the program started near the end of 1977.[17]

Reverse Engineering

Reverse engineering is a value analysis approach that is critical to value improvement and new product development efforts. Reverse engineering is a process in which companies take apart their competitors' products to find out how they work and determine the cost of performing the functions. Reverse engineering is a universal practice, especially in industries where technological change is rapid.[18] Makers of automobiles, cameras, appliances, and business machines routinely strip down competitors' products. The Ford Motor Company has a "tear-down room" where competitive components are compared

[15]"Shift to Plastic Saves Machining," *Purchasing*, March 29, 1978, p. 163.
[16]Ibid., p. 163.
[17]Zenz, *Purchasing and the Management of Materials*, p. 395.
[18]"Reverse Engineering of Microchips Is Slow, Costly and Universal," *The Wall Street Journal*, August 5, 1982, p. 1.

EXHIBIT 3-2

HOW VALUE ANALYSIS REDUCES COSTS

This insulating washer was made from laminated phenolic resin and fiber. Machined from individual pieces of material, it cost $1.23. A supplier with specialty equipment now fly-cuts the parts, nesting them on full sheets, at 24¢ each.

Standard nipple and elbow required special machining to fit a totally enclosed motor. Casting a special street "L" with a lug eliminated machining and a special assembly jig. The cost dropped from 63¢ to 38¢.

An insulator costing $4.56 was originally porcelain, leaded extra heavy. Now molded from polyester and glass, it is lighter and virtually indestructible. New cost: $3.25.

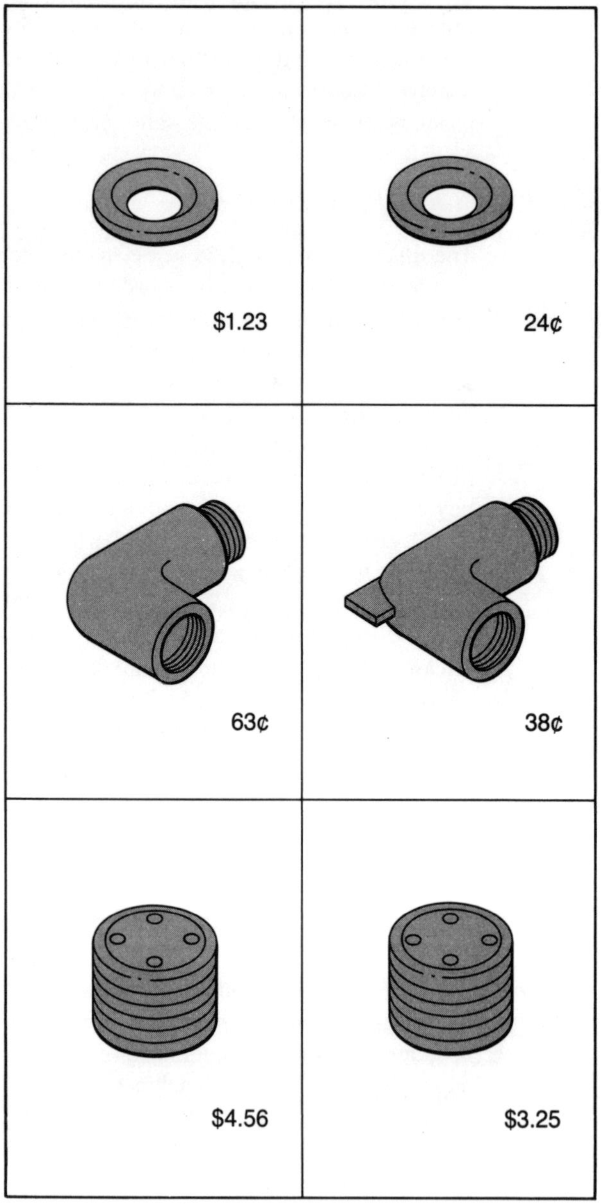

part by part for quality and design cost differences. One result was that Ford saved 45 cents in the redesign of a master brake cylinder and thereby saved $1.5 million in less than two years on this one item.

Reverse engineering per se is not illegal or immoral. Buying, analyzing, and testing competitive products is good competitive behavior. Copying that infringes on a patent, copyright, or trademark is illegal if the item has such legal protection, but many products do not have such protection. In the rapidly changing electronics industry there is considerable "technological borrowing," or learning from one another's products. There are engineering firms whose sole business is to provide reverse engineering studies and reports to clients. Many industrial firms find that their original product development efforts are complemented by reverse engineering studies of competitive products. They can build on the strengths and improve the weaknesses of competitive products in their own new product. However, a reverse engineering effort does not reveal the skill and art necessary to produce a product.

Value analysis creates threats for high-cost suppliers and opportunities for other suppliers who can accomplish the desired function for less cost. The industrial marketer should convert the initial obstacles created by customer value analysis into opportunities by updating product designs and making improvements more in tune with customers' functional needs. One producer instructs its salespeople to attempt to determine which products its customers are reviewing on a value analysis program. Often they are displayed on company schedule boards, and the customer usually does not mind if a supplier's salespeople review the projects. One customer's materials management department periodically holds sessions for all suppliers to show what kinds of problems they are currently reviewing in their value analysis program. This allows suppliers to see how and where their existing and new products might be better used or modified. The mere fact that a supplier knows a product will be reviewed in a value analysis engineering procedure should cause that firm to reevaluate its product's costs and functions with an eye toward improving performance.[19]

STANDARDS AND SPECIFICATIONS

The use of value analysis increases the use of standardization and buying by technical specifications. The setting of a so-called standard is the process of obtaining an agreement on quality, design, and composition for a material, component, or machine. Some standards are developed by governmental agencies, including the U.S. Department of Commerce, the National Bureau of Standards, and all branches of the armed forces. Trade associations and professional associations are also frequently involved in developing nationwide standards. Trade associations active in developing industrial standards include the American Society of Mechanical Engineers, the Society of Automotive Engineers, and the Underwriters Laboratory. The International Standards Association and agencies of the United Nations also seek cooperation on common standards across countries.

[19]Vincent G. Ruter, "The Success Story of Value Analysis/Value Engineering," *Journal of Purchasing*, May 1968, pp. 52–69.

Industry standards provide a sorting process to reduce the number of possible items used and thus simplify the buying decision. The existence of a standard allows a buyer to describe an item without the use of a drawing or blueprint. However, commercial or industrywide standards are often so broad that the customer must develop product specifications to meet the requirements. Such specifications are a detailed description of the desired characteristics of the specific item. Military specifications, in addition to describing technical characteristics, also often describe the method of manufacturing to be used.

Why Have Specifications?

There are a number of advantages and disadvantages for customers and suppliers when procurement is guided by specifications written by the buying organization. Developing and writing specifications require the customer to carefully review functional requirements. The process of value analysis guides the writing of specifications. When specifications are written, more suppliers will tend to bid on the business. This opens the customer's business to more vendors and may result in more price competition. With written specifications, the customer is more assured of uniformity if multiple sources of supply are selected.

If a selected supplier's product meets the customer's specifications but does not perform satisfactorily, the customer is responsible for the malfunction. However, industrial buyers generally do not like to assume such a responsibility. Once a customer writes a specification, it is difficult to change. This situation reduces the chances for different products to be considered from existing or new suppliers. For example, the aircraft industry was using a leather hide substance to seal fluid connections. The leather hides were difficult to work with and had to be soaked in oil and then stretched into a piston groove. The procedure was difficult and time-consuming, but the specifications were written for the leather substance. When another manufacturer developed a superior new Teflon composition sealing ring, it was repeatedly informed that it had to meet the existing leather hide specifications. The Teflon sealing producer had to mount a long-term and costly effort to change the existing specifications.

Whereas U.S. engineers tend to specify and develop very specific tolerances and requirements, which purchasing people pass on to suppliers, the Japanese rely more on performance specifications and less on design specifications. In the Japanese system of industrial buying, performance-focused specification might consist of a blueprint with only the critical dimensions. Kawasaki buyers ask suppliers for recommendations rather than force rigid specifications.[20]

Writing and Influencing Specifications

It is important for the marketer to know who writes the specifications for the product area so the supplier can protect, influence, or change the specifications. Manufacturing, quality control, and engineering are usually involved in developing and writing specifications. It is sometimes done in a committee, but an engineer usually has the specific

[20]Richard J. Schonberger, *Japanese Manufacturing Techniques* (New York: Free Press, 1982), p. 165.

responsibility for writing the technical product specifications and quality standards. Sometimes the specification writer inserts a brand name instead of technical specifications. The actual wording, for example, would state "Teflon or equivalent." This allows the brand name to be the standard. Specifications can also be written in such a way that only one supplier's product will meet the specifications even though there are equivalent competitive substitutes. Such a situation presents a difficult challenge for another supplier who wants to obtain that customer's business.

When a large system or turnkey operation is being built, those writing specifications are often at different geographic locations. A supplier of pressure gauges, for example, was attempting to get its product specified into a new chemical plant Exxon was building (see Exhibit 3-3). The actual writing of the technical specifications was done collectively by Exxon engineers located in New Jersey and Baton Rouge, with assistance from the construction firm's engineers in California. The supplier of pressure gauges called on the key engineers at all three locations to show the economic benefits of its new gauges and then tried to influence the specifications they were in the process of writing. The gauge supplier knew that, if it were not specified in the design and construction stage, it would be virtually locked out of the more lucrative and long-term replacement market business. For this item, the plant managers nearly always bought replacements that were specified in the OEM stage and that were earlier tested and qualified by corporate and construction engineers.

When multiple influences are involved in the buying decision, all the bases have to be covered. This often requires sales calls on different buying locations, which sometimes are located in different states and countries and generally are located beyond any traditional

EXHIBIT 3-3

GEOGRAPHIC SPREAD OF BUYING INFLUENCES COMPOUNDS SERVING TASK

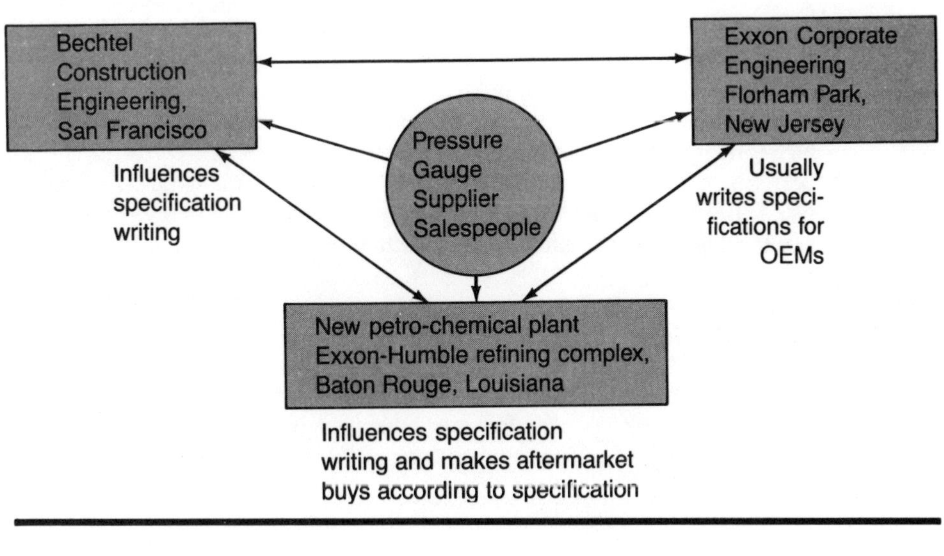

sales territory boundaries. In these situations, sales specialists or team assignments are essential to ensure coordination and open communication among all the parties involved.

Another way suppliers influence specifications is to play an active role in setting industrywide standards. At the industry level, this involves having a person from the producer's company on the appropriate association or government standards writing committee. Since a supplier's market success is often dependent on or threatened by standards and specifications, this responsibility should not be delegated to a junior person. This task is the responsibility of middle or top management or both. Specification writing by the customer is time-consuming and costly. For small-lot purchases, it may be prohibitive to prepare technical specifications. In such a situation, a supplier may literally write the specifications for the customer. An "industry standard" can also be established by a supplier providing technical information in a problem area where the product is used. In fact, a well prepared customer-user manual that provides technical assistance can actually help establish a company and its products as the "standard." This approach was employed by the Johnson & Johnson Company when it developed the first manual on sterile operating procedures for hospitals in the late 1800s. The manual was used in teaching antiseptic procedures to medical schools. Although Johnson & Johnson surgical products were mentioned only occasionally, the manual promoted Johnson & Johnson as an ethical or "antiseptic" supplier of medical products to hospitals. Interns and doctors adopted the antiseptic procedures and Johnson & Johnson products for their hospitals and office practices. Today, new editions of the manual are used as textbooks by medical and nursing students—the people who are tomorrow's buyers and specifiers.

SOURCING DECISIONS

In the business world it is imprudent to rely on a single source of supply for almost anything. A sole source supplier has too much of an advantage in the negotiating process, and too many things can go wrong. For this reason, most business organizations identify and evaluate alternative sources of supply to meet their procurement needs.[21] If alternative sources do not exist, the smart buyer will develop additional sources either externally or internally. Once a supply source is selected or developed, the buying organization usually formally evaluates the supplier's product and service performance. The supplier's performance determines whether the relationship is maintained, decreased, or terminated. But before outside suppliers are considered, many industrial manufacturing firms ask this question: "Should we make or buy the item?"

Make or Buy Situations

Customers who manufacture or have the potential to manufacture internally as well as buy externally are common in many industrial markets. The mental processes of

[21] Richard M. Cyert, Herbert A. Simon, and Donald B. Trow, "Observations of a Business Decision," *Journal of Business*, October 1956, pp. 237–48.

customers who are deciding whether to make or buy have many marketing implications for suppliers.

That the industrial buyer frequently has the option, incentive, and ability to make a product rather than buy it from an outside supply source is one of the major differences between household buying and industrial buying. The household buyer does not have this option. It is neither practical nor economical for a household buyer to even think about producing a water faucet. But for an industrial firm that manufactures sinks and bathtubs for builders and architects, it might be economically favorable, technically quite feasible, and competitively advantageous to make faucets rather than buy them from outside suppliers. If a customer decides to make rather than buy all or a portion of its annual requirements for an item, it represents a form of backward integration. Any manufacturer who buys a substantial volume of parts, components, subsystems, or assemblies is a prime candidate to begin producing the component and therefore to begin withdrawing its business from the open marketplace.

In many cases, straightforward cost or economic considerations swing the decision to internal production. Management simply determines that it would be economically advantageous to make an item rather than to continue to buy it from outside sources. In other situations, demanding requirements for quality and/or delivery are the factors that lead to the commitment to produce internally. For example, for many years General Electric purchased nearly all integrated circuits from outside. The company then decided to make rather than buy a larger percentage of the integrated circuits needed because an increasing number of its products required customized electronic components that were not readily available. Management is frequently faced with a make or buy decision whenever a component item becomes a large proportion of the manufacturer's costs for the product or a critically important part in the manufacturing process (if the producer cannot ship the final item if the component is not "on hand" or does not meet quality standards). Volume is always a consideration, but not always the deciding one. General Electric continues to produce customized integrated circuits internally, but buys the long-run standard items outside.

The decision to make rather than buy is not at all uncommon and is frequently reported in the news media. The NCR Corporation announced it would be spending nearly $200 million over four years to expand its internal capacity to develop and manufacture semiconductor parts, which are used as components in its computer systems and computer terminals. Previous to this, the company was manufacturing 40 percent of its needs internally. The added internal capacity will enable the company to produce 60 percent of its annual requirements. This action will significantly reduce the market for outside suppliers. NCR found it desirable from a performance and cost standpoint to enlarge its in-house capabilities. The firm also believes that greater in-house component capability will enable it to control quality, respond more quickly to the market, and "protect its supply of components in times of shortages."[22]

Many business markets consist of both captive producers and external sellers of the same item. The captive producers usually also buy part of their annual requirements from outside suppliers. When demand slows, the outside suppliers are usually the first to

[22] *The Wall Street Journal,* July 18, 1980, p. 5.

experience reduced orders. Exhibit 3-4 shows the major captive and noncaptive U.S. chipmakers. In 1982, the captives accounted for about 37 percent of the total market. As a result, the captive or make-buy customer is usually also a competitor.

In recent years, many backward integration situations have been prompted by extreme shortages of critical components. In addition to semiconductors, castings, forgings, and high-quality printed circuit boards have been in sufficiently short supply to prompt many manufacturers to consider internal production. Reliance Electric Company bought two small foundries to ensure a continued source of supply for an important part of its motor line. The company's president stated that he did not really want to be in the foundry business, but he recognized that environmental restrictions had forced many foundries out of business and jeopardized the company's supply lines for this critical component.

Although it is less common, industrial companies sometimes give up their make capability and turn to outside suppliers. When this occurs, it is usually because the company's make capability has become obsolete and it is too costly to bring up to date. For example, Tenneco Chemical Company discovered that it was less costly to buy a vinyl chloride monomer than it was to produce the product internally with its old and inefficient production process. In such situations, when a company does not update or reinvest in more current and efficient production processes, it may revert from being an internal producer to buying outside, as happened at Tenneco. In such situations, the supplier should analyze which internal captive sources are not updating production or processes and which may therefore become buying customers.

Customer Make Decision

There are essentially two ways a manufacturer can achieve a make position once the decision to do so has been made. One alternative is to start from scratch and make the investment necessary to get into the manufacture of the desired component or part. Another alternative is to acquire a supplier company.

The start-up alternative is generally preferable when the technology of manufacture is not complex and investment requirements are not excessive. For example, many companies have started to manufacture their requirements for standard fasteners because the manufacturing process is not a difficult one to master and the machinery can easily be obtained. Sometimes a customer is forced into a startup program when none of the suppliers are realistic acquisition candidates because of size, ownership structure, or financial condition. On the other hand, many companies have successfully implemented a make decision by acquiring one or more suppliers. For example, NCR Corporation bought a company called American Digital Data Systems. NCR was the company's largest customer, buying about 42 percent of the firm's $50 million annual output.

The decision to acquire a supplier, particularly a large one, is generally a major strategic move. Such a decision often adds significantly to the investment and fixed cost base and makes the company more vulnerable to downturns in the economy. It also frequently takes the company into new markets, since the acquired source should maintain a free market position with customers other than the parent company. This is essential to maintain a competitive position that could easily erode if all the business were captive.

EXHIBIT 3-4

THE LEADING U.S. CHIPMAKERS

Merchants

1981 rank / Company	Estimated 1981 IC production (millions)	Percent change from 1980
1. Texas Instruments	1012	+16
2. Motorola	795	+16
3. National Semiconductor	683	+5
4. Intel	544	−12
5. Fairchild	375	+7
6. Signetics	344	−7
7. Mostek	304	+10
8. Advanced Micro Devices	295	+3
9. RCA	240	−3
10. Harris	150	−19
11. General Instruments	50	+25

Captives

1981 rank / Company	Estimated IC production (Equivalent sales value in millions) 1981	1982
1. IBM	1860	2580
2. Western Electric	350	385
3. Delco	180	185
4. Hewlett-Packard	140	160
5. Honeywell	70	80
6. NCR	60	70
7. Digital Equipment	50	60
8. Burroughs	40	40
9. Data General	25	35
10. Tektronix	20	25

Source: Integrated Circuit Engineering Corp.

Selling to "Make-Buy" Customers

Selling to an existing or potential make customer is a difficult situation for any industrial marketer. In an existing make situation, where the customer buys outside as well as produces part of its requirements, the supplier is always faced with a high degree of risk. Any time business softens or turns down, the make customer will more than likely reduce or stop outside purchases to keep the captive producing facilities fully utilized.

The potential make customer is also difficult and risky to serve, especially as its annual requirements grow to a significant level. Large and growing volume requirements often trigger a make decision and leave the supplier with a costly gap in sales volume and capacity utilization. Also, the ever-present threat of making internally gives the buying organization negotiating leverage that puts downward pressure on the supplier's prices and margins. A key ingredient in selling effectively to existing or potential make customers is a comprehensive understanding of the customer's costs of producing the product. Said another way, it is essential to know whether:

1. The customer production cost is *more* than the supplier's production cost and desired profit margin price.
2. The customer's production cost is *about equal* to the supplier's production cost and desired profit margin price.
3. The customer's production cost is *less* than the supplier's production cost and desired profit margin price.

In situations 1 and 2 above, it is easier for a supplier to obtain a major portion of the business, but always with a continuing threat of losing the business if the customer's costs or situation changes. Situation 3 is a much more difficult marketing problem that can be overcome only by demonstrating noncost advantages that outweigh the straight cost comparison.

It is important for the market manager, market researcher, or industrial salesperson to identify and then determine the validity of a customer's stated reasons for making rather than buying a particular item. The respondent will typically say the company has decided to make rather than buy because the price is too high. Often further inquiry[23] will show that even though cost considerations are important, the decision to make rather than buy is based on multiple reasons rather than cost alone. As a consequence, it is important for the industrial salesperson to be aware of both the direct cost comparisons and the indirect costs or risks the customer incurs when it shifts to a make position. This requires the salesperson to have an understanding of some basic cost accounting concepts so that he or she can be sure that all indirect costs are fairly considered in the make-buy comparison. Factory or overhead costs and opportunity costs should always be considered, along with the risks that are always present when a customer moves into any new manufacturing operation.

In addition to clarifying cost comparisons, the industrial supplier should stress other considerations that need to be taken into account by the customer. For example, if the

[23]Vearl A. Williams, "Should You Make or Buy?" *Production Magazine,* June 1972, p. 79.

supplier has multiple factory locations, the salesperson can point out that they are less vulnerable to labor problems that could cripple the customer's production capability. It might also be pointed out that lack of technical experience, knowhow, and learning costs invariably inflate the estimated costs of any new production activity. In higher-technology areas, the risk associated with technological obsolescence and old inventories can be emphasized. In short, the supplier should stress any valid points it can to show the advantages of avoiding the risks and uncertainties of moving into a make position, even though there may be an apparent direct cost saving.

The unanticipated loss of a big account can have a major effect on total industry demand as well as a dramatic effect on the supplier to that firm. In many cases, the entire profit structure of the business can be unfavorably altered as suppliers with excess capacity cut their prices to compete for a smaller noncaptive market.

If the supplying firm does not continually monitor key customers who are in a position to make rather than buy, it can be in for some very unpleasant surprises. Often, the customers that choose to make are the largest in the industry and critically important to the supplier. One of the largest customers for hydraulic systems and hose connecting devices is the Caterpillar Tractor Company. Both its major suppliers were stunned when Caterpillar decided to manufacture about 90 percent of its annual hydraulic hose requirements rather than buy outside. Actually, Caterpillar's move was not surprising. These items represented a major annual purchase for final assembly of its earth-moving machines. Furthermore, these items had an annual aftermarket requirement several times larger than the original equipment requirement. When one considered both markets, it was logical to anticipate that Caterpillar Tractor would enter the manufacture of hydraulic hoses.

In one company that buys a large number of components for making its capital equipment, the materials management department created three categories of purchased parts. Category 1 lists the items they believe the company must make and reasons why it must make them. Category 2 are products and components the company has an option to make or buy along with the pluses and minuses of making versus buying each item. The third category is items the company feels it must buy outside, with the reasons for buying. Over time, and with increases in price, materials, and unit costs, the firm has found that components will sometimes move between the must-make, can-make-or-buy, or must-buy categories.

Multiple or Sole Sourcing

Multiple supply sources create a more competitive environment among suppliers. It is common for the large U.S. buyer to have its annual purchasing requirements spread among two or more suppliers and to provide enough business for each supplier to keep all of them interested. When a buyer divides business among too many suppliers, it often is not sufficiently attractive for any supplier to perform the way it should. The insightful salesperson will stress this point in seeking additional business for his or her company.

Being a second or even third source with a similar item can sometimes be as profitable as being the primary source. To be a second source usually requires less capital, less technical capability, and less risk than that faced by the primary source. One supplier sees many of its second source customer relationships as "quick cash crops."

The importance buyers attach to multiple sources cannot be overemphasized. Buyers have been known to insist that a supplier of a proprietary item (even with demonstrable advantages) license or somehow help set up a second supply source before the product is adopted. This situation can create a major roadblock for the industrial salesperson who is unable to secure large buy commitments until such arrangements are made.

Only when a product is a relatively small proportion of the total cost or price, or is not a critical item, is there a tendency for buyers to have a sole or single source. For example, in the construction of a new chemical plant that may cost $10 to $15 million, there is approximately $100,000 to $125,000 worth of small precision fittings needed for each plant. With the cost of these fittings being such a small fraction of the total construction costs, there is little economic incentive for the design engineer or procurement people to use multiple sources. They may develop functional specifications and solicit bids from vendors, but they will typically award such business to one source.

A single supply situation is also common in the introductory stage of a customer's new product, since second sources may not exist or annual volume may not yet warrant two sources. A supplier may also enjoy a single source relationship because of production know-how, a patent position, or a proprietary process. However, any of these advantages are likely to be eroded as volume requirements for any customer become larger and the smart buyer exercises its leverage to insist on a second source.

Japanese manufacturers generally do not follow the U.S. procurement practice of frequently having multiple sources for an item. The Japanese believe that multiple sources and frequent rebidding and switching of suppliers fail to build supplier loyalty and tend to emphasize price. Frequent rebidding can sometimes open the door to suppliers who buy in low for the short term and then fail to perform satisfactorily. The rule of thumb of U.S. purchasing agents is "Always have at least two sources of supply for every item." Japanese companies, in contrast, prefer to buy a given item from one supplier and preferably one that does little or no business with competitors. The Japanese also tend to buy from the same few suppliers each year so that the suppliers thoroughly understand and respond to the service and quality needs of the buying organization.[24]

Developing Sources of Supply

Industrial procurement managers are responsible for finding good suppliers. This task sometimes involves extensive research and field work by the buying organization to establish one or more suppliers as reliable sources. In some large firms procurement specialists do extensive research, including tracing the availability of an item all the way back to its origins.

A number of buyers have identified strategic components or raw materials in their manufacturing process or final products and have established long-term purchasing programs to support them. In some cases, either stockpiling or contractually securing longer-term sources of supply of the strategic item occurs. Rolls Royce in England is a major manufacturer of jet engines. The gas turbines within the jet engines need a high-temperature alloy. Rolls Royce found that two countries, Zaïre and Zambia, were pro-

[24]Schonberger, *Japanese Manufacturing Techniques*, p. 175.

viding 70 percent of the free world supply of cobalt, which was a critical metal in its gas turbines. Rolls Royce first began a major stockpiling program of the critical raw material and ultimately proceeded to buy an interest in one of the cobalt-producing mines. Similarly, backward integration through the acquisition of a critical raw material was done by a major machine tool company to establish a secure source of vanadium, which is an essential ingredient in making machine tool alloys. The ultimate goal of long-term source procurement programs is to protect stable sources of supply from economic, political, and labor instability. In some countries, the government identifies critical raw material source problems. In West Germany, the Bundesbank has provided low-cost loans to help West German corporations develop long-term sources of supply for critical key materials.

In an attempt to develop long-term sources of supply, a number of manufacturing firms have formal supplier development programs. In the development of secure and stable sources of supply, some buying organizations have spelled out their criteria for a source development program. In one company these criteria included the following:

1. Evidence of strong supplier fundamentals:
    a. On-time delivery.
    b. Low rejection rates in present work.
    c. Technical problem-solving capabilities.
    d. A good labor relations history or record.
    e. Compliance with OSHA and EEO and EPA regulations.
2. The capability to upgrade to specific requirements with minimal models or no additional capital investment.
3. An identifiable core or key group of supplier personnel who can develop production specification and documentation skills that may be required for close tolerances, such as industry or military specifications.

In supplier development programs, the buying organization may help the supplier to buy equipment; and help in job setup, quality control, raw material selection, job scheduling techniques, bid preparation, and cost accounting procedures. To have effective supplier development "reachout" programs, the buying organization should spell out the specific capabilities it is seeking. This helps the organization identify and select likely new sources of supply (see the box).

The development of new sources of supply usually takes many months and often years when there is no crisis. It requires close synchronization with the buying organization's requirements and the supplier's capabilities. Supplier and buyer staffs must work as a team to develop the supply relationship. Numerous visits to one another's plants occur before and during the startup period to achieve product features, to reduce defects, and to meet quality standards.

Evaluating Suppliers

The continuing objective of a good supplier-buyer relationship is to achieve maximum value for both parties as they coordinate and combine their actions to produce mutually profitable results. The relationship requires suppliers to make a wide range of com-

HOW TWO SUPPLIER DEVELOPMENT PROGRAMS WORKED

Proctor and Gamble is a large manufacturer of packaged household items for which it has virtually hundreds of suppliers that provide manufactured materials and containers. In such a situation, smaller suppliers often do not have the resources to develop equipment to manufacture an end product that may have a very short life cycle. For example, a bottle of antiperspirant spray has plastic extruded parts. The product may only have a market life of one or two years. To encourage firms to be suppliers in such situations, it is often necessary for Proctor and Gamble to provide financial resources to put the ingredient, component, or packaging supplier in business. In cases where special machinery or special tooling is required, it is not uncommon for the buyer to purchase or finance a large amount of the specialized tooling cost. Rather than develop these external sources, the larger buyer may choose to manufacture all or a portion of its annual needs.

The Tylenol capsule crisis caused Johnson & Johnson to look to its suppliers for a new packaging approach. A team of key suppliers worked nonstop for four months to develop and produce tamper-resistant packaging after the first victim died of Tylenol laced with cyanide on September 30, 1982. The director of materials management at the J. J. McNeil Division stated:

> We immediately called our suppliers on September 30, 1982, to consider alternatives. Gilbreth International provided the new sealing material, and Doboy Packaging Machinery provided the equipment for sealing the packages. Carton suppliers were very involved. 3M provided a cap with an inner seal. Lastly, special equipment was needed to attach the new seal-cap to the bottle. We scrambled, and all worked round the clock seven days a week to get out eight million new bottles in the tamper-resistant packages.[25]

mitments and buyers to explain the basis of their purchasing policies and practices. In maintaining stable and steady sources of supply, the purchasing department is usually responsible for performance evaluation of all supply sources. Materials, components, or products delivered late will disrupt most customers' manufacturing cycles, will cause delays that require production rescheduling, and in some cases can have a dramatic effect on a firm's profitability for that product or on an entire smaller corporation. Late deliveries inhibit an industrial customer from meeting commitments to its customers and can reduce its profitability and ultimately jeopardize reputations with customers.

Products or materials shipped to the buyer too early foster costly and abnormally high inventory levels that directly affect a manufacturing facility's space and cash flow. As a consequence, on-time—neither too early nor too late—supplier delivery is critical to the productivity and functioning of most manufacturing facilities. In most progressive procurement departments, on-time delivery is measured. Many buyers have developed delivery performance analysis systems that focus on the delivery times for a supplier on a monthly or yearly basis. Such evaluation systems compare promised delivery dates to actual dates of receipt by the customer. The rating systems award points the closer the

[25]"Drug Repackaging Is a Team Triumph," *The New York Times,* February 14, 1983.

actual delivery is to the promised date. Conversely, the later the delivery is from the promised or acknowledged date, the fewer points the supplier receives.

To avoid too much slack, many buyers will allow anywhere between one to two weeks early and up to one week late as "on-time" delivery. The Japanese "just-in-time" system usually has a much shorter time frame for "on time." A specific point system or weight that relates to how early, how late, or on-time the shipment is is preferable to systems using adjectives that say whether a supplier's delivery was unpredictable, excellent, bad, or good. A quantitative or analytical rating system also allows the buyer to rate a vendor's delivery performance against the buyer's standard and against any competitive vendors who are striving for a greater portion of the buyer's business. A delivery rating system should also factor in partial shipments that are on time compared to full shipments that are on time. Total on-time delivery should be defined as the receipt of 100 percent of the ordered quantity within the allotted early and late time period for on-time arrival. One company's delivery evaluation system for vendors is shown in Table 3.1. Industrial buyers increasingly provide all suppliers with monthly or quarterly computer printout delivery rating reports. These reports show, for each location shipped to, the number of units shipped on time, the percentage shipped early and late, and rejection rates. Some buyers seek a 95 percent "pieces on time" for each supplier to each location shipped. Supplier delivery performance rating reports are typically the first item of discussion when the supplier's salesperson calls on the account.

This emphasis on delivery performance obviously places any supplier at a disadvantage if its production scheduling system is weak or sloppy. In a situation like this the salesperson is bound to make delivery promises that are "guesstimates" based largely on what he or she thinks is required to get the order.

MAINTAINING THE RELATIONSHIP

Most industrial buying situations hinge on several buying factors. The key decision to buy from one supplier and not from another typically turns on three or four of the seven factors described below:

TABLE 3.1 ***DELIVERY EVALUATION SYSTEM***

Time Frame	*Points*
More than two weeks early	8
On time	12
8–14 days late	6
15–24 days late	4
22–28 days late	2
More than 28 days late	0

1. The unique or special capabilities performed by any one competitive product (performance).
2. Consistent quality equal to or better than the standards or specifications (quality).
3. The helpfulness of the relationship between an industrial customer and the sales or technical people that serve the account (service).
4. The promised or expected delivery date (delivery).
5. The historical experience, favorable or unfavorable, the buying organization has had with the producer (past experience).
6. Delivered per-unit price (price).
7. The cost-benefit value of alternative products performing the same or similar functions (competitive value).

How well the industrial supplier and its products serve the buyer according to these factors determines whether a relationship will occur or be terminated. A healthy supplier-buyer relationship is not adversarial or arm's-length; long-term supplier-buyer relationships are mutually dependent and beneficial.

Caterpillar Tractor, for example, has outlined the steps and basis for establishing and maintaining a supplier relationship with it. For any product, part, or subassembly, the company has outlined the following sequence of events it uses to select, evaluate, maintain, and terminate suppliers.

Stage 1. *Evaluate suppliers' quality capabilities.* Quality control performs a detailed examination of potential suppliers' control over the materials received from their suppliers. Potential suppliers are expected to show the specification requirements of *their* suppliers; an approved supplier list; a method of inspection or their supplier field auditing; and the presence of appropriately trained personnel for raw material and finished goods quality control. Any deficiencies will be improved or corrected through mutual agreement with Caterpillar and the supplier. Caterpillar quality control periodically conducts follow-up quality audit visits.

Stage 2. *Communicate quality requirements.* After a supplier has been selected, the buyer communicates the technical specifications and requirements to the supplier. Caterpillar maintains a series of manufacturing practices seminars and a manual that serves as a basis for assisting suppliers to fulfill its requirements.

Stage 3. *Preproduction sample approval.* Suppliers provide samples according to the agreed-upon sampling procedures for the item. Full-scale production does not commence until the samples are approved by the company. Preproduction sample approval does not relieve the supplier from sampling full production runs.

Stage 4. *Production shipments.* Any supplier's materials and components will be subject to dimensional, metallurgical, and functional inspection at the company. Inspection rates will be decreased as a good history is developed with suppliers and maintained or increased until a good history is developed. The company will also provide all suppliers with monthly or quarterly computerized delivery reports. These reports show the number of pieces or units shipped on time to each location, the percentage shipped early and late, and the rejection rate.

When a supplier's sales representative or executive calls on the company, these reports, whether favorable or not, are always an item of discussion.

Stage 5. Measuring supplier performance. Caterpillar continually reviews each supplier's history relating to shipments in stage 4, rejections, and any other nonconformance. Based on historical data, a status rating is assigned to each supplier. A less favorable status results in increased inspection and a decision to reduce the use of the source. Those suppliers who have continued excessive nonconformance are identified, and a program for improvement is established. Lack of response will result in reduced or terminated business. In this situation, Caterpillar will identify new potential suppliers and begin the process in stage 1.

SUMMARY

A knowledge of how organizations buy will help the alert industrial supplier in many ways. First and most important, a thorough awareness of what a customer buys, how it buys, and who buys is at the heart of the concept of industrial marketing. Such a total procurement orientation helps the supplier better serve those who are buying for others.

Second, the business-to-business marketer should take the value analysis buying tool and use it as an analytical marketing, product development, and selling tool. Value analysis concepts help to satisfy the economic need of for-profit buying organizations. Value analysis helps to provide the cost-benefit reasons for maintaining an existing customer and converting the new prospects.

The industrial supplier should never assume it will be a sole or dominant supplier forever with existing customers. It should continually work at improving and thus maintaining existing favorable supplier-buyer relationships. Similarly, the industrial supplier should be persistent in attempting to understand and better serve a potential customer that is currently being served by a competitor. By learning what, how, and who buys, a competitive edge can often be developed that will turn a prospect into a profitable customer.

APPENDIX

Government Buying

Municipal, state, and federal governmental agencies and many nonprofit organizations do much of their purchasing through a bidding system. Each year, governmental agencies purchase billions of dollars worth of office equipment, cars, trucks, computers, medical supplies, and a wide range of other products. The majority of some corporations' or an entire division's business may come from government business as prime or subcontractors. Some industrial firms began as government suppliers and then later became OEM suppliers. Marketing to a government or defense market is somewhat similar to marketing to a very large OEM manufacturer. Industrial marketing occurs in government defense contracting with prime defense contractors, but it is the subcontractors to the 50 to 100 prime defense contractors that provide most of the tooling, machinery, equipment, and finished products. Government buying is basically a specification-delivery-price buying situation, and often a winner-take-all situation with no "market shares."

The for-profit buying organization is interested in value added, lower unit cost, or whatever affects the profitability of its end products. The profit motive or return on investment are not factors in government procurement. The price paid or cost of some government contracts is based on technical requirements and the amount of government appropriations. Within those parameters, profits are distributed to the major contractors and the subcontractors to develop an "effective" system or product. Federal appropriations determine the size of the system and subsequent contracts.

A cartoon that appeared in a popular magazine showed two astronauts in a space ship ready to blast off from Cape Canaveral, with one saying to the other: "Frank, was every product in this space ship built by the lowest price bidder?" In reality this is not usually the case. Government organizations often buy less on a cost-benefit dimension than for-profit corporations. Many government contracts never are bid. If the public or government agency is a municipality or even state agency, it will tend to favor suppliers within the country, political party, town, region, or state. United States senators and representatives aggressively try to obtain contracts for corporations with manufacturing facilities in their constituents' geographic regions.

Most of the U.S. government's procurement is done by the air force, army, and navy through the Department of Defense (DOD). The General Services Administration purchases for many other agencies. The agencies or departments develop standards for most of the items purchased so they can be assured of minimum quality levels. Government agencies set specifications and then evaluate or qualify potential suppliers against these specifications. In order to become qualified, it is necessary to meet procedural standards often set forth in quality control manuals that cover each step of a manufacturing process and quality control sampling. These regulations are usually enforced by the government agency's inspectors. In many instances, the government agency continually evaluates a supplier or contractor by maintaining a resident government inspector at the supplier's production site. The inspector may be full time or may maintain an office at the site that he or she visits periodically.

Commercial firms refer to buying as "purchasing" or "procurement," but the Department of Defense refers to it as "acquisition" or "acquisition programs." The acquisition

EXHIBIT 3A-1

DEFENSE ACQUISITION CONTRACTING CYCLES

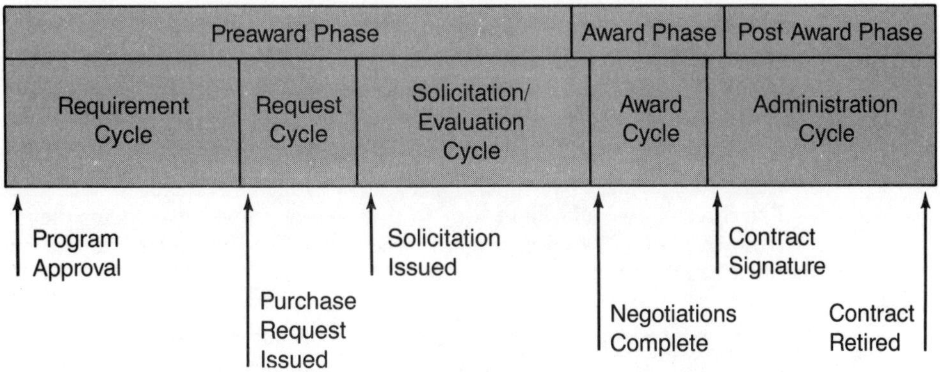

programs of the military buy a specific function that is specified by a military need. The military or "market" need is first established in an agency like the Strategic Air Command in the U.S. Air Force. These are, in essence, problems based on defense threats for which suppliers are to provide solutions. The need is budgeted by Congress and then contracts are let to suppliers to provide the products and services. Alternative suppliers are considered, and one or possibly two suppliers are then chosen. Exhibit 3A-1 illustrates a flow path for the defense acquisition process.[1] It is divided into the preaward, award, and postaward phases.

> The requirements cycle and request cycle consists of the submission and approval of the mission need statement, and the solution and evaluation cycle consists of the concept formulation stage. The preaward phase "product" is a paper product, rather than hardware. In the award phase, hardware is developed–physical, tangible products. This consists of both prototypes (development) and production items (final products). The postaward phase is the contract administration stage where progress on the production contracts is monitored and delivery and testing occurs. At the end of this phase the contract is retired. . . . New systems evolve through four design states–conceptual design, preliminary design (narrowed-down concepts), engineering design (based on engineering development), and production design (ready to go to the presses and foundries).[2]

The Department of Defense procurement or acquisition process is all initiated by, monitored by, pursued by, and approved by the buyer rather than the supplier. The suppliers rarely risk their resources. The need and supplier selection are similar to for-profit procurement, but source loyalty is less prevalent.

[1]Ronald L. Shill, "Buying Process in the U.S. Department of Defense," *Industrial Marketing Management*, 9 (1980), pp. 291–298.
[2]Ibid., p. 293.

The *Commerce Business Daily* is the traditional place the federal government uses to inform potential suppliers of forthcoming bids. Any federal order over $5,000 by law must be listed in that publication. But the astute supplier is aware of the buying need long before it is published in the newspaper. The earlier a supplier can know of a need and influence the process, the greater chance it will have to get the business.

Contrary to public opinion, many government buyers prefer a sole source. The sales manager of a large medical instrument company stated the following after receiving a large order from a U.S. government health agency:

> Regardless of the government procurement regulations against sole sourcing, the Lab directors usually find a way to sole source on whatever items they only want from one source. Before the bid is advertised or published, the chosen supplier often has the order all but signed.

Government agencies often like sole sources because they can choose a known supplier and avoid the risk of having a low-bid supplier that later cannot deliver on time or meet quality specifications. The smaller the per unit or annual purchase amount, the more likely the government agency will not put it out for a competitive bid. Furthermore, if the need is immediate, as it usually is in an aftermarket situation, it will not wait for competitive bids. Government competitive bids that specify a brand name "or equivalent" force the second source supplier to prove equivalency. The proof requires that the salespeople or proposal must often have technical product test information to show the performance of the product compared to that of the specified brand name.

High-level agency officials are usually not aware of all the sole sourcing and noncompetitive buying that occurs. Protests to high government levels can get a second source or competitive bid situation activated. It is also easier to become a second source in a nonprofit organization when it is one to three months away from the end of its fiscal year and if the budget funds are not expended by the end of the year. One major electric typewriter company instructs all salespeople to learn each nonprofit organization's fiscal year period and to make more frequent calls in the six- to ten-week period before it ends. If a budget surplus exists, the organization may also be more willing to experiment with new or different products.

II

EVALUATING THE MARKET ENVIRONMENT

4

Understanding Customers and Competition

At the monthly staff meeting, the general manager of the specialty chemical division of Dumont Chemical Corporation expressed concern about the downward sales trend and declining margins in the division's bread and butter product line. Sales were not only far off the plan for this year, but had dropped below last year's level for the same period. The general manager received several different responses. Said the sales manager: "We are being out-priced." With a better price discount structure, he felt he could restore the volume level. The division controller pointed out that a 5 percent reduction in price would require much higher volume to recapture the lost margin income. The controller also pointed out that there had been a long-term decline in unit sales growth for the past four years and that the numerous price increases had tended to obscure this fact. The manufacturing manager maintained there was no way to reduce costs further without affecting product quality and the service level.

After three hours, they were getting nowhere. Frustrated, the division general manager finally snapped: "Who knows what is really going on in the marketplace? Is the total market off? How are our competitors doing? I have a strong suspicion that a fundamental change has occurred in the way our product is being used or in the way competitors are serving these markets. A trend like this doesn't occur overnight, and we probably can't correct the problem with a short-term fix like cutting price. We need to have a very clear understanding of what is happening at the customer level and what our competitors are doing. Something fundamental is obviously affecting this product."

What is likely to happen if Dumont attempts a short-term fix?

What are the effects of the problem?

What are the real causes of the problem?

Many industrial producers often focus only on the products they produce and pay little attention to their customers' operations or to competitors who seek the same customer dollar. This is what is meant by a "product-driven" company. A product-driven industrial company is a sharp contrast to a truly market-oriented industrial company. Business-to-business marketing is too often a one-way flow of product communication to customers. But this is only part of the marketing job, since effective marketing depends on a flow of information about customer needs and competitors' actions. Vital information about customers and competition helps the industrial producer recognize, assess, and seize opportunities and counter threats. The industrial company whose products, strategies, and programs flow from analysis of customer requirements is a market-driven firm.

UNDERSTANDING CUSTOMERS

Most industrial managers know who their major customers are and generally what these customers do. However, far too few managers really have the depth of understanding they should about how their customers operate and make their money. Even worse, most fail to understand the importance of this point or do not show the interest they should in developing this understanding. Peter Drucker wrote 30 years ago: "A business is not determined by the producer but by the customer."[1] Learning everything possible about the customer's business is the very essence of business marketing. It is the foundation for designing a product and service package that will offer the customer economic value, which is the basis of business marketing. It then allows the business marketer to segment markets and to determine which customers to pursue more, less, or to avoid entirely. It is this thought process that distinguishes effective marketing from simply trying to sell more products.

Customers' Operations and Products

Each group of customers has, as the heart of its business, a unique set of functions to perform. Exhibit 4-1 shows the major functions involved in a metal production and rough machining process. Similar schematics can be developed to identify the critical functions performed by any customer group. Understanding the critical functions is the first step toward understanding the customer's operations and products. A much deeper study and analysis are required to achieve the depth of understanding that will enable the business marketer to consider ways in which its products can really help the customer become more cost effective. Many of the best business marketing companies have developed substantial banks of industry skills that help to provide this knowledge of customer operations. With this kind of knowledge, it is much easier to develop marketing strategies and sales proposals that contribute real value to the customer and are difficult for uninformed competitors to match.

[1]Peter Drucker, *The Practice of Management* (New York: Harper & Row, 1954).

EXHIBIT 4-1

METAL PRODUCTION AND FABRICATION

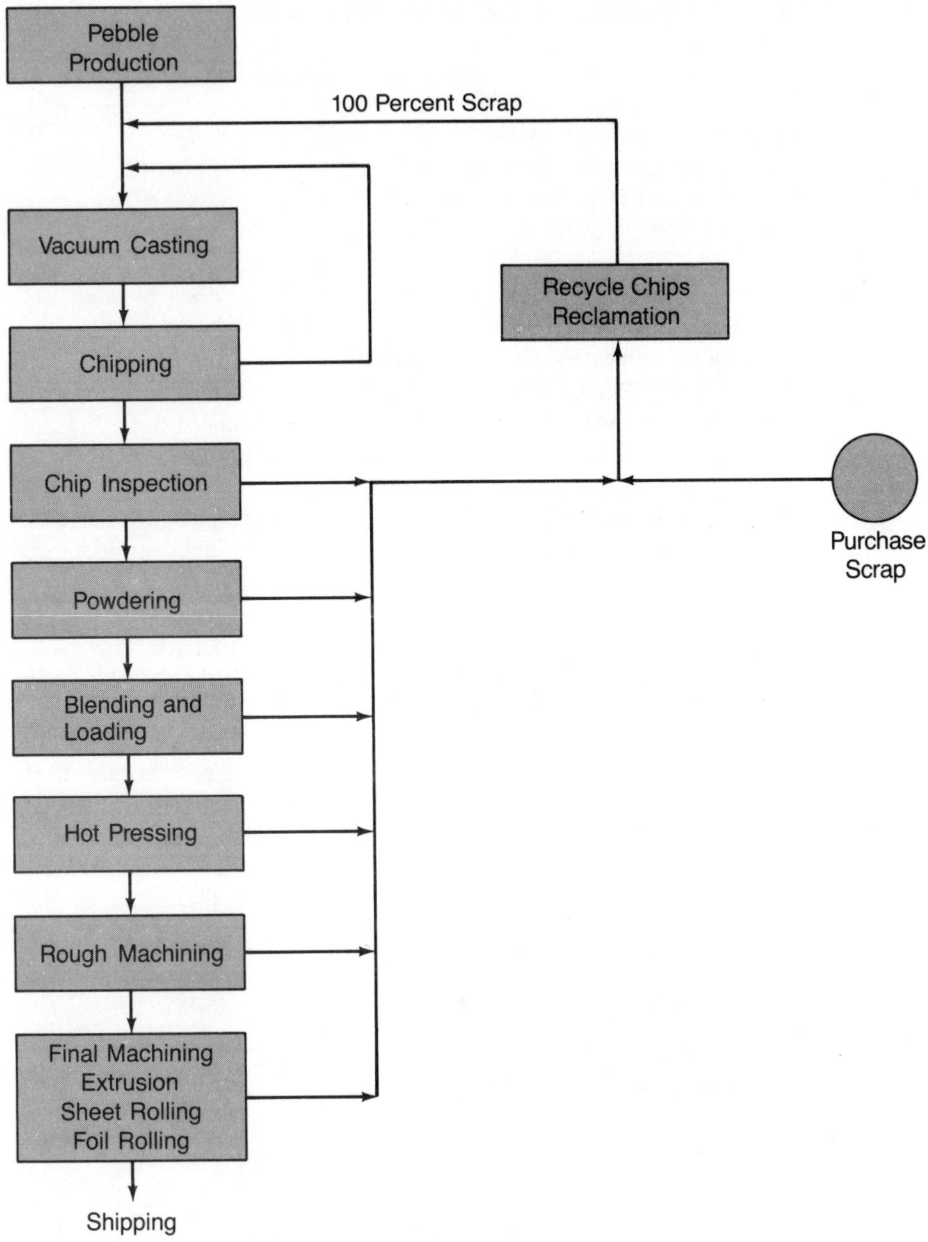

Exhibit 4-1 was helpful to a supplier in thinking through how a toxic dust and fume collection system should be designed to meet OSHA requirements. Its understanding of each function in the flow led to a system design that was more effective and less costly than those submitted by competitors. In another situation, a scale supplier sold a system that reduced waste at several points during the conversion of raw potatoes to chips. Again, the supplier's intimate knowledge of the customer's operations helped it design a system that concentrated on the areas of maximum payoff for the least investment in weighing equipment. In both examples, the supplier, rather than merely seeking an order, was able to help the customer improve performance.

Progressive manufacturers of almost anything are continually searching for ways to streamline their manufacturing processes or utilize new, more cost-effective approaches or materials. Unless the supplier keeps pace with the customer's thinking and ideas for altering the way it operates, it can easily find that new methods or materials have made its product obsolete. For example, automotive oil was packaged and distributed in metal cans for many years. The principal can supplier was unaware that oil companies were experimenting with cardboard containers that cost and weighed less and would not corrode during storage. Because these advantages were so significant, the oil producers abruptly shifted to cardboard containers and completely eliminated the metal can supplier from the picture. There may not have been any way the can supplier could have prevented this shift, but had it been aware of what was going on, it might have decided that the container business was sufficiently large to invest in equipment to manufacture cardboard containers itself, since the customer was first buying a function and then the best product to perform the function.

Learning and knowing the customer's functions and the products available to perform those functions enable the supplier to think, talk, and perform around the customer's needs. For example, the Office Products Division of IBM, which primarily manufactures and markets typewriters and word processing equipment, developed a functional approach to analyze word processing in an office. The three functions are (1) word origin, (2) production (typing), and (3) distribution and storage. This functional view of office word processing (Exhibit 4-2) allows IBM to improve products in each function and to consider combining functions in a product. A good example is IBM's memory typewriter, which now performs both production (typing) and storage functions.

Still another example points up the need to evaluate the customer's flow of work as a system to gain a better understanding of its requirements. The Pitney Bowes Corporation analyzed its customers' mailroom and mailing activities as a production system. It partitioned the mailroom "production system" of customers into identifiable functions and from this has developed a line of products beyond postage meter machines that now includes mail sealers, mail openers, folders, inserters, collators, counters, weight scales, and mailroom furniture as part of the functional system.

Customers' Costs

Once the customer's functions and production stages are identified, the supplier can develop a much clearer picture of where and how the customer incurs costs to perform the functions and where there are opportunities to improve an existing cost structure. The

EXHIBIT 4-2

OFFICE WORD PROCESSING

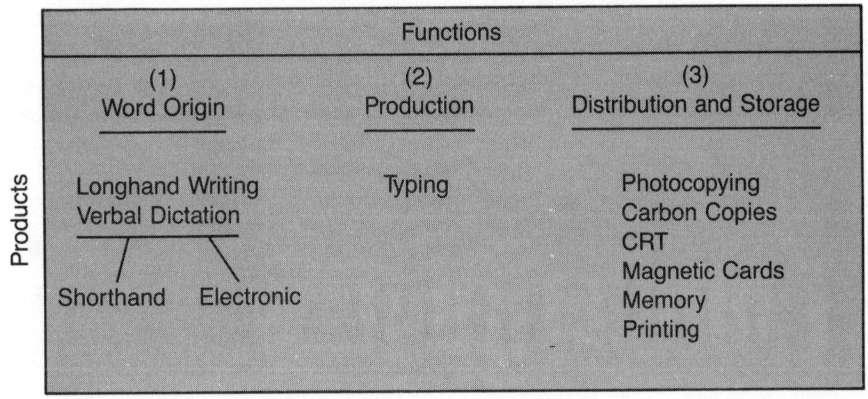

customer costs that need to be identified fall into two categories. What costs does the customer incur by buying or using a product and what costs does it recover or avoid? Although these sound like obvious questions, the answers are not so simple. Cost-benefit advantages and comparisons are not always readily apparent or clear-cut, especially when the full range of costs is considered. The range of costs to consider includes the initial purchase cost, installation costs, operating costs, and life cycle costs.

INITIAL PURCHASE COST. The initial purchase or first cost is the amount the customer pays up front. In addition to the list or quoted price of the product, there are charges for financing, freight, insurance, installation, technical assistance at startup, warranty, and/or service. It is essential to be certain that all these costs are considered in making competitive comparisons. Failing to do so can easily lead to the wrong economic decision even though the chosen supplier appears to offer the lowest price. Customers that base their buying decision primarily on initial purchase cost are a prime target for the low-cost producer that can gear its whole marketing strategy to providing the best value on this initial cost comparison.

INSTALLATION AND STARTUP COSTS. Installation costs may involve space alterations, connections to power sources, facilities for ensuring proper temperature and ventilating conditions, and arrangements for handling noise, waste materials, scrap, and so on. Startup costs typically occur after installation and involve all the activities required to ensure that the product or system actually performs to specification or the producer's claims. Both of these are typically nonrecurring, but nevertheless substantial, costs. In many cases, highly skilled individuals or teams of supplier personnel actually operate the product or system on the user's site and make the final adjustments necessary to ensure performance.

OPERATING COSTS. Operating costs are the ongoing costs of utilizing a particular product or system. They include most of the standard accounting charges like labor, material, power, maintenance and repair, depreciation, and interest charges on the purchased item or inventory. Short-term differences in these costs are typically minimal, but they often become significant when calculated over the longer term. Table 4.1 shows how an annual savings of $1,125 could be achieved by using an energy-efficient 150-horsepower motor. Although this motor would undoubtedly cost more initially, the return could be very attractive, particularly when these savings are extended for the estimated useful life of the motor and a reasonable allowance is made for rising energy costs. Similar analyses can be made for any operating costs that are reduced as a result of a higher investment in the initial purchase price.

Exhibit 4-3 shows the operating cost savings or payback for a new commercial light bulb. The initial purchase price of $10 for an electronic bulb is cost-effective when compared to an incandescent bulb over a two-year period. The more rational industrial buyer thinks in terms of operating costs after the purchase much more than the average consumer does. As a consequence, operating cost considerations often weigh heavily in industrial purchase decisions.

SWITCHING COSTS. Beyond the traditional user costs defined above, one final set of costs must sometimes be considered. These are the costs of switching from one supplier's product to another's. For example, the cost of switching from IBM equipment to another

TABLE 4.1

ANNUAL ENERGY SAVINGS*

Horsepower	*XE Eff.*	*Ind. Avg. Eff.*	*Watts Saved*	*Money Saved*
3	88.5	81.3	224	$ 64
5	88.5	83.6	252	$ 72
7-½	90.2	84.6	410	$ 118
10	90.2	85.7	434	$ 125
15	91.7	86.7	704	$ 203
20	93.0	87.8	950	$ 274
25	93.0	88.3	1,067	$ 307
30	93.0	89.5	941	$ 271
40	93.0	89.8	1,143	$ 329
50	94.1	90.5	1,577	$ 454
60	94.1	90.7	1,783	$ 513
75	95.0	91.3	2,387	$ 687
100	95.0	92.0	2,561	$ 737
125	95.0	92.1	3,091	$ 890
150	95.8	92.7	3,906	$1,125

*Based on typical utility rates of $.04 per kilowatt hour and 7,200 hours per year of motor operation.

EXHIBIT 4-3

HOW A $10 LIGHT BULB PAYS FOR ITSELF

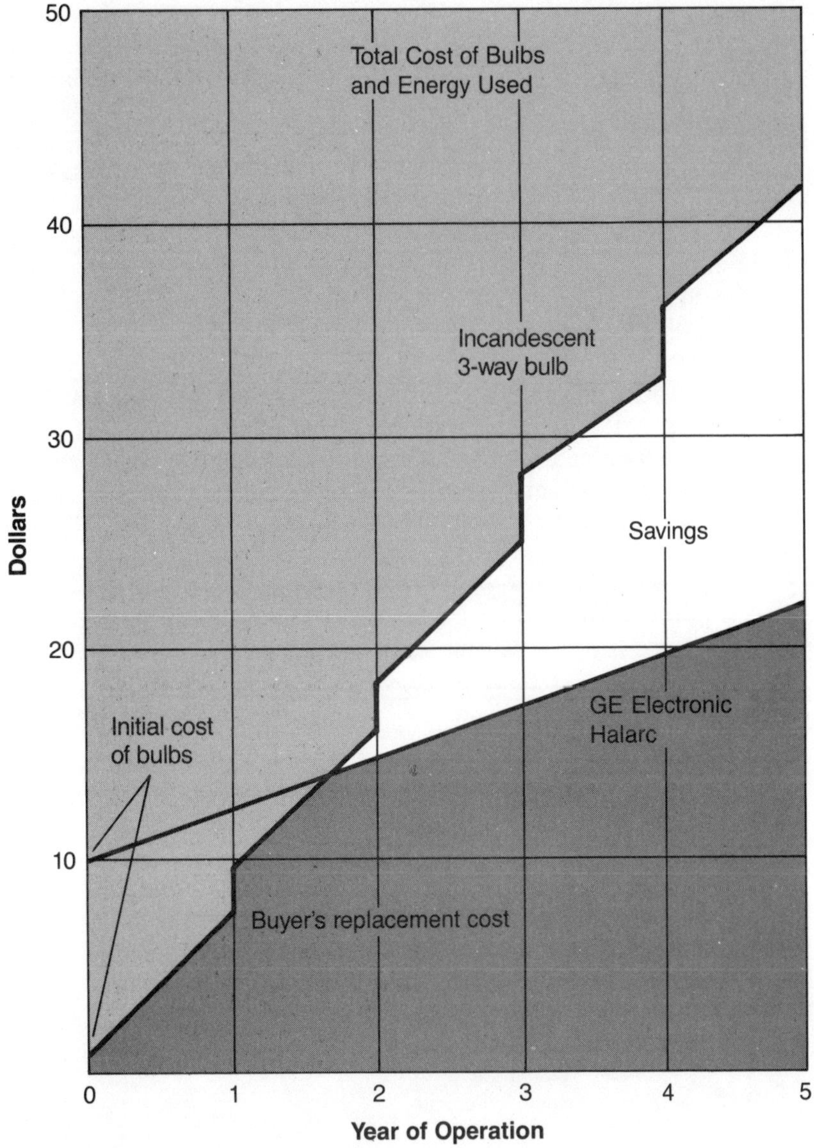

Data: General Electric Co. (assumes electricity cost of 4.6¢ per kw and use of 1,000 hours a year)

Source: Business Week, May 19, 1980, p. 124.

manufacturer's equipment is significant because in-house personnel must be retrained to operate the new equipment. Similarly, changing suppliers that provide consignment stocks can involve substantial costs unless careful plans are made to gradually phase out of one supplier's remaining stock into the other. Switching costs can be both tangible and intangible. Tangible costs include costs like those in the examples just cited. They are real and can be calculated or measured. Often equally important, however, are the intangible or penalty costs that can be incurred whenever a new supplier is brought on stream; there is always a risk that a new supplier will fail to provide consistent quality, on-time delivery, or proper service support. Although these costs cannot be calculated in advance, they can certainly be significant if the new supplier fails to perform.

LIFE CYCLE COSTS. These costs are important to consider whenever the estimated useful life of one product differs from another. In addition to all the costs described so far, they include any residual or salvage value as well as replacement costs when the original equipment has completed its useful life. Evaluating life cycle costs has assumed an added importance during the past decade because inflationary forces have greatly increased the residual or salvage value of many items and caused replacement prices to rise much faster than they had in the past. Table 4.2 shows how life cycle costing was used to compare the economics of a solar and a conventional heating system over a 20-year life. Even though the initial purchase cost of the solar system is 40 percent greater than the

TABLE 4.2 ***LIFE CYCLE COSTING: A 20-YEAR COMPARATIVE ANALYSIS****

	Type of Energy System	*Combined Solar/ Standard System*	*Conventional System Only*
P =	Initial investment costs	$20,000	$12,000
	Salvage	0	($4,000) 20th yr
S =	Present value of salvage	0	$596
	Maintenance and repair costs	0	(0)
M =	Present value of maintenance and repair	0	0
	Replacement costs	0	($6,000) 15th yr
R =	Present value of replacement costs	0	$1,434
	Base-year energy costs	($500)	($2,000)
E =	Present value of energy costs	$6,359	$25,436
LCC =	Present value of total costs	$26,359	$38,274

Formula: LCC = P − S + M + R + E

Combined solar/standard system: LCC = $20,000 − 0 + 0 + 0 + $6,359 = $26,359

Standard system only: LCC = $12,000 − $596 + 0 + $1,434 + $25,436 = $38,274

*Only present values are used in the LCC formula, and numbers in parens cannot be inserted directly into the formula.

conventional system, the costs over the full life cycle are approximately 30 percent less. The salvage and replacement costs, as well as the operating savings, are the major plus factors that offset the higher initial investment costs. If products performing the same function have different useful life periods or wear-out rates, the concept of life cycle cost can provide a favorable advantage to a supplier. Exhibit 4-4 shows the life cycle costs involved in owning a lift truck; it deemphasizes the initial purchase price and stresses the life cycle costs of owning and operating the unit. The Caterpillar advertisement in Exhibit 4-5 emphasizes the real costs a customer incurs when purchasing a machine. Caterpillar stresses that the total customer cost for its machines may be less than that of the competition, which should mean higher profit or lower cost for the Caterpillar owner.

End-User Cost-Benefit

Once cost components are quantified, it is possible to determine the cost-benefit for the end user. The cost-benefit analysis helps in determining the economic value-in-use of a producer's product in a customer's particular application. Table 4.3 shows how an end-user cost-benefit analysis was used to (1) determine the costs of activities to perform the function, and (2) compare competitors A and B on the cost components and total value.

Table 4.3 is a general framework for identifying a customer's costs for purchasing a part, machine, or materials. Some of the cost components will not be applicable for every product situation. The industrial supplier should select those costs that are applicable to the specific product and market situation. In many situations, the economic cost terms will have to be modified to the language and units of analysis of that particular industry. For example, Table 4.4 is a similar cost analysis for a finger implant for arthritic patients. It shows that although the initial purchase price is higher, the total cost to the end user (customer or patient) is lower. Since this analysis shows that end user's total costs are *significantly* lower for producer B's product, it raises a question of whether or not producer B has set its initial purchase price high enough.

TABLE 4.3 **END-USER COST-BENEFIT COMPARISON**

	End-Use Segment	
Cost Components	*Competitor A*	*Competitor B*
1. Initial purchase cost	______	______
2. Installation and startup	______	______
3. Operating cost	______	______
Yearly	______	______
Product life	______	______
4. Switching costs	______	______
5. Salvage value	______	______
6. Average product life	______	______
Total cost	______	______

EXHIBIT 4-4

LIFE CYCLE COSTS FOR A LIFT TRUCK

Source: Clark Industrial Truck

EXHIBIT 4-5

REAL COSTS OF OWNERSHIP

Profit conscious buyers know total machine cost

Total Cost Evaluation is the profitable way to examine machine costs. Buyers purchasing based only on initial price overlook very important costs that affect potential profit.

That's because true machine cost goes far beyond initial price. You must add operating and maintenance costs to your repair and downtime costs. Then subtract depreciation and resale value to get Total Cost.

And, Total Cost Evaluation demands a search for machines having high resale values and low operating, maintenance, repair and downtime costs. Lower costs mean higher profits.

Total Cost Evaluation is the objective way to select new machines. Your Caterpillar Dealer stands ready to help set up Total Cost record systems. Such professional assistance is only one of many CAT PLUS services available from Caterpillar Dealers.

CATERPILLAR

Caterpillar, Cat and are Trademarks of Caterpillar Tractor Co.

Source: Caterpillar Tractor Company

TABLE 4.4

COST-BENEFIT FINGER IMPLANT COMPARISON

Cost Components	Competitive Products A	B
1. Initial purchase price for four:		
4 × 82 (A)	$ 328	–
4 × 275 (B)	–	$1,100
2. Preoperative evaluation	28	28
3. Surgical procedure (installation)	1,100	1,100
4. Splints	65	40
5. Hospital stay:		
12 days × $300/day (A)	3,600	–
4 days × $300/day (B)	–	1,200
6. Hospital occupational therapy	280	0
7. Follow-up outpatient treatment	0	40
8. Follow-up outpatient visit	120	120
Total cost	$5,521	$3,628

The major cost benefits are not necessarily found with the immediate customer. For example, a high-temperature heat-resistant hydraulic hose that is installed on commercial bakery oven doors has a safety and downtime value to bakeries but offers little or no "cost savings" to the bakery oven manufacturers. If the major benefits are beyond the supplier's customer (in this case the OEM), the producer's selling effort must be directed at the end user to get it to specify or request the supplier's product.

EXHIBIT 4-6

PUSH OR PULL VALUE-IN-USE

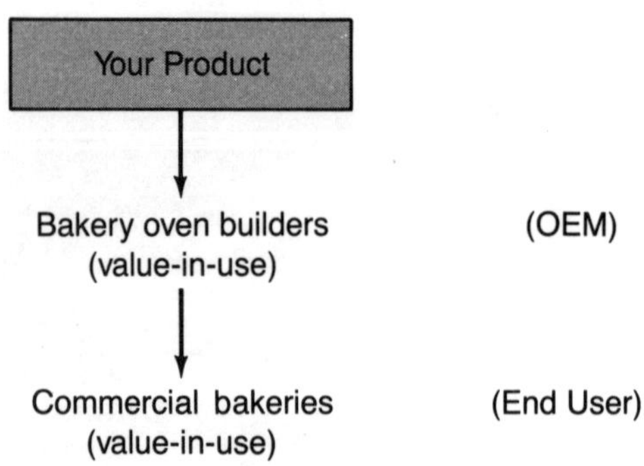

It is often necessary to develop in-depth case studies with a few customers to identify and calculate the cost-benefit value by application or market segment. This is especially necessary when the customer has not kept good cost-benefit information.

UNDERSTANDING COMPETITORS

After the business marketer knows the customer's operations and need for the product, it is necessary to examine the competitors that provide a product that performs the same function(s). A competitor may not supply an exact "pin-for-pin" product or one made of the same material, but if in the customer's eyes the competitive product fulfills the same function, it is a competitive product and therefore a competitor to analyze. An analysis of competitors is an analysis of businesses that compete for the same customer's sales dollars.

An assessment of the competition is always important—whether the company is protecting, improving, or entering a new market situation. Competitive assessment entails a knowledge of who present and potential competitors are; an analysis of how well each competitor meets the requirements of a segment; and an analysis of competitors' plans and likely reactions. Since there is usually a different set of competitors in each product or market segment, any meaningful form of assessment should be conducted for *each* product or market segment.

Competitive Structure

It is important to know the number and market share of the competitors supplying each market segment, since these factors greatly influence all marketing plans and decisions. Fragmented markets, characterized by a large number of competitors, each with a small market share, tend to be more unstable and unpredictable. Conversely, when a small number (e.g., two to four) of competitors account for 70 to 80 percent of the market, competitive behavior is more stable and predictable. Generally, the more capital intensive industries have fewer producers, whereas industries that are relatively easy to enter and leave are usually much more highly fragmented.

The existence of a captive or internal supply source is a competitor even though that source may not be selling to other customers. Some captive competitors also buy a percentage of their requirements from outside suppliers. A thorough competitive analysis should identify the total market served by those with and without captive sources. When a large or increasing percentage of a segment is supplied by captive sources, market economics are generally less attractive.

The major sources of present and potential competition to consider in conducting a competitive analysis can be classified as follows:

1. Present competitors supplying a directly competing product or a functional substitute to current and potential customers in the geographic areas the firm now serves.
2. Competitors supplying a directly competing product or a functional substitute to cus-

tomers in geographic areas the firm does not serve. This is often a foreign producer supplying customers outside the domestic market.
3. Captive sources that determine what percentage of the total market is available to outside suppliers. The make-buy customer can also compete directly by selling the captive product to outside customers.
4. Suppliers that integrate forward to earn greater profits. If the market size, market growth, and profitability of a segment are attractive, suppliers who know the business may move forward and compete with their customers.
5. Employees leaving to go to competitors or go it alone. The hiring of these employees by a current noncompetitor may signal a new competitive entrant. If these employees start their own business to compete, they frequently "cherry pick" key products and accounts.
6. Surprise sources. New competitors, especially those with a unique technology advantage, often come from outside the existing competitors or industry. The diesel locomotive was introduced by a firm that had never before made steam locomotives. Plastic beverage bottles were developed and introduced by chemical firms, not glass or metal bottle manufacturers.

Competitor Economics

Companies within the same industry can have very different cost structures, which can be due to a number of factors, including these:

1. The age and condition of their physical plant
2. The effectiveness and efficiency of their machines
3. The productivity of their labor force
4. The degree of forward or backward integration
5. Size and market share

How competitive a firm is in the marketplace often depends on the cost and productivity of its workforce and manufacturing process. This is especially true in mature industries where one must be a lower-cost producer to be an effective competitor. Many different manufacturing strategies are being employed to reduce labor costs and improve productivity and manufacturing efficiency. Many companies have abandoned their huge centralized manufacturing facilities in favor of smaller decentralized plants that typically employ 200 to 500 people. Overhead costs can be reduced in these smaller facilities, they are easier to manage and control, and the lines of communication to the workforce are much easier to maintain. Many other companies have invested heavily in robotics or other automation devices and systems in an effort to eliminate high-cost labor and build greater cost efficiency into their manufacturing process. Still other companies have migrated to other countries, particularly for high-labor content assembly operations, to take advantage of the much lower labor costs.

Some producers have a lower-cost advantage because they have integrated backward to a material source. For example, many chemical companies have become "basic" in one or more of their key ingredients in an effort to become a lower-cost producer. A firm may also become a lower-cost producer by integrating forward and acquiring a customer's products or operations, which can then be combined with its own in a cost-effective way. Still other producers have achieved significant cost advantages by setting up their operations in close proximity to a critical material source. For example, Montreal's Alcan Aluminum Ltd. has about 60 percent of its primary smelter capacity in Canada. Plentiful hydroelectric power keeps Alcan's average cost to about $.05 per pound of aluminum[2] while the major U.S. competitors, Alcoa, Reynolds, and Kaiser, spend over $.15 per pound. This cost advantage allows Alcan to compete profitably even when shipping near its competitors' plants. If the cost of electricity in petroleum-fed aluminum mills increases, the less costly hydroelectric facilities will provide even greater competitive advantage for Alcan.

Being the biggest or having a dominant market share does not assure any firm of being the low-cost producer. For example, the electromotive division of General Motors, with 1980 sales of $1.2 billion, had approximately a 75 percent market share of the U.S. locomotive market. The only significant competitor, the General Electric Transportation Systems Division, had the remaining 25 percent of the U.S. market but a lower manufacturing cost structure. General Motors' overwhelming volume and market share did not give it a cost advantage because of its very high labor costs: General Motors United Auto Workers were paid $3 to $4 dollars an hour more than GE's United Electrical and Radio Machine workers. This cost disadvantage persisted despite the fact that General Motors' electromotive division had been in the business of making diesel locomotives approximately 20 years before General Electric entered the business in 1960.[3] In short, the popular belief in experience curves and lower cost per unit of volume is refuted by such "real world" factors as labor rate differentials.

Because experience curve costs are frequently misused or misunderstood, an explanatory comment is worthwhile. The experience curve concept holds that the "costs of value added to a product decline approximately 20 to 30 percent in real terms each time the manufacturing experience is doubled." Supporters of this concept contend, therefore, that the producer with the highest market share will generally have the lowest cost because of its perceived economies of scale and greater manufacturing experience. In many cases these supporters are mistaken. They have not differentiated the degree of cost improvement that can be achieved in a mature business from that that can be achieved in a new or rapidly growing business where there is still plenty of room for manufacturing improvements.

The experience curve should not be confused with the learning curve, which was discovered over 50 years ago. The learning curve is very real for new, growing businesses and in situations where true productivity gains are achieved by working smarter. However, the opportunities for cost efficiencies diminish over the long term as manufacturing methods become routine and producers' facilities and equipment reach state-of-the-art.

Market Success Factors

Before a supplier can compete in any industrial product or market situation, there are a number of capabilities it must have in place. These market entry factors vary by market

[2]"The Sign of the Water Bearer," *Forbes,* March 2, 1981, p. 50.
[3]*Business Week,* June 8, 1981.

served, but often include having a minimum level of quality, proven manufacturing capability, technical know-how, service capability, and possibly an extensive distributor network. However, simply having the necessary capabilities does not ensure success in a competitive marketplace.

When industrial producers ask "How are we doing compared to competition?" they should look beyond sales volume or market share figures. The more appropriate question to ask might be this: "What factors cause a customer to choose one supplier over another?" One could call the "causes" the key success factors for serving the identified market. They are the vital factors on which the buying decision turns. Customers' explanations of why they buy or do not buy from a particular supplier are often different from what suppliers think. Astute suppliers recognize this point and go to their customers to find out firsthand what factors swing the buying decision.

The worksheet shown in Table 4.5 can be used to conduct a competitive analysis of the key success factors for serving a given market. Since successful business marketing involves the supplier's production, engineering, and marketing personnel, it is helpful to have the inputs of all these people.

CONDUCTING A COMPETITIVE ANALYSIS. The steps involved in conducting such a competitive analysis are straightforward:

1. List the success factors that control or influence the buying decision for a product in a defined market segment. Three to six factors are usually sufficient.
2. Rank order the competitive success factors that were listed in step 1.
3. Weigh each ranked success factor. For example, success factor 1 might have a weight of 35 percent. All the success factors must total 100 percent (see "Weights" column of Table 4.5).
4. List the major competitors that account for 80 to 90 percent of the defined market segment.
5. On a scale of 1 to 10 (10 = most favorable, 1 = least favorable), rate the competitors on each success factor.
6. On a scale of 1 to 10 (10 = most favorable, 1 = least favorable), rate your firm on each success factor.
7. Multiply each competitor and your firm's 1 to 10 rating number times the success factor weight. For example, in Table 4.5, multiply sealing capabilities (.35) times competitor 1's rating of 9: $.35 \times 9 = 3.15$.
8. Total each competitor's total in the row labeled "competitive position." The competitive position scores should compare closely to current market share. If the competitive position scores do not compare closely to known current market shares, the key success factors, ranks, or weights are inaccurate. If market shares are not known, competitive position scores can serve as a surrogate market share estimate.

A quantitative competitive analysis can be very useful when developing product or market strategies to enter a market, to protect an established position, or to improve an existing position. The analysis helps one see which competitors are strong and weak and what success factors account for their strong or weak positions. It helps a company focus

TABLE 4.5

COMPETITIVE ANALYSIS WORKSHEET

Product/Market Segment

Key Competitive Success Factors		*Major Competitors*						*Self-Analysis*	
Factors	*Weights*	*1 (Rockgood)*		*2 (Best-Warner)*		*3 (Tokyo Products)*		*(ARW)*	
		1–10		*1–10*		*1–10*		*1–10*	
1. Sealing capabilities	.35	9	3.15	5	1.75	8		9	3.15
2. On-time delivery	.25	9	2.25	6	1.50	?		2	.50
3. Technical assistance	.20	8	1.60	3	.60			5	1.00
4. Price	.20	6	1.20	7	1.40			8	1.60
5.									
Competitive position	1.00 or 100%		8.20		5.05				6.25
Current market segment share		42%		19%				32%	

on the factors it needs to improve. In one case, a company thought a price reduction would help its position. However, the competitive analysis done by interviewing customers revealed that customers were much more sensitive to rapid delivery service. It used less money than the price reduction would have cost to improve delivery and showed a significant market improvement over the next two years.

For longer-range planning and strategy development, the industrial producer should utilize a competitive analysis by asking the following future-based questions:

1. How might the success factors change in ranking and weight in the next two to three years?
2. Which existing competitors are likely to improve their competitive position?
3. Which existing competitors are likely to decline in position or exit from this market?
4. What new competitors might appear or enter the business?

Asking these questions often provides an "early alert" to competitive changes by helping the firm anticipate threats and opportunities.

GATHERING COMPETITIVE INTELLIGENCE. Gathering competitive intelligence is an ongoing process. Even the smallest suppliers can and should gather information about competitors. Competitive intelligence tends to come in fragments from many sources and often is not "hard" information. Nevertheless, it can provide very useful insights that can help formulate strategies and plans.

Competitive intelligence gathering should seek information from:

1. Product comparisons
2. Pricing
3. Expansion plans and plant closings
4. Promotional strategy
5. R&D expenditures
6. Manufacturing processes
7. Patents filed
8. Labor contract expiration dates, wages, and strikes
9. Profit and loss statements
10. Number of employees per unit or division
11. New product announcements
12. Changes in personnel
13. Interviews with competitors' personnel
14. Analysis of past bidding situations
15. An incident of very high bidding
16. Common suppliers
17. Trade shows
18. Local newspapers
19. Technical standards committees
20. Other divisions that buy from or sell to the competitor

There are many monitoring techniques a company can use to keep tabs on present and potential competitors. One technique is to buy competitors' products and evaluate them for performance and, if possible, take them apart piece by piece. This approach enabled one component supplier to market an item for less than its competitors by substituting plastic for many metal parts. A major photocopy machine producer has a full-time staff analyzing all U.S. and foreign-made copiers for performance, benefits, and features. The analysis is used for product development improvements, sales training, and product literature comparisons.

The industrial sales force is sometimes considered a biased and poor source of comprehensive information. This is sometimes true, but the problem is that the receivers and users of the information have not been properly trained. The industrial salesperson's role in understanding end-use markets is critical. The intelligence he or she develops about end users' needs, business patterns, and competition can be the lifeblood of future product-market plans and strategies. Field sales personnel should be required to obtain and should be rewarded for providing feedback on the activities of customers, distributors, and competitors. Because of paperwork and commission pressures, this approach is often not very productive. One company's division top management meets periodically with all salespeople to discuss competitive matters. At another firm, the product managers frequently travel with different salespeople to gather information.

A periodic review of patent dockets can also reveal key product features. Patent searches have revealed so much information to competitors that some firms deemphasize the filing of any patents and stress the need to guard trade secrets. Engineers and technical professionals attend the same professional society meetings where they interact with their competitive counterparts. In this situation, competitive information is often exchanged freely, especially when loyalty to one's technical discipline is stronger than loyalty to the current employer. Some of these same technical people are the company's representatives on industry standards committees. When one company desires to change a standard, it usually provides clues and sometimes technical data on a new product or material it plans to market.

Bidding situations also offer the opportunity to learn about competitors. One supplier follows a practice of submitting ridiculously high bids when it just wants to learn about the competition. A lost bid analysis in serious bidding situations helps it learn the reasons why one firm got the business and the other firms lost it. And when a customer requests a second bid from all suppliers, it often allows bidding suppliers to analyze the competitive proposals.

Common suppliers are one of the most valuable sources of competitive information. A major pump manufacturer had a buying relationship with a machine tool company salesman. The same machine tool company salesman sold equipment to the pump manufacturer's largest competitor. The salesman told the pump manufacturer the competitor's floor space, current production schedules, age and type of machines, labor costs, and explained the reasons why the competitor had purchased some new equipment.

Other divisions within a large corporation can often provide competitive information. The sister division may be supplying the competition with products, or it might be buying an item from the same competition. When sister divisions or subsidiaries are highly autonomous and geographically separated, this source of competitive intelligence is often untapped.

Top management of the division and corporate headquarters management should spend a number of days a year talking to customers in the field. This is an excellent way to gather intelligence, and the top executive will then understand comments from customers about competitors' actions. The chairman and CEO of NCR, William Anderson, believes it is a critical part of his job to keep abreast of the marketplace and therefore spends a number of weeks per year in the field gaining competitive intelligence.

Trade shows are a source of competitive intelligence and a place to leak your company's proprietary information. Salespeople, who are often extroverted and like to talk, will often tell too much about their company and products at trade shows. In one instance, a salesperson attending a trade show told "prospects" in the booth the company's profit margins on a number of products. The salesperson was not aware that he was giving proprietary information to "prospects" who were actually competitors. However, a trade show is an excellent place to learn about competition, especially about the small or private company, since this is frequently the only time its staff is accessible. A smaller company's strategy and approaches can sometimes be observed at trade shows. Some competitors disguise their trade show badge affiliation so they can learn more by visiting other competitors' booths. Other firms will hire consultants to visit competitive booths. One major office product company that always sends technical and marketing teams to visit trade shows repeatedly obtains product improvement ideas and sources of acquisitions this way.

An analysis of competitors' advertising in trade magazines and direct mail pieces usually reveals the product benefits and features the producer is emphasizing in general or to a specific segment. These advertisements should be considered when evaluating overall strategies and conducting sales meetings. Trade advertising, like trade shows, is again when the small, privately held competitor becomes more public.

A subscription to a clipping service that scans local newspapers, financial publications, and trade publications for competitive information can be an excellent investment at minimal cost.[4] After retaining a news clipping service for a nominal amount, a plastics manufacturer learned that one of its stronger competitors had had a severe fire in one of its major plants. The aggressive manufacturer knew this would disrupt deliveries, so its salespeople were advised to emphasize the risk of relying on a supplier with such a severe problem. In still another situation, a clipping service found a help wanted ad placed by its client's competitor that showed the competitor was designing a new technical capability into an old product line. It is also possible to learn an enormous amount about competitors and their intentions when interviewing competitors' personnel for job openings.

The *Wall Street Transcript* covers corporate presentations to security analysts and brokerage house assessments. The CEO of a machinery manufacturer once described the two-year marketing plan of a new machine to security analysts. After reading the speech reproduced verbatim, a competitor altered many parts of its strategies and plans for the product. The purchase of a few shares of a competitor's stock will bring quarterly earn-

[4]Robert Hershy, "Commercial Intelligence on a Shoestring," *Harvard Business Review*, September–October 1980.

ings reports, prospectuses, 10 Ks, and sometimes press releases and new product announcements. One company has managed to get on nearly all of its competitors' mailing lists.

Competitive intelligence should be maintained and kept as close as possible to the *user* of the information—that is, the one who makes product or market strategy decisions. A product manager is an obvious candidate. In one business, the VP of marketing has an assistant who works full time keeping competitor files. Assembling competitive or commercial intelligence is like putting a puzzle together, but it is one of the lowest-cost and most useful forms of market information. However, it is the customer that is frequently the best source of information about competitors. The customer's evaluations and perceptions of every competitor's practices and products is where the sale is made or lost.

Unfortunately, the notion of gathering competitive intelligence frequently connotes actions that are devious or underhanded. When we talk about gathering competitive intelligence, we mean being imaginative and resourceful in gathering and piecing together bits of competitor information that help one to assess competitor strengths, weaknesses, strategies, and plans. We are not in any sense referring to "competitive espionage" or any type of cloak and dagger activity. Useful competitive intelligence can be gathered in completely ethical ways. Over the years, Reliance Electric has done an outstanding job of gathering competitive intelligence as a foundation for developing and selecting many of its strategic moves. Like many companies, Reliance adheres to well-defined standards of ethical conduct. The following paragraph, taken from the company's statement of operating philosophy, illustrates this point very well.

> We know that solid profit growth can only come from providing customers with genuine value in a more effective way than competition and by controlling our costs. It should never come from taking unfair advantage of any supplier, employee, customer, user, business partner, or competitor. If we can't win by these rules, we don't deserve to win. And we don't want anyone on our team who doesn't want to play the game fairly.

As one can see, major emphasis is placed on never taking unfair advantage of any group, including competitors. By being smart, and in no way unfair, marketing managers in this company have traditionally done an outstanding job of gathering the necessary information about competitors to determine how and where they can gain a competitive advantage.

MARKETING STRATEGY IMPLICATIONS

Understanding a customer's costs and a competitor's situation provides a sound basis for developing better product and market strategies. Here are several specific ways that knowing customer cost and competitors can assist the industrial marketer.

REDUCES SURPRISES. Having a deep and current understanding of customers and competition can help a supplier avoid the penalties of getting "caught off base" and be more responsive to changing market conditions.

IDENTIFYING OPPORTUNITIES

The Tremco Company developed a mastic compound that was a functional substitute for putty used in glazing glass windows. Because of the higher initial price of the Tremco product, glazing contractors were hesitant to buy it because they felt the higher price would make it difficult for them to bid successfully on glazing contracts. An end-user application study discovered that wherever windows were glazed with either putty or the new glazing compound, the windows were always painted *after* the glazing was done. Special care while painting was needed to prevent smearing the window glass. This type of painting, known as "cutting-in" in the trade, was a very high labor cost. Existing putty manufacturers required the paint coating as a protection from the weather. But the Tremco mastic did not require a protective paint coating. Windows could be painted before they were glazed and then glazed with this mastic, using a colored material to blend the mastic with the color of the painted window. The study of the production work in process for the material showed it actually lowered the cost of painting contracts. The initially higher-priced Tremco glazing material actually resulted in overall lower costs per job.

IDENTIFIES NEW MARKET SEGMENTS. End-user analysis can provide hard economic facts and help identify new customer segments or market requirements. As the boxed example shows, economic analysis of a product application in a customer's operations can sometimes identify a new approach to segmenting a marketplace.

FOCUSES PRODUCT DESIGN AND DEVELOPMENT. Product design efforts can be better focused after a thorough analysis of product applications in various customer groups. For example, a product can be designed to be less costly on initial purchase than competitive products. It can be designed smaller so that installation and startup are easier and less costly. It can be designed to operate more efficiently (use less power, generate less scrap, produce at a faster rate) or to have a longer useful life. Or it can be designed to be fully compatible and easily interchangeable with competitive products. What it probably cannot be is all of the above, because tradeoffs and compromises are generally involved. If the product is designed to last longer, operate at a faster rate, or use less power, it probably requires added labor and material costs as it is manufactured, thus adding to the initial purchase price. If the product is designed around the lowest possible manufacturing costs, it probably will not have the same performance characteristics as more costly products. This is why it is so important to select the target customers and market segments to be served and then to design the product that will offer the greatest economic advantage to the users that make up those markets.

AIDS DEVELOPMENT OF PRICING STRATEGIES. Once the product is designed to enhance the operating performance and economics of a particular set of customers, pricing strategies can be developed based on value received rather than a straight writeup on costs. Obviously, this pricing for value received approach cannot be carried to an extreme, since industrial customers often have a good idea of what a product costs to manufacture and will not permit the producer to realize exorbitant profits. End-user customer cost analysis tends to cause the producer to price closer to what the market will bear, rather than using a cost-plus approach that might be below the customer's value-in-use and willingness to pay. If the competitive products are not as cost effective, competitive prices are not as relevant.

SHARPENS SALES FORCE TRAINING. The alert marketer should educate its sales force to sell its product on the strength of real economic advantages to the user. This is a difficult task, since most selling organizations tend to shy away from the costs and economics of their customer's business and dwell instead on the virtues of their product. However, the training effort required is worthwhile because it puts the salesperson in the position of being a professional genuinely interested in helping the customer improve its position rather than merely being someone who pitches the company's products.

IMPROVES ADVERTISING EFFECTIVENESS. Product benefits that are derived from a careful evaluation of customer needs and operations should be emphasized in business advertising headlines and copy. Advertising with this focus creates higher awareness and recall. Such advertising will also be more effective as a direct mail piece or as visual aids for salespeople.

SUMMARY

A close knowledge of customers' needs coupled with ongoing competitive intelligence gathering will help the alert industrial producer achieve and maintain a differential advantage. The closer a supplier stays abreast of customers' operations and changing requirements, the more market-focused the supplier will be. An intimate knowledge of how and where the customer uses the product provides information for developing competitive products and competitive product and market plans. Such close customer contact and a continuous awareness of the competitive situation help the industrial producer match the right product capabilities to the appropriate market segment. This approach also helps to avoid producing "me too" products that have no real demonstrable advantage.

5

Segmenting the Business

Ken Roy, general manager of the industrial machinery division of a *Fortune* 100 company, was surprised to find a note from the company president calling off the review session that had been set up to go over a strategic plan to enter the "flexible manufacturing system" field. Ken had given the president a draft of the plan to read for the meeting. The president had returned it along with a short note that said it was a waste of time to do a review until the market they wanted to serve was much better defined.

Ken Roy immediately called his staff together. All the members of his team were dismayed, because they had put a lot of effort into the draft. The national sales manager was particularly discouraged because he saw flexible manufacturing as a growth market the company had to enter. The director of engineering believed he had superior in-house capabilities to rapidly develop a wide range of flexible manufacturing systems that would leave competitors far behind. After two hours of discussion, it became clear that the division team did not know what the corporate president meant when he said, "We need a much better definition of the market."

Ken arranged to meet the next day with the president to discuss the problem. When the president met with Ken and his staff, he expressed a point of view that caused them to think somewhat differently about the plan:

> As I see it, flexible manufacturing is not a market. Rather, it is a product or general concept that is adapted to and then sold into various markets. We are a little late in entering this business. This means we need to identify and concentrate on selected market segments where we can secure a unique competitive advantage. Otherwise, we will be following others with a "me too" product. There are a lot of different ways to segment an industrial market. We might begin by selecting certain growth industries like electronic components or medical equipment and then identify subsections of these industries that have similar requirements. Or we might begin by examining the requirements of various sizes and kinds of machine shops that have not been automated in any appreciable way. I can't tell you specifically how to segment the market, but I can tell you it is essential to segment first before we commit a lot of time and money to an area as competitive as this one.

What was the division team's elementary mistake?

What are the strong points of the president's argument?

What are some obvious problems that would result if the company were to follow the director of engineering's advice and "rapidly develop a wide range of flexible manufacturing systems"?

Market segmentation as a business practice has long been recognized and accepted in the consumer goods sector, but among industrial or technically based manufacturing businesses, there has been no corresponding level of interest and rigor. Yet, the identification and selection of market segments is the most strategic decision facing the industrial firm. Segmenting an industrial marketplace is the starting point for all strategic planning and decision making. The selection of segments determines the business units that management will plan around. They may be defined by SIC codes, end use or application, by common buying factors, by geographic boundaries, or by size of customer. Sometimes a combination of these considerations is used to define the segments. Whatever factors are used to segment a business, the objective is always to define a market niche that can be focused on in a way that provides a distinct competitive advantage. Examples of sales, market share, and profit gains from careful segmentation are legion.

Deere, the large farm equipment manufacturer, identified a market trend to fewer but larger farms that required large horsepower tractors and equipment. Deere designed and manufactured large horsepower machinery and subsequently captured a market opportunity. The existing market leader, International Harvester, was late to recognize and pursue the new and growing market segment and lost substantial market share as a result.

Xerox, the pioneer of photocopy machines, emphasized the high-speed segment for very large customers. The Japanese competitors were the first to identify and develop a desktop plain paper copier for businesses' low-speed needs. It rapidly became the fastest growing copier market segment. The president of Canon U.S.A. stated, "It has been our strategy to identify a market demand and then create a product to fill that demand."[1] Xerox failed to resegment the marketplace and by so doing allowed Canon and other Japanese competitors to do it for them.

Both General Electric and RCA withdrew from the computer industry after unsuccessfully attempting to compete with IBM. The most successful entrants in the computer business concentrated their R&D, manufacturing, and marketing on one or a few select market segments. The chairman of Control Data stated, "We avoided going head-on with IBM but rather focused in on the largest computers, where IBM was not as strong."[2] Similar examples of successful computer market segmentation are NCR in retail systems, Burroughs in banking, and Honeywell in manufacturing and process controls.

FOUNDATIONS FOR BUSINESS STRATEGY

Over the past two decades, a number of industrial companies have rediscovered Demosthenes' idea: "Small opportunities are often the beginning of great enterprises." Unable to compete broadly against entrenched competitors, they have adopted a successful niche, or "divide and conquer," strategy: They identify a market need, then focus their resources and energies on meeting that need better than anyone else.

[1] "Copiers Still A Growth Industry," *High Technology,* May 1983, p. 54.
[2] Joel Ross and Michael Kami, *Corporate Management in Crisis: Why the Mighty Fail* (Englewood Cliffs, N.J.: Prentice-Hall, Inc., 1973), p. 80.

The identification and selection of market segments determines the producer's customer mix, what business it is in, and who the competition is. The identification and selection of industrial segment(s) to concentrate on will significantly affect all the functional areas of the firm. As Corey states:

> All else follows. Choice of market is a choice of the customer and of the competitive, technical, political, and social environments in which one elects to compete. It is not an easily reversed decision; having made the choice, the company develops skills and resources around the markets it has elected to serve. It builds a set of relationships with customers that are at once a major source of strength and a major commitment. The commitment carries with it the responsibility to serve customers well, to stay in the technical and product-development race, and to grow in pace with growing market demand. Such choices are not made in a vacuum. They are influenced by the company's background; by its marketing, manufacturing, and technical strengths; by the fabric of its relations with existing customers, the scientific community, and competitors.[3]

ERRORS IN SEGMENTING THE MARKET

How an industrial producer defines a market segment determines the boundaries of the business it is in. When the competitors' segment definitions are the same, industrial market share measurement is clear and straightforward. However, market segments are not always easily defined. The difficulty of determining market boundaries and resulting market shares can be seen in the antitrust controversy. Whether or not a firm is dominating or restraining competition depends on how one segments and defines the market. For example, IBM was accused by the U.S. Justice Department of "dominating the computer market." However, in 1981 IBM did not have a leadership position in the fastest-growing segment—minicomputers. The identification of various market segments, and an analysis of IBM's strength in each, helped dismiss the case.

Firms that consistently fail to identify meaningful market segments usually do so for one of two reasons. Many product-driven firms simply don't think enough about their markets or are not willing to commit the time or money to do the job. Instead, they concentrate only on selling their products. Others that try to think in terms of segments lack the understanding to do the job correctly.

Thinking Too Broad

An *industry* is a wide group of manufacturers producing and selling products, whereas a *market* is a much more distinct group of customers or users that have similar requirements. Sales-focused industrial firms often do not attempt to make a distinction between the two. For example, one component manufacturer stated: "We serve the computer market with solid state connectors." This kind of a statement is useless since there are many

[3] E Raymond Corey, "Key Options in Market Selection and Product Planning," *Harvard Business Review*, 53 (September–October 1975), p. 120.

distinct market segments within the computer industry, and each segment has specific customer requirements. It might have been more useful to say: "We primarily serve mainframe computer firms and some microprocessor computer builders." In still another situation, an industrial firm's division charter states: "The division is a supplier of hydraulic pumps and hoses to machinery markets." The division is again defining a general industry, not market segments. A further analysis revealed that the division was primarily supplying certain types of farm equipment manufacturers, three kinds of construction machinery producers, and heavy-duty truck makers. To avoid this kind of thinking, the president of one company told his marketing team that they were not segmenting properly if their total market was more than a hundred million dollars.

Some of these firms classify current customers by annual sales, as shown in Table 5.1. While this approach highlights the key accounts and defines them by sales volume as As, Bs, or Cs, it does not begin to be a useful form of market segmentation. This kind of a list, especially when grouped geographically, can be useful for aligning territories or making sales assignments, but is not particularly useful in making product-market decisions.

The limitation of key account or sales classification is that such classification does not reveal any differences or similarities in customer characteristics or requirements. For example, a further analysis of the customers in Table 5.1 revealed that:

1. The key customer list consisted of six end-use market segments.
   a. Construction equipment
   b. Heavy-duty highway trucks
   c. Off the road vehicles
   d. Farm equipment
   e. Materials-handling equipment
   f. Mining equipment
2. There were major differences among each of the identified six segments in annual purchase potential, growth rates, and long-term prospects.
3. The cost-benefit value of the producer's high-performance component was the greatest in two market segments where the producer had little market penetration.
4. In some segments, it was competing with different materials or technologies. In one low-performance segment, its quality was far above what was required.
5. There were different competitors in three of the six identified segments.

Thinking Too Narrow

At the other extreme, some sales-focused firms do not think beyond the needs of one or a few customers that dominate their business. One manufacturer of machining systems developed a $150 million business with the three major auto manufacturers in Detroit. This total involvement with just three firms in one industry led to myopic thinking that prevented the manufacturer from even considering other situations or groups of customers (e.g., farm implement, aerospace, oil field equipment) that had similar requirements.

Other manufacturers often think too restrictively about their markets because they are constrained by their existing products and technologies. They tend to think of expansion

TABLE 5.1

ANNUAL DOLLAR SALES—HYDRAULIC HOSE

		Dollars (000)
As	Caterpillar	$17,000
	Detroit Diesel-Allison	5,050
	J.I. Case	2,000
	John Deere	2,500
Bs	Allis Chalmers	1,200
	Clark Equipment	600
	Ford Tractor	975
	Hyster Company	588
	New Holland	610
	Rockford Clutch	1,063
	Saab Scania	675
	Twin Disc	1,000
	U.S. Government	1,576
	Warner Gear	500
Cs	Caterpillar—Mexico	250
	Clearing Division, U.S. Industries	170
	Fiat Allis	357
	Franklin Equipment	181
	Funk Manufacturing	150
	International Harvester	400
	Jeffrey Mining	268
	Joy Manufacturing	127
	Marathon LeTourneau	188
	Massey Ferguson	409
	Mine Machinery	80
	Pacific Car	201
	White Farm Equipment	12
Others		1,345
	Total	39,475

only in terms of extending their product line. They do not think about what other products or services beyond their existing capabilities could help them strengthen their position or develop more attractive markets. For example, a switch producer sold chiefly to nuclear plants where its line had been qualified and approved by the appropriate agencies. This narrow focus on a slow growth market greatly limited sales potential. Management ultimately redefined its business as one that served additional hazardous environments and, by both acquisition and internal development, added several complementary products.

Misusing the Consumer Goods Approach

Some industrial firms have been misled by advertising agencies or consumer goods marketers that eloquently tout the sophisticated segmentation approaches that work well in the consumer goods world. However, segmentation for consumer and industrial markets is as different as potato chips and integrated circuit chips. Household consumer buying can be segmented on the basis of demographic factors and sociopsychological considerations. Moreover, new consumer segments can often be defined in terms of different packaging, brand names, or advertising appeals. In contrast, industrial market segmentation must be based on common economic, application, or usage considerations, and any talk about demographic factors or sociopsychological considerations is pure nonsense. Despite the differences between consumer and industrial market segmentation, much of the literature discusses industrial market segmentation as though it could be accomplished by using consumer goods techniques.

SEGMENTING THE BUSINESS

There is no one right way for an industrial or a technically based company to segment an industrial market. Successful segmentation is both creative and judgmental. What will be an effective and profitable way to segment one market may not be a good method to segment another. However, there are a number of basic approaches to segmenting industrial markets that have proved successful.

What is most important is that the firm distinguish between the industries it sells into and the discrete markets that lie within these industries. Segmenting can be done by OEM and aftermarket, by four-digit SICs, by end use, by common buying factors, and by buyer size.

Segmenting by OEM, User, and Aftermarkets

One approach to industrial market segmentation is to classify present or potential customers as original equipment manufacturers (OEM), end users, or aftermarket customers. Aftermarket is sometimes called the maintenance, repair, and overhaul market (MRO). For farm tractors, Deere would be an original equipment manufacturer, and the individual farmer would be the end user. The repair parts bought by the farm implement dealer or the farmer would constitute the aftermarket.

All industrial products can be classified into one of three categories.

1. *Components or subassemblies.* These are parts or items used to build and repair machinery and equipment, which includes items such as switches, integrated circuits, machine tool parts, connectors, and pistons, and are often required for both the OEM and aftermarkets.
2. *Machinery and equipment.* These are end products used by the industrial users, such as machine tools, bulldozers, computers, laboratory instruments, and trucks. They require repair parts (components) as aftermarket items.

EXHIBIT 5-1

OEM-AFTERMARKET SEGMENTATION

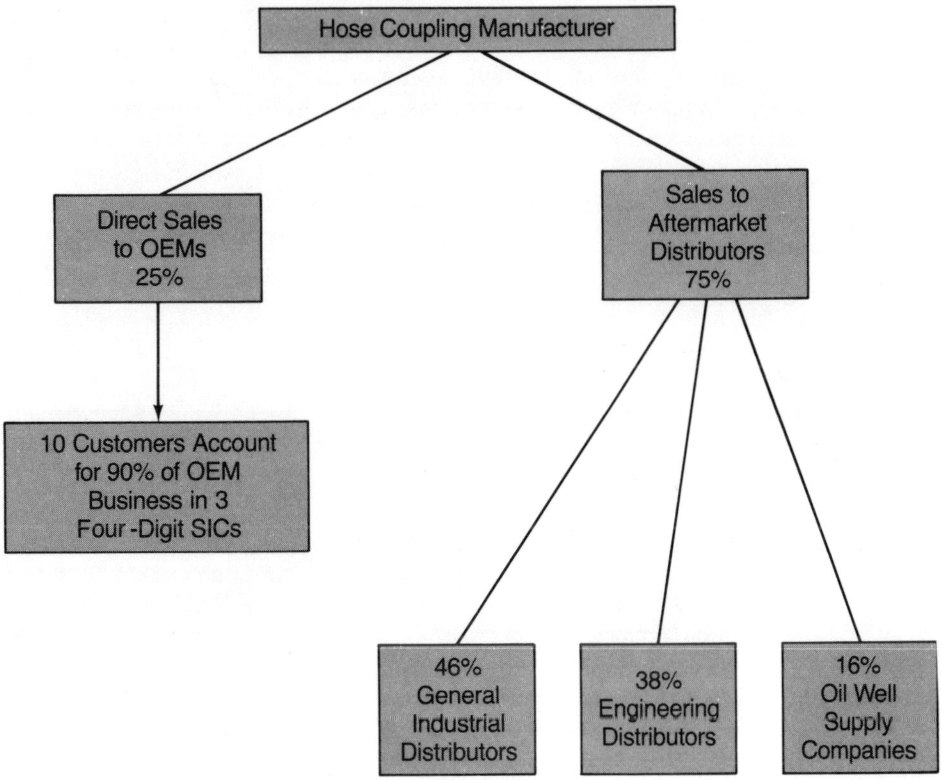

3. *Materials.* Materials are consumed in the end user's production process or components and include such items as chemicals, coolants, metals, herbicides, and adhesives. They do not usually have an aftermarket.

Materials, machinery, and equipment are typically sold only in the OEM and end-user segments. Components and subassemblies, on the other hand, are sold in the aftermarket segment, as well as in the OEM and end-user segments.

OEM, end-user, and aftermarket segmentation generally cannot be done from existing sales records as sales records do not usually show any information about the product beyond the customer or distributor. Sales personnel can be helpful in developing some of the necessary information, but they are often limited in their knowlege of end-user and aftermarket customers, especially when distributors are involved. Exhibit 5-1 shows how easy it is for a supplier to lose track of its products once they move beyond the customer or distributor level. In some cases the problem is further complicated by intermediate resellers or subdistributors that are integral links in the customers' sales chain.

Unfortunately, the OEM-aftermarket classification is far too often the beginning and end of segmentation in many industrial firms. Such companies are flying blind. This lack of knowledge of who the real customers are is especially common when producers sell primarily to industrial distributors who in turn serve other OEMs or aftermarket customers. A major manufacturer of hose couplings found segmentation beyond the OEM-aftermarket level very revealing. The manufacturer had always known that 25 percent of the coupling business was direct to OEMs and the remaining 75 percent went through independent distributors. However, until the manufacturer segmented the market further, as shown in Exhibit 5-1, it did not know that some of its products were being bought by the oil industry. A product-market plan targeted to the oil patch customers resulted in a 39 percent increase in unit sales in one year.

Segmenting by SICs

A second approach to segmentation involves the use of Standard Industrial Classification (SIC) codes, which are published by the U.S. government. This publication classifies all business firms by the main product or service provided. It then classifies all like manufacturers under broad industry groups and assigns a numerical code that indicates the basic industry and the type of product and service.

To explain how to segment by SIC codes, let's use the example of a producer of industrial brakes that wants to identify specific types of OEM prospects that make heavy construction equipment. Since the construction equipment builders are manufacturing firms, they will be within the 20–39 range of two-digit basic industry groups, as shown in Table 5.2. The next step is to look through the manufacturing subdivisions, shown in Table 5.3, to identify the manufacturing groups that represent potential users for industrial brakes. Assuming we identify Group 35, "machinery except electrical," as the most likely prospects, we would then turn to page 167 where we find the two-digit classification expanded to four digits, as shown in Table 5.4. Here we must exercise judgment to identify the four-digit area(s) where brake products will most likely fit. Each four-digit category has an extensive listing of the machinery produced in that four-digit SIC, as also shown in Table 5.4. Once this extensive list is available, it is then possible to determine what manufacturers make what products by going to one of four sources:

1. *Duns' Market Identifiers (DMI)*—computer-based records of 3 million United States and Canadian business establishments by four-digit SIC.
2. *Metalworking Directory*—a comprehensive list of metalworking plants with 20 or more employees, as well as metal distributors by four-digit SIC.
3. *Thomas Register of American Manufacturers*—a directory of manufacturers, classified by products, enabling the researcher to identify most or all of the manufacturers of any given product.
4. *Survey of Industrial Purchasing Power*—an annual survey of manufacturing activity in the United States by geographic areas and four-digit SIC industry groups; reports the number of plants with 20 or more and 100 or more employees, as well as total shipment value.

TABLE 5.2

CATEGORIES OF THE U.S. ECONOMY

Basic Industries	First Two Digits
1. Agriculture	01–09
2. Mining	10–14
3. Construction	15–17
4. Manufacturing	20–39
5. Transportation	40–49
6. Wholesale and retail	50–59
7. Finance	60–67
8. Services	70–89
9. Public administration	91–97
10. Nonclassifiable	99

Source: Standard Industrial Classification Manual, 1972 (Washington, D.C.: U.S. Government Printing Office).

TABLE 5.3

MANUFACTURING SIC SUBDIVISIONS

Group	Description	Page
Major Group 20.	Food and kindred products	59
Major Group 21.	Tobacco manufactures	70
Major Group 22.	Textile mill products	71
Major Group 23.	Apparel and other finished products made from fabrics and similar materials	82
Major Group 24.	Lumber and wood products, except furniture	90
Major Group 25.	Furniture and fixtures	96
Major Group 26.	Paper and allied products	100
Major Group 27.	Printing, publishing, and allied industries	106
Major Group 28.	Chemicals and allied products	111
Major Group 29.	Petroleum refining and related industries	127
Major Group 30.	Rubber and miscellaneous plastics products	129
Major Group 31.	Leather and leather products	133
Major Group 32.	Stone, clay, glass, and concrete products	136
Major Group 33.	Primary metal industries	145
Major Group 34.	Fabricated metal products, except machinery and transportation equipment	153
Major Group 35.	Machinery, except electrical	167
Major Group 36.	Electrical and electronic machinery, equipment, and supplies	184
Major Group 37.	Transportation equipment	196
Major Group 38.	Measuring, analyzing, and controlling instruments; photographic, medical, and optical goods; watches and clocks	202
Major Group 39.	Miscellaneous manufacturing industries	211

Source: Standard Industrial Classification Manual, 1972 (Washington, D.C.: U.S. Government Printing Office).

TABLE 5.4

MAJOR INDUSTRY GROUP 35—SUBDIVISION (MACHINERY, EXCEPT ELECTRICAL)

Four-Digit SIC	*Specific Industry*
3511	Steam, gas, and hydraulic turbines
3519	Internal combustion engines
3523	Farm and garden machinery
3524	Garden tractors and lawn equipment
3531	Construction machinery and equipment

↓

3531 Construction Machinery and Equipment

Establishments primarily engaged in manufacturing heavy machinery and equipment used by the construction industries, such as bulldozers; concrete mixers; cranes, except industrial plant type; dredging machinery; pavers; and power shovels. Establishments primarily engaged in manufacturing mining equipment are classified in Industry 3532, and well drilling machinery in Industry 3533.

Aggregate spreaders
Airport construction machinery
Asphalt plants, including travel-mix type
Backfillers, self-propelled
Backhoes
Ballast distributors
Batching plants, bituminous
Batching plants, for aggregate concrete and bulk cement
Blades for graders, scrapers, dozers, and snow plows
Breakers, paving
Buckets: clamshell, concrete, dragline, drag scraper, shovel, etc.
Bulldozers (construction machinery)
Capstans, ship
Carriers, crane
Chip spreaders, self-propelled
Cleaners, catch basin
Compactors, soil: vibratory-pan and vibratory-roller types
Concrete buggies, powered
Concrete grouting equipment
Concrete gunning equipment
Concrete plants
Construction machinery, except mining
Cranes, except industrial plant
Cranes, locomotive
Cranes, ship
Crushers, portable
Derricks, except oil and gas field
Derricks, ship
Distributors (construction machinery)
Ditchers, ladder: vertical boom or wheel
Dozers, tractor mounted: material moving
Draglines, powered
Drags, road (construction and road maintenance equipment)
Dredging machinery
Entrenching machines
Excavators: cable, clamshell, crane, derrick, dragline, power shovel, etc.
Extractors, piling
Finishers and spreaders (construction equipment)
Finishers, concrete and bituminous: powered
Grader attachments, elevating
Graders, road (construction machinery)
Grapples: rock, wood, etc.
Grinders, stone: portable
Hammer mills (rock and ore crushing machines), portable
Hammers, pile driving
Line markers, self-propelled
Loaders, shovel: self-propelled
Locomotive cranes
Logging equipment
Mixers: concrete, ore, sand, slag, plaster, mortar, and bituminous
Mortar mixers
Mud jacks
Pavers
Pile drivers (construction machinery)
Planers, bituminous
Plaster mixers
Plows, earth: heavy duty
Power cranes, draglines, and shovels
Pulverizers, stone: portable
Railway track equipment: rail layers, ballast distributors, etc.
Rakes, land clearing: mechanical
Road construction and maintenance machinery
Rock crushing machinery, portable
Rollers, road: steam or other power
Rollers, sheepsfoot and vibratory
Sand mixers
Scarifiers, road
Scrapers (construction machinery)
Screeds and screeding machines
Screeners, portable
Ship cranes and derricks
Ship winches
Shovel loaders, wheel tractor
Shovels, power
Silos, cement (batch plant)
Slag mixers
Snow plow attachments
Soil compactors: vibratory-pan and vibratory-roller types
Spreaders and finishers (construction equipment)
Subgraders, construction equipment
Subsoiler attachments, tractor mounted
Surfacers, concrete grinding
Tampers, powered
Tamping equipment, rail
Teeth, bucket and scarifier
Tractors, contractors' off highway
Tractors, crawler
Tractors, tracklaying
Trucks, off-highway: heavy duty motor
Vibrators for concrete construction
Wellpoint systems
Winches, all types

Source: Standard Industrial Classification Manual, 1972 (Washington, D.C.: U.S. Government Printing Office).

An allied source for identifying and estimating the size of industrial markets is *County Business Patterns*. This annual publication reports the number of employees and the value of shipments by the same four-digit SICs.

Segmentation by OEM and aftermarket and then four-digit SIC should always be done by the producer of industrial products. In addition, however, some very successful industrial producers have creatively segmented one or two levels beyond OEM-aftermarket and SIC levels by studying end-use application and common buying factors.

Segmenting by End-Use Application

Industrial products are used differently by different customers, and segmenting by end-use application simply means determining how the product is used in various situations. It is important to understand these differences since the cost-benefit relationship is likely to vary by end-use application. For example, a front-end equipment loader will have greater value to a customer who uses it eight hours a day in a mining operation than to a customer who uses it two to three hours a day on a construction site. Cost-benefit analysis for each identified end-use application helps to determine the economic value of the product for each segment. When conducting a cost-benefit analysis by end use, the producer must ask: "What function(s) does the customer want performed with this product?" Three steps are involved in determining which end-use market segments have the greatest cost-benefit advantages.

1. Making field visits and conducting customer studies to determine how products are used.
2. Identifying and evaluating cost-benefit relationships in different applications.
3. Verifying variables that underly different cost-benefit relationships.

Here is an example of how one company used this approach to achieve a distinct competitive advantage. A manufacturer of electric motors discovered that its customers operated at different speeds and costs and that a new, lower-priced machine introduced by a competitor wore out quickly when used in high- and medium-speed applications. Armed with this user insight from extensive field visits, it then developed segment strategies as shown in Exhibit 5-2. For customers who needed primarily medium- and high-speed use, it doubled its sales effort, stressing the superiority of its product. For users in the low-speed segment, the manufacturer launched a program to develop a competitively priced product with an added maintenance advantage, meanwhile altering the short-term sales strategy to emphasize the life-cycle cost advantage offered by its existing machines.[4]

The identification of needs by end use should include a consideration of substitute or potential substitute products that can perform the function. For example, Continental Can has found it necessary to consider the customer value of containers made of many different materials (metal, glass, fiber, plastic) for each end use. This consideration helps Continental segment markets for its products creatively when the end user is currently using a different material than Continental produces. The evaluation of functional substitutes

[4]Robert A. Garda, "How to Carve Niches for Growth in Industrial Markets," *Management Review,* August 1981, p. 16.

EXHIBIT 5-2

SEGMENTATION BY END-USE APPLICATION

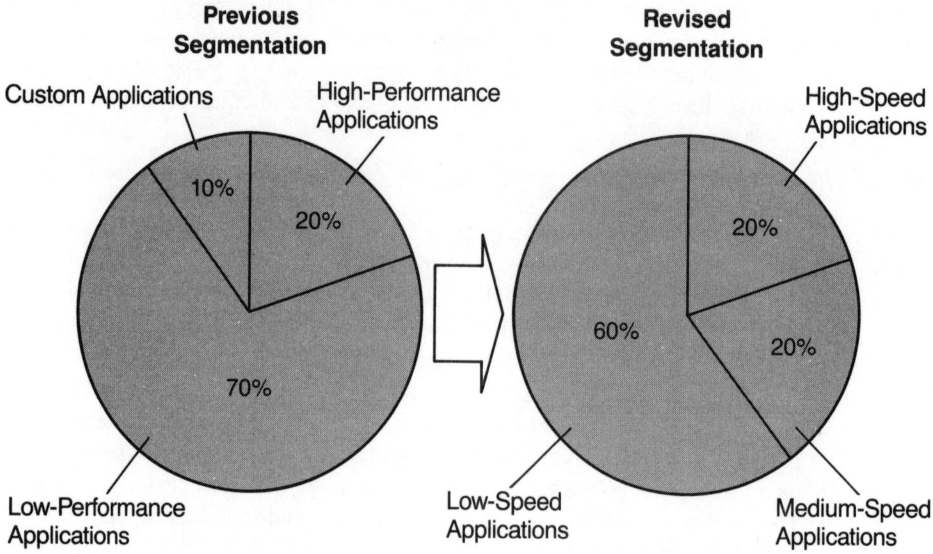

Previous strategy: Serve all segments with a single product. (Competitor's strategy: Concentrate on low-performance segment; provide higher-priced options for other segments.)	Revised strategy: Serve each new segment with separate products.

Source: Robert A. Garda, "How to Carve a Niche for Growth in Industrial Markets," *Management Review,* August 1981, p. 17.

helps producers identify end-use markets where their products have greater customer value. Many product-focused companies have difficulty breaking out of the pattern of only comparing their products to end-use segments using a very similar product. From the customer viewpoint, a product or technology is only one solution to a problem.

Segmenting by Common Buying Factors

Some industrial companies have successfully defined market segments by identifying groups of customers that attach importance to the same buying factors. Most industrial buying situations hinge on five buying factors: (1) performance, (2) quality, (3) service, (4) delivery, and (5) price. It is often difficult to define segments by common buying factors because they are not readily apparent. They often change with customer priorities, and they can vary dramatically among customers in the same business. Nevertheless, it is often worth the effort to segment this way as it can lead to significant marketing advantages, as shown in the boxed example on pages 104–105.

Two Other Segmentation Approaches

Segmentation based on geographic considerations or account size are two other alternatives that are often used in industries, particularly when the business is based on commodity type products that flow into a multiplicity of markets through a complex series of channels. Certainly the first attempt should be to segment along the lines described previously to see if discrete and meaningful markets can be defined. However, if this turns out to be impractical for whatever reasons, there are generally advantages to be gained by segmenting around geographic boundaries and/or account size.

Sales managers are accustomed to grouping customers by geography or size for planning purposes, but until recently few top managers had thought to try developing niche strategies on this basis. Yet the opportunity often exists.

An example of ingenious geographic segmentation is the case of a Midwestern commodity construction materials firm that found itself faced with overcapacity and unable to take share away from its competition in its 200-mile trading area without starting a price war. Industry folklore maintained that because of high transportation, no producer could ship more than 300 miles from plant to customer and make money. This was true on an all-in cost basis; yet, as this company discovered, the fixed costs included in its all-in costs were so high that sales to customers as much as 700 miles away would still contribute to overhead (Exhibit 5-3). The result of its analysis was three strategic market segments: core markets (up to 200 miles distant); secondary markets (200 to 400 miles); and fringe markets (400 to 700 miles). For each of these segments, the firm developed different pricing strategies. In the core market, the strategy was business as usual; in the secondary markets, prices were cut to take a few selected bids away from competitors, but not enough to provoke retaliation; in the fringe market, prices were reduced in order to fill the plants—but again, not frequently enough or severely enough to provoke retaliation. With this strategy, the company tripled its volume in the first year. Although much of the added volume was from marginal business, its profits doubled—and the industry price structure remained intact.

Another example relates to segmenting by account size. An electrical equipment manufacturer isolated 187 key accounts, accounting for 60 percent of the market, each of which bought direct and selected suppliers on the basis of price and sales coverage. These large accounts made up one strategic market segment. A second segment consisted of medium-sized OEM accounts that bought through distributors; a third comprised maintenance, repair, and operating supply accounts that required distributor servicing. Having identified these three strategic market segments, the company was able to develop programs (product pricing, distribution channels, and service policies) tailored to each.

COMBINING SEGMENTATION LEVELS

In reviewing and choosing approaches to industrial market segmentation, it is helpful to think in terms of combining approaches, as shown in Table 5.5. The first three approaches, OEM end-user aftermarket, four-digit SIC, and end-use applications, should

ADVANTAGES OF SEGMENTING BY COMMON BUYING FACTORS

In order to combat increasing price competition, an electrical components manufacturer had spent two years trying to develop detailed segment strategies for its 22 SIC markets. The breakthrough came when it discovered that the customers could be grouped or aggregated into four strategic market segments based on common buying characteristics. Segment A consisted of large-lot buyers that were extremely price sensitive (because the component was a significant portion of their product cost), did their own applications engineering, required dedicated capacity to meet their demand for a standard product, demanded only a very basic quality standard, and cared little for features. At the other end of the spectrum, segment D comprised a host of small-lot buyers, mostly makers of specialty products, that insisted on high quality and special features, relied on the supplier for applications engineering, and because they lacked buying clout, were not noticeably price sensitive. Having redefined these market segments for the total market, the manufacturer was able to develop strategies for each segment. Top management chose to price itself "up or out" of segment D by raising prices 25 percent. As anticipated, the price increase stuck; none of the competitors wanted the specialty business. Next, top management launched a facilities study that found the company could meet the low price and dedicated capacity requirements for the high-volume business in segment A.

Source: Robert A. Garda, "How to Carve Niches for Growth in Industrial Markets," *Management Review*, August 1981, p. 19.

usually be done in sequential steps. Segmentation by common buying factors, geography, and buyer size does not necessarily follow in any particular sequence, but it should always be preceded by one of the other steps.

Too Few or Too Many Segments

After conducting a segmentation analysis, many industrial firms experience one of two extreme situations. First, they may not have identified enough market segments. If too few segments have been defined, a competitor may zero in on a segment and gain a major part of the business. Large corporations frequently segment the market into too few and therefore too broad market segments. What is small to a billion-dollar company might be large to a 40 to 100 million-dollar company or division. However, if large companies do not segment small enough, competition will often do it for them. Smaller industrial firms are usually more able to think in terms of small growing segments and to position themselves within them to gain real competitive advantages.

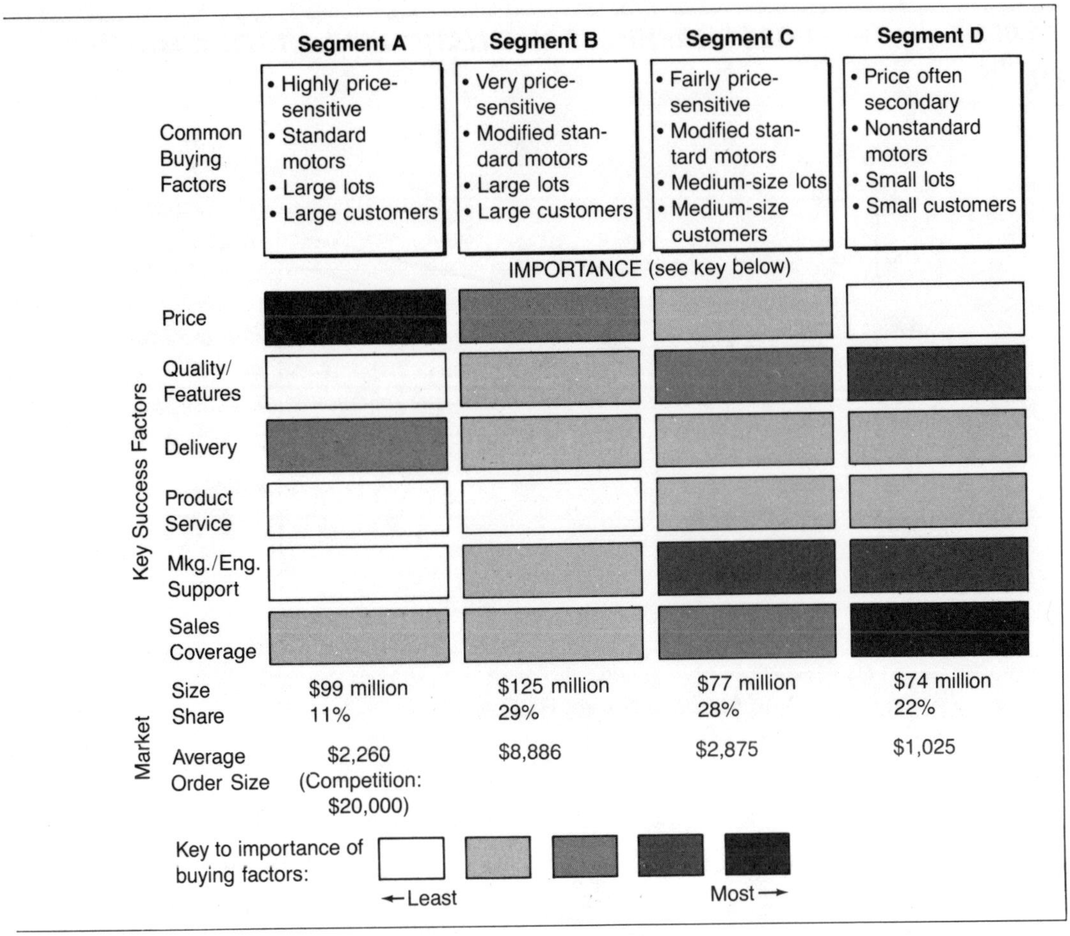

At the other extreme, some industrial companies define too many market segments. After investing in a seven month segmentation study that produced mountains of data, a division general manager stated:

> They have segmented our market into 18 segments. I've got a sneaking suspicion that's about one dozen too many. Even if it isn't, there's no way we can develop useful competitive strategies for each one in less than five years, and we haven't got five years.

VALIDATING A MARKET SEGMENT

To avoid having too few or too many market segments, there are some qualifying criteria to consider. If any one of the following six criteria is not met, the segment should be discounted. The six validation criteria are these:

EXHIBIT 5-3 ***HOW GEOGRAPHIC SEGMENTATION ENLARGED A MARKET***

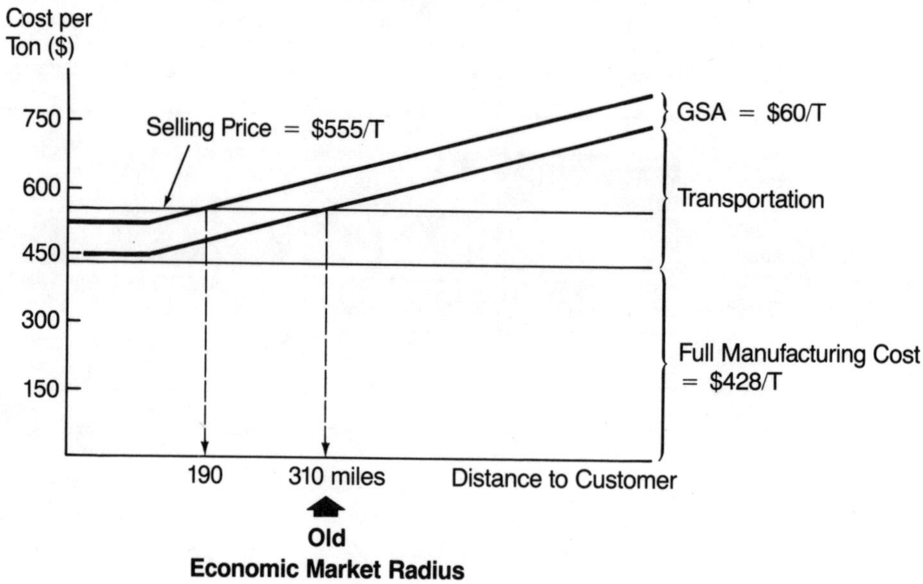

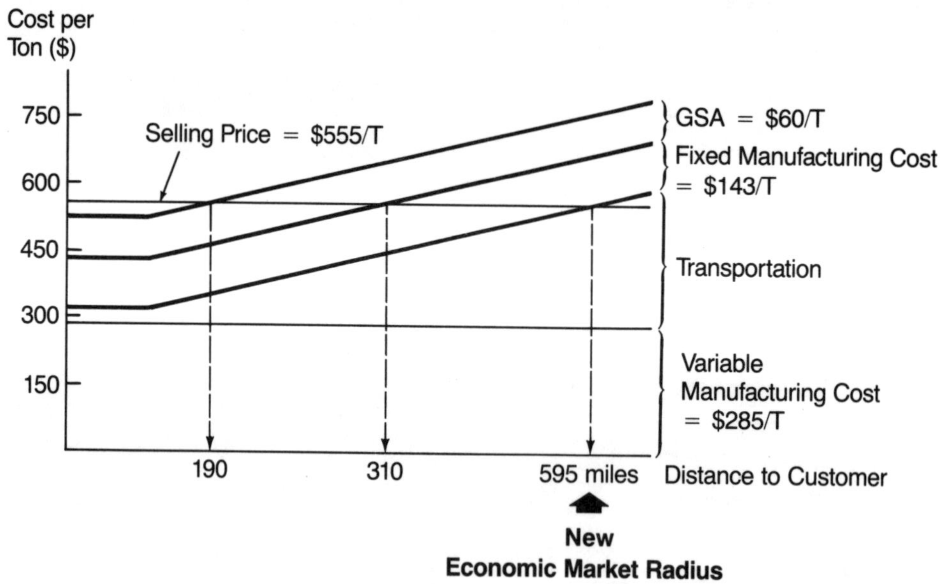

Source: Robert A. Garda, "How to Curve Niches for Growth in Industrial Markets," *Management Review,* August 1981, p. 19.

TABLE 5.5

BUSINESS SEGMENTATION APPROACHES

Machinery and Equipment	*Components*	*Materials*
↙ ↘	↙ ↘	↓
OEM Aftermarket	OEM Aftermarket	OEM
↘ ↙	↘ ↙	↓
Four-digit SICs	Four-digit SICs	Four-digit SICs
↓	↓	↓
End-use applications	End-use applications	End-use applications
	(may be considered)	
Common buying factors Geography Buyer size	Common buying factors Geography Buyer size	Common buying factors Geography Buyer size

1. Each identified segment should be characterized by a set of common user requirements.
2. Each identified segment should have measurable characteristics (e.g., customer size, growth rate, and location) per year.
3. Each identified segment should have identifiable competitors.
4. Each identified segment should be served by common sales or distribution channels.
5. Each identified segment should be "large enough" so that it represents a significant business opportunity.
6. Each identified segment should be "small enough" to protect a position against competition.

These criteria are by no means exhaustive or inclusive. However, they do help to determine if a segment does exist and whether it is attractive enough to consider further.

SEGMENTING AND RESEGMENTING

Industrial market segments are dynamic. Competitive activity, technological changes, swings in the business cycle, acquisitions, and make-buy decisions can dramatically change the boundaries and attractiveness of segments. Therefore, it is necessary to periodically evaluate existing segmentation and consider new or different approaches. Business history is replete with cases in which an existing competitor saw market segment boundaries as static or did not identify new, emerging segments and so lost out. The X-ray film market provides an example of just how dynamic a market can be. Although Kodak is the broadest line supplier of photographic film to most market segments, DuPont concentrated on the X-ray film segment and achieved a large market share. Now, developments in nuclear magnetic resonance technology promise to replace X-rays in some applications with a process that develops the "picture" electrically and displays it on a computer screen. As the X-ray market shrinks, DuPont must redefine and resegment the market if it is to hold on to its gains.

Look at the computer market for another example. With increased competition and new electronic capabilities, the computer market must be periodically resegmented with new approaches. One small computer manufacturer noticed there was a type of customer that required high reliability. This market segment included banks and other businesses where interrupted data response meant an immediate loss of customer revenue. To ensure reliability, these companies had to have backup computers or redundant systems that lay idle unless the on-line system failed. The manufacturer was able to design a fail-safe computer that would not lose any data, as the other systems did, if any part of the system went down. As a consequence, the producer was allowed three years of excellent growth and considerable lead time before it had any real competitors in its newly defined market segment.

In short, segmenting industrial markets is a creative process; management should not allow ties to how markets were previously segmented to strangle new ways to segment. In markets where there is rapid technological change, there is a need to resegment more frequently because new technologies blur segment boundaries.

RESPONSIBILITY FOR SEGMENTATION

While many product-market managers and business planners are aware of the need to do a better job of segmenting the market, their enthusiasm or ability to do so is often blunted because of short-term sales and profit pressures. Far too many general managers still regard volume gains and relationships with key accounts as the most important factors in their business. Segmentation is some kind of a theoretical exercise that is not worth much time and money, especially if it interferes with "bringing in or running the business." As this chapter suggests, segmentation requires a good deal of careful thought and creativity, and it is the primary responsibility of general management to make the money and resources available to ensure that it is done. Segmentation is not a theoretical exercise, and any general manager that skips over or shortcuts the need to define the discrete markets to be served is making a bad mistake. To ensure that the business is properly segmented, every general manager should be satisfied with the answers to the following questions:

1. How do we now segment the business?
2. Have we segmented enough?
3. Have we defined the segments in the best way possible?
4. Which segments are most attractive?
5. Is there any evidence that competitors, especially small ones, have achieved an advantage by segmenting differently?

If for any reason these questions are difficult to answer or cannot be answered at all, the chances are good that the business has not been properly segmented and that general management has fallen down on its job.

SUMMARY

Unable to compete broadly against entrenched competitors, threshold companies and those entering markets new to them have repeatedly adopted a "divide and conquer" or market segmentation strategy. Precise definition of a target market can lead to innovative product, price, distribution, and service strategies. Selective market segmentation allows a company to marshal its R&D and engineering efforts toward specific areas rather than spread a little across a wider range of vulnerable marketplaces. At the same time, market segmentation and the selection of specific segments provide direction to the business unit as to which capabilities it must develop to serve the identified market segment effectively. Knowing how to segment a marketplace is therefore one of the most important skills an industrial marketer must possess. Segmentation defines what businesses the firm is in, guides strategy development, and determines the programs necessary in cross-functional areas of the firm. Since industrial market selection is clearly a longer-term strategic decision that cannot be easily reversed, it is important that the general marketplace be first segmented into viable targets before any market selection and investment decisions are made.

6

Assessing Market Potentials

The general manager of the electronic instrumentation division asked Joyce Eichhorn, a recent MBA with a marketing background, to help him appraise the potential acquisition of a product line. The company had an opportunity to acquire a product line that many believed would be complementary to the division's business. But the division general manager wanted to know a number of things about the product and its markets before making a decision:

1. What are the present and potential market segments in which this product line is sold, and what are the key customer accounts in each?
2. What are the future growth prospects in each segment?
3. Who are the major competitors in each segment?
4. How does the product line compare to the competition in manufacturing costs and key success factors?
5. What could favorably or unfavorably affect future derived demand for this product line?

The general manager told Joyce the decision had to be made in two weeks. Joyce spent the next few days talking to friends inside and outside the company about how to get this information. One friend suggested she rely on relevant government statistics. Another suggested she locate and buy a published industry forecast. Still another told her she would not find published material that was specific enough. That friend advised doing a custom-tailored study to obtain the facts. Joyce was not sure which one or combination of these approaches she should use. But she knew she had to work out her plan soon, because she couldn't afford to waste a lot of time getting started.

What are the advantages of using government statistics and an industry forecast?

What are the advantages and disadvantages of doing a custom-tailored study?

What should Joyce do before deciding which approach or combination of approaches is most appropriate in this case?

Is the general manager's two-week deadline realistic?

Far too many industrial firms have not realized the strategic and tactical value of fact-based market information. Many industrial firms do not even have a market research unit. When an in-house marketing research staff does exist, it is typically one of the most underpaid and underappreciated units in the firm. Often it is staffed with castoffs from other departments who do not have the requisite professional skills to do a competent job of market assessment. These situations occur because top management does not appreciate the value of professional market assessment and relies instead on trade or secondary information, or "seat of the pants" estimates. As a result, the company tends to fly half blind and therefore misses opportunities, gets caught off-base by unexpected product or market developments, and is continuously vulnerable to competitors with a better base of market information.

Industrial marketers need to know the present size, potential, and competitor market shares for any market segment of interest. This includes markets the company is presently serving as well as those it is considering for entry. It needs this information to help select and then gear its operations to the most attractive market segments. The information also helps companies decide which products, markets, and individual customers to deemphasize or move away from entirely. The approach for evaluating both present and potential markets is essentially the same. The difference, of course, is that more historical sales and performance data and firsthand knowledge of the marketplace are available for the markets presently served. However, many of the market facts needed to assess either present or potential business markets are typically unavailable from existing sources. Therefore, special market analysis or study is usually needed to accurately assess market positions, potentials, preferences, and competition.

The balance of this chapter examines ways to assess the current position and outlook for markets where the company has a presence; it then goes on to describe how to estimate sales and profit potential for any market of interest. Finally, it outlines specific approaches to conducting market studies that will help determine the relative attractiveness of various markets.

ASSESSING CURRENT MARKET POSITION

Every company must have a sound understanding of where its dollar sales and unit sales come from and how its profits are generated. This statement may appear straightforward and relatively easy to follow. However, most companies report sales only by product line. Very few have regular sales reports by market segment. Even fewer have any kind of profit information by either product or market segment. The following series of exhibits shows how sales and profit data are typically reported in terms of aggregate dollar sales, unit sales, yearly profit, and ROI. Certainly one can see how the product has performed in aggregate terms and what patterns have developed in the company's business. However, these data do not provide answers to several fundamental questions.

Internal Sales Analysis

Let's look first at dollar sales (Exhibit 6-1):

1. Why was there a sudden jump in sales between 1977 and 1978?
2. Why have sales plateaued in the last three years?
3. Are there product-market segments that have different patterns than the aggregate?

Now let's turn to unit sales (Exhibit 6-2):

1. Why have unit sales declined over the past three years?
2. Is this an industry or market trend, or is the decline unique to us?

Finally, look at the profit data (Exhibits 6-3 and 6-4):

1. Why do profit and sales trends differ?
2. Which products within the line are more or less profitable?
3. Why has investment increased so sharply in a flat to declining business?

In most cases the sales account records do not identify what markets customers are in, what the customers' total purchases are, or which competitors have what share of the business. It is frequently necessary to survey existing customers to develop the necessary information required. Table 6.1 shows the data required to conduct a proper sales analysis. Table 6.2 shows how one company reclassified its major accounts under market seg-

EXHIBIT 6-1

A FITTING-DOLLAR SALES (1976–1980)

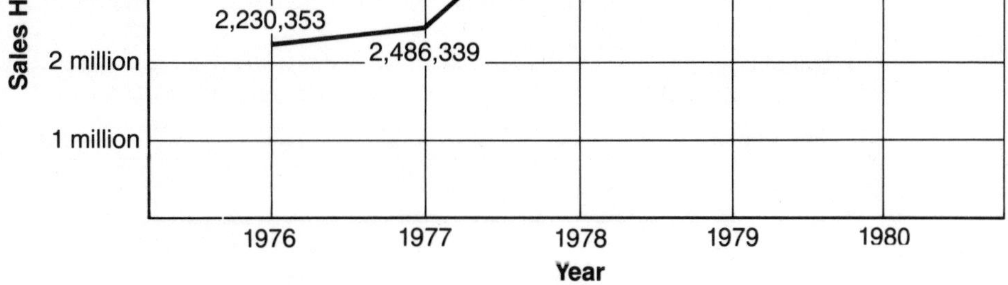

EXHIBIT 6-2

A FITTING-UNIT SALES (1976–1980)

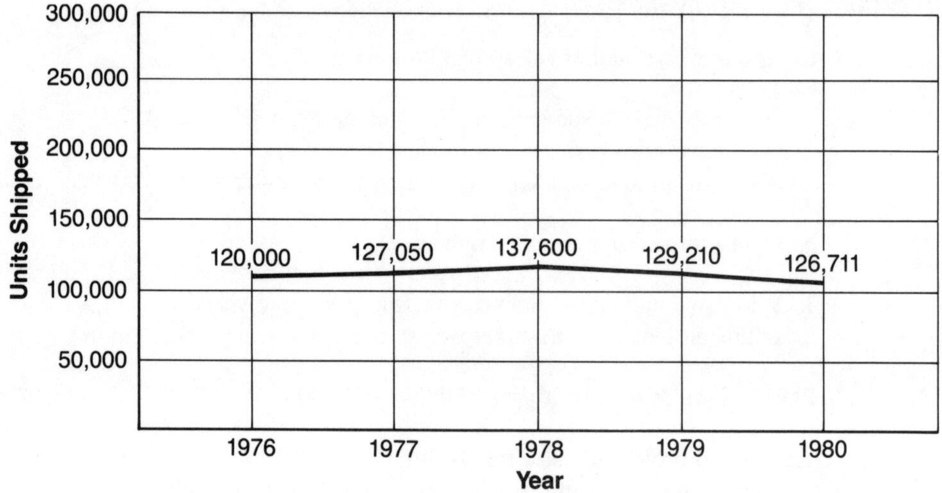

ments, which was a much more meaningful basis for developing product-market sales than the previous listing of accounts by annual purchases. Exhibit 6-5 shows how another company analyzed its sales by major accounts, market segments, customers, and geographic areas over a five-year period and saw that major shifts had occurred. This analysis led to important changes in its sales and product-market strategy.

EXHIBIT 6-3

A FITTING-ANNUAL PROFIT (1976–1980)

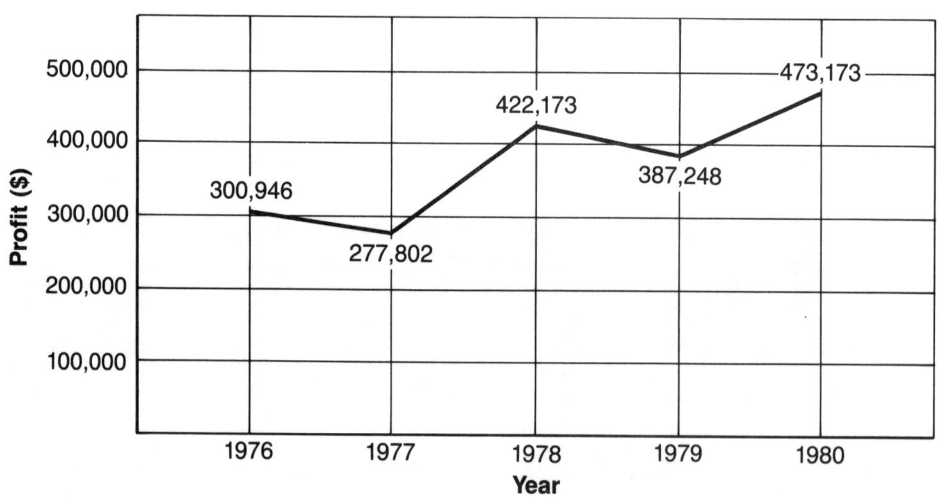

EXHIBIT 6-4

A FITTING-YEARLY ROI (1976–1980)

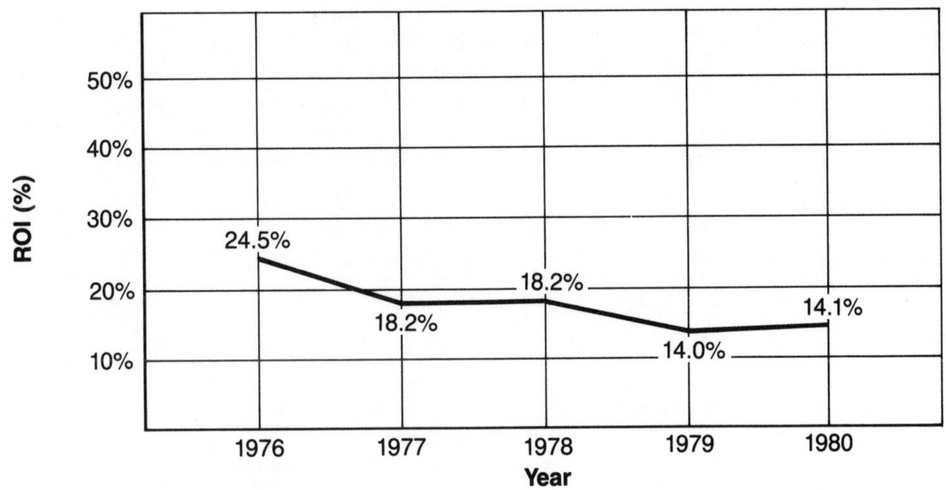

Pressure Point (Rate of Change) Curves

Probably the most important tool for management in assessing the short-term outlook for any market is the pressure point analysis or curve, which helps to predict the direction of thc product or market cycle. The pressure point curve or analysis works this way. Sales orders are posted and tracked to develop either a three-month or twelve-month moving average. Each current three-month and twelve-month average is then divided among corresponding averages for the same period of the prior year. The quotient is a numerical point that can be plotted, and when enough points are plotted the result is a pressure curve. Plotting these points shows the rate of change as sales orders move up or down and provides an early warning of trend changes that are not evident from the absolute sales data.

Exhibit 6-6 shows how pressure point curves can help management make critical decisions. The second chart in the exhibit simply tracks orders booked on a quarterly basis. Note how orders appear to be trending upward from June 1975 through December 1978. Looking at these data alone, one would conclude that the market and business outlook is attractive.

Now look at the three-month and twelve-month pressure curves. While orders moved up during the period, the three-month curve peaked in June 1976, and the rate of change started to decline. The twelve-month curve peaked six months later in December, before it too started to decline. To anyone tracking the data, this shift in the rate of change should have been an indicator that the order rate itself would start to decline, which it did in March 1978. Just think of the advantage to be gained if management can use this tool to plan ahead for changes in the order trend that are likely to occur several months ahead.

Obviously, pressure curves are more revealing if they are developed for discrete

TABLE 6.1 **DATA REQUIRED FOR CONDUCTING A SALES ANALYSIS**

Sales, Costs, Profit Analysis
1. Annual sales—dollars and units
2. Annual net profits and ROI
3. Distribution channels and costs
4. Direct selling expenses
5. Seasonal, cyclical, irregular sales
6. Gross margin trends

Customer Sales Analysis
1. Major customers
2. End-use customer segments
3. SIC of customers
4. New versus old customers
5. Size of customer's annual purchases
6. Our market share penetration
7. Frequency of purchase
8. Purchases by types of products

Geographical Sales Analysis
1. States, cities, etc.
2. Sales territory
3. Individual salespeople
4. Types of customers
5. Product types

Product Sales Analysis
1. Classes of products
2. Product lines to customers
3. Product lines to market segments
4. Product lines to four-digit SIC

product or market segments instead of aggregate sales. Whether or not this can be done, however, depends on the way a company maintains or structures its sales records.

The pressure curve is a crucial tool for management because it enables timely actions to be taken that will reduce a company's exposure as the product or market cycle turns down, and it puts the company into a position such that it can capitalize on opportunities as the cycle turns upward. In October of 1976, a large electrical equipment manufacturer reported record bookings. Sales management was euphoric because bookings had increased steadily for several months. They were dumbfounded when top management ordered a major reduction in inventory and workforce. The sales managers did not recognize that the *rate* of sales growth had declined sharply and that top management had a clear indication that rough times were ahead. Because of top management's actions, the company was able to significantly reduce its costs and was actually able to improve profits during the following year, which turned out to be a severe recession period.

TABLE 6.2

SALES—ORIGINAL EQUIPMENT CUSTOMERS (PRODUCT H)

		1981 Dollars (000)	
A	Caterpillar	$17,000	Reclassified by four segments: 1. Mining 2. Agriculture 3. Construction 4. Industrial lift trucks
	Detroit Diesel-Allison	5,050	
	J.I. Case	2,000	
	John Deere	2,500	
B	Allis Chalmers	1,200	
	Clark Equipment	600	
	Ford Tractor	975	
	Hyster Company	588	
	New Holland	610	
	Rockford Clutch	1,063	
	Saab Scania	675	
	Twin Disc	1,000	
	U.S. Government	1,575	
	Warner Gear	500	
C	Caterpillar—Mexico	250	
	Clearing Division, U.S. Industries	170	
	Fiat Allis	357	
	Franklin Equipment	181	
	Funk Manufacturing	150	
	International Harvester	400	
	Jeffrey Mining	268	
	Joy Manufacturing	127	
	Marathon LeTourneau	188	
	Massey Ferguson	409	
	Mine Machinery	80	
	Pacific Car	201	
	White Farm Equipment	12	
Others		1,345	
Total		39,475	

The key to achieving value from this curve or analysis is not in plotting the data, but in using the curve as a decision-making tool. This data is often carefully plotted in companies by someone in the marketing or economic research groups. While the exercise may provide intellectual satisfaction to those doing the plotting, little real value accrues to the company until top management recognizes its importance and makes it an integral part of the decision-making process.

EXHIBIT 6-5

SALES ANALYSIS PLANNING (PAST, PRESENT, AND FUTURE)

Sales Analysis by Major Accounts

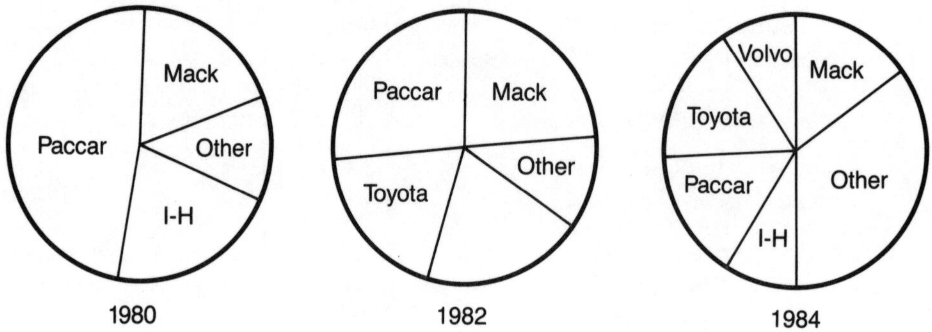

Market Segments

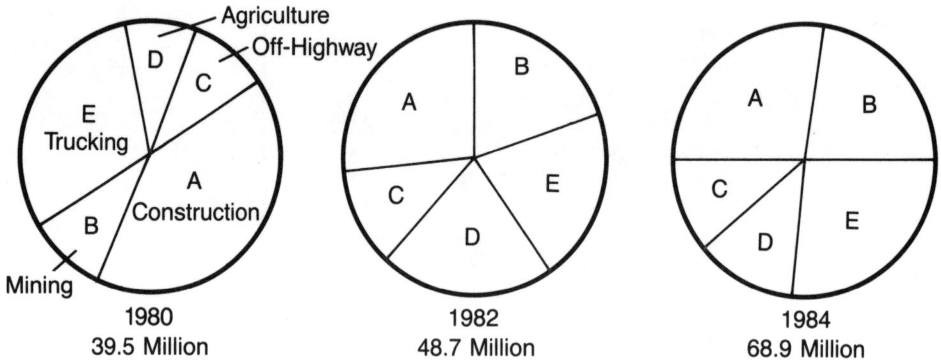

Sales/Distribution Channel Analysis

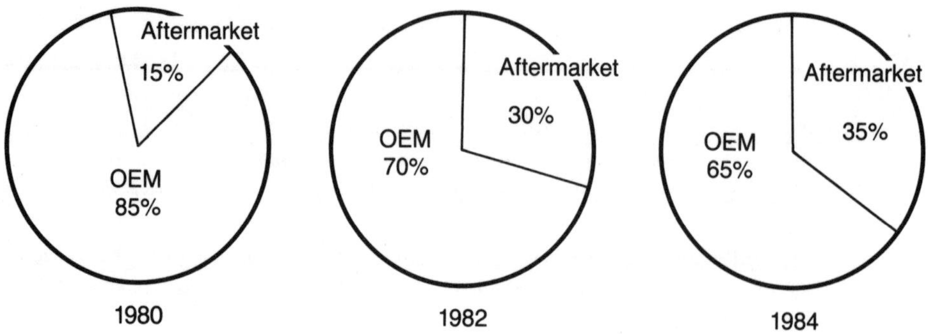

EXHIBIT 6-5

(cont'd)

Geographic Sales Analysis

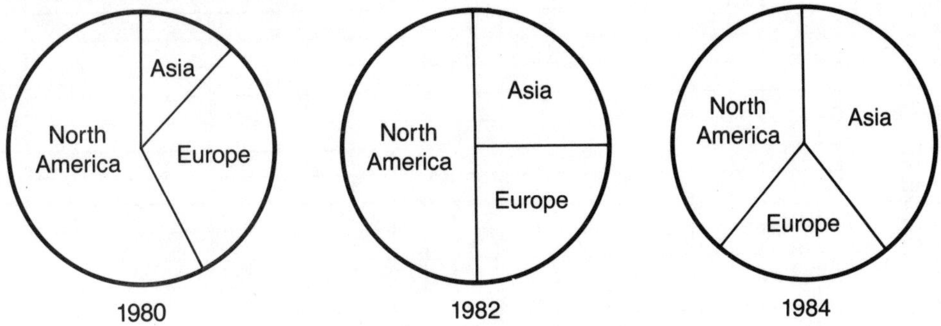

ESTIMATING MARKET POTENTIAL

In addition to assessing the company's current market position and near-term sales outlook, management is also faced with the task of estimating market potential for both existing and new markets. There are a number of ways market potential can be estimated, and how it is done depends chiefly on the sources and availability of data. However, before estimating market potentials, it is essential to carefully define the market segments.

Defining the Market

As we saw in the previous chapter, there are many different ways to define a market. As a result, confusion often abounds in discussions of market potential because those involved have not reached common agreement on the parameters of the market in question. Many times potential estimates are discussed in terms of total industry sales. Other times they are discussed in terms of certain classes of accounts. However, these estimates of market potential are of little value to anyone trying to evaluate target markets for strategic planning and decision making. To be useful, any discussion of market potential should address a specific product or a defined customer or customer group as outlined in the previous chapter on segmenting business markets.

Historical Data

Assuming the market has been properly defined, the first step in forecasting any market is to search for and examine any historical data that might be available. A translation of

EXHIBIT 6-6

ELECTRONIC COMPONENTS—TOTAL REGULAR ORDERS

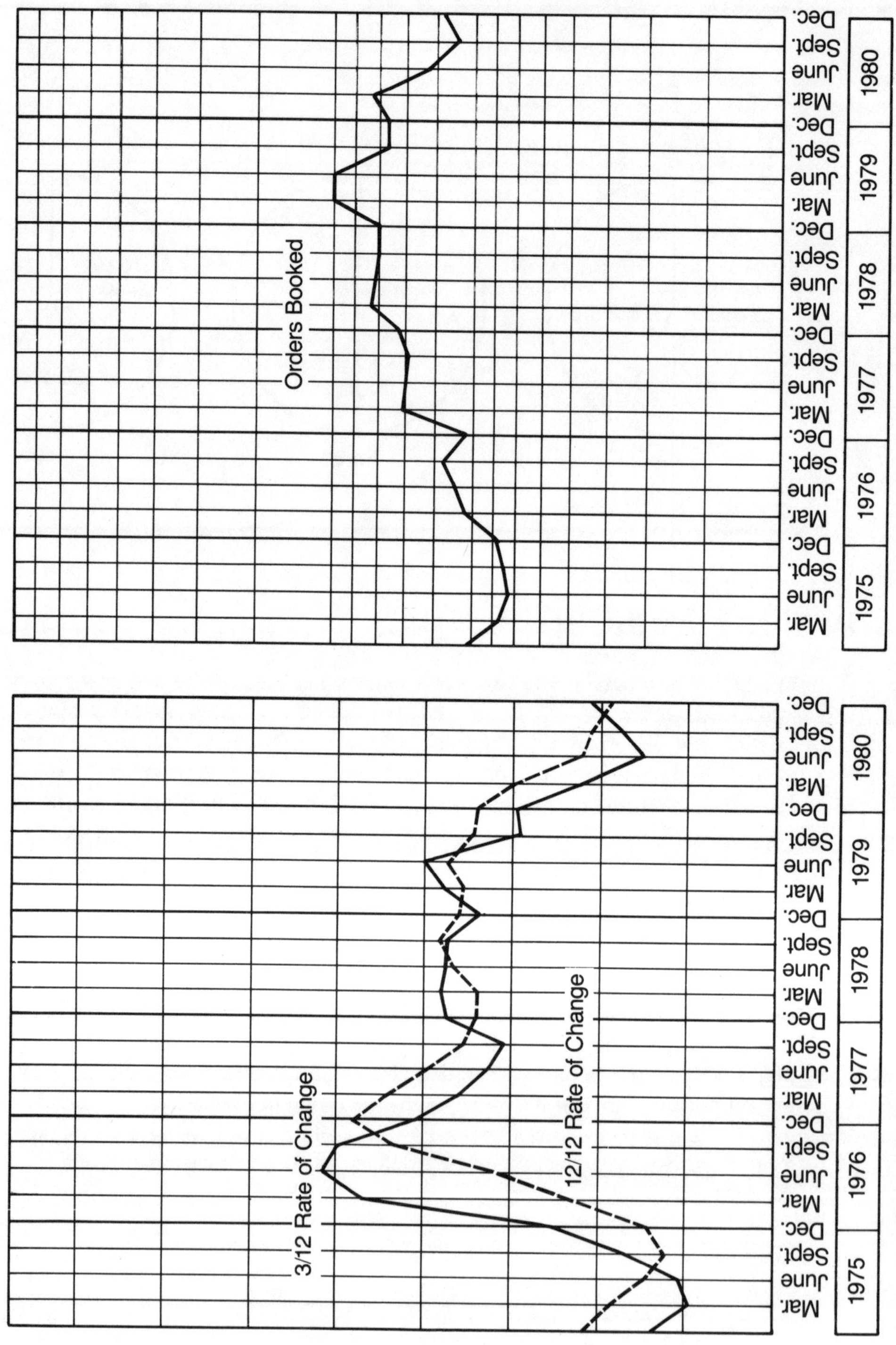

EXHIBIT 6-7

THE BUSINESS CYCLE

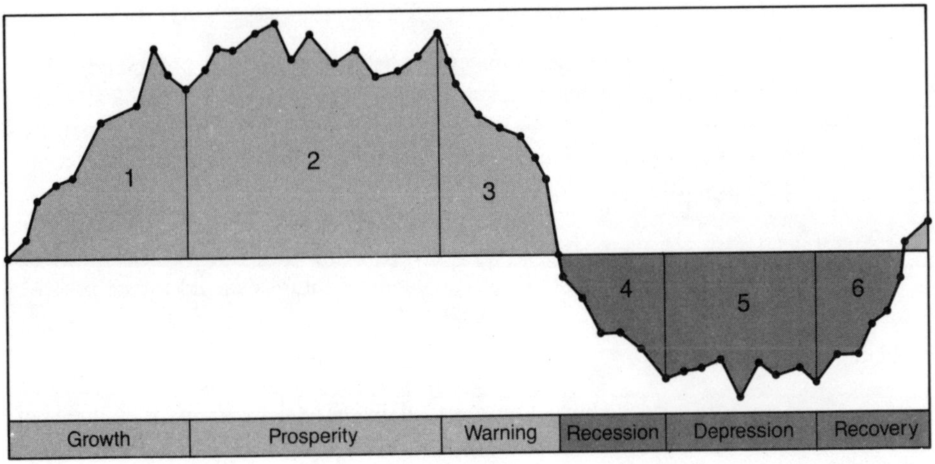

the Latin phrase on the Archives Building cornerstone in Washington, D.C., reads, "What is past is prologue." There is a good deal of truth to this phrase in business where sales into markets tend to move in repetitive cycles, as shown in Exhibit 6-7. The duration of business cycles in the United States ranges from one to nine years, with the average length about three years.[1] Thus, a historical perspective of sales trends is a useful starting point for predicting the future. It must be remembered that this is only a starting point, and any simple-minded attempt to make a straight-line extrapolation of the past into the future is likely to be a mistake, especially in our increasingly dynamic and turbulent world.

Given this caveat, it is still helpful to look for cycles or patterns in historical data that will help in predicting the future. It is also useful to determine whether there is any valid correlation between the product or market cycle and general business cycles, like capital expenditures, capacity utilization, or some other measure of business activity that is regularly plotted and forecasted in published sources.[2]

GNP or the total index of industrial activity may be useful indicators for commodity items that are consumed across all or most markets. However, these indicators are of little use to the industrial marketer struggling to estimate potential for a particular product or market. The indices are simply too broad and too hard to relate to total product or market businesses. Nevertheless, management in many companies spends a lot of money for expert opinion and wastes a lot of time developing very detailed projections or input/output

[1]James A. Estey, *Business Cycles,* 3rd ed. (Englewood Cliffs, N.J.: Prentice-Hall, 1970).
[2]Elmer Lotshaw, "All the Economics You Need for Industrial Market Planning—and No More," *Industrial Marketing Management,* 7 (1970), p. 4.

analysis for our total economy. As we see it, this is more of a theoretical exercise and is simply too far removed from the product-market segment to be of practical use.

Derived Demand

For component products or materials that are used in the production of other products, estimating market potential takes on an added dimension of complexity. Here it is essential to estimate the potential for each customer's markets, which may exist at various levels of the consumption chain described in Chapter 2. For example, a producer of ball bearings must examine a wide range of OEM and aftermarket segments where machines with bearings are used. Doing this requires the bearing producer to work closely with its customers in an effort to forecast the growth rate of each of their markets. This is the only way the bearing producer can estimate future demand for its products.

Trade Association Sources

Many trade associations forecast total industry demand for their member companies. These forecasts usually show the annual total market size and sometimes indicate competitor shares. Exhibit 6-8 shows the aggregate worldwide market for jet aircraft turbine airfoils and the respective sales by U.S., foreign, and captive suppliers. This typical industry forecast does not show the demand by market segments within the total industry, which in the case of turbine airfoils includes military, commercial, and business jets. Each of these market segments has different growth rates, different requirements, and different sets of competitors and suppliers. In short, industry associations can serve as a useful source for aggregate industry data and trends, but further refinements are required before the data can be used to estimate product-market potential.

Conversion Factors

Conversion factors can also be used to help estimate potential in some markets. A conversion factor can be used when there is a high correlation for demand in the product-market segment with consumption patterns or plans in other markets that are more visible and predictable. For example, in the biomedical industry, the type of hospital (general, teaching, specialty), the number of beds, and the occupancy rate are used to determine a weighted conversion factor by the type and size of hospital in each county. The demand for oil field pumps and parts is related to a composite conversion factor developed around the number of pumping wells, parts per type of machine, and number of barrels produced. The forecasts for new elevator systems can be related to new building permits for high-rise starts and renovation projects.

Extreme care must be used in selecting a conversion factor, even where a high statistical correlation exists, since there are many random correlations that are not based on a direct cause/effect relationship. If the wrong conversion factor is chosen, major strategic or technical errors can result. A major strategic error would be to select markets that consume considerably less than the conversion factor indicated. Tactical errors could result in the wrong alignment of sales territories, location of distribution centers, or sales

EXHIBIT 6-8

TOTAL MARKET FOR JET AIRCRAFT TURBINE AIRFOILS (1982 Forecast)

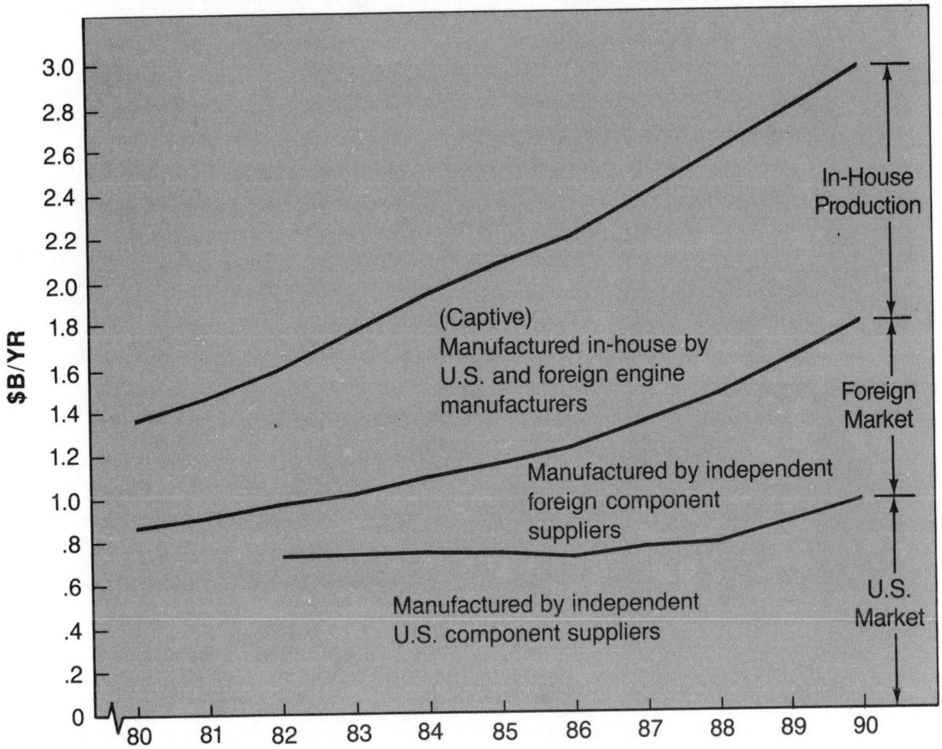

quotas. A common mistake is to regard the number of employees at various plant locations as an indicator of consumption for an industrial product. The number of employees at a plant can often be misleading as a conversion factor, especially with the increased use of automation, which reduces the employee head count. This could lead to a significant overstatement or understatement of demand estimates in geographical areas where there are heavy concentrations of new or old plants.

CONDUCTING MARKET STUDIES

The complete range of information required to assess any business market is seldom available from internal sales records or trade association data. To obtain the more precise information required, it is usually necessary to conduct some kind of a market study that involves existing customers, prospective customers, and distributors. Market studies of this type can provide firsthand information about:

Market size and growth rates
Buying influences
Supply sources
Supplier performance
Technical requirements
Product, brand, or company image
Annual purchases, needs, and trends
Competitive evaluations
New product needs
Product performance
Technological trends

Specifying Information Needed

The most important step before embarking on a search for market information is to define the problem and specify what kind of information is needed. A clearly and accurately stated marketing problem is often well on its way to being solved.[3] The definition provides the direction and control for the entire information-gathering process. If the marketing problem is not properly defined, time, effort, and money will be wasted—no matter how well the project is carried out. Who needs the right answer to the wrong question?

Defining marketing and business problems is frequently a complex process. In order to locate and define problems, a written list of all the pertinent areas to be considered should be prepared. Secondary research (research done and published by others) may help to define and develop a more specific checklist of information required before primary research is undertaken.

Secondary Market Studies

Secondary research is the search for previously published material that can provide more background information and a closer focus on the problem. Sometimes called "desk research," secondary research utilizes internal data, including sales records, salespersons' call reports, and a reanalysis of previously conducted studies. Sales analysis is a form of internal secondary research.

External sources of market information include trade associations, technical journals, government agencies, and industrial directories. The *Census of Manufacturers* and *County Business Patterns* are secondary sources explained in Chapter 5. Another source, *Thomas's Register of American Manufacturers,* classifies all manufacturers by products produced, assets, state, and city. It is used by many purchasing departments to identify suppliers and producers. Each industry or profession usually has at least one trade association. Some trade associations are little more than a public relations office; others keep close track of industry sales and trends. The name, location, and major activities performed by all U.S. associations are contained in the *Encyclopedia of Associations,* a reference that is in most libraries and should be in the industrial firm. Some of the larger trade associations have their own full-time market assessment staff. However, trade associations often do not provide member market share data, and most trade associations do not provide much information to nonmembers.

[3]Howard L. Balsley and Vernon T. Clover, *Business Research Methods,* 2d ed. (Columbus, Ohio: Grid Publishing, Inc., 1979), p. 35.

As a general rule, no market study should be undertaken before a search of secondary sources has been completed. It can sometimes solve the problem without any primary research. The cost is much less than a primary investigation, and at the least, such a search will establish a higher plateau from which a primary study can be launched. Secondary sources will often help to refocus the original problem. Secondary research is not as exciting as primary research for both the analyst and user, but because of its exploratory nature, it can establish patterns of careful, thoughtful analysis that will carry over to any subsequent primary market assessment studies.

Primary Market Studies

The quality of the data obtained from a primary market study depends on the quality and validity of the sample, asking the right questions, and employing qualified interviewers.

SELECTING THE SAMPLE. Samples for industrial marketing studies are nearly always much smaller than those used for consumer goods marketing studies because of the concentrated nature of many industrial markets. For example, a manufacturer of specialty chemicals identified a total of 20 potential users for a new high-performance chemical. The producer was able to visit personally 6 users and to conduct telephone interviews with the remaining 14 in the total market. One hundred percent "sampling" of the entire universe is not uncommon in some industrial market segments. If larger customer bases are involved, it is often best to stratify the sample by size or type of customer. The actual selecting of individual samples in industrial markets is usually based more on a judgment of which companies or personnel are most knowledgeable than on statistical models or random probability methods.

SURVEY METHODS. Survey information can be obtained through person-to-person interviews, telephone interviews, or mailed questionnaires. Person-to-person interviews allow the interviewer to see a customer's production process or system and ask some specific questions about how the supplier's product might be used. For example, one manufacturer developed a new insulating material for greenhouses that would reduce energy costs. There was no substitute for conducting person-to-person interviews in a good cross-section of greenhouses in the defined market segment. The field interviews helped the producer make a cost-benefit analysis of the energy-saving material in large, medium, and small greenhouses in each climate zone.[4] Energy costs and technical requirements were also obtained for each type of greenhouse. The person-to-person interviews also revealed some potential application problems. In other cases, a small number of interviews with customers can stop a supplier from providing an expensive function the customer does not need or want. For example, a major farm tractor manufacturer learned from farmers that a side power unit to raise and lower implements was not needed. The final engineering and manufacturing costs for the unit would have been nearly $1 million, and it would have added an unnecessary 5 to 6 percent to the purchase price of

[4]See also Chapter 4, "Understanding Customers and Competition," pp. 68–79.

the tractor. The probing nature of person-to-person interviews is excellent for learning how customers use and buy products.

Person-to-person industrial interviews typically involve small numbers. Sample sizes of ten to one hundred are far more common than the hundreds or thousands so typical in the consumer goods world.

Each business interview can last one to three hours, considerably longer than is practical for telephone or mail interviews. Person-to-person interviews are costly, especially if extensive travel is required, and may be ineffective if interviewers are not properly trained or indoctrinated. The cost of person-to-person interviews can be reduced by using focus groups. An industrial focus group consists of a small number of individuals with a common occupation. One machine tool manufacturer usually discusses a product with, and shows a prototype to, focus groups of machinists to obtain their reactions. A hospital equipment manufacturer conducts group interviews with nurses to obtain responses to its and competitors' machines. In still another situation, an electrical producer sometimes conducts group interviews with distributors at regional meetings to obtain competitive intelligence.

Focus group interviews are a relatively inexpensive and fast way to gather market information. The combined group effect often produces a wide range of information and insights, but the results are sometimes hard to interpret and quantify. The stronger personalities in the group can influence the more passive members. The tendency to seek consensus may also dampen the responses of some members. But if resources are limited, the focus group may be the best alternative to no interviews at all.

SEEKING EXPERT OPINION. Sometimes the opinions of experts on a subject are far more important than the results of any other kind of study. For example, a manufacturer of surgical hip joints wanted to determine whether hip implants made of titanium would eventually be selected by physicians over the current implants made of aluminum. Expert opinions from leading orthopedic surgeons were obtained at a national orthopedic surgeons convention. After obtaining a preregistration list of physicians, the supplier was able to schedule interviews with 30 surgeons by offering $500 to each for participation. The supplier was able to gauge the physicians' initial reactions to the use of titanium and identify sources of resistance to the new product. The expert opinion interviews were a very efficient and rapid way to obtain information for final product development, market entry strategy, and competitive promotional plans.

Expert opinions are frequently sought in high technology industries like medicine, pharmaceuticals, and aerospace. Interviewers visit key people at universities and corporations who are recognized as the innovators or leaders in the profession. The whole approach depends on knowing how to identify the real experts. True experts are recognized by colleagues and peers as nationally and internationally knowledgeable about the topic. Good interviews with true experts usually reduce the need for additional interviews with more people. It is a mistake to think that expert opinion is inferior to more scientific approaches to gathering market information. In some industrial market situations, it can be far superior to large sample information.[5] However, a small sample of experts is usually better than a single expert.

[5]Philip Kotler, "A Guide to Gathering Expert Estimates," *Business Horizons*, October 1970, pp. 79–85.

MAIL OR TELEPHONE. In situations where the cost of person-to-person interviews—either individual or group—is too high, the marketer can choose the mail or telephone approach. It is also not uncommon first to conduct a few person-to-person interviews and then complete the study with the mail or telephone approach. Telephone interviews, like the person-to-person approach to gathering market assessment information, allow marketers to reach the appropriate people and ask probing questions. A telephone interview of up to a half hour is a relatively low-cost approach. Like person-to-person interviews, it requires interviewers trained in the product or technology. Of course, complex technical questions that require seeing the respondent's situation or using visual aids are not feasible with the telephone approach. Telephone market assessment is limited to rather simple questions about annual purchases, current supply sources, and image perceptions.

Mail interviews are usually low in cost and do not require the training and supervision of interviewers. They are especially good when surveying a wide customer base with many segments about relatively few items. For example, a manufacturer of agricultural chemicals periodically surveys about 2,000 farmers to learn of different trends and purchase preferences for different chemicals. The producer supplements the periodic survey with person-to-person interviews at agricultural cooperatives and county fairs. The shorter the questionnaire, the better. Low response rates may create a strong response bias, and there is often little control over when the response is returned and who provides the information.

COMMON FORECASTING METHODS. In summary, there are a number of forecasting methods to consider when estimating or evaluating a product or market situation. The more common methods of forecasting are shown in Table 6.3. A description of each method, along with the advantages and disadvantages of each approach, is also shown in Table 6.3, and other published sources provide still more information about these approaches.[6,7,8]

One of the major advantages of personal and telephone interviews is the ability to control who the respondent is. There is little such control with mail questionnaires. A response from the wrong users, specifiers, and buyers can be harmful. Skilled interviewers take great care to be sure they are talking to the key decision maker(s) in the purchase of the item being studied.

All these approaches to conducting primary market assessment studies should be considered when a problem is to be studied. Each of the approaches is a compromise of some form. The manager or user of the market information must weigh the cost, time, and value of the project when choosing one or a combination of approaches.

ASKING THE RIGHT QUESTIONS. Once the correct respondents are identified and interview method chosen, the next problem is asking the questions in the right way. Poor wording can result in misleading and inaccurate studies. Questions that ask for ways to improve a product or "what would you like improved" will get more in-depth responses than questions that simply ask what the user likes and dislikes about an existing or new

[6]Steven C. Wheelwright and Spyros Makridakis, *Forecasting Methods for Management,* 2nd ed. (New York: Wiley, 1977).
[7]Harry D. Wolfe, *Business Forecasting Methods* (New York: Holt, Rinehart, and Winston, 1966).
[8]Richard D. Crisp, *Sales Planning and Control* (New York: McGraw-Hill, 1968), p. 42.

TABLE 6.3 ***COMMON FORECASTING METHODS FOR PRODUCT-MARKET SEGMENTS***

Method	*Description*	*Advantages*	*Disadvantages*
1. Survey	Widely used technique–mail surveys, person-to-person, or telephone approach to determine potential by segments. Helps estimate annual purchases by bridge factor in each segment.	Current. Geographic concentrations. Major accounts. Helps detect purchase trends. Can provide competitive information. Provides sales leads.	Time-consuming–1 to 3 months. Cost may be \$3,000 to \$40,000+.
2. Trend projection	Past trends are projected into the future, fitting curves to historical data.	Objective. Simple and quick.	Assumes the future is a direct extension of the past. Historical data are usually inadequate for new products.
3. Expert opinion	Obtaining opinions of a representative sample or from knowledgeable experts in the area and building projections from consensus or composite of estimates. Also used to predict technological changes.	Basis for estimating uncertainties. Provides a "ballpark feel." Provides a focus on more specific segments and for new products.	Highly subjective. Determining experts.
4. Substitution demand	Demand assumed to be related to another product. The selection of a conversion or bridge factor is a form of substitution demand analysis.	Allows rational extrapolation of limited data.	Subjective. Assumes same outside factors as for substitute product.
5. Correlation analysis	Demand related to one or more independent variables can also be shown with a regression equation.	Objective if consistent correlations are identified. Requires choice of major factors affecting demand and statement of assumptions.	Truly independent variables are sometimes difficult to identify. Other variables must first be forecast themselves. Complexity increases with more variables. High correlation does not always mean cause-effect.
6. Mathematical models	Equations developed to express interrelationships among several variables. Equations are solved to get values of dependent demand.	Same as correlation analysis. Forces "systematic" organization of data.	Same as correlation analysis. Precision likely to be confused with accuracy.

product. Here are ten guidelines to consider when constructing a questionnaire and selecting words:

1. All questions should relate directly to the research objectives.
2. Avoid examples, because they may divert the response from the research objectives.
3. If you wish to extract many thoughts on the topic, add a probing question that goes deeper into the topic.
4. Use as few and as simple words as possible in each question.
5. Make questions specific without being elaborate.
6. Avoid wording that causes ambiguous responses.
7. Use trade jargon only if all the respondents know and use it.
8. Even if it is an open-ended question, consider providing categories or precoded check boxes for the answers. This is especially helpful when asking for amounts or figures.
9. Instead of asking "how much?" indicate the units for which you desire answers—pounds, dollars, gallons, yards, percentages, or whatever.
10. Provide for "don't know" responses rather than force a guess.

SELECTING THE RIGHT INTERVIEWERS. Accurate business interviews depend on asking the right questions to the appropriate people and then listening with educated ears. Since person-to-person and telephone interviews are central for many market assessment projects, the person asking the questions and receiving the verbal responses plays a key role. The interviewer should know the industry and how the product is used and bought. Without such background knowledge, the interviewer cannot ask probing questions and will probably miss key words from the respondent. It usually takes extensive briefing and indoctrination into the industry, the technology, substitute products, and the competition to get less knowledgeable interviewers up to an acceptable level. The vice-president of marketing in a major industrial firm evaluates market studies by outside suppliers by the kind and type of briefing they do of their field interviewers. Often he personally interviews one of the field interviewers to see how well they were briefed and made aware of the problem and concerns of the study.

The business respondent's time is usually important. Therefore, the interviewer must gain as much useful information as possible within a limited time. As a consequence, industrial market research field interviewers must state questions clearly, attempt to trigger the memory, and listen very carefully. If more time and skill are invested in training industrial interviewers, smaller sample sizes may be used to yield the same amount of information in considerably less time and at a reduced cost.

One manufacturer of electronic testing equipment always sends a team of R&D and marketing people to conduct person-to-person interviews for product development. The team method allows for better questioning, note taking, and insights to better couple product development to customer requirements. R&D–marketing team interviews can also help in creative market analysis immediately following the interviews. In one case, a small number of R&D and marketing team personal interviews with customers helped to refocus product development.

The need to have expert interviewers knowledgeable in the technical language and users' needs is usually best addressed by in-house marketing research personnel. They need less timely and costly indoctrination. In a larger firm, an in-house marketing research staff is a necessary and usually cost-effective alternative to having outside firms plan market studies and conduct personal interviews.

SALES FORCE OPINIONS. The industrial sales force is sometimes considered a biased and poor source of market information. This is sometimes true, but an industrial sales representative can also be a prime source of market information. The intelligence the industrial sales representative develops about end users' needs, business patterns, and competition can serve as the foundation for future product and market plans and tactics. It is impractical for most industrial companies to structure market tests as consumer goods companies do to evaluate the needs, likes, and dislikes of market segments. The industrial marketer must gear the sales force to provide this information or in many cases do without it. One major part of the market planning and research function of any company should be to develop and provide intelligent, continual feedback from the marketplace. Industrial firms should spend considerable effort and emphasize the importance of developing market assessment information from the field sales force. Salespeople usually have well-developed interpersonal skills, are familiar with customers' operations, and speak customers' language.

Data Analysis

Most analysis of business research consists of drawing conclusions from statements made by knowledgeable people about their operations, applications, requirements, purchase plans, and buying considerations. When the results of the research are quantitative, graphs should generally be used to show trends, segments, or changing relationships. Graphs are generally limited to showing the relationship between two variables. The graph should show the manager if there is any relationship and also whether the relationship is up (direct) or down (inverse), or whether some type of curve best shows the relationship. Graphs show relationships that do not appear in various kinds of statistical analyses. Graphs help managers to make generalizations and predictions by looking beyond the data. There is limited need for the use of sophisticated statistical techniques driven by computers, and management should challenge any proposal that hinges on the utilization of these methods. There is a high probability that proposals of this type are made by people who are more interested in the technique than providing useful results.

New Product Market Studies

New product market studies, like new product development, is difficult and risky. Usually the newer the industrial product or service, the less accurate or reliable will be the prospect's responses. If the product or service is fairly revolutionary or requires a different way of using the product, evaluations tend to be more negative. In cases where the product is radically different or performs the same function but in a different way, it is often difficult for customers to visualize the value-in-use. Revolutionary products also tend to be rejected as "crazy" or strange. New products often have more credibility and understandability if they come from a well-known producer. But since most innovations come from small companies who are not well known, new product market research for these producers is often difficult.

Two independent market studies done for the then new Xerox Corporation in 1959 concluded that there was a limited market for its later successful Model 914. The studies concluded that there was no market for a large, free-standing general document copying machine. In retrospect, Xerox executives contend that those interviewed applied the criteria of the existing methods of copying or reproduction, whereas they were interested in respondents evaluating the attributes of an entirely new technology. The product the studies said nobody wanted became a product everybody wanted. New product industrial market research must carefully examine the existing production systems of potential in-use customers and the cost-benefit value and be cautious about prospective customers' negative opinions.

It is also frequently difficult to obtain accurate market size and growth information for innovative industrial products. For example, the Smith Kline Corporation found it extremely difficult to anticipate the potential success and market size of the ulcer treatment drug Tagamet, which after four years had yearly sales of about $600 million. The initial market research for this product concluded that revenues would eventually attain $100 million a year for the drug and that ultimately it could attain revenues of $250 million when it was a mature product, six to eight years later. What confounded the market researchers was the absence of statistics on ulcer sufferers. Those who were being treated by a physician showed up in the public health records, but there was no way to be sure how many others were treating themselves with diets and various nonprescription antacids. A similar problem faced Merck Pharmaceutical Company when it was attempting to obtain market information on the size of the U.S. dog worm medicine market. Incomplete statistics and lack of information about the magnitude of the problem resulted in an inability to estimate the size and growth of what was thought to be a large market.

PROJECT PROPOSALS

A sound project proposal is the framework and roadmap for conducting a professional market assessment study. All proposals should be developed with the managerial users of the information. These same managers should "sign off" on every proposal before it is implemented or before the data is gathered.

To assist the marketers in designing and implementing a market assessment study, we have provided two project proposals. The first, Exhibit 6-9, is an industrial valve study. This product has a wide potential customer base that buys primarily through local distributors. By explicitly stating the objectives of the study in the form of eight precise information needs, the problem and the specific information required are well defined.

EXHIBIT 6-9

BALL VALVE PRODUCT-MARKET STUDY

I. OBJECTIVES OF THE STUDY

The specific objectives of this marketing study are to:

1. Define the channels of distribution being used for each market segment studied.
2. Develop a list of distributors for each of the major manufacturers of ball valves.
3. Identify the major ball valve product attributes considered important buying factors.
4. Rank the product attributes in terms of important buying factors overall and market segment.
5. Rank the product attributes in terms of important buying factors by size (employment) of manufacturing plant.
6. Identify the major ball valve manufacturers' competitive strengths and weaknesses in terms of the product attributes.
7. Define the dollar market demand for brass ball valves by the market segments selected to be studied.
8. Provide a prospect list of qualified users of brass ball valves, including a dollar estimate of buying potential. This prospect list will be arranged by trading area and will include plants with more than 25 employees.

II. MARKET ASSESSMENT METHODS

1. **Literature Search** All known literature indexes and directories will be searched to gather the names of firms operating in the identified OEM markets. Examples of literature sources include state industrial directories, *Iron Age,* and major periodicals.
2. **Mail Survey** A mail survey will be used to gather the quantitative and qualitative data to measure the perceived buying factor importance ranking and the types of distributors being used to serve the various market segments. A sampling of approximately 4,500 plants is planned.
3. **Field Interviews** This marketing research technique will be used to frame and pretest the mail questionnaire and gather qualitative information concerning the major buying factors and channels of distribution.
4. **Telephone Interviews** Telephone interviews will be conducted to verify and supplement data gathered through the mail survey and field interviews.

III. METHOD OF PREPARATION

A mail questionnaire will be used as the primary research method for gathering the data. Field interviews will be conducted to pretest the questionnaire and identify the major product attributes in terms of important buying influences.

A. **OEM Markets** The OEM markets included in this study are as follows:

SIC	Market Description
3433	Heating equipment
3443	Boiler shops
3551	Food products machinery
3552	Textile machinery
3553	Woodworking machinery
3554	Paper industry machinery
3555	Printing machinery
3561	Pumps and pumping equipment
3563	Air and gas compressors
3564	Blowers, exhaust, and ventilation fans
3582	Commercial laundry, dry cleaning, and pressing machines

B. **Aftermarkets** The MRO/aftermarkets included in this study are as follows:

SIC	Market Description
1711	Mechanical contractors
2421	Saw mills and planing mills
2611	Pulp mills
2869	Organic chemicals
3069	Fabricated rubber products
3229	Glass products
3312	Steel mills
3441	Fabricated metal products
3523	Farm and garden machinery
3621	Electrical motors and generators
3728*	Aircraft parts and equipment

EXHIBIT 6-10

JET ENGINE PARTS STUDY

I. OBJECTIVES OF THE STUDY

The objectives of this study are to:

1. Identify the major buying influences for purchasing agents, maintenance engineers, and chief engineers that affect the decision to buy fuel injection and metering devices (fuel manifolds, spraybars, valves) and fuel nozzles.
2. Rank the major buying influences for purchasing agents, maintenance engineers, and chief engineers and their perceptions of the major suppliers.
    - A. Engine Prime Contractors
        1. Pratt & Whitney, Florida
        2. General Electric, Evendale, and Lynn, Massachusetts
        3. Detroit Diesel Allison Division, Indianapolis
    - B. Private Engine Rework Facilities (to be identified and sampled)
    - C. Research & Development Facilities
        1. NASA Lewis Research Centers
        2. Naval Air Propulsion Test Center (Trenton, N.J.)
        3. Jet Propulsion Laboratory (California)
        4. Arnold Engineering Development Center
    - D. USAF and USN Engine Rework Facilities
        1. USAF Bases
            - a. San Antonio, Texas
            - b. Oklahoma City, Oklahoma
            - c. Wright-Patterson, Ohio
        2. USN Rework Facilities
            - a. Alameda, California
            - b. San Diego, California (North Island)
            - c. Cherry Point, North Carolina
            - d. Jacksonville, Florida
            - e. Pensacola, Florida
            - f. Norfolk, Virginia
    - E. Aircraft Prime Contractors
        1. McDonnell Douglas
        2. Boeing
        3. Lockheed
    - F. Major Commercial Airlines
        1. American
        2. Braniff
        3. Eastern
        4. Northwest
        5. TWA
        6. United
        7. Delta
        8. US Air

II. METHODS OF ASSESSMENT

Field Interviews Based on the small number of facilities comprising the various market segments, it is estimated that approximately 12 personal interviews will be conducted.

Telephone Interviews This research method will be used for contacting the identified private engine rework facilities and performing all follow-up work that may be required.

Mail Survey In order to cut down on travel expenses and time, a mail questionnaire will be designed and sent to all facilities not personally visited. It is estimated that approximately 100 questionnaires will be sent.

III. COMPLETION SCHEDULE

This research project will require approximately 12 calendar weeks to complete, starting the day of proposal approval. The actual marketing research time allocation will be for only four man-hour weeks.

The second study (Exhibit 6-10) is for jet engine fuel nozzles. The customer base is very small, less than 25 customers, and each customer provides a significant amount of business. The products are technically complex and are used in commercial business and military jet engines. Personal interviews were the primary method for gathering information; interviews were followed up with mail questionnaires.

FRAMEWORKS FOR EVALUATING MARKET SEGMENTS

Because so many data are involved, the industrial marketer should have a framework to organize the relevant market potential information in a meaningful way. The worksheet shown in Table 6.4 illustrates such a framework. It provides the basis for presenting historical size and growth patterns, as well as estimated size and growth potential. It also provides for listing the major competitors and their market share positions along with major customers and their annual purchases. Obviously, simply filling out this form is not an end in itself. It is designed to help management evaluate and crosscheck a variety of data for various market segments into tradeoffs that must be considered before deciding which segments are most attractive.

Before a final selection of market segments is made, it is often useful to factor profit potential into the decision. In markets where a company does not have a presence, profit potential is generally not readily available. Nevertheless, profit estimates can usually be developed through published financial data, interviews with investment analysts who follow particular industries and companies, and competitor intelligence, as described in Chapter 4. Table 6.5 shows how estimated size, growth rate, and profit potential for a market can be combined to determine the relative value of a share point (1/100th of a market) on both a current and projected basis. The current value of a share point is determined by multiplying 1/100th of the market by the current profit percentage. For example, in market segment A, 1/100th of the market is $1 million. Multiplying $1 million by a 12 percent profit rate results in a current profit value per share point of $120,000. Looking ahead, the projected market size is determined by multiplying the size of the current market by the estimated growth rate. For example, market segment A, which is currently worth $100 million, is expected to grow at 15 percent each year, so the projected market five years out is $240 million. The profit percentage is expected to remain the same, and the projected profit value for each share point also doubles to $240,000.

From this table, you can see that the changes of the three key variables—size, growth rate, and EBT percentage over a five-year period—can often lead to different conclusions than market data alone might suggest. For example, compare the current and projected value per share point for market segment D. It actually shows a significant decline because of an expected deterioration in EBT percentage. And market segment E, which is currently the smallest segment, has such a high profit potential and growth rate that it becomes one of the more attractive markets five years out. Very few managers ever consider profit potential as they access various market segments. More should, however, because variations in profit opportunities can have a major impact on the relative attractiveness of market alternatives.

TABLE 6.4

PRODUCT AND MARKET SEGMENT FORECASTS

Industry Group	*Identified Market Segments*	*Segment Size Today (In units/ dollars)*	*Segment Annual Growth Rates (In % for last four years)*	*Forecast Market Size (In units/dollars)*			*Present Competitors and Market Shares*		*Major Customers and Annual Purchase*
				1 Yr	*3 Yr*	*5 Yr*	*3–5 Competitors*	*Market Share*	
							1. ____	____	
							2. ____	____	
Industrial							3. ____	____	
	Medical						4. ____	____	
	instrumentation	____	____	____	____	____	5. ____	____	____
	Process controls	____	____	____	____	____	____	____	____
	Test equipment	____	____	____	____	____	____	____	____
Computers									
	Mainframe	____	____	____	____	____	____	____	____
	Microprocessors	____	____	____	____	____	____	____	____
	Calculators	____	____	____	____	____	____	____	____

TABLE 6.5

PROJECTING THE PROFIT POTENTIAL OF A SHARE POINT CURRENT AND FIVE YEARS OUT

Market Segments	*Current Size (Millions)*	*Current Profit (Percent)*	*Current Profit Value Per Share Point (Thousands)*	*Estimated Growth Rate (Percent)*	*Projected Market Size*	*Estimated Profit (Percent)*	*Projected Profit Value Per Share Point*
A	100	12	120	15	240	12	240
B	350	9	315	7	458	10	458
C	200	14	280	8	371	10	271
D	400	15	600	5	510	8	408
E	60	20	120	20	144	20	288

SUMMARY

The day-to-day pressures of business tend to focus attention on the immediate situation. But a more systematic study and fact gathering of market trends, potentials, cyclical turns, and profitability will result in more active professional management and less defensive reaction. The time and cost required to conduct market studies that result in better direction should be considered a priority investment. The cost and risks of not having the necessary market facts can be high without such data. Wrong and irreversible strategic commitments can be made to serve markets that are rapidly declining. With slow or no growth situations and rapid technical changes in many business markets, sound market facts are even more important. When market assessment is a key input in all strategic and tactical product and market thinking, strategy, and programs, the industrial firm will have the appropriate basis for sound decision making.

III

MANAGING THE MARKETING MIX

7

Product Development

In the fall of 1974, top management of a large machine tool company made a major strategic decision. All new product development personnel and projects were pulled away from the four major divisions of the company and centralized in a new center under the direction of a corporate vice president of engineering. The technical center had cost $5 million to build and equip and was to be a showplace. Senior management was convinced that this move would put the company in a position to lead the industry in product development. Division managers were assessed 1.5 percent of sales for development projects on their products. They were also encouraged to forward their ideas for projects, but the vice president of engineering was authorized to commit funds in the best interests of the corporation.

After the recession in 1975 and 1976, the company's market and profit position deteriorated badly. The company also lost market share because it had not moved into electronic controls as rapidly as competitors. At a committee management meeting, the president complained about the lost market share and the company's poor position in electronic controls: "I can't understand it. We have the best R&D facility, the most engineers, and the highest ratio of R&D expense to sales. Why are we behind?"

In response, the vice president of engineering explained: "Things are not as bad as they seem. We are currently testing two prototype control systems that appear very attractive. We should have them ready to turn over to marketing within the next three to four months. Once these new systems are ready, our sales and marketing group should be able to regain our market share and then some." The vice president of marketing took quite a different tack: "I don't want to be the fall guy here. We are at least two years late with a competitive control system and we haven't had enough input to the systems currently on test. I don't know whether they will be competitive, and even if they are, we are going to have one hell of a job trying to recapture market share, particularly in this weak market."

The president exploded: "It's the same old story. Both of you have your own ax to grind and neither of you will accept responsibility for the problem. I don't know how good our new control system will be. I don't know how tough it will be to get back some of the business we have lost. All I know is that you two have not worked together, and our product development activities have suffered because of your failure to cooperate."

Is the president right?

What is the marketing vice president really saying?

What happens if the new products that are so attractive to engineering are not attractive to customers?

Is pouring money into R&D the key to succeeding with new products? What are some problems that could result from this action?

Developing new products that cost less or perform better has historically been a crucial activity for most industrial companies. Now, it is more important than ever, as industry girds itself to meet foreign competitors that have cut sharply into domestic markets. Product innovations that result in superior performance or cost advantages are the best means of protecting a strong market position or of taking entrenched customers away from competition without sacrificing profit margins. For this reason, new product development is typically regarded as the lifeblood of most industrial businesses. Exhibit 7-1, which is taken from a recent Booz, Allen & Hamilton study, shows that new products have contributed importantly to profits in every industry listed. Making any allowances you want for the inaccuracies that can exist in this kind of a table, one can still see that new products make a vital contribution to sales and profit growth in most industries. What is more important, the figure indicates that profit contribution from new products is expected to increase in the years ahead.

THE PRODUCT LIFE CYCLE

The importance of new product development stems from a fundamental fact of business life: Every product moves through a life cycle that eventually leads to obsolescence (Exhibit 7-2). When a successful new product is introduced to the market, it typically enjoys a period of rapid growth as it gains acceptance with more customers and replaces those products made obsolete by its presence. But this period of growth does not last forever. As competitors match or improve on the new product, it moves from its growth phase into maturity and eventually into obsolescence. When this occurs, sales volume flattens and then trends downward, prices and margins typically decline below acceptable levels, and the product is ultimately squeezed out or deteriorates into profitless price competition. The life cycle period may be relatively short (two to three years), as it is in the electronics field, where technology leaps ahead almost every day and product life cycles are often discussed in terms of months rather than years. Or it may span a decade or more, as it has for many standard mechanical products and components (screw machines, standard fasteners, or gears). But sooner or later, every product yields to new technology and is preempted by another with better cost and/or performance characteristics.

Better Mousetraps

No matter how superior a product might appear to be or how dynamic its growth has been, its leadership position is always tenuous. Modern technology is a powerful force and full of surprises; it is a serious mistake to assume that any product ever has a lock on any market. Any product can be pushed from the growth phase of its life cycle to a mature or obsolescent position very quickly by some new product or process that offers significant cost or performance advantages. Whenever a successful product enjoys a strong

EXHIBIT 7-1

CONTRIBUTION OF NEW PRODUCTS TO PROFIT BY INDUSTRY

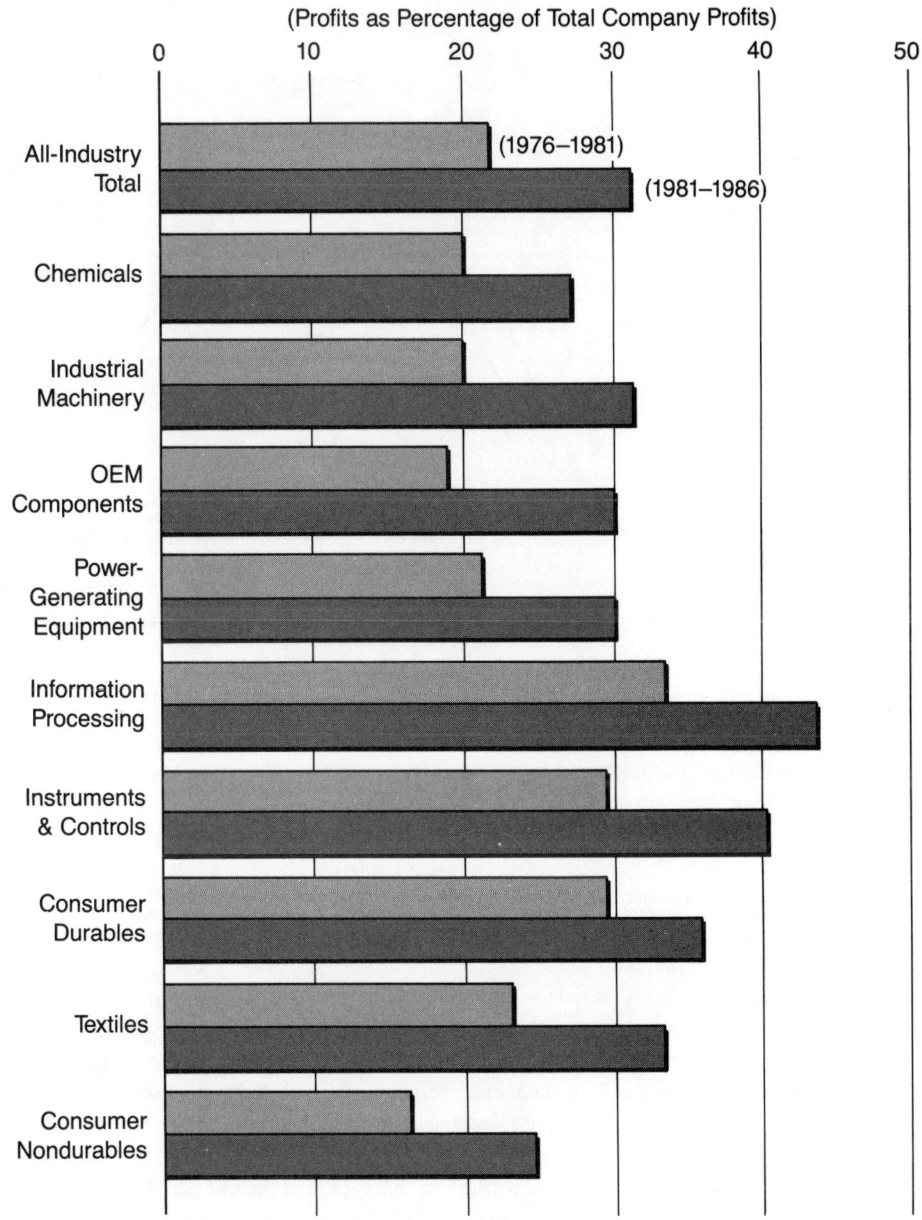

Source: Booz, Allen & Hamilton Inc.

EXHIBIT 7-2

PRODUCT LIFE CYCLE CURVE

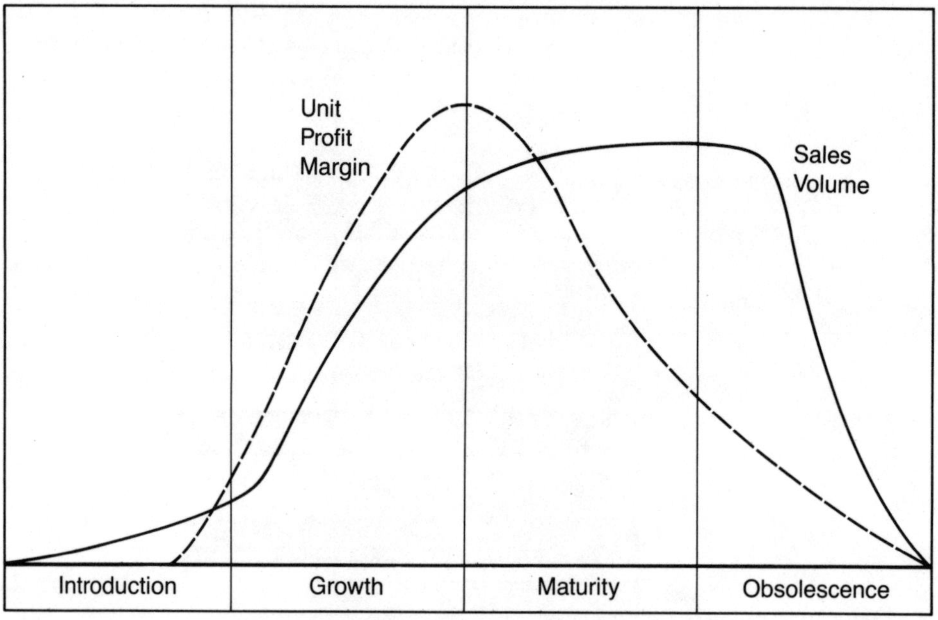

commercial position in an attractive market, management is foolish if it becomes complacent. For not a day goes by that someone, somewhere, is not working to come up with a "better mousetrap" that will weaken or possibly destroy the product's competitive advantage.

History is replete with examples of companies that have lost their competitive advantage and even their business because some competitor came into the market with a product that had superior cost or performance characteristics. This fate is not limited to small or weak competitors; even industrial giants like IBM, General Electric, and Western Electric have seen certain of their markets eroded by competition that surprised them with a distinctly superior product. IBM, despite its dominant position in the computer market, lost position in the late 1970s to several smaller companies that were first to develop powerful minicomputers to replace the large mainframe computers that were the cornerstone of IBM's business. The dramatic shift in market positions among the producers of CAT-scanning equipment in the medical equipment field is also a good example of how product innovation can pay off. Here, General Electric, which was a late entry in the field, gained significant market share over a three-year period at the expense of the companies that developed the market, but failed to keep pace with General Electric's technological advancements.

New Technologies

Management must also be aware that products can be made obsolete by new technologies as well as improved products. Technological substitution is becoming more frequent and more dramatic. New technologies create opportunities for some firms and major threats for others. With new technologies, new industries and often new competitors emerge (see the box, page 146). New technologies cause industrial firms to redefine what business they are in or should be in. For example, the market boundaries between the data processing, office equipment, and communications industries are blurring. The two rapidly changing fields of electronics and chemistry clearly show the impact of technology on industrial products and markets.

Let's look first at the electronics field. Electronics encompasses subtechnologies that affect everything from television and microwave ovens to computer and missile systems. Electronics is rapidly reshaping the world's manufacturing industries. It often results in the use of new technology in older or mature industries. What one can do for a farm combine, a tractor, a truck, or a car with a little electronics is dramatic. It enhances quality, increases productivity, reduces costs, and may permit more sophisticated designs. It also usually saves on material and labor because it requires fewer workers and typically involves substituting low-cost electronics for high-cost labor.

Factory automation has very quantifiable cost-benefits for the customer. Robots can be shown to have many applications that provide an attractive payback to the purchaser. This usually involves replacing assembly workers and semi-skilled personnel with automation. The cost savings, and the competitive impact, can be so extraordinary that suppliers and buyers may have no choice but to adopt a new technology if they want to survive. The alternative to not adopting is often a decision to not be competitive in what is rapidly becoming a worldwide marketplace.

Now let's consider the chemical field. Chemical and biochemical technologies are another example of how a new technology affects traditional industrial products and markets. A single plastic part can replace several metal parts because plastic is much easier to mold into complex shapes. A metal component would have to be divided into several simpler pieces. Super-strong engineered plastics can outperform steel and brass in many applications. A metal piston must be molded and then finished on a lathe, whereas a plastic piston can be molded very precisely to "near net shape" in one step. By rearranging the molecular chains that determine a plastic's properties, producers can tailor end-use products to specific applications. Black & Decker's cordless surgical drill uses a specialty plastic for both internal components and housing. A medical equipment manufacturer now uses the same plastic material to replace brass connectors and valves in its resuscitators.

The substitution of plastic bottles for glass is a classic example of one technology replacing another. In 1955, high-density polyethylene plastic (PVC) was introduced as a direct competitive substitute for glass containers. It could be made rigid, impact-resistant, and crystal clear. Its lightness and unbreakability were features of significant value to bottlers. Plastic bottles were several times lighter than glass bottles of equal size, which reduced shipping costs and allowed bottlers to economize by using larger-capacity bottles. As a result of these advantages, the changeover from glass to plastic bottles occurred

THE IMPACT OF ELECTRONICS

Changes in products and markets because of electronics have been dramatic. The old Frieden office calculator had hundreds of parts and sold for about $600. Its electronic version has 50 parts and sells for $80. One microprocessor replaced 350 parts in a Singer industrial sewing machine. A few dozen microchips replaced 80 pounds of switches and wiring in a vending machine. The impact of electronics on service firms can be equally dramatic. When Foremost-McKesson computerized its drug distributors and regional warehouse, it cut its warehouse personnel from 140 to 12. Operating costs were cut from 11.4 percent of sales to 8.3 percent. Inventory turns increased from 6 times a year to 7.5 times, and inventory costs were reduced accordingly.

The switch from mechanical to electronic technology in the commercial scale business substantially changed the outlook and character of that entire industry. Until the mid-1960s, most weighing in industry was done by mechanical scales and weighing systems. Some were more sophisticated than others, but all were mechanically based. The market was mature. Growth was essentially limited to replacement requirements, and the competitive structure was well established with companies like Toledo Scale, Howe Richardson, and Fairbanks Morse the major factors in the market. Then electronic technology entered the picture. It was immediately apparent that electronic scales offered major advantages. They were much more accurate, they could be programmed to compute and collect data, and they could be easily integrated into manufacturing and process control systems. Because these advantages were so significant, users replaced their existing mechanical scales, and sales of electronic units grew rapidly. The combination of more rapid replacement and higher unit price for electronic scales greatly increased the annual revenue generated and made the market for scales much more attractive.

As they attempted to convert from mechanical to electronic technology, traditional manufacturers faced many problems. Mechanical manufacturing had to be maintained at the same time the company moved into electronic manufacturing. Dual inventories had to be carried. Sales and service people had to be retrained.

At the same time new competitors entered the picture. Several smaller electronic firms saw an opportunity to capitalize on their skills and enter a market they perceived as growing away from the traditional manufacturers. Some of the larger electronic manufacturers, like IBM and NCR, recognized the need for systems integration and started to draw on their vast technical resources to move toward the scale producers' traditional business.

Source: "The Molting of America," *Forbes*, November 22, 1982, p. 165.

as shown in Exhibit 7-3. Although the substitution occurred over a 30-year period, it was steady and dramatic, and any bottle manufacturer that stayed with glass in specific applications had to lose market share. This is not an isolated case. The makeup of the textile industry changed dramatically as man-made fibers were found to have superior characteristics to wool and cotton. The increasing use of plastic or composite materials has had and will continue to have a major impact on the makeup and position of suppliers to the automotive and aircraft industries.

EXHIBIT 7-3

TOTAL MARKET SHARES FOR GLASS AND PLASTIC BOTTLES: THE SUBSTITUTION OF ONE TECHNOLOGY FOR ANOTHER

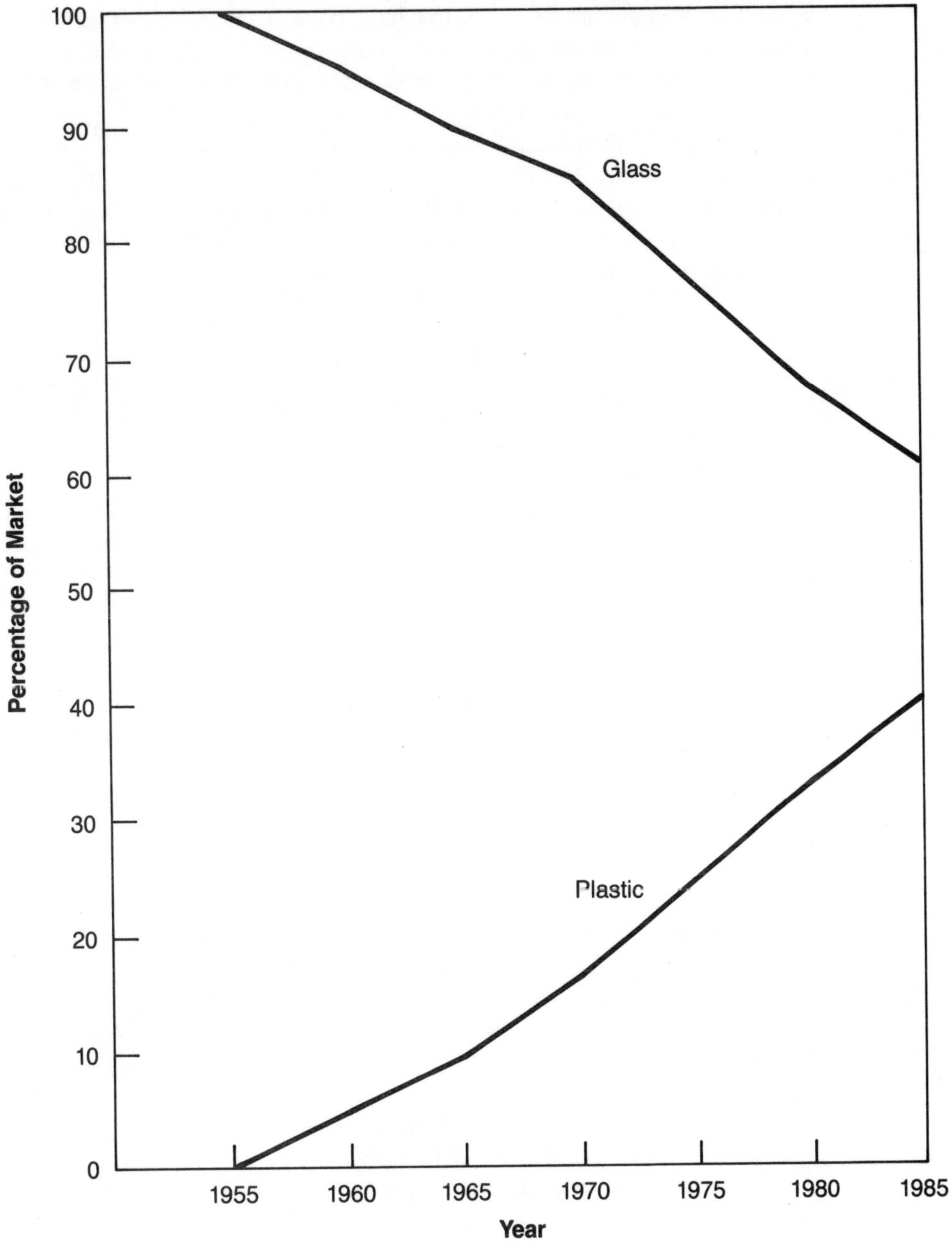

Most industrial managers recognize the importance of new product development. Billions of dollars a year are committed to this activity, but success does not automatically result from spending a lot of money. In fact, very few companies are ever really satisfied with their R&D or new product efforts. The ad shown in Exhibit 7-4, which appeared in several national publications, illustrates the point. Although cast in a humorous vein, it indicates the kinds of headaches that are all too common in most companies. If anything, the success ratio is understated. Many knowledgeable managers say that the odds are not 3 to 1 as implied, but actually closer to 100 to 1 against a product concept or idea being developed into a commercial prototype, and something like 1000 to 1 against its being a commercial success. In short, new product development is much like a gigantic crap game. The stakes are extremely high, and cost of failure by not getting into the game at all or by launching unsuccessful products is astronomical. Yet the profits to be earned by successful new products are almost without limit.

BETTERING THE CHANCES: PRINCIPLES OF NEW PRODUCT DEVELOPMENT

Even though very few companies are completely satisfied with their new product efforts, it is clear that some companies do a much better job than others—and the results show in their growth rate, market share, and profit picture. Just look at industry leaders like General Electric, DuPont, and IBM. All have a record of new product introduction that has contributed much to their success. Why are they able to achieve better results with new products than their competitors? How do they work around, or at least minimize, the risks and pitfalls in new product development that plague most companies? Each of these companies has its own set of development priorities and needs, but they all follow the same fundamental principles:

1. They think through their product-market focus to provide maximum commercial opportunity.
2. They face up to fundamental cost and performance deficiencies.
3. They rigorously prune marginal products from the existing line.
4. They ensure that all development efforts are directly linked to corporate and product-market strategies.
5. They follow an organized and disciplined process to minimize risk.
6. They strike the right balance between investing in future products and generating current profits.
7. They ensure that marketing management and field sales personnel play an important role in planning new product activities.
8. They are willing to go outside for new technology.

Let's look more closely at each of these principles to see more clearly what is involved.

EXHIBIT 7-4

3 FLOPS AND 1 WILD SUCCESS FROM GT&E RESEARCH

Let us be the first big corporation in America to admit it:

Sometimes we fall flat on our face.

That may come as a shock to you, but we've found it's a smart way to run our research laboratories.

Rather than saddle our scientists with a "Do It The Way It's Always Been Done" philosophy, we encourage them to stick their necks out—to poke around in places nobody ever poked around before.

Sometimes this philosophy makes millions of dollars for us (see Eureka!).

Sometimes it doesn't make us a penny.

Take, for instance

Flop #1: The Wam-O-Scope—a new kind of radar set that was supposed to be 10 times more sensitive than ordinary radar. (This was because we put lots of little electronic parts right inside the radar tube, where nobody ever put them before.) Theoretically, it worked fine. Practically, it didn't work at all. Which brings us to

Flop #2: The Stacked Tube. After years of work, we perfected the world's best radio tube—long lived, practically indestructible. Unfortunately, we built it the same year the transistor was invented, making our tube instantly obsolete. Then there was

Flop #3: The Omegatron—a clever device designed to tell vacuum tube manufacturers precisely how much excess gas they had in their tubes (which, you remember from Physics 1, are supposed to be completely empty). This, however, was more than they wanted to know. They wanted to get rid of the gas, not measure it. So finally, we come to

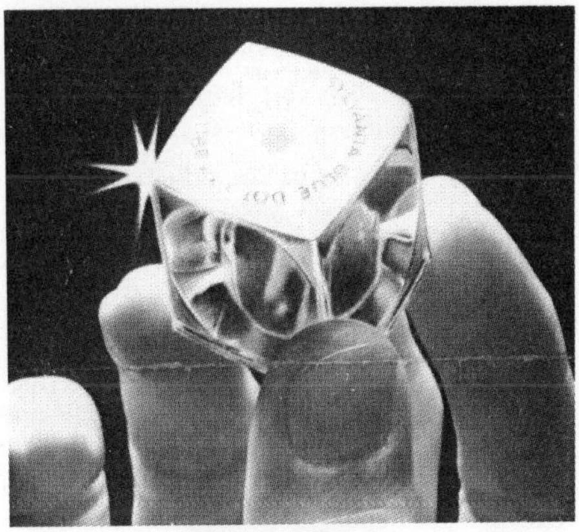

Eureka!

The Sylvania Flashcube—a little idea that revolutionized the whole camera business. For the first time, people could take flash pictures as fast as they could click the shutter—no more hot bulbs to change, no more missed pictures.

It looks simple. But it took more than 100,000 designs and years of fiddling and testing before we made the first one.

What are we up to now? Everything from laser research to pollution control.

We even have an idea that might revolutionize the entire color TV industry.

If it works.

General Telephone & Electronics

Source: General Telephone & Electronics

Defining the Right Product-Market Focus

In most industrial situations, a product-market business can be defined in different ways. And there are vast differences in the size and potential of any market, depending on how it is defined. It can be defined narrowly to focus on a particular product-market niche or much more broadly to include a range of products flowing into a large industrial market like textiles, oil field supply, food processing, or office equipment. Any company's business strategy and the scope and flow of its new product activities are greatly influenced by how the product-market business is defined. As a general rule, the business definition should focus on the customer's or user's economic or functional objective—what the customer or user is trying to gain or achieve after purchasing the product or service from a supplier. Philip B. Hofmann, a former chairman and CEO of Johnson & Johnson, frequently stated to personnel in all the J&J operating companies, "Only develop and market new products that are demonstrably better for the customer or user." This is important: No one in the industrial world buys products or services because they want or enjoy them for themselves. Business products or services are purchased only to perform a specific function that directly or indirectly improves the customer's or user's business. It is essential to understand the economic or functional objective of the customer or user and to keep this point foremost in mind so that functional substitutes do not erode the supplier's market without its knowledge and thus lose the opportunity for counter action.

Consider the case of an old line company that is a market leader in industrial drilling and cutting tools. Its management and engineers have traditionally seen themselves as being in the business of simply making and selling more and better drilling and cutting tools. But it is obvious, when you think about it, that nobody really wants to buy drilling or cutting tools. What the customer or user wants to buy is the ability to make holes or fabricate parts in the most efficient way possible. In fact, from the user's point of view, drills or cutting tools are far from the final answer. They are costly and they break or wear out, and in that sense they actually interfere with the manufacturing process. If the company had defined its business objective as helping its customers or users make holes or fabricate certain parts more effectively, instead of making and selling more and better drilling and cutting tools, it would be on much sounder strategic footing. Instead of confining themselves solely to improving or expanding its line of drilling and cutting tools, its engineers would be looking for different methods of drilling holes or cutting materials, including such new approaches as the use of lasers, electron beams, and ultrasonic waves. It would also be aware of the increasing use of materials that are easier to cut and drill with these new and unconventional methods. If the company had pursued this broader business objective, it would have been better able to respond to equipment manufacturers that introduced laser, electron beam, and ultrasonic machines to drill holes or cut material far more efficiently in many situations. The example of Reliance Electric illustrates the importance of defining a product-market focus or business objective in a way that provides the maximum business advantage (see the box, page 151).

Facing Up to Cost and Performance Deficiencies

If any statement about business or industrial marketing is axiomatic, it is the following: To be a strong competitor, a company must either be a low cost producer so it can sell

RELIANCE ELECTRIC MOVES WITH THE TIMES

In the mid-1960s Reliance Electric had between 25 and 30 percent of its defined electric motor market, which had total annual sales of about $800 million. Since both the market and the line of motor products were relatively mature, it was very difficult for competitors to leapfrog ahead with significant product innovations. Instead, they tended to concentrate on manufacturing cost improvements and looked to price competition as the major competitive weapon. Sales growth was limited, and the situation obviously created downward pressure on margins and profit results. Not satisfied with this situation, Reliance management took a fresh look at how its market might be defined to see if opportunities could be expanded. The first step was to redefine the market to include the mechanical drive linkage and systems that connected the motor to a machine. This more than doubled the potential market and opened the door to a whole range of combined electrical-mechanical developments that eliminated many of the interface problems and costs that occurred when the products were designed by different manufacturers. Reliance management further enlarged its view of the market to include a broad range of automation products and services. This shift in focus gave the company an opportunity to work with a market of some $8 billion—eight to ten times the size of its original market—and paved the way for significant growth for the next decade. Commenting on his company's success after Reliance had become a recognized success in the automation field, the chairman said: "It took us a long time to define our market in the right way, but once we did, the door was open for a whole stream of new electrical/mechanical products that we wouldn't even consider before. Getting the right market focus has contributed to our accelerated growth and profits more than anything else."

effectively to price buyers or offer a superior product to customers that will pay a higher price for the perceived value. While this point might appear to be obvious, a surprising number of industrial companies are trying to compete today with industrial products that have not improved in any way over the past several years. Product performance is the same now as it was when the products were introduced, and in many cases the cost of manufacturing and delivering the products is higher. In the meantime, competitors, particularly from abroad, have introduced new products with superior performance characteristics or adopted new manufacturing methods that enable them to sell from a lower cost base. Large areas of American industry producing many commonly used industrial items—like fasteners, standard machine and cutting tools, electrical components, castings and forgings—have been rocked back on their heels and seen their business dwindle away to virtually nothing for this reason. It is one thing if management makes a conscious decision to do nothing and recognizes that they will eventually go out of the business as a result. It is quite another if a situation like this just happens. How can this occur? How can management in any company that knows the importance of staying competitive allow their products to drift into a noncompetitive position?

First of all, many companies fail to evaluate objectively their products against competitive offerings in the rigorous way they should. If they do go through some kind of an evaluation process, it is often superficial or biased and leads to a continuation of "business as usual" rather than the dramatic cost or performance improvements that are needed. In some cases, management is not presented with the real facts because it is easier not to "rock the boat." In other cases, management may see the facts but not accept or face them squarely, since it is not easy to admit that a "bellcow" product or product line is no longer competitive. As a result, a surprising number of companies continue to rely on tired, old products long after competitors have come into the picture with better offerings.

Second, not enough importance is attached to the need to be fully cost competitive, particularly with mature products. When products like those cited previously reach the mature stage in their life cycle, it becomes increasingly difficult to come up with product improvements that distinguish them from competitive offerings. Manufacturing cost improvements, then, become the key competitive weapon, and the low cost producer generally picks up the lion's share of the market. Despite the logic of this point, a great many producers of mature products are saddled with unimproved plants and equipment, and higher-than-average labor costs. And they don't seem to have a program for making the necessary improvements. The management team in these companies may be populated with the most innovative and brilliant sales and marketing executives in the world, and they can pursue the most ingenious sales and marketing strategies one can imagine, but if they are not cost competitive, they have virtually no possibility of winning against lower cost competition over the longer term.

We are not suggesting that all old products or product businesses be scrapped any more than we suggest that all old plants be scrapped. We are saying, however, that one cannot expect a business to grow if it is built around old-fashioned products manufactured in old-fashioned plants with old-fashioned equipment. And given the accelerating rate of technological change, the possibility of simply maintaining such a business is diminishing rapidly.

While these facts may be difficult for some to accept, they represent the harsh reality of today's competitive environment. Management in the companies that are most successful in building their business through product innovations and manufacturing cost improvements recognize them very clearly. And they are perfectly willing to squarely face product cost and performance problems as they occur and do whatever they have to do to make sure these deficiencies are corrected.

Pruning the Existing Line

Product-market strategies in many industrial companies address only new products and sales growth; too little consideration is given to improving or deleting marginal or obsolete products. An objective assessment of the product lines of any ten companies would reveal a lot of tired or outdated products in nine of them. In many of these companies, management fails to recognize that its product lines are cluttered with obsolete and/or nonproductive items. In others, they may recognize the problem but fail to take the actions necessary to get rid of them. Not surprisingly, new product development efforts frequently tend to be too little or too late in these companies. They always seem to be struggling to catch up with competition and seldom achieve the advantage that a leader with new products enjoys.

The reasons for pruning a product line should be fairly clear. For one thing, when the product line is cluttered with products that have reached or are approaching obsolescence, costs tend to be high because of short manufacturing runs and excessive inventories, and sufficient money is simply not available for new product development. Moreover, it is difficult to get the kind of sales support required to launch new products effectively, since any sales force can absorb only so much product knowledge.

PRODUCT LINE ANALYSIS. Some simple analyses can quickly show whether the product line is basically competitive or whether some products need to be improved or dropped. One analysis points up which products generate what percentage of a business unit's sales and profits. As shown in Exhibit 7-5, it is not unusual to find a pattern approximating the commonly referred to "80–20" rule. As you can see from the chart, 15 percent of the products generate 75 percent of the sales and 90 percent of the profits. Of the 240 items in the total line, a large number would appear to be deadwood, or at least marginal contributors. This does not automatically mean that all these items should be dropped from the line, but their continued presence without planned improvements should certainly be challenged.

The product life cycle concept also provides a framework for evaluating a business unit's products. Exhibit 7-6 shows how the product life cycle and competitive standing of each product can be plotted to provide an overview of growth opportunities or limitations. As you can see, marketing plans for products 1 and 2 need to concentrate on improving their competitive position. Products 3 and 4 appear to be deletion candidates. Admittedly, there is always room for argument on where or how products or product

EXHIBIT 7-5

SEARCHING FOR "DEADWOOD"

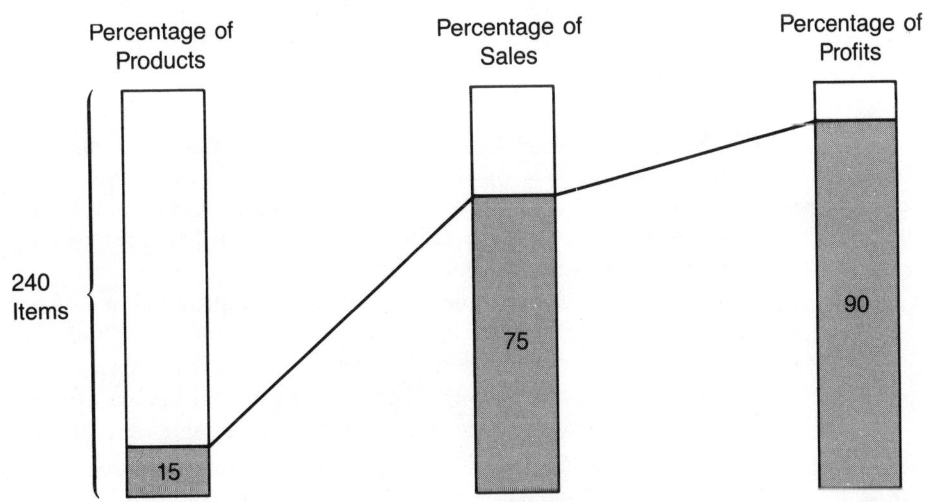

EXHIBIT 7-6

PRODUCT/TECHNOLOGY LIFE CYCLE ANALYSIS

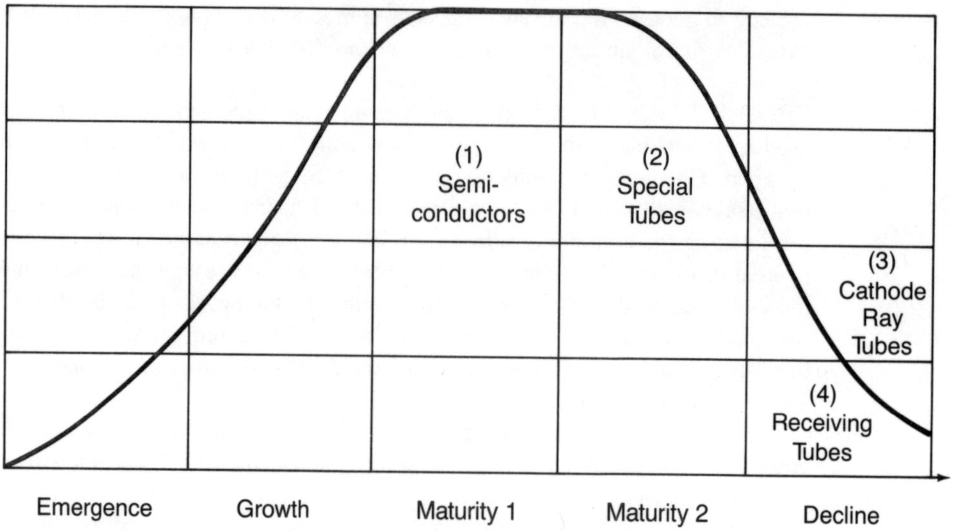

lines are positioned on this chart or where competitors' products should be positioned. However, it is a fairly simple matter to determine whether a product is in its introductory, growth, mature, or obsolete phase, and that's all you need to know. Precision is not a requirement to make an initial management judgment on the commercial health or viability of a product or product line. All you need is a reasonable perspective as to whether a company's products are positioned on the flat or downside stage of their life cycle or whether there is still plenty of room for growth.

INTERIM ACTIONS. Before a final decision to delete a product is made, a number of interim actions could extend the product's useful life. For one thing, a mature product often has a niche in the marketplace that cannot be filled by another supplier or a substitute product. When this situation exists, the product's selling price should be raised significantly. A price hike in this situation will not affect demand, and therefore will greatly enhance the product's profit contribution.

A number of other steps can be taken to improve a mature product's profitability. Reduction or elimination of costly technical support and service activities should be tested to determine if the product can survive without the associated expense. Advertising is another cost that can be removed if no new product features exist. Finally, the minimum order size can be increased to reduce handling and shipping costs and to minimize finished goods inventory requirements. Although these seem to be mundane considerations, significant savings can usually be made as a result of taking steps like these. They are frequently sufficient to bring old products up to acceptable profit levels for a considerable period of time.

Further investment in product improvement and R&D efforts should always be considered very cautiously. When a product is in its mature or declining stage, total market prospects are clearly declining, and the R&D catchup cost and risk is often greater than the potential reward. As a general rule, R&D efforts on products in the mature or declining stage of a life cycle should be approved only if there is an opportunity to make sufficient improvements in cost or performance to move the product back to the growth stage. If this is not possible, and often it is not, management should concentrate on manufacturing or material cost improvements that will enable the product to compete more effectively in a mature market.

One final point is worth emphasizing. Marginal products are often retained too long because of emotional arguments that really do not hold up under careful scrutiny. For example, the sales group frequently argues that it needs a "full line" and that the line will not be competitive if certain products are dropped. Alternatively, someone or some group almost inevitably argues that deleting certain products will increase the overhead allocation to the remaining products in the line and in turn make them less cost competitive. It is when these arguments surface that management needs to be tough-minded. A "full line" may be necessary in some cases, but not nearly as often as salespeople claim. There may be added overhead to be absorbed if certain products are dropped, but in many cases it can be eliminated if management takes a hard-line approach. It is essential for management to determine factually when the "full line" or overhead claims are real and when they are simply hollow arguments to avoid a break with the past.

More specifically, the following cost-profit considerations should be addressed:

1. What is the product's new profit contribution (after all allocated costs are considered) at current and projected sales levels?
2. What allocated or shared costs would have to be absorbed by other products if the product in question were dropped?
3. What amount of capital could be recovered if the product in question were dropped?
4. Taking the answers to the preceding questions into account, what is the net cost-profit and capital impact of dropping the product?

When a decision is made to drop a product or product line, a carefully planned exit is essential. Even though the decision is logical and correct, it is almost certain to cause some disruption in the sales force and among certain distributors, customers, or users. Sales and manufacturing activities must be coordinated to ensure minimal exposure to excess or obsolete inventory costs. There is nothing complex about a product or product line exit as long as proper steps are taken to minimize disruption and ensure an orderly transition to any new offering that is ready for the market.

Linkage to the Business Plan

Companies that have excellent records of successful new product introduction are more likely to ensure that all their new product programs flow from and are controlled by an agreed-upon business plan. This makes sense, since it is the best way to avoid the kinds of "dumbbell" mistakes described in the General Telephone & Electronics ad in Exhibit 7-4. Although this ad is obviously "tongue in cheek," it accurately reflects the kinds of results that occur in many industrial companies. From our own experience, we can cite several multimillion-dollar product development programs that resulted in products like the following:

- A high-speed printer that was three times as expensive as any competitive offering and far exceeded the requirements of any identified customer group.
- A twelve-axis screw machine that worked perfectly once set up, but only a handful of people in industry have the skill to do the setup work.
- A space-age robot designed to move material and parts to scheduled positions on the factory floor but insufficiently controlled so that it would run into or over anything that got in its way.

Many other equally ludicrous examples could be cited, but these should be sufficient to make the point. Unless product development efforts are linked to a carefully conceived product-market strategy for building the business, technical management will often assign the wrong priorities to development efforts or be led into products and markets that do not have real commercial value. Literally hundreds of millions of dollars are wasted each year because technical efforts are poured into products that are out of phase with market needs and opportunities. This is the chief reason the success ratio on new product development efforts is so low in so many companies. The plain truth is that left on their own, product development engineers will spend a lot of money developing something they are interested in or that they think is right. They will not just sit still waiting for direction. It is management's responsibility to provide sufficient direction through its business plan to avoid products that are not based on commercial reality.

Many executives will argue with this point, claiming that the idea of linking every new project to a business strategy or plan is impractical and too restrictive. We remain adamant. The only exception would be where senior management has made a conscious decision to spend money on basic or exploratory research to see what develops. This is an expensive process, however, and any company that follows this route had better have plenty of money to support "interesting" research that may not lead anywhere.

Following a Disciplined Process

Most industrial companies have had some experience with product innovations that are technological triumphs but commercial flops. The products fail to meet stated performance requirements, are too costly or difficult to manufacture, or simply miss the market. Commercial flops can never be eliminated, since product development activities often involve advancing technology or breaking new ground in terms of manufacturing know-how or market development. However, a lot of time and money can be saved by recognizing product failures before the process is too far along and before too much time and money has been committed. Although it is essential to avoid discouraging new product ideas, the risk of wasting too much time and money on ideas that have no chance of success is substantial. This risk can be reduced or controlled by defining distinct stages of development for each project and establishing stringent criteria for advancing or terminating the project at the end of each successive stage.

EXHIBIT 7-7 ***NEW PRODUCT FUNNEL***

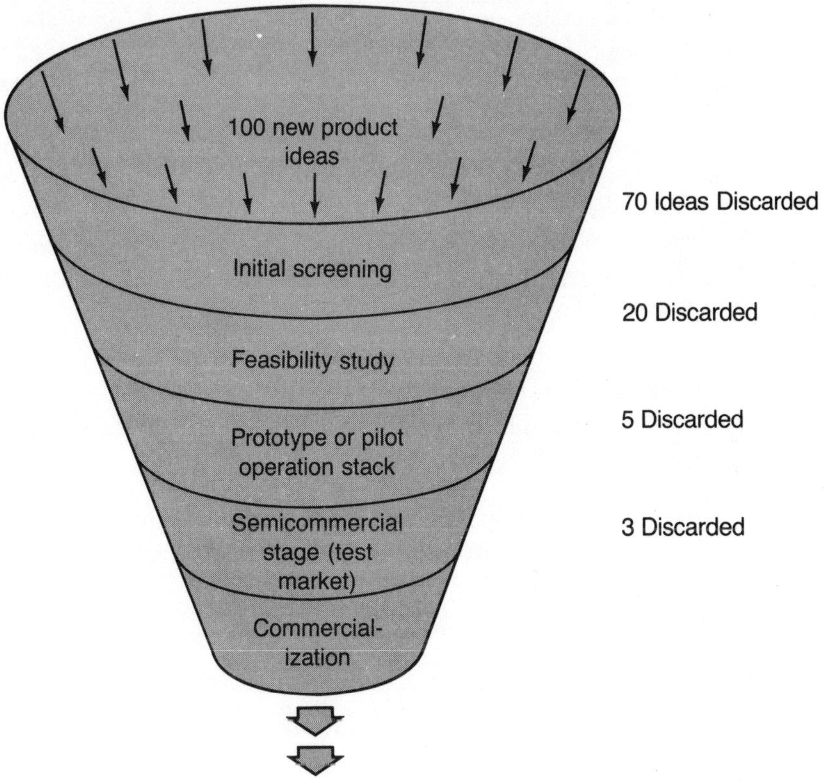

One way to think of the development process is in terms of a funnel. Exhibit 7-7 shows the typical stages of the development process in this funnel and also shows that there is always a large fallout of new product ideas between conception and commercialization. As you can see, the inputs to the funnel are ideas for new products that can come from a variety of sources. The sales force should be an excellent source of new product ideas, especially if sales personnel are trained to determine user problems and needs. Manufacturing personnel can also be excellent sources of ideas for product improvement that will improve the manufacturability and hence the costs of a particular product. First-line factory or service workers actually involved in building or assembling the product should be regarded as a part of the manufacturing group, since they often can see firsthand how minor changes in product design can improve the product itself or the way it is manufactured. Design engineers are trained to conceptualize new product ideas and to come up with functional as well as cost improvements for existing products.

All of these are traditional internal sources of new product or product improvement ideas. In addition, good ideas are frequently introduced by outside inventors or vendors who have, through research or experience, come up with something that is potentially useful. All these sources should be encouraged, since no one can predict with any degree of certainty where the best ideas will come from. The trick is to use a screening process that quickly identifies and filters out the ideas that are not technically and commercially feasible without spending an inordinate amount of time or money on the discards. The precise nature of the filtering process depends on the product. For example, the prototype stage may actually be a pilot plant operation if the product is some new chemical formulation instead of a "breadboard" model or prototype. The objective is to define the criteria that must be met before a project is allowed to go to the next stage to reduce the time and money wasted on projects that should not reach the commercial stage. These criteria will obviously vary by industry and even by company. However, they should always be developed around a few fundamental considerations that will help bring the degree of technical and market risk into focus.

Technical considerations:

1. What new technical concepts are being utilized, and what cost or performance advantages do they offer? If successful, where are we positioned on the technology life cycle curve?
2. Where does the competition stand on any new technical concepts being considered? Have successful competitors pursued other technologies that are significantly different?
3. Has the concept been commercially utilized in other products or processes, or is it a groundbreaking effort?
4. Assuming the new technical concept proves to be successful, how much of a commercial advantage does it offer, and how can you substantiate this point?

Market considerations:

1. Is the product concept basically new, or is it simply an improvement in performance or cost over an existing product?
2. Which end-use markets or market applications can be tapped most readily, and which will require further development?
3. Under what conditions (volume, price, costs) are the economics of the proposed product attractive?
4. Does the cost-profit structure of the new product match or exceed company objectives?
5. How much has the company already committed to this project, and how much time will it take to generate sufficient profits to cover total exposure?

If management does not seek specific answers to questions like these in a formal manner, you can be sure the company does not have a well-organized procedure for advancing ideas through the development process. And it would be a safe bet that whatever the company is doing about new product activities is not cost-effective and does not minimize risk.

Matching Future Products and Current Profits

In companies known for their new product success, management has mastered the ability to strike the right balance between investing[1] in future products and generating current profits. This point raises some obvious questions. How much should you invest? How much is too little? How much is too much? There are no easy answers; it is a judgment call in each situation, the kind of judgment management gets paid to make and that will haunt management for a long time if it is made incorrectly.

THE COST OF ERROR. The penalties are severe if a mistake is made either way. A company can get by and may even prosper in the short term by spending too little, because anything not spent obviously increases short-term profits. It is not uncommon for managers, under pressure to meet certain profit goals, to take this tack in an effort to make their results look good. However, such an approach is shortsighted and foolish. If the market is attractive, enlightened competitors will introduce new and improved products that will quickly erode the company's market position and cut into its future earnings stream. By the same token, many managers tend to overspend for new products without sufficient regard for the need to achieve satisfactory near-term profits. These managers are so enamored of the promise of tomorrow that they spend a disproportionate amount of money on new product efforts that will ultimately undermine the financial health of the company. Managers in rapidly changing high-technology industries face the added problem of deciding which technology to invest in as well as when to invest. By investing too early in a new technology, the industrial firm faces the risks of premature entry before the market is ready. By reacting or investing too late in a new technology, a company may fall behind its competitors and lose market position that is tough to recapture once a new technology is established. And by failing to invest at all in a new technology, a company runs the very real risk of seeing its products become obsolete in a short period of time.

Computers, medical electronics, and pharmaceuticals are good illustrations of industries in which technological change is frequent and rapid. Each product cycle often has multiple and overlapping technology life cycles, as shown in Exhibit 7-8, where T_1 to T_5 are the cycles. In these situations, it is crucial to invest in the right technology at the right time. The medical CAT-scan business has had five distinct technology life cycles over the past ten years. When the early leaders in CAT equipment chose not to invest in the latest technology, they limited their participation in the market to the cycle patterns shown as T_1, T_2, T_3, or T_4 and in effect opted out of the business when the technology shown as T_5 made all the earlier products obsolete. This pattern, which is predictable in many high technology businesses, should be a warning for any management that plans to participate. It requires a different mentality to manage in this high-risk environment. The high level of R&D expenditures makes it impossible to manage with a short-term profit orientation. Moreover, a high tolerance for stress is essential to withstand the pressures that are an integral part of any volatile business. It also takes significant financial strength to fund the development activities required to maintain a competitive line of products as

[1]The cost of product development, except for capital items that might be involved, is expensed for tax purposes. Nevertheless, the expense is literally an investment of a company's profits for future gain.

EXHIBIT 7-8

TECHNOLOGY LIFE CYCLES

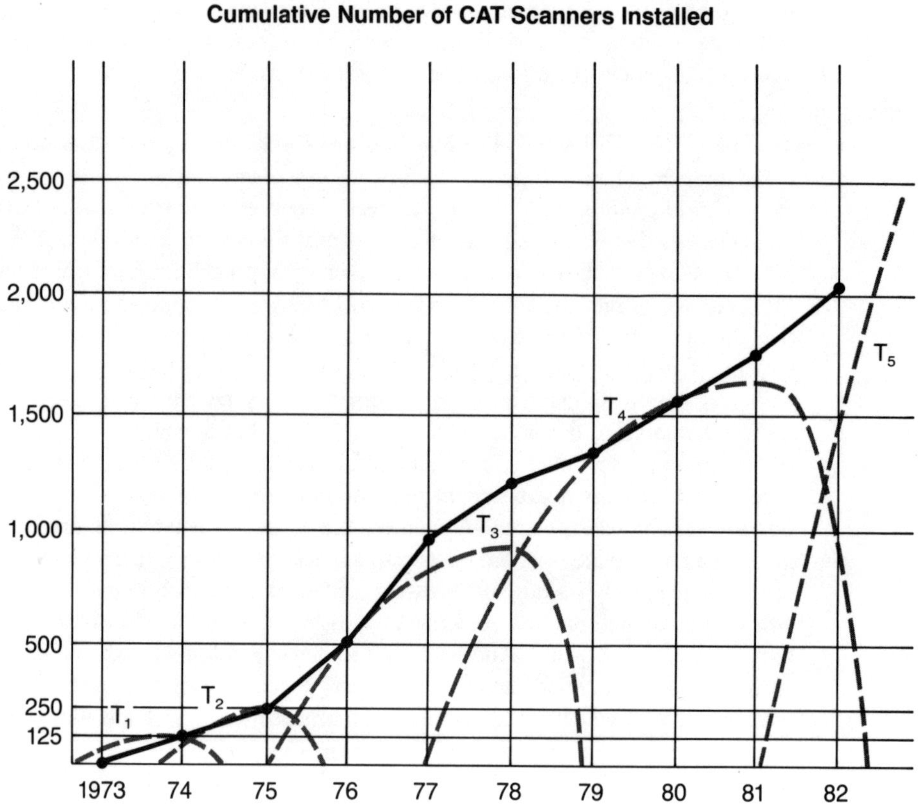

Sequence of New Technologies

1973; T_1—scan of head, 5 minutes
1974; T_2—scan of entire body, 2 minutes
1975; T_3—scan of entire body, 18 seconds
1977; T_4—scan of entire body, 2 seconds
1982; T_5—nuclear magnetic resonance replaces radiation and instantly identifies molecular structure of tissues

Source: U.S. Office of Technology Assessment

new technologies come into the picture. This is the reason so many smaller companies fail after taking an early lead in the marketplace with a new product. Even though they recognize that a new technology is clearly superior to the one they used to get their businesses started, they simply do not have the financial resources to move into a new technology (see the box).

SPENDING GUIDELINES. There is always published information available that indicates the appropriate level of spending for a particular industry. Table 7.1 shows data from a recent publication that contrast spending levels for new product activities in the information processing and farm and construction machinery industries. Although data like these are never perfect, they provide a general idea of the R&D level required in various industries. Note the difference in the composite percentage of sales in the two industries. Note also the range of ratios in each industry. The data would seem to suggest that to be competitive in the farm and construction machinery business, somewhere between 2 and 4 percent of sales should be committed to R&D activities. By contrast, 5 to 10 percent of sales appears to be the going rate of spending for R&D in the much more dynamic computer area. As you can see, the variation between the high and the low in each industry group is significant. Variances of this magnitude would be typical in any set of industry comparisons, since accounting methods for reporting R&D costs vary widely among companies, and the level of R&D expenditures for any particular company depends on its particular business strategy.

COMPETING IN HIGH TECH MARKETS

When it was introduced to the medical diagnostic field, the CAT scanner was immediately recognized as the most significant development in the field since the discovery of X-rays nearly 50 years before. In 1970 Technicare, the first U.S. CAT scanner company, was founded by two former employees of Harris Corporation with funding from a venture capital firm in Cleveland.

Between 1975 and 1981 Technicare experienced tremendous growth, with sales multiplying from $20 million to $200 million. The number of its employees grew from 200 to more than 3,000 in the same period. The CAT scanning market went through several variations or technological innovations, each of which obsoleted products less than a year old. The company managed to anticipate each step of technology. The rapid obsolescence of technology, coupled with the rapid growth of sales, fueled the company's need for cash, which nearly spelled disaster for the company.

In 1981 Johnson & Johnson Company, whose sales total more than $4 billion, acquired Technicare. Without Johnson & Johnson's acquisition and infusion of cash, most believe Technicare would have gone bankrupt within a short period of time. Reflecting on the rapid developments in this business Richard Grimm, former Chairman of Technicare, made this comment: "The way this technology moved is unbelievable. There were four major developments in three years that basically obsoleted all prior CAT scanning devices. We were smaller than some of the other competitors and if we were not quick on our feet in terms of product development we could have been out of the picture overnight."

TABLE 7.1

SPENDING FOR NEW PRODUCT DEVELOPMENT

	Sales, 1980 ($ millions)	R&D Expense, 1980 ($ millions)	Percentage of sales	
Information Processing				
American Management Systems	$ 59	$ 4.1	7.1%	
Anderson Jacobson	41	3.9	9.3	
Applied Magnetics	93	3.6	3.8	
Auto-Trol Technology	51	6.1	12.1	High
Bell & Howell	640	30.3	4.7	
Centronics Data Computer	128	4.9	3.8	
Computer & Communication Technology	46	3.8	8.2	
Computer Consoles	44	4.6	10.5	
Computervision	224	22.1	9.9	
Comshare	78	4.9	6.3	
Data Card	66	1.7	2.6	
Data Terminal Systems	118	6.0	5.1	
Datapoint	319	27.9	8.7	
Dataproducts	180	13.9	7.7	
Decision Data Computer	44	1.2	2.8	
Electronic Memories & Magnetics	99	6.1	6.2	
Four-Phase Systems	197	15.9	8.1	
MSI Data	45	2.1	4.7	
Memorex	769	34.6	4.5	
Mohawk Data Sciences	212	10.0	4.7	
National Computer Systems	39	1.8	4.6	
National Data	60	0.9	1.5	
Recognition Equipment	113	8.4	7.4	
Scope	71	2.9	4.1	
Shared Medical Systems	106	8.2	7.8	
Storage Technology	604	39.3	6.5	
System Development	168	2.5	1.5	Low
System Industries	38	1.9	5.0	
Telex	157	8.9	5.7	
Triad Systems	57	3.8	6.6	
Tymshare	235	12.2	5.2	
Verbatim	50	2.9	5.8	
Farm and Construction Machinery				
Allis-Chalmers	2064	49.4	2.4	
American Hoist & Derrick	539	3.3	0.6	Low
Barber-Greene	227	2.9	1.3	
Bucyrus-Erie	511	19.1	3.7	
CMI	115	2.2	2.0	
Caterpillar Tractor	8598	200.2	2.3	
Clark Equipment	1534	26.9	1.8	
Deere	5470	231.2	4.2	High
FMC	3482	97.5	2.8	
Hesston	241	3.6	1.5	
Pengo Industries	78	1.5	1.9	
Penn Virginia	50	1.3	2.7	
Portec	251	2.7	1.1	
Raymond	113	4.1	3.6	
Roper	428	9.4	2.2	
Steiger Tractor	121	1.9	1.6	
Toro	402	9.1	2.3	
Valmont Industries	152	2.0	1.3	

Source: "Annual Survey of R&D Expenditures," *Business Week,* July 6, 1981, pp. 67, 71.

Many companies account for some of their product development costs by conducting the final stages of development in the customer's environment and charging some portion to sales engineering expense. This is a smart approach, since it moves the product out of the laboratory and permits the final bugs to be worked out in a real-life field situation. Other companies are often successful in getting their customers to share new product development costs for certain products, which is obviously an advantageous approach. The point of all this is simply that it is important to determine what real and total R&D costs are before concluding that a company is spending at a certain level for this activity.

Another explanation for the variation is that companies in the same industry can and do follow quite different strategies to enter or secure a position in a market. Three basic strategies would call for quite different expenditure levels for R&D activities. The strategies and the requirements for each are listed below:

1. **Pioneer innovator strategy**
   Outstanding technical people
   Research-intensive
   Large development investment
   Target is dominant "niche" position
   Always ahead on "next generation" product
2. **Follow the leader strategy**
   Excellent competitive intelligence
   Technically perceptive salespeople and engineers
   Superior application know-how
   Lower R&D costs
   Good imitator; rapid product development response time
3. **Low-cost strategy**
   No R&D activity or investment
   Major emphasis on material and process cost savings
   Strong manufacturing and delivery performance
   Marketing aimed at price-sensitive segments
   Price chief competitive weapon

Any one of these strategies can be followed successfully. However, it is essential that management fully understand the need to pursue a business strategy that is fully integrated across functions and cohesively developed around the requirements listed under each strategy. As a general rule, the company that seeks to be first in the market with new products will spend more on product development because of the inherent costs and risks that always exist when one tries to keep up with technology. This fact of life has caused many successful companies to pursue a strategy that knowingly allows competitors to be first in the market with new products. For example:

> Going back to its early days, IBM has seldom put products on the market that are right in the forefront of new technology. UNIVAC and others have all showed the way; IBM has learned from others' mistakes. It was rarely the first to take a new

> technical step, but it wasn't far behind. And time after time, its new lines were better designed and more effectively sold and serviced than those of competitors.[2]
>
> Even in the world of less arcane technology, we find the same phenomenon. Caterpillar is rarely the first to come up with a new offering in its markets. But being on the leading edge has never been one of the company's goals. It has built its reputation by letting other companies go through the trial and error process of introducing new products. Caterpillar later jumps in with the most trouble-free product on the market. Indeed, Caterpillar products do not usually sport the lowest price tag. The company relies, instead, on quality and reliable service to woo customers.[3]
>
> Hewlett-Packard is seldom first into the market with its new products—Xerox and IBM, for example, were first with high-priced laser printers. The company's marketing strategy is normally that of a counterpuncher. A competitor's new product comes on the market and HP engineers, when making service calls on HP equipment, ask their customers what they like or dislike about the new product, what features the customer would like to have. . . . And pretty soon HP salesmen are calling on customers again with a new product that answers their needs and wants. The result: happy and loyal customers.[4]

As you can see, these are first-class companies that could afford to be first in the market if they wanted to. However, they firmly believe they can better serve their customers and reduce their product development expenditures by following a carefully planned "second in the market" strategy.

Although a company's spending level for R&D or product development may vary from time to time, there is not as much flexibility here as you might think. The problem is that you cannot simply turn an R&D or product development effort on and off like a water tap. You can obviously cut a program back by reducing or stopping the technical effort. However, stepping up an effort requires finding and recruiting the right technical talent, which is often much easier said than done. For this reason, most well-managed companies tend to select a reasonable spending level for R&D or product development activities consistent with their strategy and competitive requirements, and then stick pretty close to that level as a percentage of sales unless something very unusual occurs in the marketplace.

Organizing New Product Activities

Clearly, there are different approaches to managing new product development activities. But although the approach may vary, the more successful companies ensure that their product development activities are directed by marketing and/or general management. This does not mean that the organization is structured so that new product or R&D personnel report directly to marketing or general management. It does mean, however, that the organization functions in a way which ensures that marketing and/or general managers have the final say on project priorities and evaluation. Some would argue with this

[2] "What Ails IBM," *Financial World,* May 15, 1981, p. 17.
[3] "Caterpillar Is Rarely First," *Business Week,* May 4, 1981, p. 77.
[4] "The One to Watch," *Forbes,* March 2, 1981, p. 60.

point of view, however, claiming that a centralized R&D function is more efficient. In some cases this may be true, particularly when the business is based on one or two products or a single technology. Some well-known companies like General Electric have centralized R&D activities that serve separate divisions and firmly believe this is the best approach. In most multiproduct industrial companies, however, centralized R&D is not a good idea. The arrangement gives division managers an excuse when their product technology falls behind, since they can claim they are not responsible. And centralized R&D activities directed and controlled by an independent division or corporate vice president generally tend to drift into a situation where technological considerations or interests prevail at a time when marketing or commercial considerations are actually much more important.

Any function suffers when there is an absence of commercial accountability, and this is especially true for an R&D function. One could argue that R&D management can be held accountable for both technical and commercial performance, but it simply does not work this way. Most R&D managers, quite correctly, tend to focus on achieving excellent technical results, without sufficient regard for commercial considerations. Unless some provision is made to ensure that someone with profit and loss responsibility has the final say on how much money will be spent on development efforts for what projects, the chances for poor commercial results are greatly enhanced. One president who shifted away from an arrangement under which R&D controlled the new product activity to one under which product managers were held responsible for R&D spending levels and priorities for their products explained why he made the change: "There are two types of product development activities—those that have a 'market in' focus and those that have a 'design out' focus. Something like 80 percent of our efforts have had a 'design out' focus, and I think this has caused us to be out of phase with market needs way too frequently. Now we are seeking to reverse this picture to ensure that the bulk of our new product activity has a 'market in' focus, which I think is essential if we are going to make it pay off."

One other point on organizing new product activities is worth emphasizing. Managements in many companies completely overlook the contribution the selling organization can and should make to new product development. They are overlooking an invaluable resource. Who in the organization is closer to the customer than the salesperson? Who knows more about the customer's business? Who has a better opportunity to know what product changes or features are really important to the customer or user? No one. The sales force should be the most reliable source of product-market information available to any industrial company. Obviously, however, every salesperson's comments about product-market requirements cannot be accepted at face value. Because a salesperson is a salesperson, there is always a natural tendency to sell the ideas that will help most with his or her particular customers, who may or may not represent the total market. For this reason, all the ideas emanating from the sales force need to be filtered and interpreted so that intelligent product judgments or decisions can be made. How do you structure or direct the sales force to ensure that this is done?

First, it is essential to ensure that sales assignments are not so broad in terms of products, markets, or customers that representatives do not have time to get to know their customers' operations in depth. When sales assignments are too broad, the salesperson becomes an order taker. He or she has little opportunity to carry out the professional sales role and cannot be counted on for any useful feedback. Next, salespeople need comprehensive training in the company's products, training that goes well beyond the typical product explanations which are a part of most introductory sales training programs. They need to have a deep understanding of the rationale behind the design, construction, cost, and performance characteristics of the company's products so that they can talk more intelligently with the customer or user about the product and its applications. It is these in-depth product discussions with customers that often lead to ideas on how the product can be improved or what new products could be developed to fill customer needs.

A formal procedure must be established to collect and distill the ideas developed by salespeople and to make sure this information is factored into new product plans. To reinforce the idea that the sales force is a valued source of input for new product ideas, all new products should be reviewed with a small but representative group of salespeople so they can react and recommend modifications before new products are released for commercial production. Finally, the company's value system must be tailored to recognize and reward those salespeople who contribute significantly to new product activities. Some kind of formal recognition, rather than monetary reward, of the salespeople or sales groups that have made a useful contribution in new product planning is generally the fairest approach and the best way to encourage others to make a similar contribution. However, the sales compensation plan must be designed to pay off for the effort required to launch new products successfully, since this usually uses up a large chunk of time that could be otherwise devoted to selling established products.

In short, well-managed companies recognize that nothing could be a greater waste of money than to invest heavily in technical skills for new product development without providing the right kind of headquarters and field marketing support to ensure that these technical skills are properly focused on meeting actual market needs.

Going Outside for New Technology

In most industrial companies, particularly when their products are developed around different disciplines (electronic, mechanical, electrical), it is virtually impossible to stay abreast of all the technological developments that can impact the business. Recognizing this, enlightened management continuously monitors and searches for ways to capitalize on technological achievements outside the company as a means of sustaining or improving their product-market position. While this seems only logical, many companies do not do this, generally because their management has a self-centered or arrogant attitude that leads them to think that anything "not invented here" (often called the NIH factor) can't be very good. An attitude like this doesn't have much virtue in any situation, and in today's constantly changing world, it can easily trip a company into a position where its products or technology are suddenly and unexpectedly obsolete.

There is no mystery in the way management can keep up with outside developments. One way is to tie into any of the many fine university programs that exist. Most major universities throughout the world that have technical departments are involved in a variety of research activities and programs on the forefront of technology. As a general rule, they welcome and actively seek arrangements with companies that will support their efforts, and they in turn provide the company with a window into their developments. More industrial companies should follow the lead of many bio-medical companies who have built entire new businesses around their close relationships with leading scientists in medical and engineering schools.

Another way to gain technology is to participate either as a sub or prime contractor in government-funded projects that focus on or require advanced technological development. Many companies have been very successful in using this approach to capture technology for their own commercial use. Harris, Raytheon, and Motorola are good examples of companies that have concentrated on government-funded contracts that provide technological advances for the commercial side of their businesses. Technical personnel in these companies are routinely transferred from government projects to commercial business units as a means of ensuring the effective transfer of technology.

Licensing is still another way to gain new technology. Many inventors do not have the financial resources or the interest to commercialize their developments and can realize an attractive return without risk by entering a license agreement with a manufacturer that has the necessary capabilities. Many such developments exist in university research laboratories where those doing the research are more interested in advancing the state of the art than commercial accomplishments. The key here is to follow an organized approach that covers the sources where new ideas are likely to develop and ensures the early identification of developments with promising commercial potential.

Finally, new product technology can be gained through outright acquisition or through the formation of a joint venture with another company. Acquisition is probably the preferred route because any business is easier to manage when it is owned by a single entity. A joint venture is an alternate to an outright acquisition when acquisition is not feasible for any of a variety of reasons. The company with the technology may not want to be acquired; or it may be too big or too expensive, or the technology may be such a small part of the whole that acquisition doesn't make sense.[5] Whatever the reason, a joint venture that provides the basis for coupling technology with a commercial base is a very feasible alternative.[6] For example, Sundstrand Corporation, a manufacturer of machine tools and systems, developed a heavy duty automatic transmission as a result of work they had done on a government contract for Army tanks. Sundstrand management saw a potential application for this transmission in the heavy duty truck market, but did not have the marketing, manufacturing, or service capability to readily enter this market. Accordingly, they set up a joint venture with Cummins Engine, a major engine producer who had a strong position in the worldwide OEM and aftermarket for heavy duty trucks.

The most successful companies pursue some combination or all of these avenues to technological superiority. They recognize that no one has a monopoly on technological ideas or developments and constantly search the world over for opportunities to strengthen their competitive position and ability to serve their target markets.

[5]James D. Hlavacek, Brian H. Douey, and John J. Biondo, "Tie Small Business Technology to Marketing Power," *Harvard Business Review*, January–February 1977, p. 107.
[6]Lee Adler and James D. Hlavacek, "Joint Ventures for Product Innovation," AMACOM, American Management Association, p. 15.

SUMMARY

Developing new products is a chancy, difficult process under the best of circumstances, but it is vital to the long-term success of the firm, especially in a time of rapidly changing technology and worldwide competition. There are some steps firms can take to better the chances for their products: They can think through their product-market focus carefully to zero in on real opportunities; they can face up to cost and performance deficiencies in their product line; they can prune marginal products from the existing line; they can ensure that all development efforts are coordinated with corporate strategies; they can follow an organized and disciplined process to minimize risk and ensure that marketing management and sales personnel play an important role in planning; they can work to strike the proper balance between investing in the future and generating current profits; and they can look outside the company for new technology.

All this means great and continued attention to new product development on the part of marketing and of top management to be sure that the products developed fit specific market segments and are tailored to the needs of actual users, rather than being bright ideas from R&D that are not really commercial, or expensive miscalculations. New product development is a gamble, but the odds need not be suicidal.

8

Pricing for Profit

When Mark Little, product manager for small motors of the Hercules Electric Company, answered the phone and found Roger Calkins, area sales manager for the company, on the line, he knew he was in for a tough session. For the past several months, Calkins had been criticizing the company's pricing policy for small motors, claiming he had lost significant market position as a result. Mark had responsibility for setting and policing the company's pricing policy and could agree to exceptions if he thought they were in the best interest of the business. Mark had raised prices on several items in the line four months ago, which Calkins claimed had made them noncompetitive in the marketplace.

Calkins started the conversation by saying: "Mark, I have the same problem now that I talked to you about before. I'm not competitive in the marketplace on your line, and we're losing a lot of business with key accounts. It's stupid for us not to lower our prices so we can take some of the business that is here." Calkins went on to explain that several companies were offering discounts from a list price that was already 5 percent lower than Hercules. He also said he had invoice copies his sales representatives had picked up to prove these lower prices were real. Mark had received similar calls from sales managers located in other parts of the country, but none of them seemed to have the same competitive problems. He didn't want to lower the company's prices across the board, since margins on his line were already below profit objectives. On the other hand, he knew Calkins was not "crying wolf" and wanted to help him get back into the market without retreating from a pricing policy he knew was sound.

What is Mark Little's best move?

Should he make an exception in this case? Why or why not?

Does he need marketing information to make a decision?

What kind of information does he need?

Few will argue with the notion that pricing policy is an important ingredient in the marketing mix for any product or company. In the industrial world, where buying decisions are typically more rational and less influenced by promotion and advertising appeals, it is crucial. Despite its importance, not very much has been written that is useful to management in thinking through alternative pricing policies or actions. Most text material and articles on industrial pricing deal with economic theory relating to price and demand curves, and the relative elasticity of demand for various products. Although interesting from an academic point of view, this information does not offer much practical help to the manager faced with the need to make day-to-day pricing decisions that can make or break the business. What is especially unfortunate is that management too often takes decisions and actions that literally destroy long- and short-run profit performance. Examples to support this contention are not hard to find (see the box, page 172). Examples of questionable pricing policy are all too common. Pricing policies are a chief cause of poor profit performance in industrial companies all over the world. What causes these situations? Why are examples of poor pricing decisions so common?

Management's explanations for what seem to be naive pricing actions do not vary much from one situation to another: "We lowered our prices to gain market share." "The market leader hasn't raised prices, and we have to wait for him." "We needed the volume to keep our plant loaded." "Our competitors are cutting prices, and we have to stay competitive." "We can't pass on all of our added costs and still maintain market position." However, these all too common explanations are not the real reasons at all. Rather, they are symptoms of and are related to fundamental deficiencies in management thinking that lead many companies into pricing problems and poor profit results.

In the balance of this chapter we'll examine these deficiencies in some detail and then suggest actions management should take to avoid or correct them. We do not attempt to recommend pricing policies or actions for any specific situation. Rather, we outline fundamental points that should be considered in thinking through and implementing a pricing policy for any industrial or business product.

MANAGEMENT DEFICIENCIES

For purposes of clarity, we have structured our discussion of management deficiencies into five parts:

1. Inadequate understanding of the market and business economics
2. Overemphasis on volume and market share
3. Failure to comprehend the impact of inflation
4. Failure to ensure that pricing policy is linked to total business strategy
5. Inadequate administration of pricing policy

Let's examine each in some detail.

DOING YOURSELF IN WITH PRICES: THREE CASES

Case 1: A company adopted the recommendations of its consultants to sharply cut prices on many items as a means of adding to market share. Not surprisingly, since the products were relatively mature and market demand was relatively inelastic, competitors with excess capacity counteracted with even lower prices as a means of protecting *their* market share. Although the company that initiated the price cutting achieved a pickup in volume, it was not profitable and the company's overall profit structure was severely damaged. Equally important, the company did not achieve a lasting gain in its market share position, and a vicious cycle of price competition was introduced that ultimately weakened the profit structure of the entire industry.

Case 2: A large company with a leadership position in its industry watched a small competitor cut steadily into its business with lower prices for competing products. Management's analysis of competitive product offerings indicated that material content, quality, performance characteristics, and presumably costs were essentially the same. Management concluded that the competitor was simply willing to operate at little or no profit and that ultimately this policy would lead the competitor to financial disaster. Unfortunately, this did not occur. In fact, the competitor flourished at the leader company's expense, and when it went public, management was surprised to see how profitable it really was. The leader company could not figure out how such high margins were generated with such low prices. What it had completely overlooked was its own bloated overhead costs.

Case 3: A product manager was reluctant to raise prices in his product area even though labor and material costs had increased dramatically. His major competitor, which was historically the price leader, had not raised prices, and he was concerned about losing volume and share position. As you would expect, profit margins declined. His response was to eliminate some of the product features that added to cost. Once this was done, some key customers turned to competitors to get the products they wanted, and volume as well as profit margins declined. Faced with another round of labor and material cost increases, the product manager concluded that the situation was hopeless and recommended to top management that the line be dropped.

Inadequate Understanding of Market and Economics

Many managers simply fail to develop the deep understanding of their market and how and where the business generates profit to the extent required to make intelligent pricing decisions. There is nothing complicated about the information that is needed; it simply takes some digging and tough-minded thinking to put it together. For example, these kinds of questions about the market require specific answers:

1. How is the market segmented? What factors (such as performance, price, delivery, service) control or influence the buying decision in each segment? Which specific segments or customer groups are you seeking to serve and why? What is the value of the product or service to the customer or user?

2. What is the competitive structure in each segment? What is the relative market position of each major competitor? How do competitors match up on the factors that control or influence the buying decision?
3. How does industry capacity compare with total market demand? What significant changes in capacity are likely? Why? How does the changed capacity outlook compare with estimated demand for the future? How have industry or company pricing practices shifted in the past with changes in capacity or demand relationships?
4. To what extent does market demand vary with price? What underlying factors cause the relative elasticity or inelasticity of the demand curve (such as commodity product, unique product advantage)?

All these questions about customers, product demand and usage, competitors, industry capacity, historical patterns, and relationships provide the background essential to making intelligent judgments on how various pricing policies or changes in pricing policies will be received in the marketplace.

Now let's look at the questions about the company's profit economics that need definitive answers.

1. How much profit contribution and absolute profit (after all allocations) is generated by each product?
2. How does the cost and profit structure for each product vary with changes in volume?
3. How and where in the overall make and sell cycle are significant costs and value added?
4. How many dollars of assets are committed where, and what return is being earned on each major chunk of investment?
5. How sensitive are profits to changes in key variables, such as price, mix, costs?
6. What are true idle plant costs for abandoned or underutilized capacity?

As you can see, these questions are designed to generate the information about the cost and profit structure necessary to quantify the effect of pursuing one pricing policy versus another.

Without being able to answer these kinds of questions, it is impossible to make intelligent pricing decisions. For example, will a reduced price actually generate incremental volume? How much incremental volume is required to offset a lower price that reduces unit margins? Are competitors likely to react to a pricing action in a way that will damage the overall profit structure of the business? None of these questions can be answered without a deep understanding of the fundamental market and economic characteristics of the business. Managers typically rationalize their inability to answer these questions by claiming that their market research and accounting systems do not provide this information. To some extent this is true; most traditional information systems do not automatically generate the data necessary to answer these questions. But this deficiency is not a valid excuse for not knowing the answers. The data do not have to be 100 percent accurate or complete. In the vast majority of cases, the information can be developed simply by reordering existing data or even by making estimates that allow intelligent judgments to be made. Blaming the system is simply an excuse for the kind of sloppy thinking that inevitably leads to faulty pricing decisions.

Overemphasis on Volume and Market Share

Recent emphasis by professional consultants and planners on the importance of volume and market share to profit performance and the experience curve to cost performance has led a lot of managers on a volume chase that does not make sense. These experts claim that the producer with the highest market share will have the lowest cost and greatest profit because of economies of scale. Their reasoning is based on the theory that the costs of value added to a product decline approximately 20 to 30 percent in real terms each time accumulated manufacturing experience is doubled. Believers in the theory advocate pricing below competition and sacrificing current margins as a means of gaining volume and market share. They argue that the higher profits achievable as volume grows and manufacturing experience is gained will more than offset the profit shortfall from lower prices.

There may be isolated cases where this strategy pays off in the industrial world, but it is an impractical approach in the vast majority of cases. Although it is quite reasonable to expect and plan for 20 to 30 percent cost improvement during the early stages of manufacture of a new product (or even of an old product in a new manufacturing facility), the picture is quite different for almost any established or mature product. As Exhibit 8-1 shows, there is a learning curve in these situations, and costs should improve dramatically as workers and management gain experience with a new manufacturing process. However, the curve is a curve, and the potential for further gains through additional manufacturing experience diminishes rapidly after the process reaches maturity. This does not mean that manufacturing costs cannot be reduced by 20 to 30 percent after the initial learning period, but it will not happen automatically when manufacturing experience doubles and certainly not without major investment and a specific plan for achieving this kind of improvement.

A lot of companies have fallen into the trap of cutting prices with the expectation that increased volume or "tonnage" alone will automatically lower manufacturing costs sufficiently to offset lower margins and add to profits. The results have been disastrous. Nothing is more painful to senior management than listening to some marketing manager try to explain why profits are down even though volume is far above plan. Anything the marketing manager might say about gaining market share through aggressive pricing or counting on some kind of experience curve to improve future profits does not go over very well with senior managers who know better from experience.

The Impact of Inflation

It is essential to understand the impact inflationary pressures have or should have on pricing policy. Failure to recognize just how important this inflation factor is and how to adjust pricing policy to take it into account have triggered serious profit problems in many companies.

Nobody has to look very far to find examples of companies that have been seriously hurt because of management's inability to operate effectively in an inflationary environment. On standard products with short delivery cycles, there are myriad cases where

EXHIBIT 8-1

THE EFFECT OF THE LEARNING CURVE

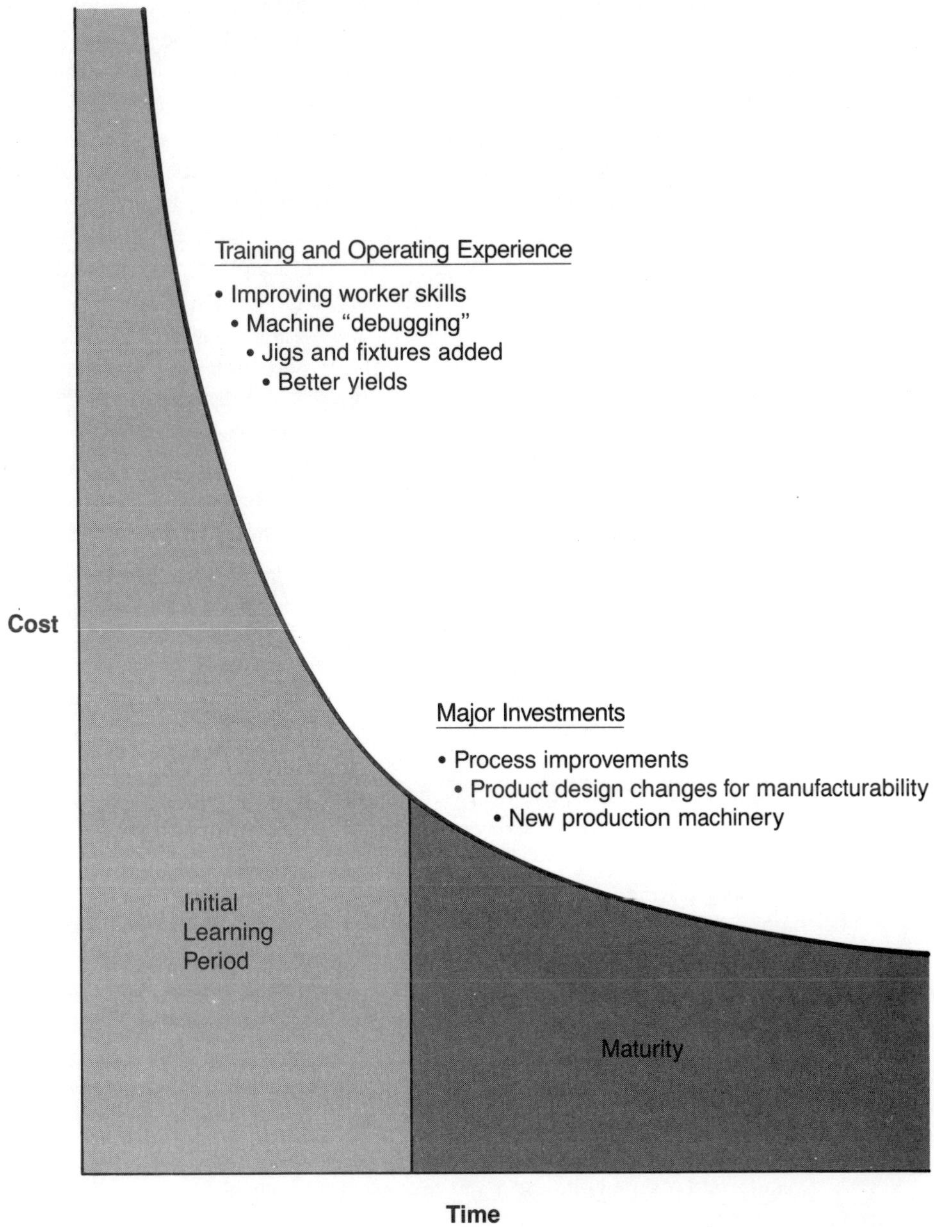

costs escalated ahead of prices and profit margins showed a steady decline, frequently on greater volume. On longer-cycle products or systems sold on contracts that might call for delivery one or two years ahead, there are just as many cases where anticipated profits suddenly turned into red ink because inadequate allowance was made for cost escalation during the manufacturing cycle. The pattern of profit decline may vary somewhat in different situations, but the cause is basically the same. Stated simply, management does not anticipate or react effectively to the inflation spiral that quickly and inexorably pushes labor, material, and overhead costs higher and higher.

Business managers and governments in countries like Brazil, which has lived for years with an annual inflation rate of 40 to 50 percent, have a better grasp of the problems caused by high inflation and have adopted economic and pricing policies to protect profits and assets against its impact. Wages, rent, contract prices, assets, and other values that are affected by inflation are frequently and automatically indexed by government data, and managers move aggressively to adjust any values that are not indexed so that parity is preserved. But most managers in countries where high rates of inflation are a new phenomenon have not adjusted their thinking to the realities and tend to lag or fall short in their reactions. To start with, they don't understand the extent to which inflation affects profit requirements. Higher inflation demands higher returns just to stay even. Although this may sound like an amazing discovery of the obvious, far too many managers have not as yet adjusted their thinking to the realities of inflation economics. They are content with profit returns that are way too slim when the impact of inflation is taken into account. As a result, the company's return on capital and even its capital base can actually erode while management thinks the company is turning a satisfactory profit. Also, most managers are far too slow to react, and price adjustments tend to lag farther and farther behind increasing cost curves. Profit margins deteriorate and the business gets caught in a cost-profit squeeze. In some cases, managers simply don't move quickly enough or simply don't understand what is happening. In others, they are afraid the market won't accept a price increase and don't want to lose volume. Whatever the reason, profit results are severely penalized and never seem to catch up as costs move relentlessly ahead.

Making price adjustments to track inflation is unquestionably a high-risk exercise with high stakes. The precise inflation rate can never be known in advance because it is an approximation of the weighted average price shift of a "market basket" of values. It doesn't take much insight to see that there is a penalty for changing price too soon, too late, too much, or too little. However, the heaviest penalties are inflicted on those who do not adjust prices to inflation at all. Since it is a good bet that we will be plagued with inflation problems for many years, it is essential that managers start to think logically about the futility of chasing volume while costs continue to rise. Otherwise, as economists point out,[1] we will see a continuing erosion of industrial profits and capital that will lead ultimately to the liquidation of many important companies.

[1]George Terborgh, *Inflation and Profits,* Machinery and Allied Products Institute, October 1976 (5th printing).

Link to Business Strategy

Few generalizations are useful in industrial management. However, one that is deals with the importance of ensuring that all parts of the business are linked together in a cohesive strategy geared to the fundamental characteristics and requirements of the market being served. Otherwise, impact in the marketplace will be diffused and profit results will not be satisfactory. This general principle applies especially to a company's pricing policy. For example, if the business strategy is aimed at participating in a mature, price-sensitive segment of the market, the business is likely to be structured around a narrow line of "bread and butter" products, high-volume–low-cost manufacturing operations, minimal engineering and redesign capabilities, and a selling effort targeted at price-oriented accounts. In this kind of situation, a pricing policy designed to achieve high-volume goals even at the expense of some unit margin probably makes sense. But this same pricing policy would make no sense at all if the business strategy were focused on a segment of the market where custom product design and superior performance features were the key factors in the buying decision. Here a more logical policy would be to price at a premium and be willing to sacrifice volume to preserve unit margins and a reputation for superior performance.

Differences in product design, manufacturing operations, or selling approaches obviously lead to substantially different cost structures for what may appear to be similar products. For example, a plant structured to produce a narrow range of products will generally have more automated equipment, lower direct labor costs per unit, higher fixed and indirect manufacturing costs, and a higher breakeven point than one set up to manufacture a similar product for a custom market in small quantities. However, when the business comes under tough competitive pressure or the market softens, these fundamental differences in economic structure are often forgotten and pricing policies or actions are implemented that are totally at odds with the profit-making strategy management originally set out to follow.

During the past few years, Cleveland Twist Drill, a broad-line manufacturer of high speed cutting tools, found that smaller specialty producers were cutting into its business by selling below cost on certain lines with selected high volume users. To preserve its position with these accounts, Cleveland Twist Drill matched the lower prices, but did not intend to lower prices across the board. There are few secrets in the marketplace, however, and once the lower price was granted to certain customers, other customers heard about it and demanded the same treatment. As a result, the price eventually dropped across the line and margins deteriorated. The narrow line producers then retaliated with an even lower price and again started taking market share from Cleveland Twist Drill. Discussions with vendors indicated that, even with the lower prices, at least three of the four specialty producers could still make satisfactory profits.

Inadequate Administration

Once a pricing policy is defined, you might think that everyone will automatically follow it. Unfortunately, this isn't the way it works in the real world. Unless management takes positive steps to ensure that the policy is explicitly followed throughout the company, exceptions will occur at a phenomenal rate. A few exceptions to any policy are to be expected, but too many exceptions and the policy becomes nonexistent.

One might wonder how this happens, but it is easy to explain. There is almost always pressure from some quarter for a lower price. Salespeople the world over can always find persuasive reasons why prices below policy are required to be competitive, or to "crack a new account." A plant manager sees a costly gap in a near-term production plan and calls on the sales force to help him fill it by taking some short-cycle business (short period from sale to delivery) at reduced prices. A product or sales manager sticks to the list price, but offers the buyer some form of price concession through extended terms, a longer warranty period, a break on return goods, prepaid freight, or some other advantage that costs money. A systems marketing manager accepts an order within current price policy, but for delivery 12 months from now with no escalation clause to adjust the price at delivery for inflation. In short, any salesperson, market, product, or plant manager worth his or her salt can always find a hundred reasons and ways to deviate from stated price policy. Unless top management exercises tight control, the company's pricing policy will become a joke or, at best, simply the starting point for price negotiations. Most companies think they have the tight control necessary to avoid these situations, but they really don't. It takes a lot of top management attention and discipline in an organization of any size to make sure that unauthorized price concessions or policy deviations do not occur. And the plain truth is that management in many companies simply does not exercise the kind of tough-minded discipline required to make a pricing policy stick.

MANAGEMENT SOLUTIONS

Let's turn now to the actions management can take to prevent or correct these problems. There are no easy answers or pat solutions. Preventive or corrective actions should be designed to keep a strong focus on bottom-line profits and the impact that changes in a product's cost structure and alternative pricing actions will have on these results. All these actions revolve around basic management requirements that are essential to success in any industrial operation.

Establish Growth and Profit Targets

The first requirement is to define and communicate an explicit set of growth and profit targets. To be meaningful, the targets must be balanced to cover the expected return on sales and capital as well as a profit growth objective. To be worthwhile, they need to represent a level of performance that yields an attractive return on capital and provides the means to create an attractive work environment for employees. For example, an after-tax return of 7 percent on sales, 20 percent on capital employed, and a 15 percent growth rate would represent a satisfactorily explicit and balanced set of targets. These target numbers are precise and require balanced performance. They cannot be achieved by concentrating on sales growth alone without regard for the investment in working capital required. Nor can they be achieved by sacrificing growth and scaling back investment and costs to improve returns. Conversely, some vague statement about earning attractive profits or achieving large sales gains would not be worthwhile. The emphasis must be on profits and profit growth to counteract the strong volume orientation that commonly exists in most industrial companies.

Given the dynamic nature of our business environment, these targets (like interest rates) should be reviewed regularly and adjusted for changing inflation rates and economic conditions. It is clear that profit returns, like interest rates, require upward adjustment with the rate of inflation. In other words, if management expected to earn a 10 percent after-tax return on its capital with inflation at 3 to 4 percent, it makes no sense at all to settle for the same return when the inflation rate doubles. In the mid-1970s, many companies determined that their growth and profit targets had to be adjusted when the annual inflation rate jumped to double-digit numbers. Although they may not know it, those managers who failed to recognize this need actually suffered an erosion in their capital base when inflation rates exceeded profit returns.

A different set of targets needs to be developed for international operations. International targets must take into account differing inflation and tax rates, as well as the inherent economic and political risks in each country. For example, it simply doesn't make sense to settle for the same profit returns in a soft-currency country like Mexico or Brazil, where high inflation erodes half or more of the monetary value each year, and a hard-currency country like Switzerland, where inflation appears to be under control. Nor does it make sense to overlook the volatile political climates in some countries that greatly increase the risks of getting a payout on invested capital. Obviously, high-risk situations demand a higher return and a shorter payout period.

As important as defining these targets is the need to make sure they are communicated throughout the organization and that everyone understands the business strategy and basic pricing policies designed to achieve them. Special emphasis should be given to explaining these targets to the sales force and relating them to the company's sales and marketing plans and pricing policies. Communication with the sales force is crucial, since the sales organization is where most of the pressure for volume and deviations from pricing policy starts. Getting the sales force to understand how the company's pricing policies relate to achieving overall growth and profit targets and the importance of adhering to these policies will put a cap on a lot of this pressure.

Determine Product Line Costs and Profits

A second requirement is to have an accurate picture of the cost and profit structure for each product line. Management in most companies has some means of knowing the relative profitability of its key business segments. Some rely on statements that show gross margin dollars and percentage of gross margin to sales; others use contribution dollars (sales dollars less "out of pocket" costs equal contribution to overhead and profit). These data can lead management to wrong pricing decisions because they do not include all the costs of doing business and thus do not fully reflect the true cost and profit picture. Unfortunately, even so-called fixed costs tend to increase steadily when inflation rates are high. As a result, what are traditionally regarded as relatively stable overhead costs (insurance, taxes, supervision) can escalate unexpectedly and dramatically affect any cost and profit structure. Relying on profit statements that do not take all these costs into account can easily lead to pricing decisions that generate more gross margin or contribution dollars but less bottom-line profits.

To keep the true profit picture in focus, net profitability statements need to be developed on a regular basis for each major product line. This is not an easy task, but neither is it impossible. Most accounting systems identify the direct costs (labor, material, direct overhead) for each major product line. Allocations of indirect costs, including corporate charges, can be assigned to each product line on some kind of rational basis. There will be plenty of arguments by those responsible for the profitability of one product line or another about the fairness of these allocations, and undoubtedly periodic adjustments will have to be made. However, all indirect and overhead costs must be completely allocated. None of them is going to go away, and they must be assigned somehow to specific product lines to reflect a true profit picture. The allocation process should not be arbitrary or left entirely to the accounting side of the business. Getting the managers with profit and loss responsibility involved is a good way to improve their understanding of the economics of their business and will help gain agreement on the fairness of allocation methods.

Once developed, these net profitability statements should serve as a starting point for regular review sessions to bring necessary management actions into focus. Estimated cost increases for labor, material, and overhead should be made frequently so that management can see how each product line statement will be affected. Doing this should highlight the need for management action to reduce material or labor costs, cut back overhead spending, defer major programs, or initiate price increases. Management needs to use these statements aggressively. They should be reviewed regularly as a formal part of the management process so that problems can be pinpointed quickly. Once problems are identified, strong action to raise prices or reduce costs should be initiated to ensure that target profits for each product line are achieved. Finally, management must take a hard line on product lines that do not meet profit objectives and be willing to drop them if necessary unless realistic plans to achieve satisfactory profits are presented. The whole idea is to get a regular and all-inclusive look at the cost and profit structure for each product line so that appropriate action can be taken to achieve satisfactory profits for the total business.

Develop and Enforce Pricing Policy

A final requirement calls for top or general management to define and articulate the pricing policy and then provide strong follow-through to ensure that it is effectively administered. Although it sounds difficult, defining pricing policy is not the toughest part of the job. To begin with, there are only a limited number of pricing policies to choose from for any market segment. You can price low to build volume and market position. You can price high to hold or improve margins. You can tie price to the customer's perceived value. You can match or price off certain competitor prices. You can be a price leader or a follower. There are not many other alternatives.

The key is to determine which of these policies is most appropriate for each market segment of interest to the company. Exhibit 8-2 shows the network of interrelated considerations that need to be evaluated as a basis for selecting a pricing strategy for any busi-

EXHIBIT 8-2

DEVELOPING PRICING STRATEGY

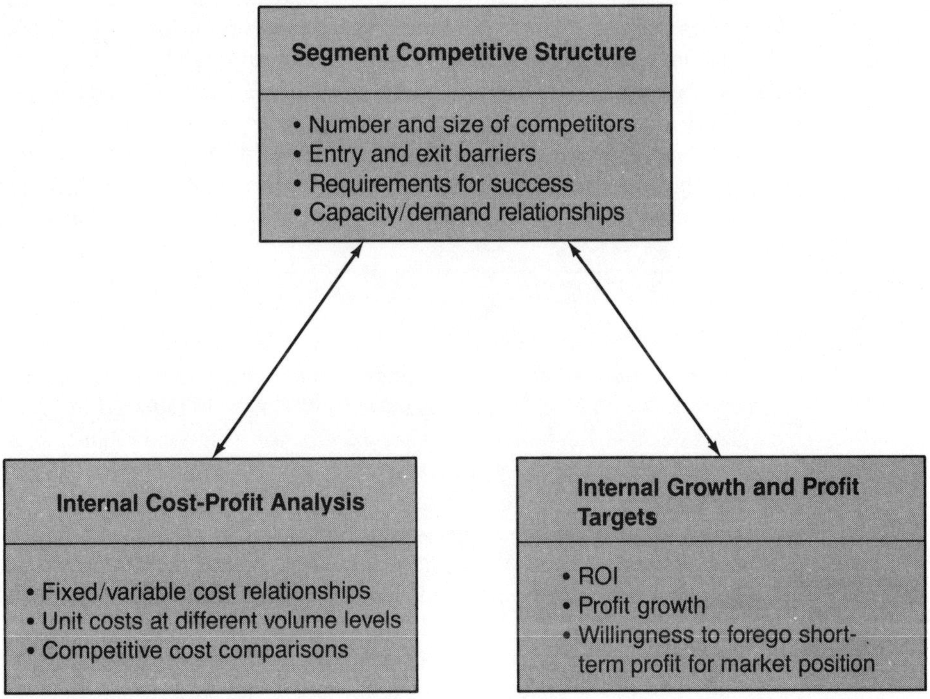

ness. Exhibit 8-2 illustrates the need to have *both* market and economic facts on which to base pricing decisions. It also shows that pricing strategy decisions are in effect investment decisions, which commit the resources of the firm and which therefore must be directly linked to the company's overall business strategy. It is not necessary to define pricing policy in a way that covers every conceivable situation or set of circumstances. Broad but definitive statements, like "We intend to adhere to our standard list or discount structure and will make no special deals with anyone," or "We intend to price in a way that achieves our margin objectives on each sales transaction," or "We want to price at a 5 percent premium over certain competitors," are totally adequate pricing policy directives.

The most difficult part of management's job is to take the actions required to show that the policy is not just words. To start with, someone with an eye for profits has to be given the responsibility for monitoring individual pricing actions to ensure that unauthorized deviations do not occur. In some cases, the general manager may want to maintain this responsibility. In others, especially where multiple product-market businesses are involved, general management may delegate the responsibility to a product or market manager. In still other situations, the general manager may decide to give this responsibility to the controller as part of the overall accounting-control assignment.

Whoever has this responsibility must clearly play the role of enforcer. Carrying out the job will not win any popularity contests, for it involves such things as making sure any orders taken that do deviate from policy without appropriate authorization are turned back and the responsible party ordered to explain the situation to the customer, seeing to it that those who try to slide around established price policy in some clever way get their wrists slapped and everyone knows about it. Admittedly, actions like these are tough medicine, but they are essential to let everyone know that top managers really mean it when they say: "This is our pricing policy, and we intend to make it stick."

Strengthen Ability to Compete

Beyond actions designed to ensure tight control over pricing, other management actions are required to make it practical to stick to a firm pricing policy in the face of competitors that may not. Continued or even increased investment is required in product development activities that can build greater proprietary value into the product or service offering. It is essential to put the salesperson in a position where he or she can emphasize new product features, shorter delivery cycles, quality assurance and reliability programs, product training, or any other conceivable advantage that provides genuine value to the customer. Arming salespeople with advantages like these enables them to sell in a way that takes the emphasis off price and encourages the customer to think about total value instead of which product is the cheapest.

Management must also place constant and heavy emphasis on cost reduction to help offset inflation-driven increases in material, labor, and other product costs that are certain to occur. Successful programs that take costs out of a product without penalizing its quality or performance are essential to preserve profit margins without passing every increase on to the customer. When inflation is running at a double-digit rate, however, it is unlikely that even the most successful cost reduction programs can completely offset spiraling cost increases, so timely price adjustments must be implemented along with the appropriate customer explanation. Timely means planned well in advance, and not waiting until accounting records show that profit margins have declined. This is not as difficult as it might sound. Most cost increases are predictable, and operating plans should include schedules that show both the cost reduction programs and the pricing actions that will be taken to preserve or enhance profit margins.

Stand Firm When the Market Turns Soft

The acid test of management's determination to stick with a firm pricing policy comes when the market turns soft and a struggle develops to achieve volume goals. When this occurs, management can expect to see proposals to lower price as a means of picking up incremental volume or marginal contribution to help absorb overhead. On the surface, these proposals have a lot of appeal. Why not lower price to pick up volume you would not get otherwise? Why not take your price down even below full cost to pick up added volume that will help absorb a fixed amount of overhead that you have to pay anyway? There may well be times when it is smart to lower price to achieve objectives like these, but in most cases the proposals are ill-conceived notions that represent a snare and a delusion.

Think about what happens if competition matches or goes below a lower price and as a result captures some of your established business or customers. Consider how effectively you can compete if your action to lower price triggers an all-out price war among competitors who also have idle capacity and would like to have incremental volume to fill it. Or assume you are able to pick up low price volume that absorbs overhead without competitive retaliation. Have you really achieved an economic gain? Is there a real advantage in wearing out machines and people just to gain contribution dollars instead of scaling back capacity so that underutilized capital can be redeployed?

Pricing actions like these are never made in a vacuum. Aggressive competitor reactions should be anticipated, particularly in mature market situations where demand is relatively inelastic and competitor share positions are relatively stable. This does not mean that such pricing actions should never be taken. It does mean, however, that management must be judicious and consider probable competitor responses and the ultimate economics of such actions after all factors have been taken into account.

When it looks as though the market is turning soft, management needs to move quickly to cut back costs; otherwise, the fears of those arguing for lower prices will prove valid and lower volume will create an intolerable profit pattern. If management is on top of the business, it should be able to anticipate soft market conditions so that actions to reduce inventories, staff levels, and indirect costs can be initiated prior to the actual volume decline. Waiting until the condition actually reflects itself in the profit and loss statement is at least several months too late and often leads to panic reactions that penalize the firm over the longer term.

In most make and sell situations, the economic structure of the business is not totally dependent on volume, and market declines tend to be cyclical rather than permanent. Given these characteristics, it is surprising how well profit margins and even absolute profits can be preserved if management moves quickly and aggressively to scale back costs in anticipation of lower volume. As a general rule, a volume shortfall from plan of up to 5 percent—and in some cases up to 10 percent—should be absorbed without penalizing planned profits if the plan is soundly conceived and management moves quickly enough to make appropriate changes in its cost structure. If the volume shortfall is deeper than 10 percent, cost reduction efforts should be targeted at reshaping the cost structure so that planned profit margins are achieved on a much lower volume base.

Admittedly, these are demanding objectives that cannot be achieved with a "kid glove" approach to cost reduction. But it is clear that they can be achieved. History has recorded plenty of examples of businesses that actually generated the profit dollars and margins necessary to achieve these objectives on lower volume as those businesses grew through various stages to their present size. During the 1975–76 recession, one of Reliance Electric's plants operated at about 35 percent of its rated capacity and still broke even. It was able to do this for two reasons. First, the plant was basically an assembly operation, and the fixed cost base and breakeven point were relatively low. Equally important, operating management anticipated the decline in business and moved quickly to reduce both its direct and indirect costs. The direct workforce was cut from 700 to 200, and the ratio of indirect (supervisors and support personnel) to direct was improved from 1:3 to 1:5. When the economic cycle turned upward, the plant achieved higher profit levels than it had in prior years because management was able to return to former volume levels with fewer direct workers and with the stronger indirect to direct ratio developed during the recession period.

With proper management, a business can generate the same profit dollars and margins as volume slides down. To be successful, management must understand that discretionary costs tend to be regarded as variable when volume increases and fixed as volume goes down. These discretionary costs are the ones that must be attacked and scaled back to ensure a cost configuration that will yield satisfactory profit margins and profits on a lower than planned volume base. Belt tightening is always tough, but it is a necessary course of action for management when the market turns soft. And it is the only way to build real integrity and believability into a company's pricing policy.

Of course, if the economic structure of the business is volume-sensitive, as it is in many industries that operate with an unusually high percentage of fixed costs, there may be no alternative to lowering prices. And if at some point the total market really dries up, prices may have to be lowered and lower margins accepted in any business just to keep the doors open, since some contribution to overhead and profit is better than no contribution at all. However, unless the business is extremely sensitive to volume, cutting prices should be a last resort and seriously weighed against the alternative of scaling back or going out of the business so capital can be redeployed in areas where profit opportunities are more attractive.

SUMMARY

Pricing policies are a vital part of the marketing mix for any company, and they need management attention if they are to foster the long-term success of the firm. Panicky decisions under market pressure, naive decisions made without proper marketing information, and chasing short-term gain at the expense of long-term success are common in industrial firms, although they need not be.

Most of the trouble stems from management deficiencies—not understanding the market and the economics of the business; overemphasizing volume and market share; failing to keep a step ahead of inflation; failing to link pricing to the total business strategy; and failing to administer a pricing policy consistently and carefully. All these mistakes can cost the company profits and even its existence.

Certain procedures can take the mystery and the danger out of pricing. One is to establish growth and profit targets and make sure they are communicated throughout the company; another is to determine actual product line costs and profits. One of the most important is to define and enforce a pricing policy, and to stand firm when the market turns soft. A management with a clear idea of where the company is going and a good grasp of economics can make and administer a firm, consistent pricing policy that will work to the company's advantage.

9

Competitive Bidding

Jerry Potter, senior sales engineer for Custom Machinery Company, was excited about the verbal agreement he had just received from the purchasing and engineering groups at U.S. Can Company, an account that could give him his largest single order. Jerry had worked closely with U.S. Can for several months to develop the parameters and design concept for a new machine that offered potential cost and performance advantages over the machines U.S. Can currently had in place. He had been assured verbally by an engineer at U.S. Can that he stood to get an order for another 35 machines if the first one met cost and performance specifications. At approximately $300,000 per machine, the total order could amount to over $10 million.

Jerry forwarded all the necessary information to the home office to enable it to prepare a firm quote and proposal. Several weeks passed with no response. Worried, Jerry called Fred James, the national sales manager, to see what was going on. Jerry opened the conversation by saying: "Fred, we'll lose this sale if we don't get the proposal in to U.S. Can. I promised it within a few weeks, and six weeks have already passed." Said James: "We've got a problem, Jerry. I think it's a heck of an opportunity, but the boss has a lot of concerns, and I have not been able to convince him that we should go ahead with the bid." "How can he have any concerns when such a huge piece of business is staring us in the face?" Jerry asked, astonished. "I agree with you," Fred said, "but let me read you the comments the boss made on your transmittal memo."

> Even though this might be an attractive piece of business, it looks very risky to me.
>
> 1. We have no proven position or record with U.S. Can as a supplier. What is to stop U.S. Can from just picking our brains and sharing the ideas with their traditional suppliers?
> 2. We have no experience in making a machine that matches these specifications. How do we know we can build a machine that will perform at this cost?
> 3. What assurance do we have that there will definitely be follow-on business or that we will get any of it if it does develop?
> 4. As I see it, it would cost us $60,000 to $80,000 to prepare a definitive proposal. That's a lot of up-front money with these risks, especially compared to other opportunities we have with customers we know well.

Jerry, dismayed, answered: "I don't know how we will ever get new business with this kind of potential if we aren't willing to take some risks."

What else can Jerry do to prove his point?

Should he come back with more facts and more arguments? What kind of facts would he need?

What might be done to prevent this situation from happening again?

Good procurement practice dictates the need to seek competitive bids on most purchases of any consequence. The buying need may be a one-time capital equipment purchase, or it may involve long-term repeat purchases over many months or years for a material, manufactured component, or service. If the customer needs a long-term steady and stable source for a critical item, a competitive long-term supply contract is often sought.

Products that require a long manufacturing cycle of many months are typically conducted on a competitive bid and supply contract basis. Most job-shop manufacturers secure business on a bid-contract basis. Major OEMs with large annual requirements for an item will seek competitive bids before selecting one or two long-term supply sources. Large corporate headquarters purchasing units, sometimes called national accounts, frequently buy centrally on a competitive bid and supply contract basis. For example, IBM now offers contracts for most products that include a "volume procurement amendment," which grants customers a discount for agreeing to buy a set number of units by a given date. These discounts and contracts appeal mainly to large customers. Once an end user signs an 18-month contract to buy IBM products, which is common in a volume deal, competitors find themselves locked out.[1] Finally, most municipal, state, and federal government purchases are conducted by requesting competitive bids and then awarding a contract. In most of these situations, large sums of money are involved.

If a bidding situation is not properly thought through, there can be significant long-term risks for the supplier. The most common areas of risk are these:

1. Not thoroughly understanding the customer's requirements.
2. Making wrong assumptions about the future and the competition.
3. Making wrong estimations of costs, purchase quantities, and expected profits.

Competitive bidding situations are like military warfare. The prudent supplier must select bid situations or "battles" that fit its capabilities and provide attractive profits. The technical challenge or "interesting project" has caused many suppliers to pursue bids for which they did not have the capabilities or resources. Technical or engineering driven bids without a close customer-market orientation can result in a lot of unprofitable "won" bids and lawsuits for failure to deliver. So can the pushing of a sales manager who says: "This could be a 'showcase account' that will result in a lot of follow-on business from the customer." This form of wishful thinking is usually nothing more than a desire to grab any business for the sake of volume. A statement like "Everyone else is submitting bids" is also not a valid reason to bid. In one company, the sales manager influenced the division president to sign bid proposals to fill a plant that was running at less than 50 percent capacity. The company bid low for one larger OEM's component needs and was locked into three years of shipments in which increases in labor and material costs nearly bankrupted the division.

[1]Peter D. Petre, "Meet the Lean, Mean New IBM," *Fortune,* June 13, 1983, p. 74.

SOME COMMONSENSE PRACTICES

There are a number of sound business practices to follow *before* pursuing a competitive bid situation. These practices will help an industrial marketer decide how to bid, and equally important, when *not* to bid.

Understand the Customer's Requirements

When examining any bidding situation, it is important to consider each customer or buyer individually. The astute marketer or salesperson will first identify the people who write the requirements and product specifications. This requires close contact with technical and purchasing personnel, and often top management. Every step in a government or private customer review process is a marketing opportunity to influence specifications or conditions so that the company becomes or remains a qualified supplier. But the first step is to identify the network of line and staff influences in the procurement process for the item.

Identification of the decision makers and the requirements of the account usually require numerous visits to the potential customer's organization. This interaction helps the supplier to discover the customer's real needs and lessens the chance of the supplier becoming preoccupied with a technology or a preconceived solution to a situation that may not exist. Repeated on-site visits, questions, and cross-questioning help a supplier better understand the customer's requirements. It is also helpful to verify with the customer what you believe its requirements are. This approach helps avoid misunderstandings that could misdirect a proposal. A team of marketing and engineering personnel listening to the customer is most helpful. Often random customer statements and information help get to the real requirements. In-depth discussions with one large potential customer, for example, revealed that it expected the chosen supplier to invest in special quality-control equipment, which would have had a very negative impact on the supplier's profits. In another situation, a thorough understanding of customer requirements revealed that, on smaller production runs, the customer would provide or pay for the costly injection molds. Armed with this information, the supplier bid only on that portion of the business.

The supplier considering entering a bidding position is usually putting a lot of eggs in one basket for a considerable time period. For this reason, there is a great need to learn as much as possible about the customer's requirements before deciding whether or not to bid and how to bid if the decision is yes (see the box, page 190).

When company or division top management teams are really customer oriented, they will have plenty of firsthand data on customers' requirements and competitive offers. Staying close to the customer also helps the supplier learn about a new technology or application. The result is a tailored product with a lot of value for the customer. This focus is contrary to the typical sales orientation that stresses a large number of calls per day. In short, the field people should be problem solvers rather than salespeople with a canned pitch.

Once the customer's requirements are understood, it is important that the potential customer understand the solution you have for his or her problem or requirements. Since there is rarely one person who influences the choice of supplier, it is important to get the solution to all the decision-making parties. In some situations, the supplier can know what the customer's requirements are before they issue the request for a quote (RFQ).

STAYING CLOSE TO CUSTOMERS

Boeing designs and assembles jet aircraft for each customer's specifications. In its metamorphosis from a military to a commercial company, Boeing states:

> We built teams that were customer and not technology oriented. We came to a realization that if we were going to succeed in the commercial business, the important ingredients were the immediate customer and his customer's needs. . . . It took us a long time to recognize the customer's problems. Now this point of view percolates throughout our entire organization.

An accountant at a major specialty chemical company was at first surprised when, after two months on the job, he was asked to spend more time accompanying a salesman making calls. The accountant, who later became the division comptroller, commented afterward:

> If you don't understand how the customers use and buy an item, you won't understand the business and how to submit bids. All of our contract administrators spend time in the field with each customer before we decide to bid.

Much of IBM's data processing computer equipment is sold on a proposal-bid-service contract basis. The corporate vice president of marketing at IBM stated:

> Every proposal to a customer should be overwhelmingly cost-justifiable from the customer's standpoint. Such an orientation requires in-depth knowledge of what each customer can do with the machine. We want our salesmen to act as if they were on the customer's payroll. IBM is customer driven, not technology driven.

When Hewlett-Packard engineers make service calls, they ask customers what they like and dislike about the existing product. They also ask customers what specific new features they would like. The computer system division general manager at Hewlett-Packard stated:

> If we don't stay close to our customers, the Japanese or another competitor will leapfrog our position. As the division general manager, I still spend 1 week per month in the field, visiting installations, talking with customers and attending sales meetings. This helps us learn from others' mistakes, and it helps to avoid designing systems that are technically interesting but don't provide enough customer value.

Source: Thomas J. Peters and Robert H. Waterman, *In Search of Excellence: Lessons from America's Best-Run Corporations* (New York: Harper & Row, 1982), p. 169; and a personal conversation with F. G. (Buck) Rodgers, IBM Corporation, Armonk, New York.

Analyze Past Bids

Armed with an exhaustive knowledge of the present or potential customer's requirements, the supplier should conduct a bid-history analysis whenever possible. A *bid-history analysis* is a systematic consideration of why bids were won or lost. Some executives are reluctant to conduct such analyses because they are a review after the fact. However, projections and decisions based on 20/20 hindsight are one of the most reliable forecasting tools available to management. Objective after-the-fact examinations can be most revealing and promote better account planning, better price determination, and the development of sales tactics that take advantage of patterns of customer requirements and competitive behavior.

Historical bid and contract award analysis should be conducted with both internal data and firsthand information from buyers. Internal data sources include salesperson call reports and past correspondence with potential and existing customers. The analysis should consider the economic, technical, competitive, and political reasons a contract was won or lost.[2]

The industrial supplier might initially analyze just those bids that were lost. Purchasing departments, buyers, and key customer executives are some of the best and most accurate sources for analyzing lost bid situations. Some purchasing departments have a policy of explaining to the losing bidders why they were not awarded the business. This practice helps the buyer develop better supplier relations and often increases competition for the buyer's business. An analysis of the customer's reason for lost business frequently refutes the salesperson's common reason of "price-buying" as the umbrella explanation for all lost business. Lost bid analysis may instead reveal that a technical proposal was unsound or that delivery dates were unacceptable. The specific reasons for the loss of business will usually focus on one or more of the following: quality, delivery, service, long-term availability, supplier's technical assistance, and price. IBM, for example, conducts monthly "lost account reviews" with its branch and regional people to discuss why business was lost and what needs to be done.

Lost bid reviews should also be done in face-to-face meetings with the customers. Often customers will not only explain why the business was lost, but suggest ways that near misses can be turned into hits. In one case, such a visit revealed that the quoted delivery of 12 weeks was the weak factor; the winner's delivery quote was 5 weeks. Bid-history analysis ultimately allows a supplier to profile both customers and competitors and better anticipate customer requirements and predict competitor responses.

Know Whether to Bid for the Short or Long Term

In many industries, suppliers encounter situations in which the firm winning the initial contract has an advantage in obtaining the longer-term follow-on business. This situation typically results in suppliers "buying in" by offering low initial prices or other inducements to tie customers to them for long periods. This practice is often referred to as "getting well" on the "follow-on" business.[3] The initial sale is often made at less than desirable profits or possibly at a loss in anticipation of the more lucrative subsequent sales of the same or related products and services. For example, Goodyear bid $1 for the initial Boeing 757 order for the landing gear and wheel assembly. The aftermarket unit sales in

[2]Paul L. Smith and Lawrence G. Regau, "Before You Bid, Know Your Competition," *Aerospace Management*, March 1963, pp. 24–28.
[3]Robert E. Weigand, "Buying into a Market," *Harvard Business Review*, November–December 1980, pp. 141–49.

that situation are hundreds of times larger than the initial OEM sale. By winning the original order for $1 Goodyear is assured of the replacement part business because it is unlikely that another supplier will be qualified on the original equipment.

A basic issue in bidding and pricing for follow-on business is to ask: How likely or probable is it that the firm will obtain the follow-on business? The link between the initial buy-in business and the follow-on sales must be strong if this approach is to be profitable. If the link between the two is not strong, the supplier has probably obtained a low-profit or money-losing contract. Here are five ways to build strong links for more follow-on business:

1. Patents and proprietary products help build the link between initial and follow-on sales. However, other firms can sometimes "reverse engineer" around the proprietary product if there is not a strong patent position.
2. Noninterchangeable machines or parts tie the customer to additional purchases of your system, parts, or service. This type of customer dependence is commonly practiced in the computer and word processing and photocopy machine businesses.
3. Customers usually want to keep the number of parts, spares, and inventory to an economic minimum and therefore will often provide follow-up business to one supplier. Airlines are a good example. They will specify a jet airplane engine from one supplier and buy replacement engines and carry spare parts only from that supplier. In situations where multiple follow-on supply sources are sought, the link is less effective.
4. The cost of retraining employees can also keep customers loyal. Many manufacturers will provide full training to a customer's employees to ensure proper use of the product and to create high retraining or switching costs if the customer does not buy the follow-on products. For example, Airbus Industrie, the European airplane consortium, encountered difficulty in selling jet aircraft to flight and maintenance personnel who had been exclusively trained on U.S. equipment. To overcome this link to U.S. producers, Airbus invested in the training of hundreds of airline flight and maintenance personnel in how to operate and repair their airplanes.[4]
5. By influencing the specifications in the initial order, a producer can be presented as the only one with the performance capabilities for that application. One firm was able to influence the braking system specifications of two major truck manufacturers in such a way that there were not any available functional substitutes. The aftermarket repair manuals carried the same specification and referred to the sole supplier's brand name.

Without some of these links between initial and subsequent sales, producers should not price low or seek lower ROIs for the initial sales. If a supplier does not have enough current capacity or the funds to increase capacity to satisfy the follow-on business, it should not pursue the initial buy-in. Suppliers who have made this mistake have only primed the follow-on market for other suppliers.

Bidding or buying-in low for higher prices and better profits later is often limited to medium or large firms that have strong capital bases. A small one-product company or

[4]Ibid., p. 143.

a highly leveraged one often does not have the financial base or staying power to buy into long-term situations. In larger firms, with interdivisional buying, selling, and transfer pricing, a division may be asked to reduce its profits to allow another division to buy in with low prices. Top management must resolve this conflict by deciding where it wants to take the profit.

If there is a high probability of winning the follow-on contract with some strong links, the supplier must then determine what combination of bid prices on the initial purchase order and follow-on business will lead to an acceptable overall rate of return. Exhibit 9-1 shows how a series of purchase orders over time improves the supplier's ROI as additional profits accrue and original investment costs are amortized. The time intervals between orders and the quantities of subsequent buys are key pricing strategy considerations.

In complex follow-on business situations that require the supplier to think through the initial competitive bid prices, the probability of follow-on or subsequent business, and the ultimate profit payoff, it is helpful to sketch out the possibilities. A decision tree analysis with pricing alternatives, business volumes over time, and ROIs is a means to think through the alternative "what ifs." A decision tree analysis also helps to model competitive situation and potential profitability levels.[5,6] Exhibit 9-2 shows three possible bid prices considered by a supplier and the probability of profit payoff from different levels of follow-on business. As you can see, it probably makes sense to consider the $510 unit price since the probability of a large follow-on business is attractive. The required investment and additional operating cost can also be added to a decision tree framework to analyze more accurately a competitive bidding cost situation with successive orders, volumes, and resulting profits.

EXHIBIT 9-1

BIDDING FOR FOLLOW-ON BUSINESS

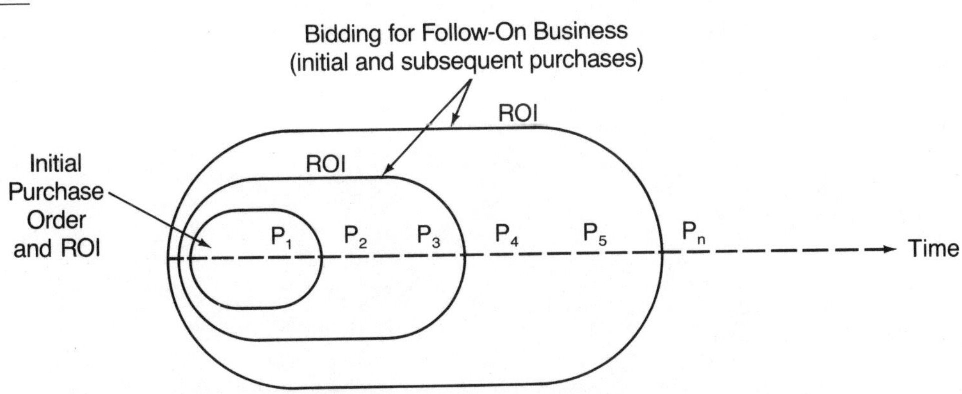

[5]John F. Magee, "Decision Trees for Decision Making," *Harvard Business Review*, July–August 1964, pp. 126–38.
[6]Jacob W. Ulvia and Rex Brown, "Decision Analysis Comes of Age," *Harvard Business Review*, September–October 1982, pp. 130–41.

EXHIBIT 9-2

EVALUATING INITIAL PRICE VERSUS FOLLOW-ON

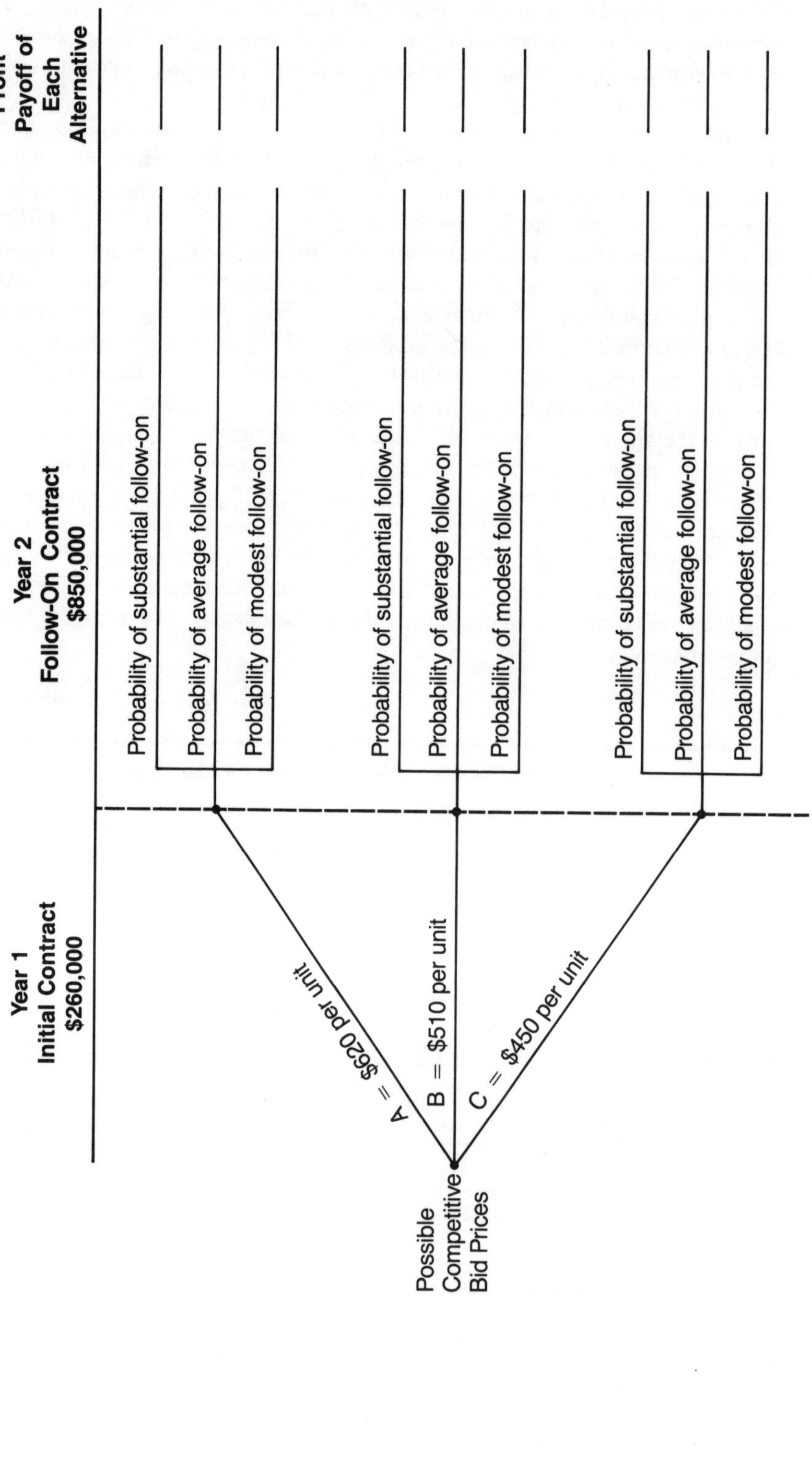

Set Proper Pricing Terms

Once a business strategy is chosen for the customer or account, the supplier must determine what pricing terms to put in the proposal. There are essentially four different ways bid or contract pricing terms can be structured: fixed price, fixed price with escalator, cost-plus, and PETS.

FIXED-PRICE BID. In this system, the producer and buyer agree on a firm price and delivery dates. When cost increases are predictable, the producer bears less risk with this type of quotation. Since costs invariably increase with time, fixed-price bids are typically for less than one year. In high inflationary periods and over time periods of more than one year, a fixed-price contract substantially increases the producer's risk. For example, in 1972, a manufacturer of electrical products significantly underestimated the rate of material inflation for switchgear assemblies to be delivered in 1974. Table 9.1 shows the anticipated and actual percentage increases in labor and material. The higher actual material costs resulted in losses for each unit shipped. Producers can guard against these types of losses by employing either escalator or cost-plus clauses.

FIXED-PRICE BID WITH ESCALATORS. When a supplier is not confident that major costs will remain stable during the contract period, a fixed-price bid with allowances for price escalation should be considered. The producer still assumes the risk of performance on all costs except those indexed according to escalator clauses. Escalator clauses result in a contingency pricing approach that usually moves more risk to the buyer. Producers should not quote fixed prices without escalators for any delivery dates more than a year ahead. Escalator clauses that typically cover increases in labor and material are usually tied to government statistical indexes for the appropriate industry.

COST-PLUS BID. Cost-plus contracts were commonly used by government agencies during the late 1950s and early 1960s to purchase sophisticated weapon systems from suppliers who did not have the necessary experience base to submit fixed cost quotations. Profit targets ranging from 10 to 15 percent were negotiated before bids were awarded. These cost-plus contracts were highly criticized—and for good reason. Under the terms of these contracts there was absolutely no incentive for the supplier to control costs. In fact,

TABLE 9.1 ***SWITCHGEAR ASSEMBLY COST-PRICE STRUCTURE***

Cost Component	*Price (%)*	*Anticipated Annual Increase*	*Actual Annual Increase*
Material	35%	6%	22%
Labor	55%	6%	7%
Profit	10%	–	–

in some cases where fees were negotiated as a percentage of costs, it was to the supplier's advantage to build up the cost base as high as possible. Cost-plus contracts were largely to blame for many of the huge overruns that occurred on major defense programs. A cliché commonly heard in defense marketing circles stated that "an elephant is really a mouse designed to produce the military specifications under a cost-plus contract."

PRICE IN EFFECT AT TIME OF SHIPMENT (PETS). PETS bids allow for posting price increases to all buyers before shipment. PETS are desired escalation clauses when the producer must buy from a volatile supply market. General Electric uses PETS bids to market steam turbine generators, but with the limitation that the increase will not exceed 10 percent if delivery is taken within one year, 20 percent if within two years, and 30 percent if within three years.[7] PETS are also suitable in foreign export-import situations where currency rates often fluctuate widely.

Progress payments may be a part of any of these pricing approaches. General Electric and Westinghouse bid on all power generation systems for utility customers with progress payment in the bid. The generation systems require up to two years to deliver from the awarding of the bid. With such long manufacturing cycles, the supplier should always receive monthly progress payments. Progress payments are especially important to the supplier because they help its cash flow. If an entire company is essentially a job shop, progress payments may be a key to the producer's financial stability. McDonnell Douglas lost a $3 billion order for 60 jets from Delta Airlines because of a disagreement on progress payments.[8] Delta actually preferred the DC-11 to the Boeing 757 jet, but McDonnell Douglas wanted progress payments as each phase moved through production.

Make the Proposal—A Total Business Plan

Understanding the customer's requirements, analyzing past bids, the potential for follow-on business, and pricing strategy are all combined in the preparation of a proposal. The development of a proposal is essentially the writing of a total business and marketing plan. Proposal and bid preparation is a costly activity. In the high-technology aerospace industry, a component supplier estimates it costs more than $100,000 to prepare and submit one proposal. Some companies maintain a substantial budget item called "new business development" that is primarily a pool of money to support proposal writing. In some situations, the customer will fund proposal submission by three to five potential suppliers before selecting one or two for the business. Bid preparation funds should be prudently allocated. Bid preparation or proposal expenses should be closely controlled and allocated only after a "to bid" situation is decided on by senior management. Otherwise, a lot of money will likely be wasted on proposal writing where there is little chance for success.

Bid and proposal preparation is a multifunctional effort. But if the effort is dominated by engineers, it may be doomed to failure. Good marketing people know what the customer needs or requires. If this concept is kept clearly in mind, the industrial marketer should never lose an argument to the engineer on what the customer needs. A careful

[7]R. G. M. Sultan, *Pricing in the Electrical Oligopoly* (Cambridge, Mass.: Harvard University Press, 1974).
[8]"The Big Deal McDonnell Douglas Turned Down," *Business Week,* December 1, 1980, pp. 81–82.

review must also be made of the supplier's technical and manufacturing capabilities and the customer's requirements. Accurate and successful proposal preparation requires a close working relationship between sales, marketing, engineering, accounting, and estimating personnel. On large projects or for large customers, it is common to have project teams submitting sections of the proposal from each functional area. If such teams are led by marketing, they will produce proposals that show closer understanding of a customer's needs and more accurate cost estimates of the requirements.

In the development of the proposal, which is also a marketing plan, it is important to anticipate the likely competitive responses. It is common to see five or six firms bidding on a large contract worth millions of dollars. Probably two or three are serious contenders for the contract. One should ask, "Why are these other firms submitting a bid?" The reasons are as many as there are firms. The contract may be related to the bidder's pet technology interest. It might be a bid from a desperate firm or a desire to fill in when business is slow. Someone's ego may be the driving force at another competitor. A firm should prepare a proposal and bid only when there is a good chance of winning against the known competition.

NEGOTIATING BID-CONTRACT SITUATIONS

Most competitive bidding situations can be categorized as serious bids or courtesy bids. Courtesy bids are situations in which a buyer would like another bid for his or her management and to enhance his or her negotiating position. Some friendly suppliers will submit extremely high courtesy bids with little supporting documentation to earn other business. It is important for the serious supplier to know whether courtesy bids have been submitted. In a serious bidding situation, a supplier should first consider whether there will be a ritualistic first-round submission with the real decision in a second round, or whether the first bid of each supplier will be the final or last bid. The possible bids of identified competitors that have been profiled in the analysis stage should help to anticipate their pricing strategies. The more differentiated the product or service, the more that seller has control over price. Also, the closer a supplier is to full capacity and large backlogs, the more likely its bids will be on the high side. One division president stated: "We price low only when we're hungry for the business." Bids of survival-crisis firms or marginal divisions are often "low ball" prices.

Large Customer Advantage

Most competitive bidding opportunities are characterized by one or two large customers and relatively few potential suppliers. Any one customer's business can represent 20 to 100 percent of the annual total market requirements. A typical supplier-buyer bidding business with few suppliers and few customers is shown in Table 9.2. This typical situation results in very large and concentrated purchasing power by the customers. Their purchasing power often results in customers' playing one supplier against the other in negotiating the final bid and terms. The larger customer will frequently use its size as an advantage or to leverage the relationship. For example, in June 1980, the Ford Motor

TABLE 9.2 **SUPPLIERS AND USERS FOR JET ENGINE TURBINES**

Number of Suppliers	*Number of Customers*
1. TRW (U.S.)	1. Pratt & Whitney
2. Howmet (France)	2. General Electric
3. Walbar (U.S.)	3. Rolls Royce

Company sent letters to 1,600 suppliers asking them to reduce their prices by 1.5 percent to ensure Ford as a customer. The letter stated: "Without this support and cooperation, the future market for our vehicles and in turn your products may be in jeopardy." Ford, in 1980, was having a profitless year; and 1.5 percent off its material cost would favorably affect its profit situation.

In heavy fixed-cost industries, capacity utilization may have to be running at 75 to 80 percent just to break even. This can be a bargaining chip for big customers in negotiating bids with suppliers. For example, when General Motors purchases commodity steel, it is aware that most steel companies need a minimum of 80 percent capacity utilization to break even. Such large customers can promise extra business, which steel producers may desperately need in times of falling demand, in return for holding the line on price increases. Smaller customers have considerably less or no effect on suppliers because of their smaller annual purchase requirements.

Large customers often also use the threat of future or more self-manufacture as a bargaining tool. When a large customer's purchases are a major portion of the supplier's business, the supplier frequently will concede to the large customer's desires. In situations where the supplier has a dedicated production line exclusively for the large customer, the supplier is even more dependent and vulnerable. The highly dependent contract industrial supplier is usually left stranded when the business from one customer is lost or reduced. These suppliers typically have a narrow product, little or no developed marketing capability, and little or no image among other potential users.

It is important for the supplier to avoid becoming dependent on a narrow customer base. To reduce this vulnerability, some OEM suppliers try not to have any one customer account for more than 7 to 10 percent of its business. One supplier of machine components, for example, has successfully sought out and bid on fragmented segments in which each customer is quite small. By doing this, the machine component supplier substantially broadened its customer base and per-unit profit margin.

Price Gambits

The large purchasing power of some customers allows them to exert considerable influence on the pricing terms. Large customers with prudent procurement departments will learn as much as possible from potential suppliers before selecting sources. In situations where customers also have an internal supply source, they will usually have more cost information than buyers that do not have an internal self-manufacturing source. The more a large customer knows about a supplier's costs, the more negotiating leverage it has. The more prudent procurement organizations often seek comparative supplier information on cost, quality, performance, and delivery dates. In an attempt to obtain the best supplier information, some buyers request very specific line item bidder quote information. For example,[9] IBM's centralized procurement personnel are responsible for purchasing office furniture for all sales offices. IBM requested bid quotes from each supplier in the following form:

1. Separate price quotes for five major furniture items
2. Separate price quotes for one and two years' annual purchasing requirements
3. Separate price quotes for each of three shipping zones

This type of supply request allows purchasing managers to examine and compare supplier prices precisely. It provides the buyer with information to portion business out to one or multiple suppliers for each item. When buyers seek such specific information, there is often great emphasis on price and less on product quality and delivery capabilities.

The lowest price does not necessarily always get the contract. If supplier A's bid was not as low as supplier B's bid, the higher bidder might successfully challenge the lower bidder's capability to perform and deliver—especially if the lower bidder is a much smaller company. Furthermore, if the buyer is convinced that one firm is buying in low for the follow-up at much higher prices, the higher-bid firm might be chosen. The slightest deviation in the bid from customer specifications and requirements can also swing the award to another supplier. In addition, buyers and production personnel want secure and stable supply sources, especially for items that are key to their product or service offering.

SUPPLY CONTRACT OBLIGATIONS

The pricing terms and supplier obligations in a competitive bid are usually formalized in a contract between supplier and customer. A basic question in most supply agreements is this: How will risks be assigned or shared by the two parties? The key areas of risk are inflationary cost increase factors and the risk of a buyer's earlier stated volume requirements fluctuating downward. If the stated volume amounts are firm, the buyer is obligated to purchase that volume at an agreed price, or pay penalties. However, large customers will often attempt to renegotiate in such a situation. Some supply contracts will have cancellation charges if cutbacks do occur. If the supplier had to incur considerable investment, there may be cancellation payments required of the buyer to cover all or part of the supplier's costs. This is an especially important clause if the supplier cannot sell the product elsewhere at the agreed-upon price.

Suppliers have firm legal obligations in contracts with customers. In the takeover battle

[9]Raymond R. Corey, *Procurement Management: Strategy, Organization and Decision Making* (Boston: CBI Publishing, 1978), pp. 212–30.

between Bendix, Martin Marietta, and Allied Corporation, Martin Marietta borrowed $900 million to keep its independence. In searching for ways to reduce its large debt, Martin Marietta was considering selling some of its divisions. Martin Marietta is in the aerospace, chemical, cement, and aluminum businesses. All these businesses have supply contracts with major customers. In light of the debt, the need for cash, and the existing supply contracts, Martin Marietta's options were greatly reduced. Their president and CEO stated: "We have long-term contracts with important customers. We just can't vacate the scene willy-nilly."[10]

Air Products and Chemicals received $50 million in a litigation settlement from Tenneco for failure to supply Air Products with contracted natural gas.[11] Air Products claimed it was forced to buy more expensive natural gas on the open market. The risk of delivery at agreed-upon prices nearly always falls on the supplier.[12,13]

Relief from cost increases is not usually granted if such contingencies were not anticipated and written into the contract. Rolls Royce, a major jet engine builder, got locked into export supply contracts that were written principally in dollars. Rolls Royce's costs were mainly incurred in British pounds. As the pound strengthened and the dollar fell, the company's expenses soared to nearly $66 million.[14] The currency fluctuation helped plunge the division operations into the red for the year.

Purchasing departments often prefer long-term contracts at relatively fixed prices for major items. Continued inflation, increased labor and maintenance costs, and foreign currency fluctuations create an even greater desire to have more stable supply sources and prices. Furthermore, in market situations where there are relatively few producers and relatively large buying organizations, bids and supply contracts may increase in use. The major municipal, state, and federal government markets will continue to buy on a bid-quote basis. The legally bound but prudent supplier must systematically decide whether it wants to participate in each particular situation. In all such situations, industrial suppliers should attempt to share more of the risk with buyers. They should proceed cautiously before committing themselves to an agreement. Thorough preparation and caution are the watchwords.

BIDDING GUIDELINES

All competitive bidding situations should be considered in terms of both potential risks and potential rewards. There are a number of guidelines or questions to ask before submitting a proposal or entering into a supply contract with a customer.

1. Knowledge of all the customer's requirements. The technical parameters are just the beginning of the customer's total business requirements.

[10] "Martin Marietta Looks for Ways to Reduce Its Large Debt, But Shuns a Fire Sale of Assets," *The Wall Street Journal*, January 12, 1983, p. 1.
[11] "Air Products Settles Tenneco Litigation," *The Wall Street Journal*, June 10, 1981, p. 32.
[12] K. S. Rosenn, "Protecting Contracts from Inflation," *Business Lawyer*, 1978, pp. 729–49.
[13] T. R. Hurst, "Drafting Contracts in an Inflationary Era," *University of Florida Law Review*, Summer 1976, pp. 879–903.
[14] *Business Week*, October 29, 1979, p. 65.

2. Our capabilities. Can we meet the customer requirements with existing capabilities? How difficult would it be to develop or acquire the additional capabilities? Are our firm's capabilities and past performance thoroughly known by all key people at the customer? Has any past poor record or problem been improved and made known to them?
3. Bid history. On what basis were past bids lost or won at the particular customer? Will these factors be the same or different in this situation?
4. Costs. Do we really know our costs to make this item or meet the requirements? Can we secure appropriate escalator clauses in the more volatile or unknown material and labor cost components? Do competitors have lower or more favorable cost structures?
5. Plant capacity. A supplier operating at 95 percent of capacity will not be eager to receive a bid that would add 20 percent more business. Conversely, a firm operating at 50 percent capacity would be eager to obtain the bid or long-term contract. The supplier's backlog also affects capacity utilization. A shrinking backlog may create a need to bid more aggressively.
6. Follow-up opportunities. Winning an initial contract or bid may yield much greater repeat orders. The concept of buying-in should be considered only if there are strong links to the follow-on business.
7. Quantity requested. The quantities the customer desires must be evaluated against plant capacity and production economics for various levels of orders.
8. Delivery requirements. Does the customer want periodic shipments or a "one-shot" shipment? The ability to meet customer delivery dates may determine whether or not to consider the business.
9. Competition. Who will be the likely or known competitors? How and what will they bid? Wherever competitive bid histories are known, they should be analyzed. Does one competitor have a strong inside position? What is the backlog of each likely competitor?
10. Special requirements. Are there specific qualification tests that only one supplier has equipment or ability to perform?
11. Wired bid. Is the bid wired to favor a specific supplier? Are the specifications written to fit only a favored source? Are there specifications directly from a supplier's product information? Are there short deadlines to favor an existing or favored supplier?
12. Customer information bid. Some customers request bids to help them decide whether to make or buy the product. Potential suppliers often help them by providing the comparative cost-price information needed. Sometimes the RFQ is written so that outside suppliers cannot perform as well as the customer's inside source.
13. Profit prospects. The contract or price should meet the supplier's rate of return objectives. If the initial price is a buy-in price, the secure repeat business prices should recoup the supplier's rate of return objectives over the time period. If the profit prospects are not attractive in either the short or the long term, the business should not be pursued.

SUMMARY

Central to good competitive bidding by suppliers is practice of the industrial marketing concept. First, thoroughly understand the potential customer's requirements before deciding to pursue or not pursue the business. An attractive profit in the short term or a protected longer-term buy-in must be coupled to the industrial marketing concept. The customer and profit criteria will help guard against commitments to technically challenging and high-risk business with low profit rewards. The decision to bid or not to bid is as important as or more important than the decision to bid on many situations. A high bid-win ratio goal should never override a desired profit goal. The prudent industrial supplier should never gear up its operation for a large customer until it thoroughly understands the customer's requirements and its own costs, and truly believes it can earn an attractive profit if the business is won.

10

Linking Sales to Marketing

Charles Wilson, vice president of sales for a large specialty steel company, was called into the president's office to discuss several major sales problems. Total industry prospects had declined, and the company's sales had dropped by 25 percent from the same period last year. The president started the discussion by saying: "I've just been going over our P&L projections, and we've got a real mess on our hands. With volume down as it is, your sales costs are way out of line. They've never been more than 8 percent of sales as long as I've been with the company, and they're now running closer to 12 percent. As I see it, you have to get rid of at least 25 salespeople and streamline your management structure to get costs back in line."

Charles was aware sales costs were a little high as a percentage of sales. He had added eight new salespeople last year in anticipation of increasing industry sales, and travel costs had moved up sharply with inflation. But even though industry sales had declined, Charles was reluctant to cut back; he knew the decline was temporary and believed the company should just ride it out. "I know our sales costs are a little high, but we have the best sales force in the industry. We have more sales experience and better customer relations than any of our competitors. It would be a mistake to get rid of anyone now when what we need more than anything are a lot of people who can get purchase orders."

The president listened while Charles made his arguments, but they didn't change his mind: "Charles, I have heard all this before, and I don't buy what you are saying. To avoid wasting any more time, I'm giving you a direct order to reduce the size and costs of your sales force by at least 25 percent. We have to weed out our marginal order takers and get rid of a lot of unnecessary management structure. You should also think about replacing some of our narrow-focused, product-oriented people with representatives who have a broader ability to evaluate, understand, and serve customer requirements effectively. Our long-term strategy is to focus on target markets with a broader and more complex range of products. A lot of your old-time product people simply can't do this job."

Charles left knowing it was impossible to change the president's mind. From Charles' point of view, the president, who had come up through the engineering side of the business, simply didn't understand what it took to sell effectively in today's market.

Who is actually more up to date?

What are the major requirements for successful selling in industrial markets?

What is the president's order designed to do? Where does he think the company is going?

In the industrial world, sales force performance has always been a very important contributor to marketing success. Other elements of the marketing mix—advertising, promotion, and merchandising—simply cannot have the same impact in industry as they do in consumer goods. There are very few situations in industry where the buying decision is made impulsively or clinched by some especially creative advertising or promotion appeal. Of course, advertising, promotion, and merchandising activities are important for communicating the company's image and product or service capability, and thus breaking the ground for the sales contact. But by themselves, these elements never close a sale and seldom even provide a competitive advantage, no matter how costly they are or how brilliantly conceived. Only the salesperson can carry out the lengthy transaction that characterizes industrial selling and finally gets the commitment to buy. Three forces are certain to make the role of the industrial salesperson even more important to marketing success:

1. Purchasing practices all over the world are becoming sharper and more sophisticated as more companies recognize the tremendous profit potential of building economic and value analysis into all major purchasing decisions.
2. The technical complexity and sophistication of products, systems, and applications are continuing to increase.
3. Competition from foreign producers will remain intense and even increase for many products.

The first two considerations will place a much greater premium on intelligent selling to help customers and users perceive their needs and to demonstrate the economic worth of the product in meeting these needs. The third consideration means that many companies will have to rely on a creative selling effort to overcome cost—and even technological—disadvantages. For these reasons, most industrial executives are quick to agree to the importance of having an outstanding selling force. As a general rule, industrial management supports this position by paying somewhat higher compensation to sales personnel than companies in the consumer products field. Despite their conviction and willingness to pay more for outstanding performance, however, only a few companies are fully satisfied with the quality and productivity of their selling organizations. Although executives in these companies voice their concerns in different ways, the concerns are all traceable to one root cause. Stated simply, the sales force in many industrial companies does not function according to the marketing concept, which holds that every business activity in the company should be responsive to market conditions and requirements in a way that generates maximum profits. More specifically, their industrial selling operations fall short of this objective in these critical ways:

1. They do not identify creative ways to establish a proprietary edge with customers or to take pressure off price as the key buying consideration.
2. They do not search for the new markets or applications necessary to achieve maximum growth and do not provide a flow of market intelligence to aid management in planning new product offerings.

3. They do not balance their efforts between long- and short-term selling needs to achieve marketing objectives.
4. They do not maintain the level of productivity necessary to keep abreast of constantly increasing costs of selling.

In short, the sales force in many industrial companies functions more as a collection of independent sales and distribution agents than as the integrated marketing arm it should be.

Why is this the case? Why, when its importance is generally recognized, is the sales force often relatively ineffective? We submit that the problem can be traced to failure to follow one or more of six principles that lead the sales force to function as a marketing arm. We'll discuss each of these principles in turn.

USE SIMPLE ECONOMIC ANALYSIS TO MAKE KEY SALES DECISIONS

Total selling costs–that is, those costs recorded in the typical general selling and administration account–are not only the largest chunk of marketing expense, but also in many cases one of the largest annual expenditures an industrial company incurs during the normal course of business. When one looks at a compensation scale, and makes reasonable allowances for travel and entertainment expenses, benefits, supervision, and other overhead, it is very easy to come up with a cost of $60,000 to $80,000 for each salesperson in the field. When this figure is multiplied by, say, 50 salespeople, the annual cost can quickly amount to several million dollars for the smaller sales organization; multiplied by a few hundred, the selling costs can total $10 and even $20 million for companies with large-scale organizations.

With these huge amounts at stake, all sales decisions must be made very carefully. Yet in company after company, sales management is permitted to make decisions that have a significant cost and profit impact without really thinking through the market and economic consequences. Here are several examples of the kinds of decisions that are frequently made without sufficient thought being given to the economic implications:

Whether and where to add a new salesperson or a new sales or branch office.

Whether to engage in a greater or lesser degree of sales specialization.

Whether to sell directly or through agents, dealers, or distributors.

Whether a price concession should be granted to get more volume.

Whether certain customer demands (quick delivery, small orders, and customization) should be met.

Whether certain sales calls are productive.

Whether certain accounts are most or least profitable.

These considerations and others like them clearly have major cost and profit implications. For example, adding people or sales branch offices without ensuring an economic

WHEN IS A SALES FORCE TOO LARGE?

In the late 1960s, Addressograph-Multigraph Corporation was a supplier of office equipment and charge card impressors. The company's sales organization of several hundred representatives was structured around more than 60 district sales offices throughout the United States. A routine economic analysis of the company's sales costs and productivity revealed several important factors.

Addressograph-Multigraph had at least 20 more district sales offices than its major competitors.

The average sales revenue generated by each salesperson was significantly lower than its competitors.

The total cost of the sales force as a percentage of sales was 2 to 3 percent higher than its competitors.

Over 200 salespeople did not appear to be generating sufficient revenue to cover the cost of maintaining them in the field.

When made aware of these facts, management replied that the sales force had always been a major strength of Addressograph-Multigraph and it would be criminal to think in terms of scaling it back. Shortly thereafter, the company encountered serious financial difficulty, and financial analysts who followed the company attributed many of its problems to higher selling and administrative costs.

payoff from incremental volume can easily lead to sales costs that are way out of line (see the box). Similarly, acceding to customer demands for unusual delivery schedules, small-order lots, or custom work without a clear fix on the economics can easily chew into the profit structure of the business. Deciding to grant some kind of price concession to pick up "plus business" without really evaluating the cost-revenue tradeoff can quickly lead to an untenable profit structure.

We are not suggesting that sales management decisions like these can be made by numbers alone. In today's fast-moving, competitive environment, none of these issues has one sure answer. Nor are we suggesting that sales executives be financial experts. However, all these considerations can be brought into much sharper focus through a few fundamental economic analyses that any controller's staff can make very easily. For example, Exhibit 10-1 shows simple economic analyses that were used in one company to determine the net contribution required to support the acceptance of an order and the relative profitability of accounts. Making these analyses helped management see the economic impact of accepting small orders and calling on marginal accounts. Once these facts became clear, management quickly decided to raise the minimum order level and to stop calling on unproductive accounts. Some volume loss occurred, but this was more than offset by the cost savings from dropping marginal accounts. More important, the move freed a lot of sales time that could then be focused on developing more profitable business.

EXHIBIT 10-1

ECONOMIC ANALYSES OF COMPANY X

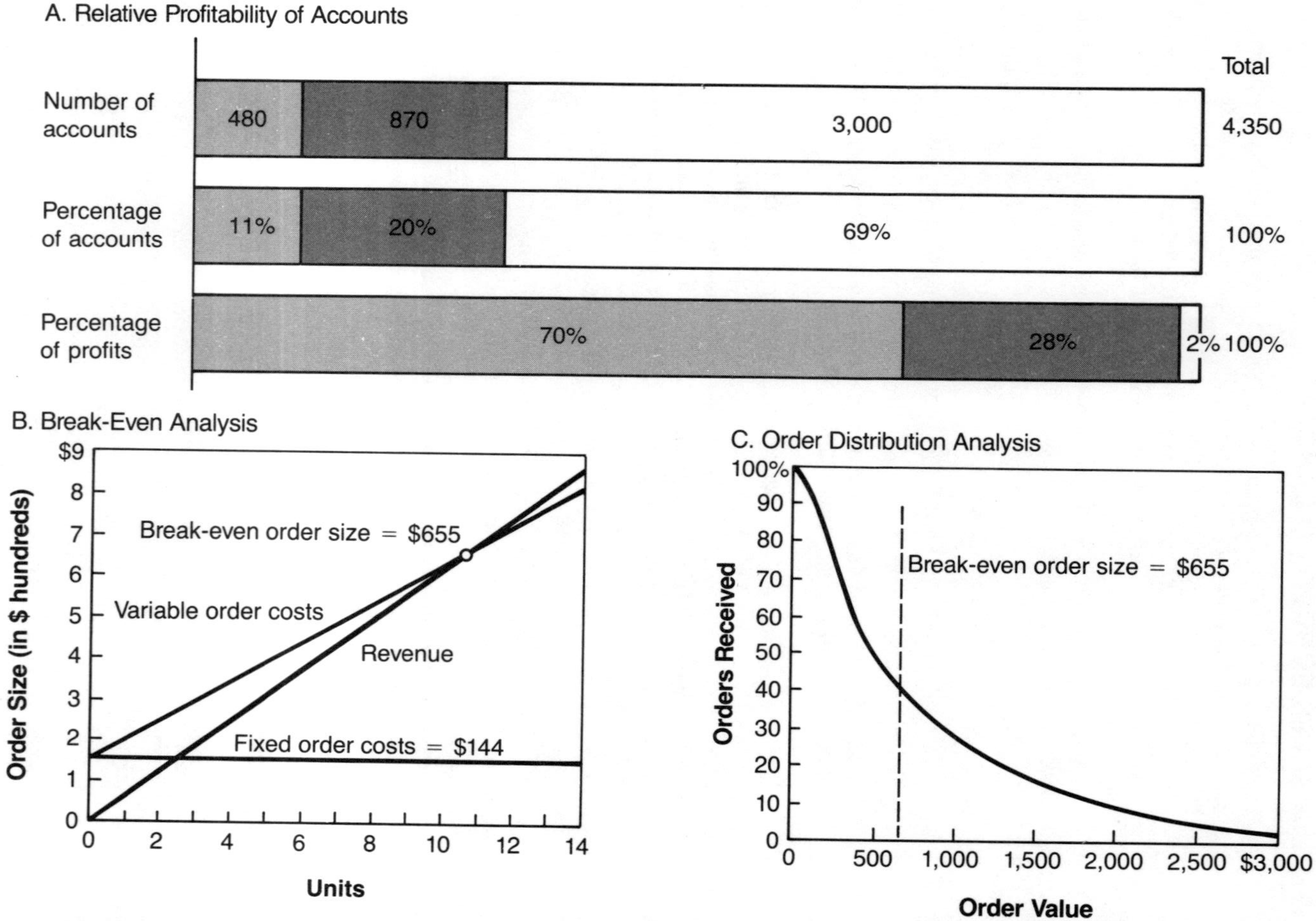

Source: B. Charles Ames, "Marketing Planning for Industrial Products," *Harvard Business Review*, September–October 1968.

Some sales managers say that although these calculations can of course be made, differences in the mix of sales from salesperson to salesperson or changes in the mix or margins over time render them useless as a measuring device. Others say they have too many products or too many accounts to even think about attempting to deal with them in terms of their individual profitability. The contention that the account list or product line is too long to permit analysis for relative profitability is easily refuted. If many products or accounts are involved, they can always be grouped according to their profitability and dealt with as classes of accounts or products instead of on an individual basis. The argument on differences or changes in mix or margins has some validity, since variation does add complications. But when one thinks of the amount of profit that can be dissipated if the economics are not clear, it makes no sense not to commit the time and effort required to work around the complications.

Still others argue that even though these kinds of economic analysis might be made, they really cannot be put to use. They maintain that most salespeople and many sales managers are not responsible enough to handle this information with discretion, and that they might unwittingly let it get into competitors' hands. This argument is nothing more than an excuse. If management does not want the salespeople to know actual cost and profit figures, it can easily have them coded in a way that gives a general picture of the margin structure on different items, yet preserves the confidentiality of the information. The salesperson still has a much better basis for concentrating on business that will generate the most profit dollars than if he or she is flying blind.

The key in making and using economic analyses is to recognize their limitations. They should be regarded neither as substitutes for managerial judgment nor as hard-and-fast rules that crank out answers. Rather, they are guidelines that provide sales management with a much better basis for making many fundamental decisions that affect the ability of the sales force to be productive, to compete effectively in the marketplace, and to serve as the marketing arm it should be. If sales management, in making its case for adding staff or seeking a "low ball" price to get a certain piece of business, is allowed to "fire from the hip" instead of relying on solid economic calculations, an insidious process is started that eventually undermines its image and effectiveness. When this kind of image is developed, it is virtually impossible for the sales staff, or any members of the sales organization, to make a contribution to the marketing effort.

DEFINE AND ARTICULATE THE STEPS NECESSARY FOR A SUCCESSFUL SELLING JOB

In today's industrial climate, the sales job is a great deal more complex than simply selling the product. Management expects the salespeople to build a proprietary position with key customers, to provide market feedback, and to bolster profits by enriching the sales mix.

Rarely, however, does management give salespeople any explicit instructions on how they should accomplish these objectives. Usually, salespeople are given a quota, along with a pep talk, and told to "get out there and sell." This is not very helpful to the typical salesperson, who is constantly faced with a choice of how to allocate time among various products, customers, users, or other contacts that could influence the sale. Nor does it help the person to plan the specific actions he or she should take when the priorities have been decided.

Many sales executives are likely to take comfort in the thought that their training programs are designed to tell salespeople all they need to know to do their jobs. But most programs focus almost entirely on fundamental selling approaches, such as how to tell the product story, combat customer objections, refute competitor claims, pique customer interest, and close the sale. This kind of training is useful, of course; every salesperson must know the basics before he or she can make an effective sales call. But such knowledge alone is not sufficient in most cases to help salespeople do an outstanding job. To be in a position to accomplish that, they must have guidelines to help them decide such things as these:

Which activities (identifying potential applications, telling the product story, generating or following up on bid inquiries, preparing proposals) are the key to selling success, and the standards of performance in each of these activities.

What selling strategy (emphasis on cost savings, product reliability, product performance features, ease of operation) to use with various customers and products to take the emphasis off price as the dominant buying consideration.

How to divide their time between servicing existing accounts and prospecting for new ones.

How much emphasis to place on new product introduction, and which applications represent the best targets.

One could argue that any salesperson worth his or her salt should be able to figure these things out. But a recent confidential survey on sales effectiveness shows that only about a third of the typical sales force has demonstrated the capability to do this, and two-thirds flounder badly without adequate management direction. Thus, we submit that any management failing to provide the kind of training and selling guidelines that give salespeople the answers to the kinds of questions we have raised cuts sharply into the competitive effectiveness and productivity of its sales force (see the box, page 211). Defining the salesperson's job is not as easy as it might seem; however, if the job is not defined, management may find that its people are wasting their time or—even worse—working at cross-purposes with the company's marketing objectives. To avoid this possibility, the job for any sales force—regardless of its size or the complexity of its product line—should be defined with sufficient specificity so that any representative has a guideline to point him or her in the right direction in any given situation. This is a crucial step in forging the link that ties the sales force directly into the marketing effort.

PROVIDE CAPABLE, FULL-TIME FIRST-LEVEL SUPERVISION

Most sales executives agree that strong first-line sales supervision is a key ingredient in building an outstanding selling organization. The reason for this is clear. The sales force is typically made up of a collection of people with widely diverse backgrounds, experience

HOW NOT TO USE A SALES STAFF: THREE CASES

As you can see, failing to provide specific direction to a sales force is analogous to a quarterback's giving mixed signals to his team.

Case 1: Management knew that selling a certain mix was essential to the company's profit structure, but the salespeople were not advised specifically about how much of each product they should sell to help optimize the mix. As a result, many salespeople had the frustrating experience of not being able to get reasonable delivery commitments on orders they had worked hard to get because manufacturing was locked into a production plan that did not have room for the products they had sold.

Case 2: Although management knew that opening new accounts was more profitable than servicing existing ones, no one had bothered to tell the salespeople how much of their time was to be spent on new account development. Since breaking new ground is always a more difficult task than staying in friendly territory, most of them spent very little time on this activity.

Case 3: Management decided (as many companies in many industries are doing today) that the salespeople should try to sell a total system in certain situations, rather than individual components. The idea was fine, but management made no effort to define the situations where systems selling was appropriate, or to provide training for this more complex selling job. Not surprisingly, many of the sales representatives never even tried to sell systems; and when management made its disappointment clear by suggesting that the salespeople lacked the basic intelligence to do the job, turnover increased sharply and morale took a nosedive.

levels, and perceptions, and often they are separated from headquarters by thousands of miles. The first-line supervisor is the only manager physically close enough to them to direct their day-to-day efforts, coach them in the company's sales approach for various products and markets, and help them resolve problems in light of the company's marketing objectives and local market conditions. But although most sales executives agree with the idea that providing strong first-level supervision in the field is essential, many have not taken steps to ensure that it exists in actual practice. All too frequently, the people they are relying on to provide first-level supervision simply do not or cannot perform as they should. Let's see why.

Conflicting Demands

In some cases, the performance of first-line supervisors falls short because their job is structured so that they have a supervisory title in name only. They are really supersalespeople or bureaucratic administrators, with the bulk of their effort focused on direct selling activities or paperwork. One company, for example, relied on its branch sales managers to handle the first-level supervisory role. Each manager was expected not only to watch over three or four salespeople, but to take on a sales territory of his or her own as well. The results were not at all what management expected. The branch managers spent the great bulk of their time in selling and developing their own territories, and thus provided little real supervision for their salespeople. Although their individual sales records were satisfactory, overall sales were below management's expectations. This should not have been surprising, for whenever salespeople must choose between doing the sales job that is second nature to them and carrying out the difficult tasks inherent in any managerial role, they tend to take the easiest path. Our experience shows that most people who have this combined sales-supervisory role quite naturally and honestly get so deeply involved in their own direct selling activities that they have little time for the coaching, training, and follow-up responsibilities that are the heart of the supervisor's job.

This dual-role approach to the first-line supervisory job may well be a practical necessity in outlying areas where a full-time supervisor cannot be economically justified. But in far too many cases the approach is followed throughout the sales organization. This is dead wrong. We are not suggesting that it is totally inappropriate for a sales manager to have any direct sales or account responsibility; we are saying that this responsibility must be strictly limited. Whenever a first-line supervisor has a direct sales responsibility that places major demands on his or her time, the odds are stacked against the organization having truly effective first-level supervision.

Inadequate Training

In other cases, first-line supervisors fail to perform well because they do not know what the supervisory role is or how it should be carried out. In fairness, this is frequently not their fault, for surprisingly few companies provide any kind of training program to help new supervisors learn how to carry out their responsibilities. Most first-line supervisors are in their first managerial position, which they have typically earned by doing a superior selling job. Shifting their sights from managing their own time to managing the time and coaching the selling efforts of others represents a quantum jump in responsibility few people can accomplish without help. Most need assistance in learning how to carry out the sales management process that represents the heart of their job. In particular, they need to be shown:

How to determine which people or sales problems deserve the most time and attention.

How to make territory and/or market analyses, and how to determine market potential.

How to help salespeople plan their time and selling activities so they can be most productive.

How to evaluate the performance of their salespeople and to identify training and development needs.

How to carry out the on-the-job training and coaching activities necessary to improve selling performance.

Unless most first-line supervisors are taught how to do these things, they will drift into a pattern of operation that keeps them busy—but not on the right things. As a result, they never really provide the quality of supervision they should. In some cases, former star salespeople who can never make the transition to manager, no matter how much training is provided, are allowed to stay in supervisory positions far too long. Management often finds it difficult to face up to the fact that this situation exists, or to take the necessary corrective action once it is recognized.

Discussions with a number of sales and marketing executives indicate that this situation is more common than one would think. The consequences, of course, go beyond the reduced effectiveness of the sales force. Eventually, the management career path becomes clogged with people who are going nowhere. Understandably, this frustrates outstanding younger salespeople who are looking for an early promotion and leads to a high turnover of people who should not be lost. This situation starts a vicious circle that results in mediocrity at the supervisory level and ineffective training and direction for the sales force.

Excessive Paperwork

A further problem that cuts into the effectiveness of first-level supervisors is the improper use of daily call reports. In many companies, the daily call report is sacred because it gives management a feeling that it knows what is going on. More likely, all management has is a massive paper flow that generates phony data. These are harsh words, but they are true. We know of company after company that looked to its call reporting system as a reliable means of control. In actual fact, however, the salespeople were simply going through the motions in "filling out their forms" and doing as they pleased in terms of the way they spent their time. Sales personnel for a large rubber company used to joke about the fact that they would meet at a local tavern late every Friday afternoon to fill out their call and trip reports. When anyone was stuck on what to put down to cover a block of time, others were quick to pass on ideas. The joke was that the ideas for fictitious calls or trips often became outlandish after a couple rounds of beer. It didn't really make any difference what the salespeople put on the reports, however, since no one in management followed up; in fact, most of the reports were not even read.

Clearly, some form of planning and control system is essential in every sales organization, but it should be designed around a weekly or monthly cycle to minimize the paperwork involved. And it should not be so form-oriented that it creates a burden for either the salesperson or the supervisor. Moreover, the supervisor must be taught to use this system as a tool for working with and providing active direction for salespeople. Whatever form this system takes, management must not allow it to degenerate into a paper-shuffling exercise that encourages the supervisor to function as a desk-top administrator.

Four ingredients are required to ensure strong first-level supervision:

1. The sales organization must be structured so that a capable, full-time supervisor exists for every eight to twelve salespeople. There may be exceptions to this ratio, but it is a good general rule to follow. Going much beyond twelve people starts to stretch the span of control; moving below eight pushes the supervisory costs out of line and, more important, creates a make-work situation for the supervisor.

2. Provision must be made to ensure that each supervisor has the proper training and tools to do the job.
3. Each supervisor should spend the bulk (75 percent or more) of his or her time in face-to-face work with salespeople to provide the on-the-job coaching and direction that is needed.
4. Senior sales management must be very tough-minded in evaluating supervisory performance and in weeding out supervisors who perform below expectations or who lack the capability to take on additional management responsibility.

USE THE COMPENSATION PLAN AS A MANAGEMENT TOOL

No matter how strong or effective sales supervision is, all salespeople are on their own most of the time in deciding which accounts to call on, which products or applications to emphasize, or even whether or not to make another call. So it is essential to design and administer the sales compensation plan to motivate them to concentrate on activities that will contribute most to the achievement of marketing objectives. This sounds so fundamental the reader may wonder why it is included in this discussion. Obviously, no one can expect the sales force to function as a marketing arm unless the compensation system is designed and administered in a way that motivates people toward the accomplishment of marketing objectives. Nevertheless, in a great many cases the system is actually in conflict with marketing objectives.

In some cases, the levels of compensation are simply too low to attract and retain the caliber of people and to build the kind of sales force essential for marketing success. Exhibit 10-2, which shows the compensation opportunities in two sales organizations that competed head to head in the marketplace, brings this point sharply into focus. Comparison of the salary levels for various sales positions and the average time required to reach these positions shows clearly that company B offers a much more attractive career opportunity. Little wonder that company A's force was regarded as substantially inferior by many major customers. And since these major customers accounted for the bulk of the business, it is clear that company A had very little chance of doing the job it should in the marketplace.

As a matter of fact, many incentive arrangements actually work at cross-purposes to what management is trying to do. For example, many companies still pay salespeople strictly on the basis of volume, even though selling a certain product mix, or opening new accounts, or developing certain end-use markets is an equally or even more important objective in terms of ultimate success in the marketplace. Just think of this arrangement for a moment. Who in his or her right mind would spend time on longer-term sales development activities when the payoff is for orders written today? Some commission arrangements encourage salespeople to "skim the cream" from the market by concentrating on quick volume from smaller accounts, when the emphasis should be on developing the potential in larger accounts. Several salespeople from one company that sold powered hand tools freely admitted they set a daily volume quota for themselves that would yield

EXHIBIT 10-2 ***AVERAGE COMPENSATION LEVELS OF TWO COMPETING SALES ORGANIZATIONS***

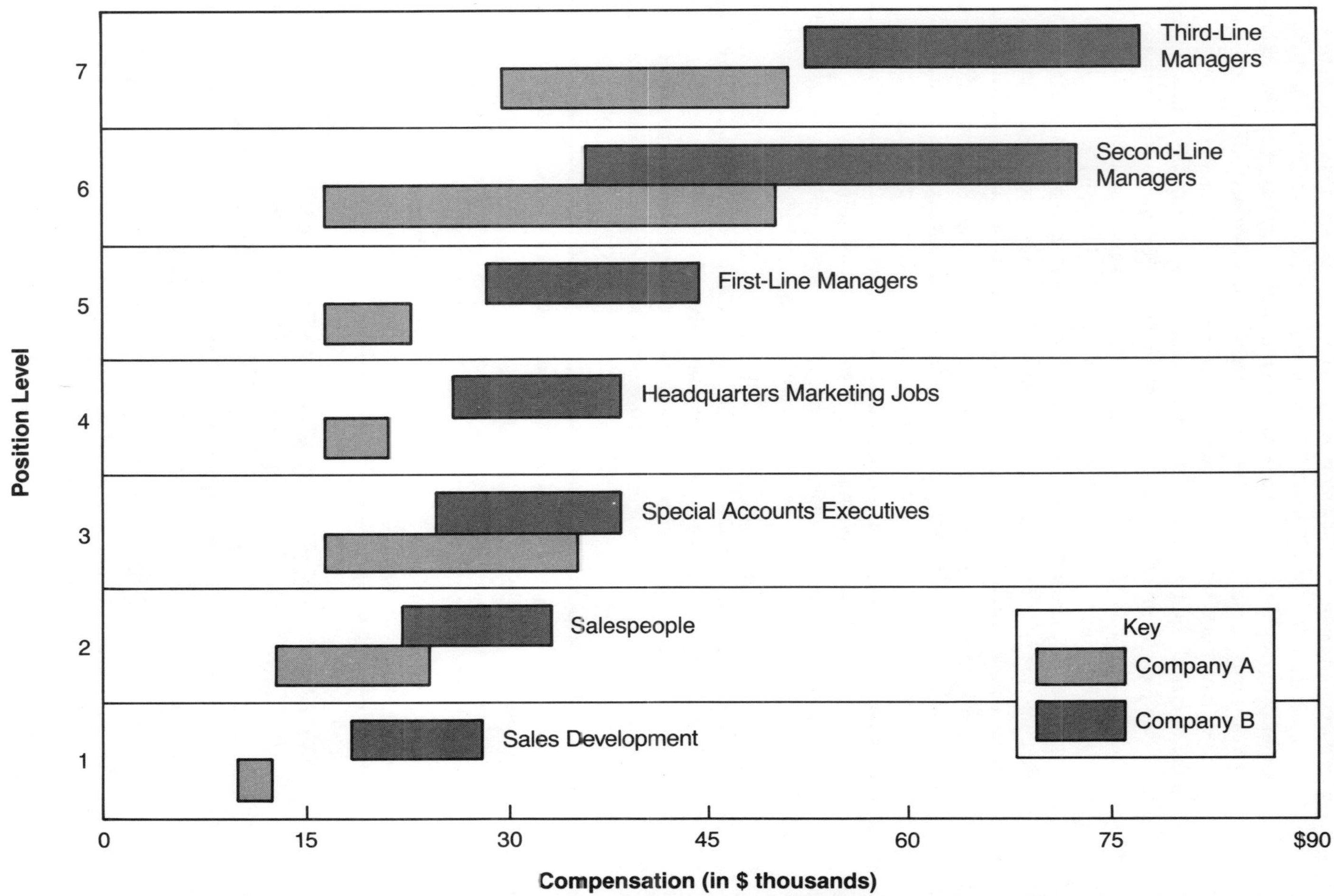

Source: B. Charles Ames, "Marketing Planning for Industrial Marketing," *Harvard Business Review,* September–October 1968.

enough commission to meet their needs. They frequently bypassed high-potential accounts that required development in preference to small, "sure thing" orders.

Other compensation systems are designed in such a way that they reward seniority rather than performance. This arrangement has a double-barreled effect; senior people tend to relax their efforts, and young, aggressive people are frustrated. One company that sold in the electrical equipment market was a classic example of this situation. Incentive payments were made out of a group bonus pot, and each person's award was based on a percentage of his or her salary. Since no adjustment was made to reflect individual performance and since senior people tended to have higher salaries, many hard-working younger people became discouraged and left. Equally important, when management looked into the situation, it found that many of the senior salespeople were relying on the younger people to build up the pot and thus were not pulling their own weight.

It is hard to see how any company could allow situations like these to develop, but they are all too common. Generally, one of the following reasons is at the heart of the problem. In many cases, sales executives are so concerned with the idea of keeping their compensation plan simple they fail to take into account key variables that affect performance. It is not at all uncommon to hear executives say something like this: "We know that our sales compensation plan is not right, but it is simple, and we don't have any difficulty getting the salespeople to understand and believe it." This holdover attitude that the sales force is a collection of not-too-intelligent drummers is not justifiable in this day and age. The typical industrial salesperson in today's complex technological environment has a college degree or the equivalent, and many have advanced degrees. Certainly, people of this caliber can cope with a compensation system that involves several variables. In still other cases, executives feel that once a system is in place, it should not be changed because the staff will become confused or suspicious. Of course, making any midstream changes that would be unfair to the salespeople should be avoided at all costs. But the fact is that marketing objectives do change frequently, and unless the compensation system is adjusted to reflect these changes, it is certain to drift out of phase with the company's goals.

As we have indicated, the paramount need is to tailor the compensation system to meet the particular requirements of the situation at a given point in time. There is no way to prescribe a compensation plan that is right for everyone. However, every compensation system should be designed and administered to:

Ensure a balanced selling job by paying off for new account openings, new applications, new product introductions, and other sales development activities essential to strengthen the company's short- and long-term market position.

Provide an attractive entry level for new people so there is adequate raw material to build the kind of organization necessary to achieve marketing objectives.

Provide an especially attractive earnings opportunity for career salespeople so there is a cadre of highly skilled, trained, and motivated people to serve as the cutting edge of the marketing effort.

Draw a sharp distinction in the rewards for average and outstanding salespeople, and penalize below-average performers severely.

The successful compensation plan is one designed and administered to help management achieve these four objectives. If these objectives are not accomplished, the plan is of little value, no matter how complex or sophisticated it might be.

STRIVE FOR A SHARP END-USER FOCUS

Industrial products are typically sold to a number of user groups, each of which has particular application requirements. This diversity means that the requirements of each market or user segment must be understood and dealt with individually to ensure a successful sales and marketing effort. All-purpose products or buckshot approaches to the marketplace simply will not work in a world of increasing specialization. Industrial companies do not have access to market information sources like Nielsen, SAMI, and others that are available to guide product and market planning efforts in consumer goods. And it is not practical for most industrial companies to structure market tests as consumer goods companies do to evaluate the needs, likes, and dislikes of different user groups. Industrial management must gear its salespeople to provide this kind of information or do without.

Achieving this end-user understanding is, in many respects, the most important activity the industrial salesperson performs. The intelligence he or she develops about the end user's needs, business patterns, economics, and so on, are the foundation of future product and market plans. To carry out this activity, the sales force must be set up and trained to provide organized feedback on such questions as these:

How does the product fit into the end user's operation, fill a need, and compare with competitive offerings?

What features of the product are really important in the end user's mind?

What current or potential developments in the end user's business could change the product's cost or design requirements?

What changes in the end user's operation or the competitive environment could affect the customer's business, and how could these changes, in turn, affect selling requirements or demand for the product?

Management must do more than simply insist that the salespeople provide end-user feedback information; it must take three important actions.

First, organize the sales force to give each person a chance to achieve an understanding of what is going on at the end-user level. Typically, some degree of specialization by market or application is required so the person has a chance to learn about specific end uses in depth. Just how much specialization is required boils down to an economic tradeoff between the added costs of specialization and the payoff anticipated. Achieving the appropriate degree of specialization may require restructuring the entire force around end-use markets or applications. Frequently, however, the economics prohibit this kind of a move. In these situations, a selected group of salespeople may be assigned as full- or part-time specialists to cover the most important user and application segments.

Second, install a formal system for distilling and interpreting the information received from salespeople so it can make intelligent judgments. Time after time we have heard salespeople say: "I send the market information in to headquarters, but nobody ever listens to me or believes what I say." This does not have to happen very often or very long before the person concludes, "Why bother?" Companies that do, in fact, regard and use the sales force as their eyes and ears in the marketplace have designed their planning process so that the collection and distillation of field sales intelligence is an important part of it. This not only ensures that plans are developed in the light of real-life market conditions, but also has the positive effect of showing the salespeople just how important their feedback is. With this encouragement, their natural inclination will be to try to do an even better job of sharpening their end-user focus.

Third, ensure that the company's value system reflects the importance management places on a clear perspective on end-user needs. This may be manifested in a compensation structure that pays a premium for developing business in certain end-user groups or for certain applications. Then again, it may simply show up in the way management compliments those who do a good job—or, more important, chastises those who do not. How it is done is an individual matter, and no one approach is necessarily better than another. Whatever the approach, however, management must support its point of view with actions as well as words, or the salespeople will never be convinced that they should make any extra effort to understand what is really going on at the end-user level.

CARVE OUT A STRONG MARKETING ROLE FOR SALES MANAGEMENT

The top sales management of any industrial company—that is, the national sales chief and subordinates who typically have responsibility for sales performance in the largest geographic divisions—have an important role in the marketing-planning process. Their participation is essential to ensure that the company's product and market plans reflect customers' changing needs. It is also essential to gain the wholehearted commitment of sales management to the successful execution of the company's product-market plan. If the salespeople are enthusiastic about the plan and genuinely believe they can sell the volume and mix that is expected, they will do a good job. If they feel the expectations are unrealistic, or that unfair sales goals have been imposed on them, the plan will not be successful, no matter how brilliant it may be. It is not unusual for salespeople and field supervisors to charge: "Our sales quotas have nothing to do with rhyme, reason, or the marketplace. They are just 10 to 15 percent higher than last year." With this feeling, how can they be expected to do all the hard work that is necessary to achieve demanding sales targets?

Considering the importance of sales performance to the success of product-market plans, it is only logical to give top sales managers a voice in their development. What they should be doing is this:

Closing the feedback loop from the field by distilling and interpreting information on local market conditions and competitor moves.

TURNING A BAD SITUATION AROUND

Top executives of a large company serving the building products field were concerned over a general deterioration in the company's marketing effectiveness. Share position in traditional markets was slipping badly, and important new markets were emerging in which the company had no position at all. The company's product edge had been lost, and new products were not coming along as they should. Finally, sales costs were increasing steadily while productivity (average sales per salesperson) was trending downward. In short, the current marketing situation was bad, and the outlook worse.

In recognition of the gravity of the situation, the marketing vice president called in his product managers and key sales managers for an emergency planning session. Including sales management in the planning session was more of an afterthought than anything else, since planning had traditionally been a headquarters marketing function, while sales had responsibility for execution. To the marketing executive's surprise, the most imaginative and effective ideas came from the sales managers. They recommended product modifications that could be made quickly, well before new products could become available to meet important needs in emerging markets. In addition, they suggested dropping a collection of low-volume products so that the sales force could be cut back, territories enlarged, and overall productivity increased. And they proposed a volume discount plan that would provide the basis for recapturing business which had been lost with large customers while still preserving the integrity of the company's pricing structure. The marketing vice president and the product managers were so impressed with the contributions made by the sales managers that they made it a regular practice to include them in planning sessions from that point on.

Participating in discussions with other functional managers about various strategic options for building the business.

Helping to select the most promising options, and considering the commitments and programs necessary for each alternative.

Agreeing on realistic volume and share of market targets under various options, and helping to decide which options are most attractive.

By having its top sales executives function in this way, a company can ensure that the sales force does in fact serve as a marketing arm, instead of as an independent sales and distribution system. The box above gives a good example.

SUMMARY

Clearly, a host of things needs to be done to build an outstanding sales organization. Here, we have emphasized six principles that cause the sales force to function as a strong marketing arm.

Basing sales decisions on economic analysis

is necessary to ensure that sales productivity keeps pace with increasing selling costs. Defining essential selling activities gives the salesperson the platform of understanding he or she needs to view the job as more than simply selling the product at any price. Providing appropriate supervision and compensation are the mechanisms for ensuring the sales capability and focus necessary to accomplish marketing objectives, and for adjusting that focus as priorities change. Linking the planning and execution arms of the marketing department and ensuring that a firsthand understanding of market needs and opportunities is factored into product-market planning make it possible to achieve overall company objectives.

None of these principles is difficult, but in many cases implementation requires overcoming traditional ideas and methods, reeducation of managers and salespeople, and possibly even personnel changes. And it always requires a great deal of management thought and attention. However, all this effort is clearly worthwhile, for failure to manage the sales force according to these principles can cost any company a fortune in excessive selling costs and lost market opportunities. Many successful industrial companies have taken a hard look at their selling effort and made the changes necessary to build these six principles into their sales operation. In doing so, they converted a volume-conscious sales force into a team that followed a cost- and profit-conscious approach to developing the company's sales position in every present and potential market. This, in turn, has given these companies clout in the marketplace that has significantly strengthened their competitive position and ultimately accelerated profit growth.

11

Marketing with Distributor Partners

John Rogers was the newest and youngest district sales manager for one of the country's largest standard and special purpose fastener companies. He had joined the company four years earlier as a distributor sales representative on the West Coast. Because he had done an exceptional job of helping his distributor accounts to build their business, he was promoted to a district manager job much earlier in his career than most of his counterparts.

After spending a few weeks evaluating his district's sales and distributor operations, he prepared a report to his boss, one of four regional sales managers, and sent a copy to the manager of distributor development at the headquarters office. The thrust of his report featured three points:

1. There are too many weak or poor-performing distributors in this district. Many of them have been with us for years, and the principals are good friends with many of our senior managers. Nevertheless, we need to cut back on the number of distributors we have and make sure those that remain have both the financial strength and the ambition to do the job we want.
2. Our policy of selling only through distribution is killing us with our major accounts. We are losing a lot of business to our competitors, who are willing to sell direct at a price much closer to our distributors' cost. These are big-volume accounts, and they simply do not want to pay a price that includes a distributor profit.
3. We need to set up some arrangement that enables our most aggressive distributors to earn price breaks on large-volume orders. It doesn't make sense for a distributor that buys in truckload quantities to pay the same price for a product as distributors that buy in broken lot quantities to fill particular orders. The smart distributors know this and won't work with us unless we come up with some kind of volume break program that makes sense.

The regional manager found the memo very disturbing. He had worked with the distributors in that district for nearly 30 years. He knew some of them were not as aggressive as they should be, but they were loyal to the company and they had made a real contribution during the company's initial years. He was even more disturbed about the idea of selling direct. The company's policy had always been to sell exclusively through distribution. He couldn't imagine trying to explain a shift in this policy to the distributors. He thought, however, that the last point had some merit. He and other senior sales managers had talked many times about the advisability of developing a pricing structure that allowed a better price for large quantity orders, but again they were concerned about offending some of the smaller old-time distributors that were not large enough to take advantage of quantity offerings.

As he picked up the telephone to talk to John about the memo, the manager couldn't help but remember that he had been opposed to appointing anyone to a district manager's job with such limited experience. He had found it was much easier to work with people who had been around for awhile and better understood the company's business.

Is the problem really the "new broom" syndrome?

What positive results may come from taking the proposal seriously, even though the proposal is ultimately rejected?

What are some obvious advantages of using distributors?

What are some alternative ways to reward old distributors' loyalty?

A significant and growing[1] percentage of the GNP every year is marketed through independent distributors or dealers. Industrial giants, including 3M, Caterpillar, Pfizer, and Mead Paper, market a major portion of their yearly sales volume through this channel. To counter competition from Japanese photocopy machine manufacturers, both IBM and Xerox named independent distributors to market lower-priced copiers and typewriters.[2] The distributor selling any industrial product, whether it is a machine, a pharmaceutical, a chemical, or a repair part, is a major avenue through which large, medium-size, and smaller producers serve key markets. The reasons are clear. The cost to the producer of making direct calls frequently becomes prohibitive in relation to the price of the product the customers buy. Furthermore, if customers reorder or repair the item, they often want rapid delivery, which is usually best provided by a local distributor or dealer that buys and maintains a local stock of products to sell to customers.

In the aftermarket or MRO market, the industrial distributor is often a vital link between producer and user. When a bearing or a hydraulic cylinder needs to be repaired, the user usually wants the product in a hurry. Availability and rapid service are critical and are usually best provided by a local distributor with the appropriate inventory (see the box). For more technically complex customer needs, the industrial distributor will be

WHY CATERPILLAR USES DISTRIBUTORS

Due to the importance of rapid repair, parts delivery, and field services in the construction equipment industry, Caterpillar believes local distributors can best serve key customers. Caterpillar is not just selling machinery; it sees itself as marketing equipment and a parts-service package. The local distributor provides the basis for achieving maximum uptime or minimum downtime for very expensive machines. When a $200,000 machine is down because of a $50 part, every hour represents a significant loss of money to the user. To minimize downtime and the resulting financial loss to customers, local Caterpillar distributors carry parts for all Caterpillar equipment—including parts for equipment Caterpillar hasn't manufactured for the last 30 years.

When a Caterpillar road grader was an integral part of a road resurfacing crew in the Arizona desert, the breakdown of the grader idled four other pieces of road building equipment, seven asphalt trucks, and twenty workers. The local Caterpillar dealer sent a radio dispatched repair unit to the field with the appropriate parts for that model road grader. The 2.5 hour downtime could have been days had there not been a local distributor with the right parts in its inventory ready to provide prompt service.

[1] "36th Annual Survey of Distributor Operations," *Industrial Distribution,* July 1982, p. 37.
[2] "IBM Expands Outside Its Sales Channels, Names Concerns to Distribute Two Products," *The Wall Street Journal,* October 7, 1981, p. 2.

called to help solve specific problems or to install an item. Technical service, or "engineering in the field," is vital to repeat purchases for many industrial products. These service levels are sometimes quite intangible in the short term, but they often pay big long-term dividends. Exhibit 11-1 shows the important intermediate role between producers and users played by industrial distributors. Marketing through a distributor can save the user time and money in the item's purchase price. Industrial distributors can reduce the producer's selling cost and thereby reduce the selling price of the product to users. So paying the distributor a profit is not the same as paying a "double profit." If the functions performed by the distributor are shifted, they must be performed and paid for by the producer or the user. When distributors perform these functions effectively and customers benefit, the distributors are entitled to a profit for their efforts.

EXHIBIT 11-1

LINKING PRODUCERS TO USERS

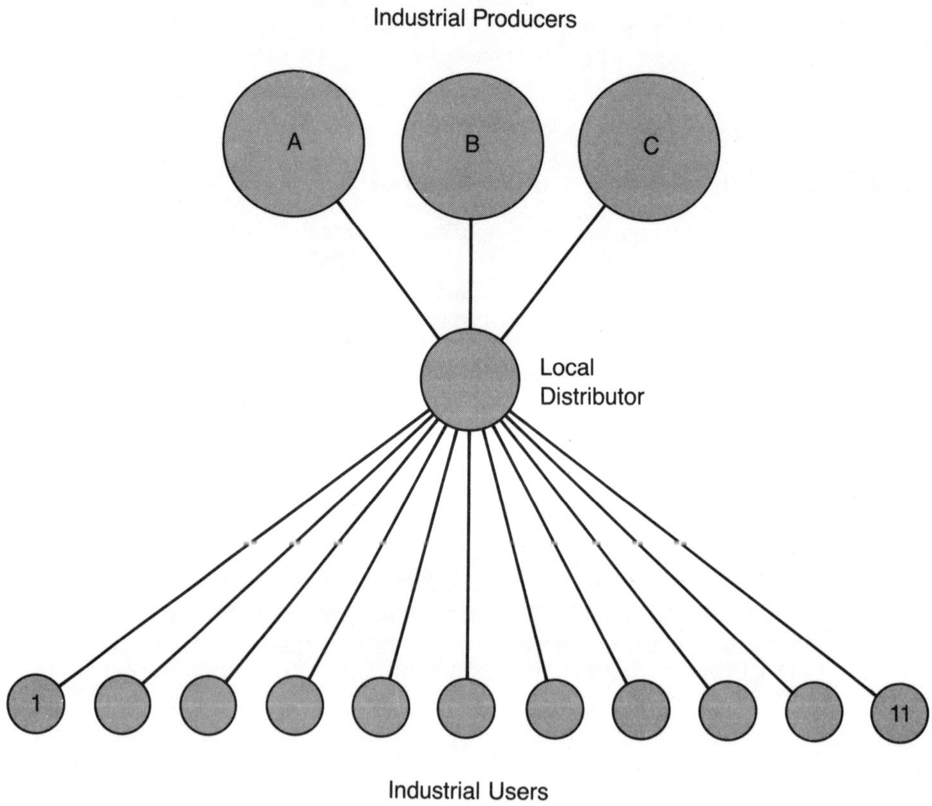

PRODUCER-DISTRIBUTOR RELATIONSHIPS

Most industrial producers use distributors to achieve some of their sales and marketing objectives. But the marketing of products through distributors is frequently badly done, and the results are often poor for both producers and distributors. Far too many industrial firms see the distributor as merely an intermediary for pushing products through and are continually disappointed with this means of serving customers. The following statement by a marketing manager with a major chemical company captures the essence of this all too common problem:

> Since I've taken over this job, I've experienced a lot of difficulty in putting together an acceptable distribution system. Traditionally, our products have been sold direct to end users. This worked well when all of our customers were large volume purchasers. Within the last ten years, there's been a dramatic increase in the number of small accounts using the product, causing our firm to alter its strategy and sell through distributors. Sure, the prospects of added sales are fantastic, but listen to some of the problems we face: The discount system is falling apart because distributors are "giving away" portions of their discounts in the form of lower prices to gain business. Unfortunately, some distributors are even being forced into bankruptcy; our distributors on the West Coast are not pushing the products; in the Cleveland area, distributors are not utilizing our co-op funds properly; although we have five distributors in Chicago, their sales are far below a market potential prediction; perhaps more distributors are needed there; and our distributor in northern New Jersey won't tell us who he's selling our products to. Top management of our division feels that these difficulties can be eliminated through a return to aggressive direct sales. I'm not so sure we can make any money that way with these smaller accounts.[3]

Many industrial producers treat their distributors as stepchildren and fail to get the cooperation they need to capitalize on the distributors' sales and profit potential when large amounts of business are at stake. The same producers often use bullying or brinksmanship tactics to achieve their goals without regard for the distributor's needs. The result is a "relationship" that is far from a partnership. Other producers go to the other extreme and become totally dependent on what distributors do or don't do in the marketplace. This inevitably results in little or no knowledge of end-use customers and their changing requirements, and frequently places the producer at a serious competitive disadvantage.

Many distributor networks have been put together on a random basis that results in poor or no coverage in some markets and overlapping coverage in others. In both situations there are nearly always too many marginal distributors. The comment of a progressive cutting tool distributor in southern California shows the problems that can result from this kind of approach:

[3]James A. Narus, "The development of a marketing channel selection process model and its demonstration in an industrial chemicals business and in an electronic components business," unpublished doctoral dissertation, Syracuse University, 1981.

> They signed up anybody and anywhere in Los Angeles for so long that we all felt they were not really serious about distributors. I get slow inventory turns from their line and if the large margin wasn't there, I'd drop them tomorrow.

One of the largest U.S. industrial corporations surveyed its marketing and sales executives to identify the most common problems encountered with their distributors. The survey was completed by 188 marketing and sales personnel in the firm's 24 operating divisions. The 14 most frequently reported problems with distributors are shown in Table 11.1. A key reason for all these problems is that the independent distributor is generally a small entrepreneur. The independent industrial distributor will work *with* a producer and follow its lead if properly coached. However, the distributor will never work *for* the producer in a subordinate relationship. The industrial distributor is not typically an "organization person." In fact, the personality and independence of the distributor is often in direct contrast to the producer's tendency to be more bureaucratic.

It is useful to examine the question of the distributor's independence more carefully, since it is such an important factor in the producer-distributor relationship. Although producers and distributors would seem to have the same objectives in terms of achieving sales and market share, their priorities are often different and even incompatible. To start with, the distributor is typically dealing with its own money and incurs all the risk, whereas the producer has stockholders, so the risk is syndicated. The cost-profit structures of producers and distributors are typically quite different. The producer generally has a relatively high capital and fixed-cost base and a longer-term business horizon. It is interested in building volume, even at lower margins, to gain profit leverage after covering its fixed costs. The distributor's operation, however, is totally different. The distributor operates a buy-sell business with low fixed capital cost and is interested in maximizing profit on each dollar of sales over as short a time period as possible. These economic

TABLE 11.1

PROBLEMS WITH DISTRIBUTORS

1. Want all customers to come to them.
2. Don't provide us with information about who and where "their" customers are.
3. Are not good at problem solving—assistance with customers and our products.
4. Don't effectively use our factory personnel or territory managers.
5. Don't emphasize our lines enough.
6. Don't follow our suggested pricing.
7. Primarily sell on price, not the product's value.
8. Don't carry appropriate inventory levels to serve customers rapidly.
9. Don't stress our brand name.
10. Don't utilize promotional materials.
11. Have no succession plans.
12. Are very independent business people.
13. Can't or won't meet our territory goals.
14. Have objectives different from ours.

differences help explain the different business orientation and value system that make the whole concept of working with distributor partners a lot easier to talk about than accomplish.

The successful distributor can afford to be independent. He or she can probably secure a competitive line if he or she is threatened or sees the possibility of a better relationship with another producer. But their independence notwithstanding, distributor activities must be managed like any other marketing function. To develop, improve, and continually refine an effective distributor network always involves hard and uncomfortable work, and many sales and marketing executives do not have the will or the personality to do this job. Let's see what it entails.

MANAGING THE DISTRIBUTION NETWORK

Attention to a few fundamentals is the key to developing and managing an effective distribution network. None of these fundamentals would be difficult to follow in a start-up situation. However, they are very difficult to implement in an established business with a distributor network already in place. Traditional relationships, values, and commitments to ways of doing things are serious roadblocks to thinking through and carrying out the required corrective steps. But because marketing with distributors is so necessary for many industrial firms, all levels of management must be concerned with building and maintaining an effective network. Lack of interest by any level of management and especially by senior management generally means the job will not be done the way it should. The first step, in any case, is to decide whether or not the product should be sold through distributors.

The Distribution Selling Decision

The industrial producer must decide whether or which of its products fit logically into a distribution channel. Several considerations[4] need to be examined. If any one of the following criteria are not characteristics of the customer or market being served, the product should probably be sold directly by the producer.

RAPID DELIVERY AND SERVICE. Probably the most important criterion is the need for rapid service, which is often stated in hours rather than weeks or months. If the product is needed immediately due to equipment breakdown or operating supply shortage, the customer needs the item as fast as possible. The driving force behind rapid delivery is also how practical it is to plan the purchase. The cost of downtime for an oil drilling rig is over $100 a minute; the downtime on an automotive engine assembly line is over $100,000 an hour. Minutes can be a matter of life and death when a hospital operating room needs a small piece of surgical tubing or parts for a life-support machine. In all these situations, the greater the downtime, the more costly the situation and the greater the need for prompt delivery and possibly technical service by a local distributor.

[4]James D. Hlavacek and Tommy J. McCuistion, "Industrial Distributors—When, Who and How?" *Harvard Business Review,* March–April 1983, p. 97.

LARGE POTENTIAL CUSTOMER BASE. If only a handful of customers will ever buy the product, it is unlikely that a distributor will do as satisfactory a job as the direct sales to user approach. Producers often allow custom-tailored products to become distributor items. For example, one company's special gasket products designed for customers' unique requirements were given to distributors to sell. Virtually no new accounts were created. After several years, it became clear that the distributors received repeat orders only from the few customers originally obtained by the producer's salespeople. The broader the customer base with standard requirements, the greater the need for a distributor network.

STOCKABLE PARTS. Most customer-designed parts, chemicals, or machinery, which are made to order, are easily eliminated as possibilities for distributors. Most of the product line should be able to be stocked and serviced locally. This implies catalog or standard items manufactured in large quantities and sold locally off-the-shelf a few at a time.

QUANTITY OF PURCHASE. Items selling for a few dollars are the most likely distributor products to be sold off-the-shelf. If the yearly purchase volume of OEMs is large, they are usually not served through a distributor. On the other hand, maintenance, repair, and overhaul replacement parts for the same item are often best sold by the local distributor. For example, bearings are used in tractors, motors, and machines. When they wear out, they need to be replaced in the aftermarket. The small unit value purchase rule also applies to heavy equipment items like construction machinery and trucks. The customer buys one or a few at a time, and is often buying on the basis of later service and parts availability. Repair parts for the original equipment are nearly always of smaller unit value. Frequently the distributor or dealer in machinery and equipment has the larger items on consignment from the manufacturer or has one demonstrator and then orders for each customer from the producer.

CUSTOMER BUYING LEVEL. The lower in the organization an item is bought, the more likely it will be sold through a distributor. The producer often does not consider at what organization level the large customer will buy the product. The flat organizational structure of an owner-operator business has little or no buying specialization, and therefore buys most frequently from a distributor. Some products, such as aircraft landing gear, are bought directly from the producer by very high levels within the airframe manufacturer; such items seldom become products bought through a distributor network. When designing and producing landing gear for a specific airplane, the supplier needs highly skilled engineering interaction with the customer's design engineers and procurement people. However, other products sold to that same airplane builder, such as o-ring seals or fasteners, are bought through distributors at lower levels in the organization. Here off-the-shelf service is important and the products are standardized. In this situation, the distributor's salespeople may need to know only the size and specification for the item.

Recognizing Market Differences

Once the producer's target market segments are identified, management must determine the size, growth potential, and requirements for each segment and decide whether to serve that market with distributors or with its own direct sales force. Two producers successfully serving the same market segment with similar products will usually use the same selling approach. If one producer emphasizes the OEM market segment for the product, it will usually sell directly to users. If another producer of a similar product emphasizes the aftermarket segment, it will sell primarily through distributors. Many industrial or technical product producers think first in terms of geographic coverage and then of distinct markets or customer segments. Thinking this way can result in the wrong selling approach and limited sales. The marine and forest product industries, for example, are both located in the Pacific Northwest. But these two market segments generally buy the same product from different types of distributors in the same geographic area. The marine customer buys mostly from a marine supply distributor which stocks special products for customers' needs, speaks their language, and knows marine applications. For example, it is often necessary to have products with technical U.S. Coast Guard approvals for salt-water corrosion resistance. The wood products customers in the same geographic area often require many of the same products as marine customers, but they buy from a distributor that serves the forest products industry. Due to differences in marine and wood products customer needs and the trade languages that are so much a part of each business, customers and distributors in one market in many cases do not know the other exists. There are numerous end-use markets in each major industrial area (mining, railroad, trucking, oil well drilling), and they must be served by distributors set up to talk their language and meet their special needs. Deere, for example, employs different distributors to serve its agriculture and construction equipment market segments. Caterpillar frequently uses different sets of distributors to serve the construction equipment, lift truck, and diesel truck engine markets in the same geographic territory.

The specialized distributor serves and stocks the special needs of these respective markets, whereas a general distributor may not be as effective. If a producer's existing distributors are not able to penetrate the different market segments in the same geographic area, management would be wise to consider different types of distributors to serve different or specialized market segments. If one producer is already successfully penetrating the identified market segment, the second or third producer coming into that market segment should carefully examine what type of distributor the successful first entrant chose.

Matching Distributors to Segments

There are different types of distributors for reaching and serving distinct market segments. In order to reach and penetrate multiple market segments effectively, it is often necessary for the producer to market through multiple channels. Exhibit 11-2 shows a producer of diesel engines that markets to three general types of markets: governments and municipalities; OEMs; and MRO-replacement markets. The government market (federal, state, and municipality) is often a direct sale because of the buying practices of these organizations. The OEM and MRO aftermarkets require distinctly different channels to serve the respective ultimate users. However, OEM and MRO channels are not always totally separate. As Exhibit 11-2 shows, MRO engine distributors may sell to OEM dealers, ultimate users, and engine rebuilders. As a consequence, the OEM and MRO channels compete.

EXHIBIT 11-2

MULTIPLE DISTRIBUTION CHANNELS

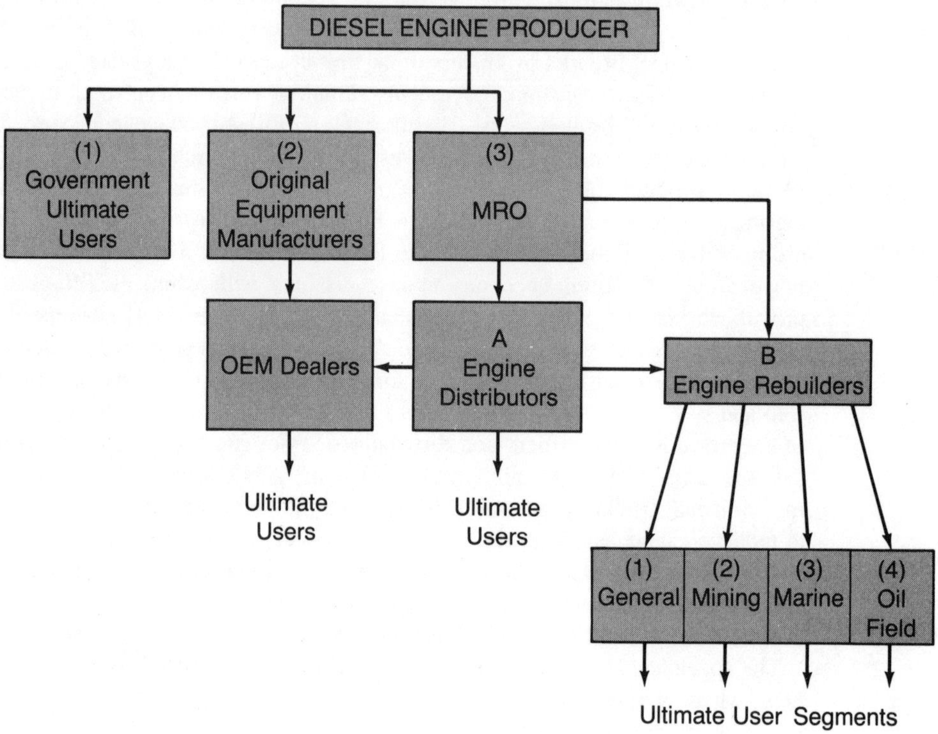

This particular diesel engine producer has further divided MRO engine rebuilders into four segments with distinct distribution channels: (1) general, (2) mining, (3) marine, and (4) oil field. Different marketing programs and distributors might be used to reach each of these subsegments of the aftermarket. In situations where there are multiple and complex channels and competition among a producer's channel members, special care must be exercised when developing strategies and prices for each channel. For analysis and strategy development, it is helpful to develop a scheme like that in Exhibit 11-2. Such schemes also help to isolate competitors, specifiers, and buying patterns in each segment.

Assigning Distributor Territories

A distributor's suggested territory may range from part of a large city like Chicago to three or four counties in a state. If a distributor's business is based essentially on product lines from one producer, the distributor will typically ask for some protection from other distributors selling in the same area. Some distributors selling more technical products that must be specified or "designed in" will usually want some kind of protection to prevent another distributor in the same geographic area from getting the business after he or she has done all the work. Many distributors will simply not carry a producer's item unless some specific territory is assigned to them. Their investment in space, inventories, and time is simply too great if they do not have the assurance that they will be credited for sales in their area.

Producers, however, should be careful not to assign "exclusive" or "protected" territories in which the distributor is compensated for all sales irrespective of whether it participates in the transactions or contributes to the selling effort. Generally designated territories can be assigned to specific distributors. But the producer should not be trapped into paying a distributor commissions on direct sales to accounts that have the buying power to demand direct sales. Nor should the producer be obliged to pay a double commission on occasional sales made in one distributor's territory by another distributor that has aggressively pursued the business across designated distributor lines.

Developing Distributor Policies

To avoid problems in working with distributors, all producers should define how they plan to work with those distributors before a distributor agreement is signed. It is essential to state clearly what products the producer wants the distributor to sell, what market segments or customer groups to focus on, and what geographic territory the distributor is expected to penetrate and serve. These ground rules should also spell out inventory requirements and what sales volume of the items the producer expects over time. If these conditions are not spelled out and understood by potential and existing distributors, a lot of time and effort will be wasted, and a lot of profit lost to competitors.

It is important to think through the common areas of potential producer-distributor conflict and then set down in writing specific policies for dealing with these situations that are fair to both parties. These policies should be discussed with all existing and prospective distributors. At a minimum, specific policies should be developed to address the areas of pricing, inventories and returns, sales to large accounts, market coverage, market volume penetration, and ultimate user information. For example, industrial manufacturers should have clearly defined pricing policies that encourage adequate distributor inventory levels. In many cases, the bulk of a distributor's capital is committed to producers' inventories. The supplying producer's pricing practices can enhance, protect, or penalize the market value and profit margins on these inventories. Some enlightened manufacturers have a policy of paying salespeople who call on distributors only for what the distributor sells, and not for what he or she buys. This reduces the tendency to overload the distributor with inventory.

Producers should also develop policies defining how large OEMs and end-use accounts will be served. Will large accounts that have been developed by a distributor ever be taken away from the distributor and sold on a direct basis? If so, when and under what circumstances? Some producers leave the distributor-developed account with the distributor as long as the distributor delivers an acceptable share of the account's business and can profitably serve the account with its normal price structure. This is admittedly a touchy subject, but specific written policies must be developed. Being completely open is the only way to minimize potential conflict and misunderstanding. There should also be specific written policies on the kind of sales information the producer requires from a distributor. Without information from distributors that shows who their customers or users are, or who is buying how much, the producer will not know what amount of penetration, if any, exists in a particular market or account. One successful producer has a policy, which is a condition of being a distributor, that calls for all distributors to report sales to every ultimate user by part number, customer, SIC, where shipped, and where billed. Another producer requires warranty cards to be completed and returned so it can track this same information. This kind of information enables the producer to evaluate distributor performance, set distributor quotas, and provide market direction by market segments.

In considering such policies, one caveat is worth emphasizing. Industrial distribution channels are outside the company, and therefore policies cannot be developed and implemented by issuing directives. This means that the industrial producer must carefully develop policies that are fair and consistent with the idea of the producer and distributors working together as partners to serve common customers.

Once the key areas and responsibilities of distributors are developed and written, they should be communicated to the producer's salespeople and to all present and potential distributors. A sound producer-distributor relationship should be regarded as a long-term partnership for profit, so the need to establish a solid foundation for that partnership is important. Exhibit 11-3 shows how the NAMCO Controls Division of Acme-Cleveland has defined its distributor policies. Exhibit 11-4 shows the same company's guiding "Distributor Partnership Philosophy."

Sales management in many companies often resists developing written policies like these. They argue that being so specific often creates hard feelings among distributors and reduces their flexibility to deal with distributor problems. We don't believe this is the case at all. As long as the policies are fair and responsive to market needs, they will be welcomed by distributors. And where there are honest differences of opinion, it is much better to get those into the open so they can be resolved. Allowing them to smolder under the surface will only lead to problems that will ultimately strain or destroy the relationship.

Providing Training and Support

Often the distributor's sales force is undertrained and undersupported by the producer. This is commonly called "franchise 'em and forget 'em." Training a distributor sales representative to sell a new product takes many hours of instruction. The producer must demonstrate the product features, advantages, and benefits for many different user situations or applications. The more technical the product or "art" required to use or apply it, the more time necessary for training. Sometimes such training must be done by the producer for both the distributor and the first customers who use the product. Product literature must be supplemented with trade magazine advertising to generate inquiries and new sales leads for the distributor. The producer, in turn, must promptly channel inquiries to the appropriate distributor to have a local sales call made.

Improving the effectiveness of industrial distributors can be approached in many ways.

EXHIBIT 11-3

PRODUCER AND DISTRIBUTOR RESPONSIBILITIES

NAMCO's RESPONSIBILITY

NAMCO agrees to make products, which are included within the product line for which Distributor is authorized, available to Distributor for purchase on the same terms and conditions of sale which such products are made available to authorized NAMCO distributors generally. Additionally, NAMCO will:

- Make available its staff and facilities to provide adequate training for Distributor employees and for technical and marketing liaison with them.
- Provide Distributor with a reasonable number of its catalogs and other advertising matter for use by Distributor for display or other marketing purposes.
- Attempt to maintain an inventory of the most commonly purchased items based on overall demand. NAMCO shall not be liable to the Distributor for direct, consequential or exemplary damages arising out of NAMCO's failure to have any NAMCO products in inventory or of NAMCO's failure to meet a delivery commitment.
- Refer orders or inquiries from non-authorized customers to the Authorized Distributors in an area of primary responsibility.
- Provide Distributor with all technical information available for NAMCO products.

DISTRIBUTOR'S RESPONSIBILITIES

While an authorized NAMCO distributor, Distributor shall:

- Maintain adequate stocks of NAMCO products for which Distributor is authorized, to service the needs of its customers, to allow NAMCO representatives to perform monthly stock reviews, and at least once each year participate in a business review with NAMCO.
- Actively promote all of NAMCO's products, for which Distributor is authorized, to its customers and aggressively solicit business for the products within the Distributor's areas of primary responsibility.
- Maintain a place of business with all necessary services and sales functions to service its customers and promote goodwill for NAMCO.
- Promote NAMCO products by inclusion in Distributor's advertisements and displays.
- Make its personnel available to NAMCO for training programs.
- Distributor specifically agrees to keep confidential all technical information made available to it or its employees except materials designed for promotional purposes such as specification sheets.

Source: NAMCO Controls Division, Acme-Cleveland Corporation

For example, a producer can open regional warehouses or depots to provide the means for the smaller but growing distributor to expand its volume for the line or item. Sometimes a good cooperative advertising program that provides leads and inquiries will help get new accounts. In dealing with larger customers, specialized sales support may greatly strengthen a distributor's performance. Under extreme circumstances, it may be necessary to give financial aid in the form of inventory, equipment, or accounts receivable financing.

When a distributor needs technical field assistance for a potential key account, the producer should ensure that such support is provided. Most producers have regional sales representatives who can accompany distributor salespeople on calls and provide the first

EXHIBIT 11-4

DISTRIBUTOR PARTNERSHIP PHILOSOPHY

Distributors play a vital role in helping NAMCO reach its market penetration and sales coverage objectives. Whenever and wherever practical, NAMCO will go to market with our Distributor Partners. Since we do consider our distributors as business partners, we intend to have clearly defined policies designed to make this partnership concept equitable and beneficial to both of us. We will have only authorized stocking distributors.

We want to work with distributors who are financially strong and who are geared to service our end user markets. These distributors will be willing and able to grow in strength and market coverage, with increasing capabilities of servicing our customers. These distributors will provide a positive contribution in sales to our joint customers, and, in return, they should expect to earn a satisfactory profit. It is NAMCO's responsibility to provide quality products, product and application training, promotional support, market guidance and prices which allow these distributors to maintain a competitive position in the market. In turn, these business partners are obligated to represent NAMCO in a business-like manner, to aggressively promote sales of our products, to carry inventories of NAMCO products adequate to service local customer needs.

A Distributor Agreement will be of interest to our distributors only if there is sufficient profit potential to support their sales effort. NAMCO will follow a selective distribution policy, authorizing only the number and type of distributors necessary to meet our marketing objectives in a geographical territory. NAMCO's first priority will be to authorize distributors who will market all of NAMCO's products within their trading area. Our second priority will be to authorize distributors for a portion of our products where they service specific market segments. A single distributor cannot always provide total market coverage, particularly within a large trading area. We will continually monitor each trading area to provide balanced coverage. We are willing to review our analysis with distributors at any time, and will advise current distributors if we plan any additional distributors in their trading area. NAMCO will drop ship to end user or OEM customers within a trading area only, for distributors authorized within that trading area. We will maintain recommended trade discounts for various classes of end user and OEM customers, to provide a pricing structure that protects our authorized distributor partners' investment in inventory.

NAMCO may sell direct to User and OEM accounts, but only when technical or other special conditions warrant direct sale. We will advise our distributors who will be sold direct and the reasons why. Our field sales employees and representatives will call on major User and OEM customers to gain approval and specification for NAMCO products. We will endeavor to direct the resulting business through our distributors.

We do not expect to compete with our distributors for any NAMCO business. Any distributor that develops an account, no matter what the volume, as long as they can service the account satisfactorily at normal distributor pricing will continue to service the account. However, we expect our distributors to call us in if customer needs or competitive direct selling jeopardizes the business. We will discuss with our distributors any situation where it appears we are competing with our distributor for NAMCO business.

When it becomes evident that a distributor's goals and objectives are significantly different from NAMCO's market objectives, we will discuss this with the distributor and recommend appropriate action. If that distributor does not act on our recommendations within a reasonable time, we will seek a replacement distributor whose objectives more nearly match ours.

To document this philosophy and to assure equal treatment of all distributors, we will have a signed agreement with each distributor. A standard policy, including terms of sale, will also be provided. Any differences from standard policy will be granted only where special market needs and conditions or specific performance logically and legally justify such action.

This is a statement of our philosophy of doing business with our distributor partners. We will make every effort to follow it. If changing conditions dictate changes in these policies, we will make them. And, we will always welcome constructive comments from our distributor partners.

Note: This particular philosophy was developed by E. G. Orahood of Reliance Electric and later adopted and modified by Jon Slaybaugh of NAMCO Controls.
Source: NAMCO Controls Division, Acme-Cleveland Corporation

level of technical backup. Although some might regard this as an inordinate cost or a luxury the producer cannot afford, it is often a smart investment. The producer's sales rep, with his or her greater product and technical know-how, can help analyze an account's needs and get a product specified, which in turn will build volume six months to a year later. It is usually a mistake to assume that distributors will get the producer's product specified. If a product requires some specification work and that work is not done by the producer, the distributor will generate little or no business in that territory. In the health care market, drug company salespeople or detail people (who explain the technical details of the drug to the physicians) must first influence physicians to specify or prescribe one drug brand over another before the local drugstore or distributor can fill and possibly deliver the order to the ultimate user. Similarly, architects must be encouraged to specify one producer's product, or the local building material distributor will not get the business from the local user account.

Sometimes a product is technically specified in one geographic area but is bought in another. For example, General Motors in Michigan specifies what make of valve it wants on machine tools it is having built by a machine tool builder in Ohio for a production line in California. In order to sell to the machine tool builder who is selling an automated production line to General Motors, it is first necessary to meet the specification and get approval by General Motors' corporate office. Without General Motors' corporate approval, the Ohio distributor cannot serve the Ohio machine tool builder. It frequently pays big dividends for producers to have a person who does nothing but get their products specified or qualified at OEMs, government agencies, automotive companies, and railroads.

Manuals or handbooks that help people to design or use a product or solve technical problems have proved to be excellent "silent salespeople" that help get a producer's products specified and then ordered from a local distributor. Well-known examples exist in many industries. The *Merck Manual,* which first appeared in 1899, was written to meet the needs of physicians in selecting medications. It stated that "memory is treacherous and that even the most thoroughly informed physician needs a reminder to enable him to prescribe exactly what is needed for the patient."[5] In 1983, the *Merck Manual* was in its 14th edition, with 2500 pages covering disorders (problems) and suggested therapy (solutions). The *O-Ring Handbook* by Parker Hannifin Corporation helps a design engineer design a product or specify a solution to prevent leakage in an oil or air system. Ingersoll-Rand produced the *Drill Doctor's Book* for drillers to select the bit, speed, and setup in various rock and coal mining situations. All these manuals are designed to support the distributor in its efforts to sell a complete array of technical products and services.

Turnover and Yearly ROI

It should be obvious that an independent entrepreneurial distributor is motivated primarily by profit margins and financial incentives. For this reason, distributors will typically emphasize the higher-margin lines and often carry lower-margin items as complementary

[5] *The Merck Manual,* published by Merck, Sharp & Dome Research Laboratories, Division of Merck & Co., Inc., Rahway, New Jersey, 1983.

fill-ins. Many distributors and industrial marketers do not fully understand the dynamics of inventory turnover as they affect yearly ROI. For example, if one manufacturer's product has a gross margin on an item of 20 percent and the inventory turns two times per year, the yearly gross margin is 40 percent. However, if the number of inventory turns for a similar competitive product also with a 20 percent margin is four times per year, the distributor receives a yearly gross margin of 80 percent. So there is more pricing flexibility on high-turnover items.

Many industrial producers have found it worthwhile to explain turnover to their distributors to help them improve their businesses. The price-turnover relationship is shown in Table 11.2. For this situation, we can assume a distributor desires a 120 percent gross margin of profit per year for the sales, investment, and working capital being used to cover all overhead and receive a 7 percent profit on sales per year after taxes. A distributor that receives a lower *unit* gross margin on a higher *yearly* turnover item will receive greater yearly returns.

Distributor Councils

As we emphasized, industrial producers should view the distributor as a business partner with a common customer. The end-use customer is not considered to "belong" to the distributor; the distributor serves the customer with the producer's product. The producer

TABLE 11.2

PRICE-TURNOVER RELATIONSHIP

% gross margin per year

Turnover per Year	*Gross Margin on Sales* 10%	*20%*	*30%*	*40%*	*50%*	*60%*	*70%*	*80%*	*90%*	*100%*
0.5	5	10	15	20	25	30	35	40	45	50
1.0	10	20	30	40	50	60	70	80	90	100
1.5	15	30	45	60	75	90	105	120	135	150
2.0	20	40	60	80	100	120	140	160	180	200
2.5	25	50	75	100	125	150	175	200	225	250
3.0	30	60	90	120	150	180	210	240	270	300
3.5	35	70	105	140	175	210	245	280	315	350
4.0	40	80	120	160	200	240	280	320	360	400
6.0	60	120	180	240	300	360	420	480	540	600
8.0	80	160	240	320	400	480	560	640	720	800
10.0	100	200	300	400	500	600	700	800	900	1,000
12.0	120	240	360	480	600	720	840	960	1,080	1,200
24.0	240	480	720	960	1,200	1,440	1,680	1,920	2,160	2,400
52.1	521	1,042	1,563	2,084	2,605	3,126	3,647	4,168	4,689	5,210
365.0	3,650	7,300	10,950	14,600	18,250	21,900	25,550	29,200	32,850	36,500

assists in the promotion and specifications process. As an aid to maintaining closer distributor relationships and ensuring good feedback on markets, customer needs, and competition, some leading producers have formed very effective distributor councils.

A distributor advisory council should consist of six to twelve members that represent other distributors in their respective geographic regions. Each member serves for a maximum period, such as three years, and every year a specific number of members go off and new ones come on the council. The rotating membership keeps distributor councils from becoming just social gatherings of old friends. The full council might meet twice a year. Council members sometimes have regional meetings with the distributors they represent to raise and discuss common concerns. Minutes should be kept at meetings of the national distributor advisory council and then distributed to all distributors as well as to the appropriate producer personnel. The distributor meetings are conducted at a high level and address issues that include the producer's policies, the competition, sales, technical and promotion support, and needed products. Other topics might include return goods policies, a quality problem with a particular product, the need for new catalogs, new industry standards, a product line gap, or the training of inside salespeople to handle distributor problems. General economic trends and business conditions are also useful discussion topics for council meetings, as long as they are tied to specific actions the distributor and/or producer should take.

Properly directed, a meeting of a distributor council is an opportunity for the producer to capitalize on the distributors' direct contacts with hundreds of end-use customers. The council can provide reliable feedback on common problems that need attention from the appropriate division or from top management. The points of view expressed by council members can be very helpful to a division marketing manager or product manager attempting to think through a new program or policy.

Assigning Responsibility for Distributor Development

In many manufacturing firms, no one person has responsibility for distributor development. In theory, the top marketing or sales executive bears this responsibility, but in practice it is often fragmented or even neglected. Merely writing the responsibility into sales representatives' job descriptions is seldom enough to ensure that the job is done properly. To most salespeople, loyalty to long-time distributors, the pressures of meeting the current quota, and earning bigger bonuses are usually more important considerations than the tedious assignment of keeping tabs on all the distributors in his or her group. Unless this duty becomes a real part of a salesperson's job performance standards, it will almost surely be neglected. Moreover, sales managers struggling to meet current quotas are unlikely to make distribution changes that might hurt the current quarter's sales. Finally, marketing executives usually have more exciting and seemingly more profitable projects to think about—such as new product introductions, sales promotion campaigns, and strategic planning needs. Not having the time or staff to spare, they will seldom be inclined to invest the necessary time and effort required to strengthen the distribution network. Some leading companies have established a position that is responsible for distributor development. However, the job really belongs to the marketing management executives, and they need to make sure it is done.

At Caterpillar, for example, the support and development of distributors is a concern that permeates the entire corporation. The Caterpillar chairman states: "We all approach our distributors as partners in the enterprise and not as agents or middlemen to pass products through. We worry as much about their performance as they do themselves."[6] Caterpillar dealers are effusive in their praise of relations with Caterpillar: "They have consistently supplied us with superior products and a high-quality program of parts and product information."[7] Every year, Caterpillar conducts dozens of intensive training programs for distributors and product demonstrations for end-use customers. Field demonstrations are common to show the distributor the competitive advantages of Caterpillar's track-type tractors, front-end loaders, graders, and other excavating equipment. The company even conducts a course at corporate headquarters in Peoria to encourage and show distributor families how the business can be passed on to the next generation. The average Caterpillar distributor tenure is 35 years, and most stay within the family for generations. Caterpillar's loyal distributor relationships are quite possibly the greatest barrier to its competition.

EVALUATING DISTRIBUTOR PERFORMANCE

The starting point for evaluating distributor performance is a thorough knowledge of the market potential in each distributor's territory. To be meaningful, total potential should be established for each product-market segment in the territory. The marketing research staff should be able to determine the market segment or territory potentials to a county and major account level. No industry or marketplace is static: New uses are usually found for existing products. New products displace older ones. New market segment opportunities emerge, and other markets stagnate or shrink. As a result, end-use markets change in size and importance and producers' and distributors' market shares typically increase or decrease over time. Therefore, it is extremely important continually to survey and track market segment changes in size, growth, and buying locations. Market facts provide the base information necessary to determine where stronger, more, or new distribution coverage is needed.

Exhibit 11-5 illustrates the importance of this point. A nationwide market study revealed that a major gasket manufacturer had weak sales through distributors that served the two fastest-growing market segments, instrumentation and oil fields. Exhibit 11-5 also shows low market penetration in the fluid power market segment. These lost opportunities, and areas needing additional marketing emphasis from distributors, would be missed unless the producer first assessed what was happening in each key market segment. Once market share data have been developed, distributor quotas should be established. The distributor's initial quota should be established from these market facts and then adjusted by sales and marketing management to reflect the producer's marketing objectives and the realities of the competitive situation.

The next step is to track distribution sales in each product-market segment. Many com-

[6]"Caterpillar: Sticking to Basics to Stay Competitive," *Business Week*, May 21, 1981, p. 77.
[7]Ibid.

EXHIBIT 11-5

GASKET DISTRIBUTOR PROFILE

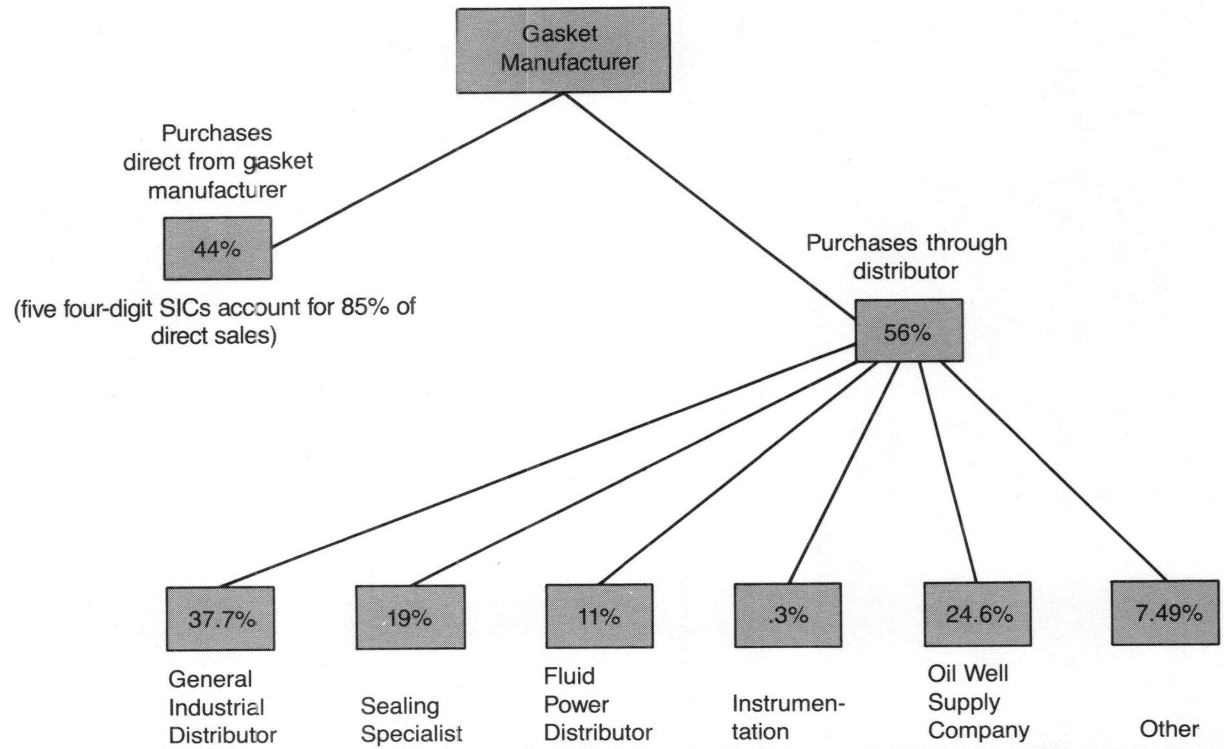

	General Industrial Distributor	Sealing Specialist	Fluid Power Distributor	Instrumentation	Oil Well Supply Company	Other
Annual Segment Real Growth Rates	1–2%	2.5%	3%	8%	6%	
Total Market Size	Large	Medium	Large	Small	Large	
Market Share	21%	17%	6%	1%	4%	

EXHIBIT 11-6

CLASSIFYING DISTRIBUTORS BY PERFORMANCE

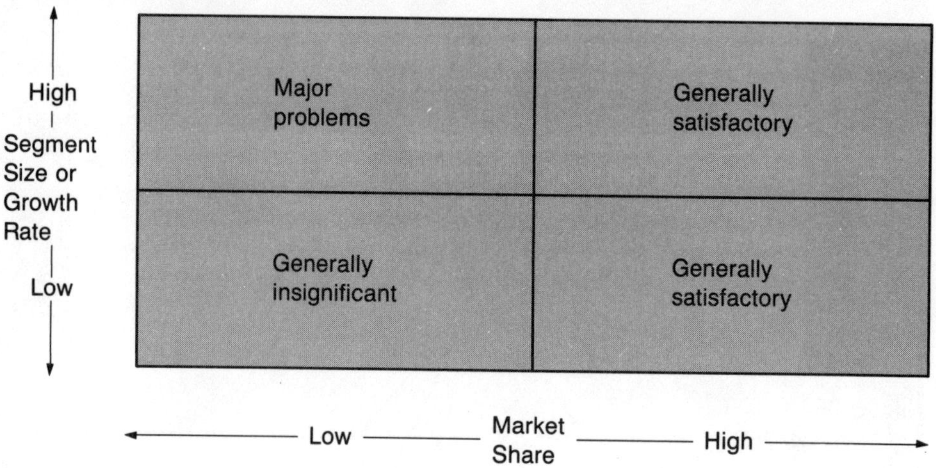

panies have no idea where their product goes after it leaves the distributor's shipping department. As a result, they lose touch with their ultimate customers and do not have a sound basis for evaluating distributor performance. Many sales personnel will argue that this kind of information is not available. This is not true. It is available and can be obtained with the distributor's cooperation. If a distributor is unwilling to cooperate or does not keep appropriate sales records, he or she shouldn't be allowed to carry the producer's line. As we mentioned earlier, some producers require each distributor to submit monthly sales information to them by product, customer name, and location as a condition of carrying their lines. When a motor, machine, or large piece of equipment is sold with a warranty, customer information is much easier to develop. Most of the ultimate customers fill in and return the warranty card directly to the producer. This means the producer should be able to track sales to the ultimate user without any distributor involvement. However developed, a system that reports sales to ultimate customers provides invaluable information for a wide range of distributor and marketing management decisions.

Another step in analyzing distributor performance is to determine which distributors are performing well or poorly in high- and low-value market segments. The matrix in Exhibit 11-6 shows an approach that is helpful in classifying distributors into these categories. This analysis can be developed for each distributor to determine how it has performed for each of the manufacturer's products. Or it can be used to compare the relative performance of all distributors in the producer's network. A common pattern to watch for is strong market share positions in the smaller or lower-value markets that are usually less competitive, coupled with a weak market share in the higher-value markets where competition is more intense. This reflects a serious weakness in the distribution network and results in a lower than average market share overall.

Once unsatisfactory or "problem" distributors have been identified, the person responsible for the territory should study the distributor's operation in more detail. Here factors like the following should be examined.

Annual inventory turns

Adequacy of business experience as reflected in quality of customer service

Coverage of assigned area and time available to seek new accounts

Distributor's competence in managing the business (sales management, financial control, recordkeeping, warehousing, and inventory control)

Historical trend of volume as measured against performance requirements established by the producer's regional sales manager

Share of market or penetration in assigned area

Willingness to carry a full line of products to service all customer needs

Condition of equipment and warehouse facilities

Financial position (accounts receivable, cash position, debts, inventories, fixed assets, and payment record)

Ability to grow in the assigned area

Almost every manufacturer periodically faces the task of getting much more effort out of certain distributors. To accomplish this successfully, management must be able to grade the performance and potential of its existing distributors and concentrate its support programs on those distributors that can generate the most sales and profit dollars by achieving realistic goals. For example, bringing the distributors in the top 20 markets up to the average market share performance levels of the entire group would seem to be a reasonable goal and can often generate significant sales dollars.

Complete and periodic distributor evaluations require considerable time and diplomacy. When distributors have interests or goals that are not consistent with the manufacturer's market objectives in the defined market and geographic trading area, producers should first try to explain what must be done and the payoffs for such efforts. If a distributor has not achieved satisfactory penetration or growth in a key market, the producer should establish an improvement plan with target dates. If no real improvement occurs after a reasonable time and appropriate producer assistance, a decision must be made. It is crucial to face up to the task of replacing distributors who will not or cannot upgrade. The producer's determination to improve a distributor network has proved to be the key to more than one outstanding marketing success story. For example, in 1974 Ray Snyder, Manager of Distributor Sales at Reliance Electric, made an analysis of distributor sales and found that the proverbial "80/20 rule" was in effect. Twenty percent of the company's 1,200 distributors accounted for a little more than 80 percent of total distributor sales. Faced with the obvious question of why carry a lot of nonproductive distributors, he launched into a program to upgrade the distributor group. Within 24 months, the number of distributors had been reduced by nearly 50 percent, average sales per distributor increased by 20 percent, and total distributor sales were up sharply.

SELECTING NEW DISTRIBUTORS

After concluding that new or more distributors are needed to serve the market, a careful selection process must be followed so that the problem is not compounded. Many producers frequently choose additional distributors who are already overloaded with products. The successful distributor is usually courted by numerous producers and is frequently carrying as many product lines as it can effectively handle with existing sales and service capabilities. Producers also frequently make the mistake of choosing the more mature distributor with a successful history who has forgotten how to be aggressive. Admittedly, the credit rating on the newer, more aggressive distributor will rarely be something that excites the home office financial people. However, the producer often errs by not attempting to find a way to help finance or support a newer distributor who could do a good job with the right kind of assistance.

Distributors are never very happy when they are told that they are being canceled or that an additional distributor is being franchised in what had been their exclusive territory. Many producers are reluctant to take this step because they are unwilling to upset the longstanding personal relationship with the low-performing distributor. However, when the decision is made forcefully and objectively on a base of solid market facts and the distributor's lack of performance, the producer's market position inevitably improves. Conversely, procrastination or rationalization typically leads to further market deterioration.

Identifying and adding the specific distributors is generally a local or regional decision. Regional sales managers should be the first people to do an exhaustive search for new candidates. Since it is a regional decision, the search is frequently narrowed down to one or two key cities in the region. Trade directories and local Yellow Pages are typically used as sources for existing distributor candidates. Sometimes the number two person in an existing or competitive distributorship becomes a candidate to start a new distributorship. In some situations, the existing distributor may be interested in opening a new branch to provide the necessary coverage and is aware that if he or she doesn't, the producer probably will find a new distributor for the area. As a last resort, some producers will consider opening a company store on a temporary basis with one of its salespeople managing the distributorship. Often producers continue the person's salary, finance the new inventories, and provide management assistance to help get the operation running in the black. At this point, the company employee is often given the opportunity to arrange his or her own financing to buy out the producer's assets and become an independent business that will remain and develop accounts in that territory.

MULTIDIVISION PRODUCTS

In many corporations, several different divisions often manufacture related products that are sold to common customers. In these situations, it is advantageous for the manufacturer to sell through a common distributor network. This enables the distributor to become a single-source shopping place where a customer can buy all related requirements. This common distributor concept has provided a focus to some producers' acquisition and product development activities as they sought complementary products or product

EXHIBIT 11-7

MULTIDIVISIONAL OR GROUP DISTRIBUTION

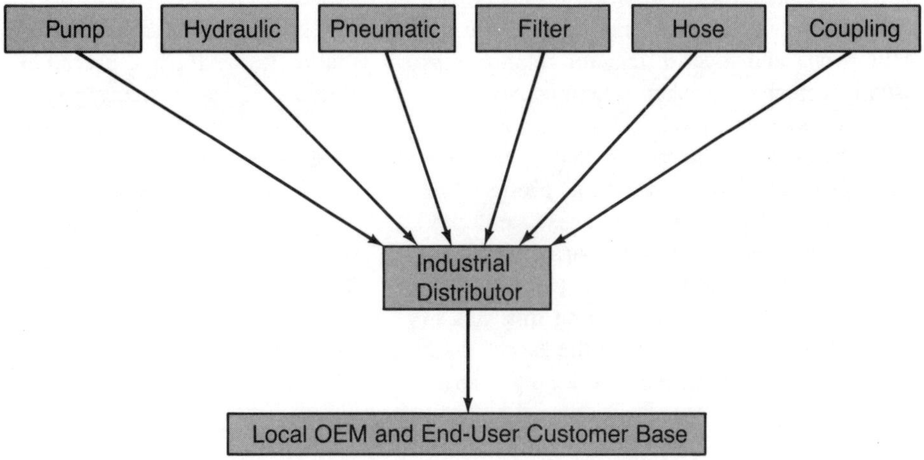

lines that fit with their established common existing distributor network. Exhibit 11-7 shows how complementary products from six separate divisions flow through a common distributor network to local customers.

Although this arrangement offers many advantages, it adds to the complexity of the management task. This is particularly true when the divisions involved were acquired rather than internally developed and have successful sales histories based on quite different distribution policies and practices. In these situations, buying terms and conditions, stocking requirements, returns and allowances, and credit evaluation are most likely to be different and often in conflict. On the surface, it would seem that problems like these are easily corrected. In practice, however, they are not. First, the divisions are generally autonomous and typically have a vested interest in distributor policies and practices that have proved successful in the past. Distributors will also want to preserve the policies and practices from each division that are best for them and will argue strongly against any change that is not in their best interest. This arrangement also can create difficult operating problems, particularly if division performance is uneven. Even though the manufacturer's divisions are separate operating entities, distributors will tend to evaluate the performance of all the divisions as a group. As a result, all divisions end up with a tarnished image if one division falls short with missed delivery dates or quality defects.

Given these concerns, the best management approach is to work toward a common set of distributor policies and practices acceptable to all parties. This will take careful thought and time as well as skillful negotiation, but it is do-able. At the same time, it is essential to preserve the individuality of each division and the brand name of the division's products. If this can be accomplished, it will provide the manufacturer with the leverage that results from being a major source to each distributor, while still permitting each division to stand on its own performance.

SUMMARY

Experience shows that all too few sales managers understand how to market products with distributors successfully. Industrial producers with strong and loyal distributor relationships usually perceive distributors as business partners and not just as vehicles to pass products through. Such producers see that distributors must earn satisfactory margins and profits while serving their joint customers. These same producers cement the distributor partnership with market guidance, training, and technical and promotional support. By avoiding mistakes in distribution and taking care of the essentials in evaluating, selecting, and developing distributors, they substantially increase their chances of market success.

A good distributor network is often the key to market leadership and overall business success. Because it takes many years of continuous attention to develop and maintain, a sound producer-distributor organization is often a high barrier to competitors. Without a solid network, even a manufacturer with a superior product can fail in the marketplace. A producer that recognizes the importance of distributors has a major competitive advantage that can reap attractive profits for itself and its distributors.

12

Advertising and Promotion

Ursula Hartmann, advertising manager, Peter Fraser, marketing services manager, and Bill Lewis, the new controller for a large Midwestern materials handling company, were reviewing the results of their recent participation in an industry trade show. Ursula was particularly pleased with the show: "We had the best display by far. We showed more bells and whistles and had better attendance than anyone else in the industry. At least 200 people attended our reception." Peter was equally happy: "This is the tenth year we have been in this show, and this was the best ever. No one else even came close to us." With a typical controller's perspective, Bill raised a question that led to the following discussion.

Bill: How much does a show like this cost?

Ursula: About $250,000.

Bill: Is that the total cost?

Ursula: Sure. My budget was $218,000, and we had a few thousand dollar overrun.

Bill: Does the $250,000 amount include travel and living costs for everybody from our company who attended the show?

Ursula: No, that's a sales expense.

Bill: Do you know how much was involved for travel and other associated costs?

Ursula: No, it's not my cost.

Bill: Do you know how many of our salespeople attended the show?

Ursula: I don't know that either, but we usually try to have enough sales representation so customers can be handled properly.

After the meeting, Bill talked with Gordon Jones, a product manager for a major segment of the business. Gordon didn't have much more information, but said he knew that travel and other costs were significant because a big chunk of the total costs were allocated against his product line. He also said that he wasn't very happy about this charge and questioned what benefits his product or even the company got for all the money that was spent. "It's just a big ego trip for the advertising and sales guys" was his parting comment.

Bill did some research and found that the travel costs involved amounted to $121,000. Despite the glowing comments of the advertising and marketing services managers, Bill had real misgivings about the value received for the total amount of money spent on the show. He wrote a brief memo outlining his concerns to the vice president of finance and sent a copy to Ursula and Peter. Ursula reacted angrily: "This guy's only been here three weeks and already he's stuck his nose into an area that is none of his business." As she started toward Bill's office, Ursula thought about the effort she put into the trade show and wondered if Bill had any idea how important this activity was to the company.

If this isn't Bill's business, whose is it?

What are the criteria to use in judging how well promotion money is spent?

Who should decide how promotion money is spent?

Are there any hidden benefits of participating in trade shows?

Does the controller have the right to ask the questions he did?

Properly planned and controlled, advertising and promotional activities are useful recognition and volume-building tools in the industrial world. They can introduce a new product or service to established or new markets in a cost-effective way. They can explain cost benefits to a much wider potential customer base than the typical industrial sales force can possibly reach. They can effectively turn up sales prospects or leads that help make the time of the sales force more productive. However, in reviewing advertising and promotion activities, it is important to keep this statement made by a cost-conscious businessman foremost in mind: "I know that 50 percent of the money we spend for advertising and promotion is wasted; I just don't know which half." There is a good deal of truth to this point in any advertising situation, and it is particularly true in the industrial world, where advertising and promotion expenditures are sizable.

THE PROBLEM OF WASTED EFFORT

Responses to criticism about waste from those involved in business-to-business advertising and promotion activities can be anticipated: "You have to keep your product and name in front of the customers." "We must keep building the company's image." "Giveaways are a constant reminder of our product." "We lose face if we don't continue to make major commitments in our trade shows." As we see it, none of these responses are valid. In fact, they represent the kind of superficial thinking that is the root cause of much of the waste in industrial advertising and promotion. Our point of view is not simply an unsupported bias; there is plenty of evidence that is consistent with our thinking. For example, L. W. Rodger makes these comments about industrial advertising expenditures:

> The advertising budget probably represents the largest amount of money disbursed by manufacturers with no precise measure of what it can be expected to achieve. The spending of large sums of money on advertising without some system of accountability can be compared to conducting a business without a bookkeeping or accounting department. Advertising accountability has lagged far behind general management accountability in that the latter is held responsible for accomplishing certain specific and usually measurable results in relation to money spent.[1]

A recent *Wall Street Journal* article[2] reported that Edward MacEwen, director of advertising at General Telephone & Electronics, says: "All that most corporate slogans do is waste space. Such slogans rarely are remembered and even less frequently identified with the proper corporation." To prove his point, MacEwen developed a brief quiz that called for participants to match the advertiser with the appropriate slogan. Included in the list of companies that had spent millions of dollars on their corporate image were such well-known names as ITT, Bendix, W. R. Grace, Monsanto, 3M, U.S. Steel, LTV, Allied,

[1]Leslie Rodger, "Marketing in a Competitive Economy," *International Industries,* 1971, p. 110.
[2]*The Wall Street Journal,* December 9, 1982.

and others of equal stature. When MacEwen gave this quiz to about 250 advertising executives, only 6 entrants could correctly identify more than 10 of 31 slogans. The winner matched 19.

Trade shows are an advertising/promotion activity that is certainly subject to question. Some recent publications include these quotes:

> It is strange to find that so little is known about the usefulness of exhibitions (trade shows), that they are so often an expression of faith rather than fact, with such factors as size of stand (display) and budget determined intuitively by some senior executive. Evidence of this is to be found by discussing the matter with exhibitors and is confirmed by the random way in which in one year a company invests in a substantial stand, next year pulls out altogether, then later comes back with an even larger display.[3]

> Trade shows are terribly expensive and of limited value for the business you do versus the dollars spent. Once we did cut out a show, but there was such buyers' remorse that we were forced to reinstate it. Everyone wondered if we were having some financial difficulties and couldn't afford to participate! For us, trade shows are a self-perpetuating problem. If I could just throw that money into operating profit each year, I'd be a superstar. But we go, we go.[4]

> Everything nowadays is done for the show management, not for the exhibitors. The only other ones to get anything out of trade shows are the hotels and the prostitutes.[5]

All these negative comments do not mean that money should never be spent for advertising and promotion. Rather, they mean that careful consideration must be given to determining the role advertising and promotion can realistically play in the particular industrial marketing situation. When it is determined that these activities can make a useful contribution, they must be carefully planned and controlled. One must always remember, however, that the industrial buying decision typically swings on more important components of the marketing mix, like product performance, price, delivery capabilities, and service. Even the most creative or ingenious advertising and promotion will never offset deficiencies in these areas (see the box, page 249).

The Money Involved

Although far from perfect, there are data which show that most industrial companies spend money on advertising and promotion, and that the sums involved are substantial. In a recent survey of 483 industrial companies of varying sizes, 93.1 percent responded positively to the question, "Does your company advertise?"[6] Although one can always find deficiencies in survey data, our experience with a wide range of industrial compa-

[3]Norman A. Hart, *Industrial Advertising and Publicity* (New York: Halsted Press, 1978), p. 17.
[4]Thomas Bonoma, "Get More Out of Your Trade Shows," *Harvard Business Review*, January–February, 1983.
[5]Ibid.
[6]"Highlights of Sales Management and Marketing Survey on Industrial Advertising," *Sales and Marketing*, June 8, 1981, p. 53.

THROWING MONEY AWAY

It doesn't require any particular genius to see a lot of wasted dollars spent on advertising and promotion in the advertising world. Some common examples:

- Repeated pictures in trade journals of old, mature, or "me too" products that don't talk about or offer new benefits to anyone.
- Myriad giveaway items (golf balls, tee shirts, bottle openers, paperweights) and other promotional gimmicks that have no relationship to the company's products or capabilities.
- Countless TV and radio spots, as well as newspaper and magazine ads, devoted to so-called corporate image building developed around some catchy slogan designed to express the company's business purpose or accomplishments.
- Costly trade show participation that is more of a social get-together for competing sales personnel than a forum for showing and selling new products and technology.

nies suggests that this ratio is certainly realistic. And although the amount of money spent for business-to-business advertising and promotion is far less than that spent by consumer goods companies, the amount is still significant. Table 12.1, prepared from these same survey data, shows 47 percent of the companies had annual expenditures over $100,000, 13 percent over $500,000, and several companies had budgets running into the millions.

Like most other business expenditures, ad budgets continue to spiral upward. Table 12.2, again from the same survey, shows that most advertising budgets in the sample companies call for significant planned increases in 1981 over what was actually spent in 1980. Given the hundreds of thousands of industrial companies, it is safe to conclude that if aggregate data on their advertising expenditures were available, it would be expressed

TABLE 12.1 ***INDUSTRIAL ADVERTISING BUDGETS, 1980***

Amount	*Percentage of Companies*
Less than $100,000	49.1%
$100,000–$499,999	34.4
$500,000–$999,999	6.4
$1 million–$2,999,999	5.6
$3 million–$4,999,999	0.8
$5 million or more	0.4

TABLE 12.2

INDUSTRIAL ADVERTISING INCREASES, 1980–1981

Comparison	*Percentage of Companies*
Up 9% or less	21.1%
Up 10%–19%	27.7
Up 20%–29%	8.3
Up 30% or more	8.3
Same	21.3
Down	7.7

in hundreds of millions or possibly even billions of dollars. And as we have seen, the trend in spending is definitely upward. These numbers relate only to print, TV, and radio advertising; they do not include money spent for all the other activities generally considered to be a part of an industrial advertising and promotion budget, such as trade shows, catalogs, product literature, price lists, business cards, company signs, sales ads, giveaway items, slide shows, films, video presentations, direct mail, and product seminars. Obviously, the costs and importance of these activities vary widely by company, but as a general rule they typically match the amount spent for print, TV, and radio advertising.

The Special Problems of Industrial Advertising

The difficulty of avoiding waste in advertising and promotion is certainly not limited to industrial companies. Anyone who advertises or promotes anything to any market is always concerned about this point, since the money spent is lost unless it ultimately generates sufficient additional volume and profit to cover the cost. Business-to-business advertising, however, is more susceptible to waste for several reasons. To start with, it is harder to do well and to quantify the results. The chairman of one of the largest and most successful advertising agencies expressed this point very well when he said: "Industrial advertising is tougher to create than consumer advertising. There are more facts required and less puffery. You have to convince a better informed and more knowledgeable audience. Emotional appeals are not particularly useful, since the benefits one communicates must be in dollars and cents and not emotions or dreams."

This comment accurately reflects three points that are facts of life in the industrial world. First, industrial customers tend to be fewer in number and make less frequent and higher-volume purchases of any particular product than customers for consumer items. Moreover, the lag between the time an impression is made through some advertisement or promotional offering and the time of need or purchase is generally much longer for industrial products. Finally, the industrial buying decision is generally more rational, and those making the decision are less likely to be swayed by advertising appeals, claims, or promotional offerings. For these reasons, it is far more difficult to test and measure the effectiveness of advertising or promotion activities in the industrial world and thus far easier to spend a lot of money on these activities without knowing whether the investment is paying off.

A revealing piece of research work from McGraw-Hill's *Special Report on Buying and Selling Techniques Used in the British Engineering Industry* supports this point.[7] Among other things, the research showed various methods of arriving at the advertising and promotion budget, as Table 12.3 shows. Although this survey reflects the practice in British industry, our experience suggests it is not far off the mark from what we would find in the United States if a similar survey were conducted. Making any allowance you want for greater marketing sophistication in the United States, the results still reflect the fundamental problem. Far too few industrial companies develop and carry out their advertising and promotion activities as an integrated part of their marketing and business plan. Budgets for these activities are frequently established independently or on an ad hoc basis that is difficult to track. Even when the budgets and programs are included in the plan, they are generally not subjected to the same rigorous challenge and review as other elements of the marketing mix, such as product development, pricing, inventory levels, and direct or distributor sales costs.

Contrast this situation with what occurs in consumer marketing. Here, the success of the product and even the company often depends on how effectively advertising and promotion funds are spent or invested. In fact, these activities are so important and the expenditures so large that consumer marketing is frequently referred to as "the science of spending" for these activities. To enhance their chances for success, consumer goods marketers routinely evaluate and measure the effectiveness of alternative advertising and promotion programs and spending levels in test markets before major recommendations or commitments are made. Moreover, any advertising or promotion program of consequence is presented as a vital and an integrated part of a marketing or business plan with quantifiable objectives designed to provide a basis for measuring actual performance against each planned expenditure. Management then monitors sales and profit results

TABLE 12.3

BASIS OF ADVERTISING BUDGETS

Basis	*Percentage of Respondents*
Percentage of last year's sales turnover	7%
Percentage of this year's expected turnover	17
Percentage of last year's actual and this year's estimate	4
A fixed figure without specific reference to sales	39
No known basis	29
Other	4

[7]Hart, *Industrial Advertising and Publicity,* p. 132.

against advertising and promotion costs and makes appropriate adjustments in spending levels to improve the chances of an attractive payoff. This approach obviously increases the opportunity to base advertising and promotion decisions on profit economics rather than intuition, individual preference, or historical patterns.

There is one more contributing factor that needs to be pointed out. Many advertising agencies are not particularly well suited to working effectively on industrial advertising and promotion. Agency personnel are certainly knowledgeable about advertising and promotion techniques, but most agencies find it difficult to attract and retain personnel with the technical knowledge and understanding required to market industrial products effectively. Of course there are exceptions, especially in agencies geared primarily to serving industrial companies, but as a general rule this point holds true. A recent survey[8] highlights the deficiencies many industrial companies see in their advertising agencies. Responses were given to this open-ended question: "What added strengths should your agency develop to serve your company more effectively?" The answers were coded as follows:

A A significant number of answers along these lines, and therefore a key factor.

B This view was repeated a number of times, and some attention should be paid to it.

C Mentioned only once or at most four times; much less significant.

Here were the responses:

1.	Need for greater technical and product knowledge	A
2.	Improvement in creativity in all senses	B
3.	More comprehensive promotional planning	B
4.	Knowledge of technical media	B
5.	Complete involvement in clients' business	B
6.	Market orientation	C
7.	Less staff turnover	C
8.	Better production efficiency	C
9.	Greater use of free-lance talent	C
10.	Higher caliber of personnel	C
11.	Initiative	C

The results of this survey are not surprising, since it is difficult for an outsider to develop the deep understanding of a company's technology, products, customers, and competition when it takes the company's full-time employees many years to learn the business. The business skills required to develop more technical or product knowledge to contribute to marketing plans or even to manage the sums of money involved prudently are simply not there. Of course there are many exceptions to this generalization, but it contributes to the waste that occurs in many industrial advertising and promotion programs.

Despite these problems and negative comments, advertising and promotion can be very cost-effective tools for the industrial marketer.

[8]Ibid., p. 133.

THE INDUSTRIAL PROMOTIONAL MIX

Exhibit 12-1 shows a typical pattern of cost effectiveness for various industrial advertising and promotion activities. This illustration obviously reflects a generalization; variables, such as the type of product, stage in the life cycle, market-customer makeup, and competitive structure, would alter the picture in any particular situation. Nevertheless, it clearly shows the range of costs per contract for various promotional approaches that can be used to reach the customer. Obviously, each of these approaches has its advantages and disadvantages and is more or less effective in varying situations. Let's take a closer look.

Catalogs are next best to the salesperson for giving a customer what it needs to make a buying decision. Catalogs reach more people than the individual salesperson and are there with a product message when the prospect is ready to buy. Design, printing, and

EXHIBIT 12-1

THE INDUSTRIAL PROMOTIONAL MIX

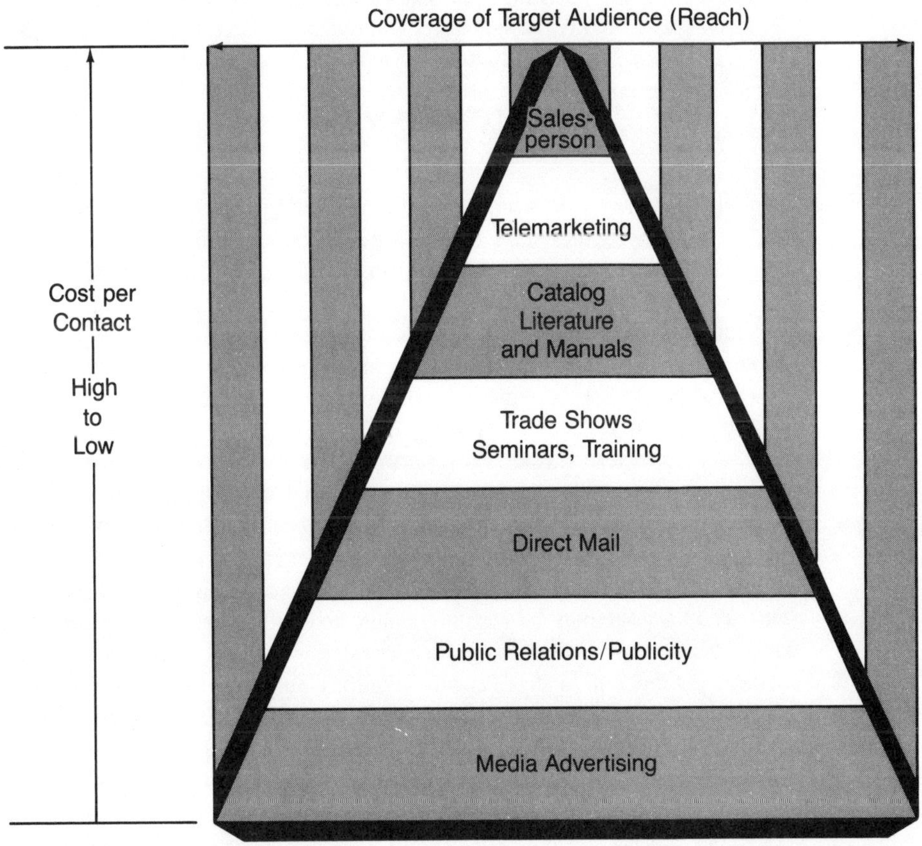

THREE USES OF TELEMARKETING

(1) The B. F. Goodrich Chemical Group uses a telemarketing center for order taking, customer service, and information dissemination purposes. When customers call, a center specialist brings up the customer's file on a data terminal screen, records the order, checks inventory, and, when necessary, talks with production and shipping to schedule the shipment. Field sales personnel are also supported by being provided current inventory data and estimated arrival times. High volume accounts are scheduled for field visits, thereby increasing the number and quality of contacts between B. F. Goodrich and its best customers.

(2) The 3M Company relies on a telemarketing center to assist customers with equipment trouble. After calling 3M's 800 number, the customer describes the problem to a skilled technician with access to an on-line computer system. On more than 30 percent of the calls, 3M finds that the equipment difficulty can be solved in minutes without having to dispatch a service technician. This has improved customer service activities and provided a valuable service at a very reasonable cost to 3M.

(3) The Parker Hannifin Corporation utilizes telemarketing to sell to marginal accounts and keep closer contact with distributors. Telemarketing helps both Parker's and its distributor salespeople "call" on customers that would not be reached. Finally, new product features are quickly explained and questions answered for distributors and end users by telemarketing.

Source: Roy Voorhees and John Coppett, "Telemarketing in Distribution Channels," *Industrial Marketing Management,* 12, 2(April 1983), 106.

distribution, however, can be costly. Telemarketing is a form of marketing communication that utilizes telephone technology (WATTS lines, 800 numbers, and so on) to make sales "calls" and receive information from markets. Telemarketing is effectively used to generate sales leads, qualify customers, receive sales and service inquiries, and finally to substitute periodically for person-to-person sales calls (see the box).

Trade shows, seminars, and training are the only industrial communications vehicles through which prospects come to learn more about a product or service offering. Having made the effort to come, attendees represent a select target for some direct selling opportunity. An alternative to trade show participation (or a possible next step following an expression of interest) is scheduled plant visits that show the potential customer how the product is designed, manufactured, and serviced, and how it performs under various conditions.

Direct mail is the only mass medium that can be directed toward target groups or prospects. The message may be highly personalized and can also be designed as an effective market research tool. But rising postage rates make this an increasingly costly method to reach potential prospects. Public relations publicity has believability through perceived public endorsement and wide coverage of target audience. However, it is impossible to control the timing or content of the message. Direct mail is the only mass communication vehicle that can be controlled completely. You control what you want to say, when you want to say it, and to whom. It is the least effective in terms of actually closing a sale, but can be the most effective in low-cost coverage of an entire target audience with a controlled message. It is often difficult to use media advertising effectively because it is often hard to define a message or appeal that is truly meaningful to a sizable cross-section of potential customers.

The direct sales contact is clearly the most effective means of closing a sale, but far and away the most costly. As Exhibit 12-2 shows, the average cost of each industrial sales call has risen dramatically over the past 15 years and is probably well over $200 at the present time. Driven by inflation, direct sales costs will continue to rise and increase

EXHIBIT 12-2

COST OF AN INDUSTRIAL SALES CALL

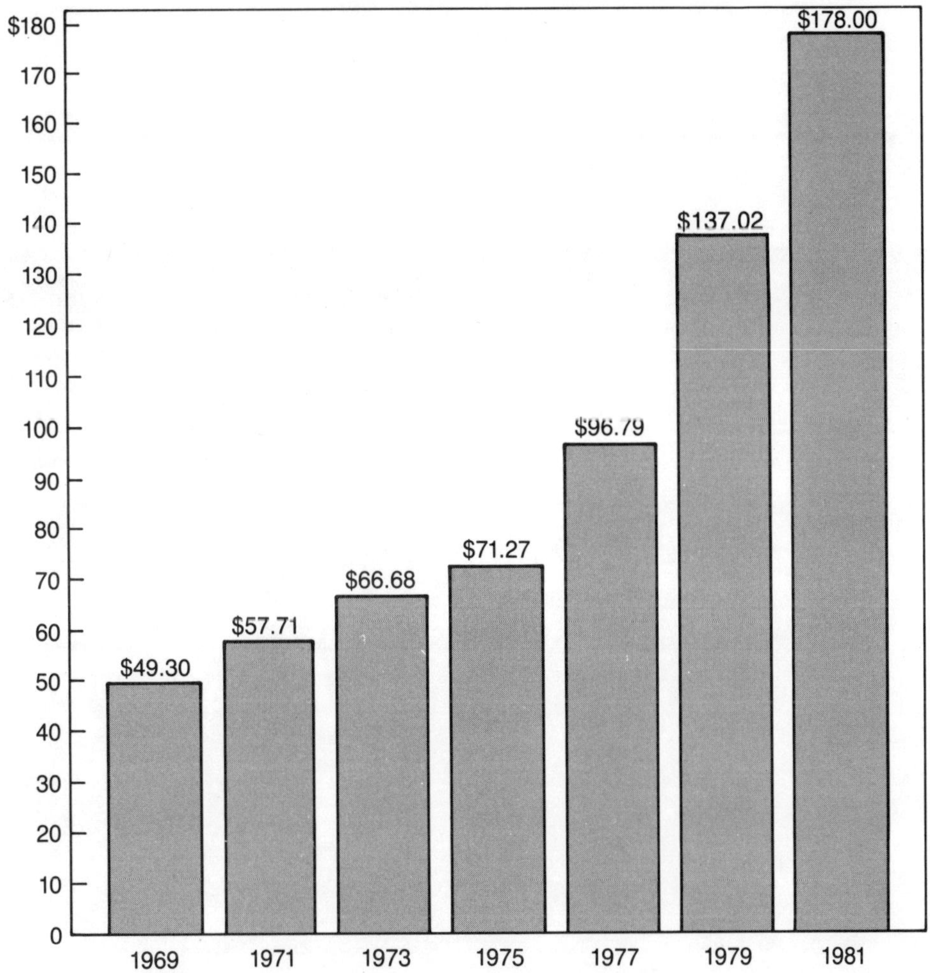

Source: McGraw-Hill Research

the need for productivity improvement in most industrial selling organizations. For this reason, it should be clear that if advertising and promotion activities can be used to make the sales representative's calls more productive, they can provide a real economic benefit to the company.

SOME EFFECTIVE PROGRAMS

Many companies have successfully used their advertising and promotion programs to generate sales leads and improve the salesperson's hit ratio. For example, the ad shown in Exhibit 12-3 for a wind deflector, a totally new product designed to improve fuel efficiency for long-haul truckers, appeared in many leading trade journals and other national publications. As you can see, the ad clearly shows how the deflector is mounted and how it works. More important, it specifically describes how much efficiency can be

EXHIBIT 12-3 ***THE KENWORTH VARASHIELDS™ AD***

Source: Paccar

achieved and the kind of economic gain that results from investment in this device. Finally, the reader is told how and where to contact a local dealer for additional information. The response to this ad and others in the series provided the salespeople with a large number of leads and put them in a much stronger position to close a sale than when they simply made cold calls. Effective media advertising like this can be very useful in generating sales leads and contributing to the success of the new product or a product with distinctly new features.

Another good example is a series of General Electric ads that featured its new line of energy-saving motors. The ads shown in Exhibit 12-4 illustrate how the company used two different approaches to promote energy-saving motors across all industries and in selected market segments. The first ad appeared in broad-based purchasing and production-engineering magazines. The second ad for the same product was designed specifically for pulp and paper mill customers and appeared only in trade publications reaching that market. Both ads emphasize the savings potential from the motor, but the first describes the savings in general terms, and the second describes savings potential in terms related specifically to mill usage.

Many other companies have booked a substantial volume of new orders by participating in trade shows with the right kind of product exhibit. One independent manufacturer of telecommunications equipment regularly planned new product introductions to tie into the schedule of key industry trade shows and developed a very aggressive promotion and sales solicitation program to make sure potential customers were in attendance at these shows. Sales and marketing management were able to predict with a high degree of accuracy how successful the product would be by initial customer reaction at the trade show. Manufacturing and sales plans could then be realistically geared to high-probability volume estimates. This approach enabled the company to get a running start on new product sales that it would not have achieved if it had relied solely on the sales force to do the job.

Another group of companies has developed a strong position with customers by providing them with problem-solving handbooks that are of genuine value to potential users or specifiers of the company's products. Although some advertising experts may not think of these handbooks as a form of advertising, they are often the most effective promotional vehicle in the company's entire communications program. One reason advertising personnel are often less than enthusiastic about handbooks as a communication vehicle is that they have a limited role in their development. The handbook is generally organized around common customer problems that require technical data for solution, and there is simply no place for advertising puffery. Parker Hannifin's *O-Ring Handbook* is a prime example. It is in its 12th printing and is used by engineers the world over to help solve hydraulic sealing problems that may be encountered in any operation where fluid must be contained. Tommy McCuistion, a former vice president of marketing at Parker Hannifin, referred to the *O-Ring Handbook* as "a silent salesman that is always there when a customer needs help to solve a problem." Another very effective handbook was developed by the Crawford Fitting Company for the SWAGELOK tube fitting line. Exhibit 12-5 shows the contents page. As you can see, the book has been designed to help the engineer trouble-shoot and map out the connection and fitting requirements for many machines and applications.

EXHIBIT 12-4 (a)

GENERAL ELECTRIC'S AD FOR BROAD BASED PURCHASING MAGAZINES

Get a 50%, 100%, even 200% ROI with Energy $aver™ motors.

The more you use Energy $aver ac motors from GE, the more you'll profit from them. As the chart shows, your return on investment can be 200% and more. Few other motor lines can pay back your investment as quickly or as handsomely.

From their first day of operation, Energy $aver motors start paying for themselves. Thanks to their higher energy efficiency and because their operating life is up to four times longer than standard motors, these GE motors can save you thousands of dollars in energy costs. And keep plant operating costs low year after year.

All of which means Energy $aver motors are a smarter investment from every key financial standpoint — including return on investment, annual savings, life-cycle costs and after-tax savings.

So insist on Energy $aver motors from GE — the ones whose high return on investment adds up to higher profits. For a free copy of our booklet, "How to be certain you're getting the maximum return on investment on your high-efficiency motors," write today to: General Electric Company, Section 295-09, Schenectady, NY 12345.

TM — Trademark of General Electric Company

GENERAL ELECTRIC

Source: General Electric Company

EXHIBIT 12-4 (b)

GENERAL ELECTRIC'S AD FOR PULP AND PAPER MILL CUSTOMERS

Turn a profit in your mill year after year with Energy $aver™ motors.

Downtime costs American industry millions of dollars in lost profits every year. But a simple switch to reliable Energy $aver ac motors from General Electric can help you cut this profit-draining downtime in your pulp or paper mill. Because Energy $aver motor insulation lasts up to four times longer than that of standard motors, GE motors can help you avoid expensive replacement and rewinding.

The reason? Energy $aver motors run much cooler under load. As the chart shows, the addition of more magnetizing steel and more copper results in a motor that runs 20 to 30 degrees cooler than normal-efficiency motors. And Energy $aver motors' superior aluminum-alloy frame and endshield efficiently transfer heat — up to three times faster than cast iron.

In addition, Energy $aver motors are far more energy-efficient than standard motors. Just one 125hp Energy $aver motor can save you $1,277* in the first year of operation in your pulp or paper mill. And $11,283 in just seven years.

So insist on Energy $aver motors from GE — the ones whose longer life and energy savings add up to lower life-cycle costs in your pulp or paper mill. For a free copy of our booklet, "How Energy $aver motors can help you turn a profit year after year," write today to: General Electric Company, Section 295-35, Schenectady, NY 12345.

TM — Trademark of General Electric Company
*4¢/KWh initial power cost, 10% annual increase

On Reader Service Card **Circle 114**

GENERAL ELECTRIC

Source: General Electric Company

EXHIBIT 12-5

THE SWAGELOK™ TUBE FITTING AND INSTALLATION MANUAL

CONTENTS

iv

Source: Crawford Fitting Company. SWAGELOK is a registered trademark of the Crawford Fitting Company. Reprinted with permission.

Many industrial companies have successfully employed some form of corporate advertising to help open the door for their salespeople. The ad from a Reliance Electric series shown in Exhibit 12-6 is a good example of this kind of an effort. As you can see, it clearly shows a broad range of capabilities in one of the company's target industries and emphasizes the company's growth record and financial strength. This ad and others directed toward other target markets were featured in *The Wall Street Journal, Fortune,* and other financial publications to present a successful picture to the investment community. They were also featured in appropriate trade publications to help promote the company's capabilities in the marketplace. The ads made a very favorable impression on potential customers, and Reliance salespeople were able to use them very effectively in their sales presentations.

The money spent in all these efforts contributed importantly to the sales performance of the companies involved and represented attractive investments. With proper marketing management and control, there is no reason why the great bulk of the money spent on advertising and promotion activities cannot yield the same kind of result.

PLANNING AND CONTROL

To achieve this benefit and make these activities pay off requires the same kind of tough-minded management attention that prevails in any other aspect of business. And one principle of good business management must be rigorously applied to ensure that advertising and promotion activities are cost effective: Never spend any money without a plan, and never waste time planning anything that cannot be controlled.

Stating this principle is a lot easier than actually following it. As a general rule, advertising and promotion managers in the industrial world do not tend to be tough-minded themselves. Moreover, many senior managers find it difficult to "ride herd" on these activities in an effective way because they are generally unfamiliar with the jargon and techniques commonly employed by advertising and promotion managers. When review sessions are conducted, they more often than not degenerate into a discussion of the merits or demerits of a particular ad or promotion and seldom get into the managerial considerations that really count, like target groups, specific marketing objectives, and the basis for measurement. As a result, very few senior managers know how the total budget for advertising and promotion was established, what cost-benefit expectations were planned, and how actual results measure up against original objectives.

Budgets Versus Plans

As we have stressed, the key to managing these activities is to ensure they are planned and controlled, with the emphasis on *planned.* What are often passed off as advertising and promotion plans in far too many industrial companies are actually only budgets established by calculating some percentage of sales, matching competitive expenditures, or plusing last year's expenditures by some amount. This sets up a budgeted amount of money for spending, but it is not a plan and does not establish an adequate basis for

EXHIBIT 12-6 (a)

THE RELIANCE ELECTRIC SERIES

AA-1212

Reliance Electric interaction helps turn a city on.

The job of putting "juice" into a city's power lines gets more challenging every year. But through successful interaction of technologies, products, and services, we help utility companies operate more efficiently to meet that challenge.

Reliance Electric has valuable firsthand experience in meeting the unique needs of nuclear power plants, including the requirements for software and drawings, seismic analysis, and radiation-resistant materials.

For fossil-fuel plants, Reliance V*S Drives power limestone slurry pumps in SO_2 removal systems.

Throughout the industry, Reliance supplies a broad line of Duty Master® A-C motors to power fans, pumps, and auxiliary equipment. And in the control room, Reliance control panels and consoles monitor complex operations and systems.

Successful Reliance Electric businesses interact in other important areas.

Dodge pulleys, clutches, and couplings are an integral part of handling systems that move coal from hopper cars, barges, and stockpiles.

Master gearmotors and speed reducers and Reeves variable speed drives provide precise power to control the motion of auxiliary systems handling coal, ash, and limestone.

Toledo Scale equipment weighs and identifies — in motion — loaded railroad cars that deliver coal and oil. And Toledo Weighveyors® measure the flow of coal on moving belts, automatically.

These complex, automated systems receive instructions and sequencing from AutoMate® programmable controllers that replace maintenance-prone relay panels.

Lorain Products provides inverter systems for power-failure protection of computerized grid control networks and for critical instrumentation and controls throughout the power plant.

Haughton elevators provide fast vertical transportation for people and equipment within multilevel generating plants.

Reliance Electric is also people. More than 20,000 people interacting around the world, including application engineers and industry managers concerned with the immediate and future needs of utility companies. They offer industrial and commercial automation components, systems, and services that no other company can match. And they're backed by networks of distribution and service centers to maintain the equipment they supply.

For fiscal 1974, our policy of disciplined acquisitions and interaction paid off with record sales of $580 million and record earnings of $2.10 per share, fully diluted. Records achieved by sales to the commercial, industrial, service, and international markets.

This multinational interaction is outlined in our new corporate profile. For a copy, write B. C. Ames, President, Reliance Electric Company, 29325 Chagrin Blvd., P.O. Box 22280, Cleveland OH 44122.

Successful businesses interacting.

RELIANCE ELECTRIC

This advertisement appears in FORTUNE (Financial), June; and FINANCE, July, 1975
M&F Advertising / S-8503

Source: Reliance Electric Co.

EXHIBIT 12-6 (b)

THE RELIANCE ELECTRIC SERIES

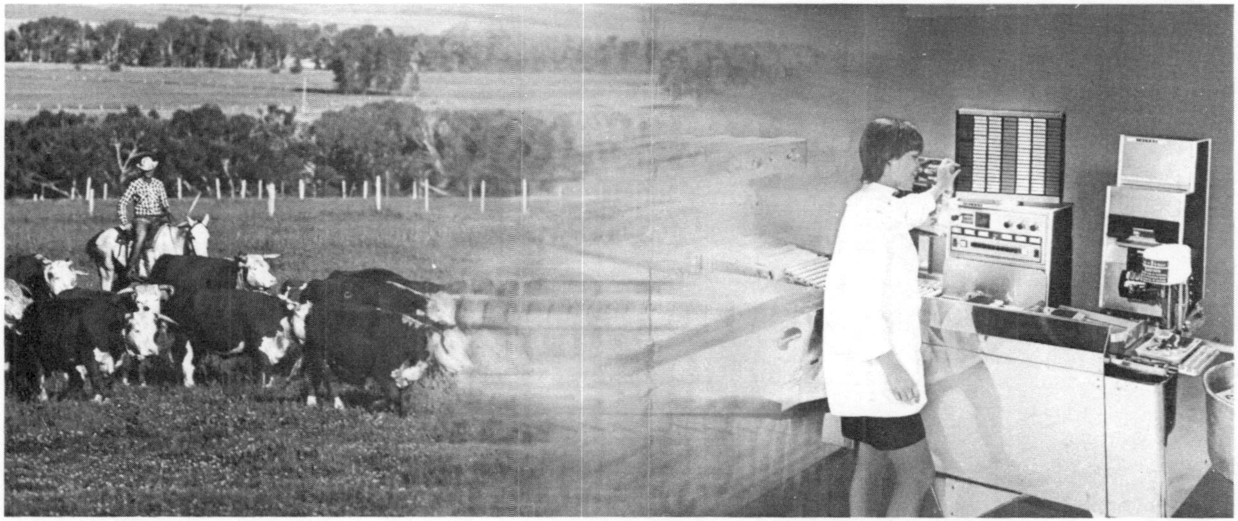

AA-1177

Reliance Electric interaction...automates beef from way out to weigh-in.

Putting meat on America's tables is no simple process. But through successful interaction of technologies, products, and services, we help cattle feeders, food processors, and supermarkets reduce the costs and speed the distribution of meat products.

Toledo Scale is Reliance Electric, supplying feeders with automated batching systems that carefully measure, weigh, and blend ingredients and supplements for livestock rations. Supplying automatic equipment to help packers weigh dressed sides — in motion — and keep track of inventories. Then, in retail supermarkets, Toledo automated wrapping machines, scales and checkout systems package, weigh, price, label, and count the items that appear, ready-to-buy, on today's meat counters.

Successful Reliance Electric businesses play other important roles in our interaction story.

Reliance electric motors power pumps and refrigeration equipment. Reliance electrical V★S® drives control conveyors that move perishable meat products quickly and reliably through packing and processing lines.

Dodge bearings, screw conveyor drives, pulleys, couplings, and fixed speed drives are essential to material handling systems that move feed to fatten cattle for market.

Master gearmotors, speed reducers and Reeves variable speed drives provide precise power to control the motion of processing and packaging machinery.

Haughton elevators and escalators provide vertical transportation for people and materials in processing plants and shopping centers.

Lorain Products provides Uninterruptible Power Systems to protect the accuracy of computer inventory and distribution controls activated by entries from electronic point-of-sale cash register terminals.

Reliance Electric is more than 20,000 people interacting around the world, including application engineers and industry managers concerned with the needs of the food processing industry. They offer industrial and commercial automation components, systems, and services that no other company can match. And they're backed by distribution and service centers to maintain the equipment they supply.

For 1973, our policy of disciplined acquisitions and interaction paid off with a record $484 million in sales and a 51 percent increase in earnings. Sales to the commercial, industrial, service, and international markets in the first half of 1974 were a record $271 million, and earnings were up 37 percent over the same period in 1973.

This multinational interaction is outlined in our new corporate profile. For a copy, write B. C. Ames, President, Reliance Electric Company, 24701 Euclid Avenue, Cleveland, Ohio 44117.

Successful businesses interacting.

RELIANCE ELECTRIC COMPANY

This advertisement appears in
BUSINESS WEEK, July 20; FORTUNE, July; INSTITUTIONAL INVESTOR, August; MEAT PROCESSING, June; NEWSWEEK, August 12, 1974.
M&F Advertising / S-7122

Source: Reliance Electric Co.

EXHIBIT 12-6 (c)

THE RELIANCE ELECTRIC SERIES

Photo courtesy American Airlines AA-1181A

Reliance Electric interaction makes connections at the world's largest airport.

Passengers making connections at the spectacular new Dallas-Ft. Worth Airport get lots of help from Reliance Electric. Our successful interaction of technologies, products, and services helps keep people, baggage and freight on schedule.

Lorain Products is Reliance Electric, totally involved in telecommunications through a complete telephone exchange built right on the airport grounds. A broad range of Lorain telecom power and line treatment devices helps assure dependable phone service throughout the sprawling flight complex, from a routine time check to an emergency phone alert in the world's largest control tower.

Even the unique "people movers" that make connections within and between airline terminals and the hotel are controlled by a computer system that receives non-stop power from a network of Lorain Uninterruptible Power Systems (UPS).

At airports across the land, Lorain UPS helps make connections by providing continuous power to computerized hotel and airline reservation systems.

Successful Reliance Electric businesses help make connections in other important ways.

Toledo Scale equipment quickly weighs baggage and freight for incoming passengers and records the totals for conformance with load-limit requirements.

Haughton elevators and escalators whisk passengers from ticket counters to check-in gates. Haughton service specialists maintain all types of transportation and handling equipment in vast and busy terminals.

Reliance electrical drives control conveyors on X-ray and inspection equipment to speed passengers through security areas.

Master gearmotors driven by Reliance electrical V★S® drives control the exact positioning of telescoping boarding ramps for weatherproof direct access between aircraft and terminal.

Reeves mechanical variable speed drives control the movement of handling systems for fast loading and retrieval of passenger baggage.

Dodge couplings, torque-arm speed reducers, bearings, and pulleys on conveyors from cargo holds to carousels help deplaning passengers make connections on the ground.

Reliance Electric is more than 20,000 people interacting around the world, including industry managers concerned with the needs of the transportation and communications industries. They offer industrial and commercial automation components, systems, and services that no other company can match. And they're backed by distribution and service centers to maintain the equipment they supply.

For fiscal 1974, our interaction policy paid off with sales of $580 million and record earnings of $2.10 per share, fully diluted. Sales to the commercial, industrial, service, and international markets in the first half of 1975 were $326,564,000, and fully diluted earnings were a record $1.23 per share, compared to $.96 per share for the same period in 1974.

This multinational interaction is outlined in our corporate profile. For a copy, write B. C. Ames, President, Reliance Electric Company, 29325 Chagrin Blvd., P.O. Box 22280, Cleveland OH 44122.

Successful businesses interacting.

RELIANCE ELECTRIC

Source: Reliance Electric Co.

control. Many advertising and promotion managers will react defensively to this criticism by showing that their overall budget is broken down into detailed expenditures for different activities and programs so that each component part can be controlled. In most cases they are correct. The detail does in fact exist, and they in fact manage the component pieces of their advertising and promotion budget closely. However, it is still a budget and not a plan. You can control actual expenditures within the budget and still not know whether the money was worth spending. For example, what were the budgeted expenditures designed to do in terms of achieving added volume, or gaining new feature recognition or new account interest? When were these accomplishments to occur? What profit impact was anticipated, and how does it relate to the advertising and promotion costs? These are the kinds of questions that need to be answered as part of the advertising and promotion plan to justify budgeted expenditures and provide the basis for determining whether the funds were well spent.

Many of those involved in advertising and promotion activities will argue that you can't define what you are trying to accomplish with advertising and promotion dollars in such precise terms. They claim the dollars budgeted or spent should be regarded as an investment that will somehow pay off in terms of a better image for the company or a better reputation for a product. Those who take this point of view are asking management to accept a lot on faith—which simply does not make sense when so much money is involved.

The Policy Statement

To be effective, planning and control must begin with an outline of a policy that defines broadly when and how advertising and promotion dollars should be spent. Ideally, the president of the company should take on this task, since he or she is in a better position than anyone else to provide a statement that will set the tone for the way these activities are managed throughout the organization. The responsibility may be delegated to a division general manager or even a product or market manager as long as they have direct responsibility for profit and loss in the area where the dollars will be spent. The president of one industrial company clearly established the parameters for advertising and promotion spending with the following memorandum:

> January 15, 1981
>
> To: All General Managers
>
> Subject: Advertising and Promotion Expenditures
>
> I was appalled to find that we spent $3.7 million, or nearly 1 percent of sales, for various types of advertising and promotion last year. Moreover, expenditures for these activities have grown at better than a 15 percent rate each year for the last five years. I don't know how all of this money was spent, but I do know that a lot of it is wasted on repetitive type product ads in various trade journals, giveaway pen and pencil sets, golf balls, and calendars, uncontrolled attendance at trade shows, corporate promotional brochures, etc.
>
> The main reason these expenditures have gotten out of control is that they have been managed at the corporate level and no one with a direct profit responsibility

has felt the burden of responsibility for them. Effective February 1, the corporate advertising and promotion function will be disbanded and each division manager will be responsible for the advertising and promotion required in his operation. While each division will be responsible for their own advertising and promotion budget, all budgets should be developed around the following ground rules:

1. No more giveaway items that don't have a direct tie to our business;
2. No more loosely controlled participation in trade shows;
3. No media advertising unless it is specifically designed to:
   a. introduce a new product or new product features;
   b. introduce an existing product to a new market;
   c. introduce the company to some user or customer group or some important part of the financial community that does not know us.
4. No expenditures for any advertising and promotion activities that are not backed by a solid plan that can be used as a vehicle for measurement and control.

As a result of this memorandum, the company's advertising and promotion expenditures were reduced by 60 percent without any loss of market position or selling effectiveness. The approach outlined by the president in this case may be too tough and not applicable in every situation, but it is the kind of a starting point that is essential to ensure proper planning and control.

The Plan

Once this kind of direction has been provided, the next step is to make sure that a comprehensive advertising and promotion plan is developed to support all proposed expenditures. When completed, the promotional plan should become part of the overall marketing and business plan for presentation to senior management. No special format or approach is required as long as the promotional plan includes the following:

1. A brief statement that defines the objectives of advertising and promotion in meaningful terms, with emphasis on the word "meaningful." For example, a broad statement claiming that advertising and promotion will be used to promote product recognition and the corporate image is not worth saying, since it doesn't mean anything. A statement like the following expresses a serious intent to manage these activities in a businesslike way that provides the best possible chance of generating a return for the dollars spent:

   All our advertising and promotion activities are designed to help sell our company and its products. We expect to work closely with sales and marketing management to ensure that every dollar we spend *supports* their efforts and will ultimately contribute to profit results. We will always ensure that our activities are integrated into sales and marketing plans and that every spending proposal is accompanied by a specific set of goals that will provide the basis for measurement. We will never commit or spend any advertising or promotion dollars on the basis of vague hopes or objectives or without the approval of the line manager responsible for profits.

2. A summary of the budgeted costs for each project or program and a brief written description of the specific marketing and business objectives to be accomplished. Most objectives should be stated in quantifiable terms so that performance can be measured.
3. A measurement program to determine whether approved advertising and promotion goals have been achieved as defined and whether expenditures for these activities were cost effective.
4. A schedule of advertising and promotion events designed in such a way that spending can be cut back without destroying the entire program if the business runs into a difficult period.

Following an approach like this is not easy, but it is well worth the effort. It imposes a discipline on the advertising and promotion management team that helps them function as business partners to support sales and marketing management. It forces an objective analysis of individual projects or programs and expenditures, highlights weaknesses in the overall communications program, and allows selective pruning of nonessential items. And most important, it provides a solid basis for review and control.

Review and Control

Assuming the advertising and promotion plan has been developed along the lines described above, the final step for management is to ensure that satisfactory results are achieved. This can be done through a full marketing review, or it can be done separately if management chooses. However it is done, a formal review should be conducted at least quarterly and those responsible should be required to explain any variance from planned objectives, timetables, spending levels, or results. If management fails to conduct such a review on a regular basis, you can be sure that the planning process will deteriorate and that a lot of dollars will be wasted on ill-conceived activities that contribute very little to market performance or profits.

As in any business situation, the key to effective review and control is the quality of the plan. There is simply no way to effectively review performance unless you know what it is you want to do in the first place. This is why the detailed planning described earlier is so important.

Many people in the advertising and promotion world will argue that you can't be as specific as we have suggested. Don't buy this argument. If those making the advertising and promotion proposals can't define specific economic benefits they intend to achieve with the expenditures they propose, the money would be better spent if given to charity. When the advertising and promotion budget is based on a sufficiently detailed plan, the review sessions can focus on planned accomplishments and adjustments can be made to ensure objectives are achieved. Alternatively, if it is clear that the objectives cannot be achieved for whatever reasons, spending for advertising and promotion activities can be scaled back or stopped so that more profit flows to the bottom line.

SUMMARY

Advertising and promotion activities are useful tools for any company: they can build recognition and volume, introduce a new product or service, explain cost benefits to a wide potential customer base, and turn up sales prospects. The key, however, is planning and control so that the dollars spent on this activity have some chance of bringing the company the return it wants. A lot of money is involved, and a lot of it is often wasted because it is difficult to construct the proper mix of activities and to quantify the results.

Business-to-business advertising has special requirements if it is to be successful, and it is up to the marketing organization to get the type of advertising that will work. Most important is planning and control; an advertising budget is not a plan, and occasional checks on how the budget is being spent is not an effective review and control program. The budget must be related to a detailed plan that is formally reviewed on a regular basis to see that the company gets its money's worth from its advertising and promotion effort.

IV

DEVELOPING AND EVALUATING PLANS

13

Developing Strategies and Plans

In the fall of 1978 Joe Cohen, a two-year associate with a well-known international consulting firm, was assigned to a study project for a large pump and valve manufacturing company. The study was designed to help the company strengthen its approach to planning so that it could be more responsive to changing market conditions. The company's management believed that outside assistance was necessary to integrate the best features of the planning process that had been developed in its individual subsidiaries, which had been brought together through acquisition.

Each of the four consultants on the study team was assigned to different areas of the business. Joe's assignment was to work with the electronic valve division of the company to define its planning requirements and to recommend a planning approach for the division that would tie in with the planning requirements of the other divisions and the whole corporation. Joe had worked as a product manager for a large food products company and had been very involved in designing and implementing a planning process for that operation. Because of his strong sales and marketing background, he spent a good deal of time with sales and marketing management in the division. After several weeks, he thought he knew enough about the client company's requirements to develop a schematic drawing of the planning and control process that should be followed. As you might expect, he drew heavily on the successful experience he had had with his former employer.

Joe reviewed his work with two division product managers as well as the marketing vice president of the client operation and found that they were generally supportive and enthusiastic. So he was very surprised when the partner in charge of the consulting assignment reacted very negatively to Joe's efforts during the study team review meeting. The partner was blunt: "You have developed an approach for marketing planning and control that may make sense in a package goods business, but is not at all applicable here. You are getting paid to think deeply about the particular planning requirements of our client's operation. If you can't do a better job of discerning these, you can't be a very effective consultant."

When the review meeting ended, Joe sat there. He looked over the schematic he had prepared. Where had he gone wrong? What was so different about the planning requirements of this industrial company?

What are probable differences between this company and Joe's former employer?

Why would a business plan for an industrial firm require a different approach from one for a packaged goods company?

What should be Joe's first step in rethinking his plan?

Corporate life would be a lot easier if management could forget or wish away the whole idea of formal business planning, for no one yet has been able to figure out how to get business plans into written form without a lot of hard work. But planning is likely to become a more important management tool in the future as companies face increasingly more complex and difficult situations and continue to scramble to add new products and markets to their base.

WHY PLANNING IS IMPORTANT

Formal planning, which means committing plans to writing, has been accepted as a way of business life for the past 20 years. The discipline helps managers avoid the mistakes that are bound to occur when they try to ad lib their way through a complex situation. Planning has taken on added importance in recent years as the world has been caught up in a maelstrom of change that has greatly increased the risks and chances of failure for any business venture. Of course, there is really nothing new about change, especially in business. What is different is the velocity with which change is occurring and the sudden impact such change can have on almost any business. Businesspeople all around the world continue to reel from a series of events that are clear evidence of the increasing velocity of change: exploding technology, rapidly increasing foreign competition, the energy crisis, and changing interest rates and currency values. Beyond these, a number of fundamental social changes, like declining birth rates, fewer marriage and family formations, and more two-worker households, have far-reaching implications for most industrial activities. They have caused and will cause real growth to decline in certain markets and to explode in others. They have made or will make dinosaurs out of some products and processes that have historically been mainstays of the American economy. They have caused or will cause other products or processes that have been considered uneconomic in the past to become much more attractive in the future.

Many people tend to view these developments as unusual dislocations that will become less disruptive over time. We don't believe this is the case at all; we believe these developments will have greater impact on industrial operations of all types in the years ahead, and that others like them are going to occur with greater severity and frequency. Many people also argue that it is impossible to plan in an environment characterized by so much change and uncertainty. Actually, these conditions make planning more important. It is essential, not helpful, for management in general and marketing management in particular to devote much more time to thinking about: (1) the direction of these trends and developments; (2) what impact they are likely to have on various businesses; (3) what can be done to minimize the risks or capitalize on the opportunities likely to occur as a result of these changes; and (4) what to do if things turn out differently than expected. Developing answers to these questions and finding responses to a number of scenarios are essential for survival in a period of accelerating change and increasing uncertainty.

Despite the need for and inherent logic of formal business planning, very few companies are really satisfied with the results they achieve for all the time and effort involved.

The comment of one vice president typifies the frustration and disappointment of many executives:

> We knock ourselves out every year with a major time commitment and massive paper flow to put together a strategic plan for the business that is heavily based on marketing input. But we can't really point to any substantive benefits that are directly traceable to all the extra effort. As I see it, our marketing group has not done the job it should in thinking through a strategy. If it had, we'd have a lot stronger edge in the marketplace. At this point I am not sure whether it is something important that we ought to do better or whether it is just a fad that we ought to get rid of.

Why should his reaction be the rule rather than the exception? What are the pitfalls that cause planning results to fall short of expectations? Most important, what lessons can be learned from the experience of those few industrial companies that can honestly point to concrete results from their planning efforts?

SOME PLANNING PITFALLS

Ignorance of planning theory or mechanics is not the cause of the disappointments so many companies are experiencing. Most industrial managers in both line and staff positions are well aware that effective planning depends on market and economic facts, results in detailed operating programs (not just budgets), and provides the best basis for measurement and control. Few executives are unfamiliar with the concept of formal planning. Various approaches to formal planning have received their share of emphasis in the business literature and the academic world over the past several years, and apparently most executives have tried them. Yet major problems crop up in many companies when they set about putting some kind of a formal planning approach into practice. These problems fall into four categories:

1. Failure to fit the concept to the industrial context
2. Confusion over types of planning
3. Overemphasis on the system at the expense of content
4. Lack of alternative strategies

Let's examine each of the problem categories a bit more closely before moving on to see what steps have been taken by companies that have successfully integrated an effective approach to business planning.

Matching Concept and Context

Planners often run into trouble when they try to use, without change, concepts developed for planning in consumer goods companies. To a large extent, the disappointing results encountered by industrial companies reflect their failure to recognize two distinguishing characteristics of most industrial companies that dictate a need for a particular planning approach.

The first is the multiplicity of markets and channels discussed in Chapter 2. This diversity of market and channel combinations requires discrete marketing strategies. A consumer goods company typically markets its several brands through one or two channels to a common consumer group. A multiproduct industrial manufacturer is likely to sell in a wide range of different markets through a variety of channels. For example, it would not be uncommon for a manufacturer of electrical components to sell its major product lines in as many as 30 distinct markets through several different channels and face different competitors in different markets. As you can appreciate, anyone who tried to cover this complex network of markets and channels with a single marketing plan would be doomed to failure. What is actually needed is a number of discrete plans, one for each combination of products and markets that can be managed as a discrete entity (often called a product-market business).

Juggling a large number of markets and channels is not the only problem facing planners in industrial marketing. They must also plan around and with the other functions of the business, since marketing simply does not control factors like engineering or manufacturing that typically make or break performance in the marketplace. As we have stated, marketing success in the industrial world depends largely on the activities of functions like engineering, manufacturing, and technical service. This means that changes in marketing strategy are likely to be based on product design, manufacturing cost, or service innovations, rather than on advertising, promotion, and merchandising—the core elements of the consumer goods marketing plan. Because the success of marketing plans depends to a large extent on activities in other functional areas and on the share of total company resources each product-market business receives, it is unrealistic to expect product managers, market managers, or even the head of marketing to handle the job without the full participation of operating managers. The role of the marketing planner in an industrial company is to analyze and interpret market requirements and determine what operating managers in all functional areas of the business must do to meet these requirements. The planner draws together ideas for an assigned product or market, but the resulting plan is a total business plan, not just a marketing plan.

Obvious as this point might seem, it is frequently overlooked in industrial companies. Having embraced formal planning as a sophisticated way of running the business, many executives try to turn the entire job over to marketing or sales management. After a couple of years of frustration, they are ready to write off the whole effort as a monumental waste of time. The real cause of their disappointment lies not in the concept, however, but in the way it has been applied (see the box). Unfortunately, this has been the experience of a great many otherwise well-managed companies. Far too much planning is carried on as a parallel activity that gets plenty of lip-service, but little real attention from the line decision makers.

Confusing Various Types of Planning

Confusion over the distinctions among strategic planning, long-range planning, operational planning, corporate strategy, and product-market strategy also leads to major diffi-

PLANNING ISN'T WORTH THE EFFORT

A major chemical company added a group of six managers to its marketing organization, gave them a planning format to follow, and told them to develop a written plan for achieving a stronger and more profitable position in their assigned markets. All six managers, eager to earn their spurs, embarked on a massive fact-gathering and writing effort. After several months, hundreds of pages of plans and supporting documentation had been written, but no one in top management was much impressed. The president put it this way:

> I'm being generous when I say the end products are only slightly better than useless. Admittedly, we have some better market facts now, but the plans are based on a lot of ideas for product and market development that just aren't in line with my idea of the direction this business should take. On top of that, they've left out a lot of technical and capital considerations that really count. I've concluded that our market managers are simply too far out of the mainstream of the business to do an intelligent job of planning for us.

Not surprisingly, the market managers felt they too had good cause for complaint. As one of them put it:

> The first month of effort was worthwhile. We were putting a fact base together that is essential for intelligent planning. But after that we were flying blind. We never had any idea from top management on the kind of business the company wanted or didn't want, the minimal return it expected, or the kind of support it would be willing to throw into various markets. Worse still, we had no cooperation from the development group, the plants, or even the sales force, where decisions that really influence the business are made. The planning we did was bound to be a bust.

culties in accomplishing the planning job. These are all distinctly different types of planning, and the terms cannot be used interchangeably without creating confusion. To start with, it is useful to point out the differences and the relationships between strategic and operational planning.

STRATEGIC PLANNING VERSUS OPERATIONAL PLANNING. *Strategic* planning defines the basic direction of the business and provides the basis for allocating and committing resources, both labor and capital, to a course of action designed to achieve corporate objectives. The distinguishing feature of strategic plans or decisions is that they typically involve a commitment of resources to a particular course of action. And once these resources are committed, it is difficult to change directions. This is not to say a commitment to a strategic course of action is irrevocable, but a penalty is incurred if directions are changed once a company starts to implement a strategic decision. For example, there is no way to reverse a decision on an acquisition once it has been made or to retract funding commitments for new product or market development once the project is underway without suffering some kind of a time and cost penalty.

The time frame involved is another distinguishing characteristic of strategic planning. Generally, strategic planning covers a period of several years. Three to five years is a reasonable period in industrial manufacturing companies, since most strategic decisions or actions (such as building a new manufacturing facility, developing new products or a position in new markets, or completing acquisition or divestiture programs) can be implemented within this period. Heavy manufacturing or resource companies may need to plan over an even longer period to allow sufficient time for completion of the huge capital projects often required to add new capacity or to develop natural resources.

Operational planning, on the other hand, is typically done annually, and operating plans should be designed to implement strategic business decisions. They also provide management with an annual budget for controlling performance year to year, quarter to quarter, or even month to month. Many of the cost and time commitments reflected in the operating plan are the result of strategic decisions to develop new products, build new plant facilities, strengthen positions in new markets, or make an acquisition effort in one direction or another. Since the operating plan is a vehicle to help implement the strategic plan, it is obvious that the two types of plans must be directly linked. In effect, the first year of a strategic plan serves as the foundation for next year's operating plan.

HOW SALES FORECASTS TIE IN: THE LEAD NUMBERS. The pivotal factor in any operating plan is the sales forecast. Manufacturing levels as well as expense budgets are related to the sales forecast when the operating plan is put together. The sales forecast is also the most variable and least controllable set of numbers in any business plan. Manufacturing costs are far more predictable since there is generally an experience base from which manufacturing costs at various volume levels can be predicted with a fair degree of accuracy. Also, expense levels for most sales, general, and administrative activities or programs are known from prior experience and are therefore more predictable. Sales results on the other hand are dependent on a host of uncontrollable factors like the economy, competitor actions, industry or user developments, and so on.

There arè a variety of techniques for making sales forecasts that range from simple trend line extrapolations to sophisticated statistical and computer based projections developed around relevant market and economic indicators, as we've shown in Chapter 6. Regardless of how the sales forecast is made, however, it is still a guess about future events and has all the uncertainty of any prognostication. In most manufacturing companies, multiple forecasts are prepared by different individuals or groups within the organization, and it is general management's job to sort out these forecasts and ensure that they are properly used to plan, manage, and control the business. Let's examine the different types of forecasts that are likely to be made in any industrial concern.

First, most salespeople are asked to make a "grass roots" sales forecast for their accounts and territories. The aggregate of individual sales forecasts typically reflects the optimistic view of an enthusiastic sales force and is generally an unrealistic set of numbers for making operating or financial commitments. Recognizing this point, sales management usually scales back the salespeople's forecast and recommends a lower set of numbers for planning purposes. If product managers are involved in the organization, they will make sales forecasts for their assigned product line, based on their best estimates of market conditions and the competitive situation. The aggregate of the product forecasts is a good cross-check against the forecast made by sales management, but also may be on the high side since it is unlikely that everything will turn out the way all the product managers expect. Many companies also have additional sales forecasts made by independent market or economic research groups to get still another picture of sales expectations. Finally, it is not unusual for manufacturing management to "second guess" any of these forecasts and make a forecast of its own to schedule its manufacturing operations. A manufacturing manager for a bearing company put it this way: "The sales guys always have a 'pie in the sky' forecast that they never make, and I am not going to build product to a forecast like that."

It is general management's job to make certain that everyone in the organization has a clear understanding of what forecast is going to be used for what purposes. Probably the best approach is to use one of the more optimistic forecasts as a basis for setting sales quotas, establishing incentive programs, and evaluating individual sales performance. This avoids the need to set sales goals that are lower than the salespeople think they can achieve and hopefully will stretch the sales force toward better performance. A second, more conservative forecast, however, should be used to make operating and financial plans and commitments. It is always much easier to adjust these plans and commitments upward if higher sales are achieved than it is to scale them back if actual sales results fall below forecast. Following this approach will help management avoid the embarrassment of having to explain that profits suffered because sales were lower than forecast and that operating and expense ratios got out of line.

PRODUCT-MARKET STRATEGY VERSUS CORPORATE STRATEGY. Beyond the distinction between strategic and operational planning, a distinction needs to be made between the two categories of strategic planning that should be carried out in any multibusiness company.

The first category of strategic planning is product-market strategy. We noted earlier that a separate strategy is needed for each identified product-market business. A well-defined product-market strategy should show where the business is heading and what kind of growth and profits can be expected. Division marketing and general management have the major responsibility for developing product-market strategy by helping to determine answers to questions like these:

1. Is the basic cost and profit structure of the business competitive? If not, what does it take to get marginal operations on a competitive footing?
2. Is the business focused on the right market segments? If not, how should the focus be shifted?
3. What external factors are likely to affect growth and profit potential favorably or unfavorably?
4. Is the operation's technology even with, ahead of, or behind major competitors?
5. Should investments be made in engineering, marketing, or manufacturing to enlarge or improve the business?
6. Should investments be made to integrate forward to strengthen market position or backward to improve the profit structure and/or ensure a stable source of supply?

7. Is plant capacity available to handle increased volume expectations? If not, when will new capacity be needed, and how much?
8. How much new capital is required for what projects, and what payoff is expected?
9. What is the sales, profit, and cash flow outlook for the business, and what is the probability of achieving these results?

Once product-market strategies are developed for each business unit, corporate management has the basis for deciding what strategic moves, if any, are required at the corporate level. This leads to the second type of strategic planning typically done by corporate management, which is designed to answer two fundamental questions:

1. Does the outlook for all the company's strategic business units, in the aggregate, meet corporate growth and profit goals?
2. If not, how big is the gap, and what are the ways to close it?

Exhibit 13-1 shows how a gap can be calculated by aggregating the planned performance of all business units and comparing the result with corporate goals. As you can see, the company's operating divisions have projected earnings well below the corporate objective of 15 percent compounded growth each year, and an earnings gap of $1.20 per share is expected. If we assume there are 5 million shares outstanding, the company needs to pick up $6 million of after-tax earnings over the next five years to close the gap. In this kind of situation, corporate management has three alternatives:

1. Change the corporate earnings target.
2. Restructure division plans to close the gap.
3. Redeploy capital into new businesses with sufficient earnings power to close the gap.

Obviously, some combination of these alternatives is also a choice, and probably the most prudent approach to follow when a strategic planning gap occurs. Whatever the decision, it is likely to change the structure or even the basic direction of the company.

It is strategic planning gaps like these that cause companies to expand certain businesses, sell off others, make acquisitions, and take other actions that reshape the basic character and earnings stream of the business. When you read that some company has sold one of its business units or diversified into a completely new area, you may be seeing the actual results of a shift in corporate strategy. Corporate management has decided that the current structure of its business is not satisfactory to achieve its goals and has carried out a strategic decision to change that structure.

Warner-Lambert and Diamond Shamrock are two companies that have undergone a major restructuring of their businesses. Warner-Lambert sold off its Entenmann's bakery products unit and used the proceeds to buy Imed, a west coast manufacturer of sophisticated medical electronics equipment. These moves were designed to take the company deeper into the medical equipment field. Diamond Shamrock sold off certain of its chemical and plastic units and acquired Sigmore and Natomos to further its objective to become an energy resource company.

EXHIBIT 13-1

CALCULATING THE AGGREGATE OUTLOOK

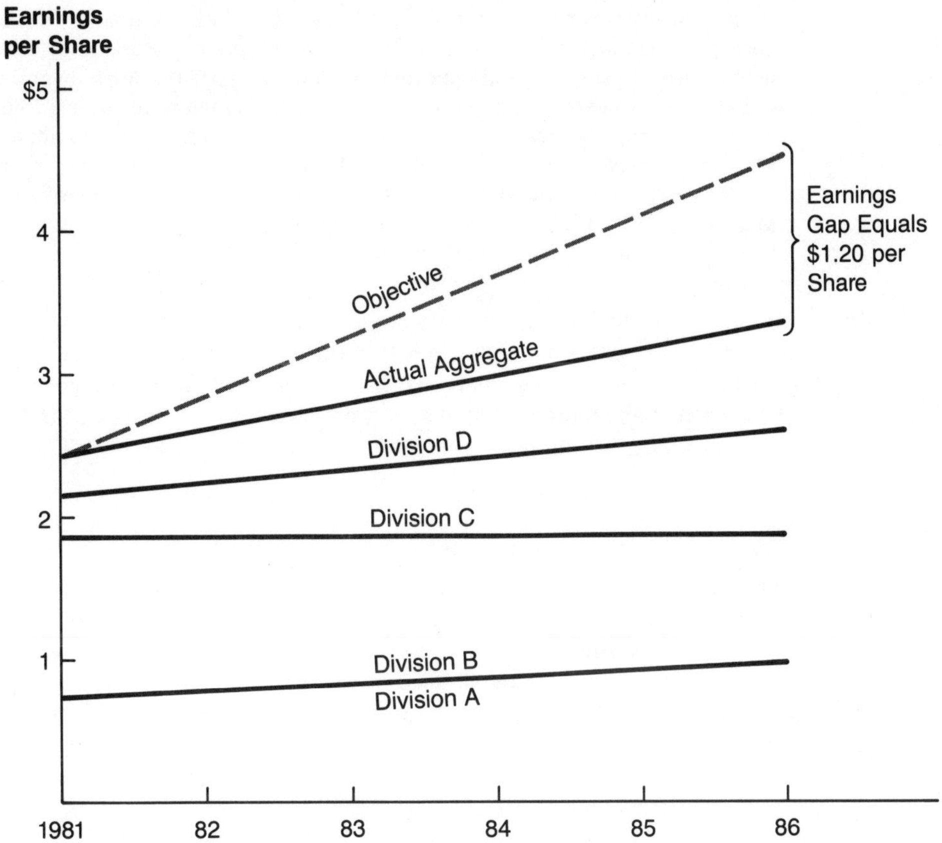

Overemphasizing the System

Many companies have developed comprehensive planning systems that define formats and procedures in great detail. Although some of this structure is necessary, in too many cases the system is so detailed and so rigid that it is a hindrance rather than a help to the planning process. In effect, the system becomes the end product rather than the means to an end, and management is deluded into thinking that it is doing a good job of planning when in fact it is not. Of all the roadblocks, the problem of structure is the most frustrating to managers charged with the responsibility for planning. They recognize that good planning is hard work and cannot be done without a certain amount of pencil pushing. But they bitterly resent demands for excessive written material or filled-in forms that serve no practical business purpose. A product manager for an electronic equipment manufacturer voiced this complaint:

> As part of my planning responsibility, I have to follow a format prescribed by the corporate planning group that calls for a point-by-point discussion of history and a laundry list of problems and opportunities. I'm "gigged" if I don't cover every point in the format, and there's no way to do it in less than ten pages of text. That takes a lot of time—mostly wasted time. All the product managers are sore about it. Much of what we have to write is a rehash of the same old things year after year. In effect, we're being discouraged from concentrating on the issues of the business that are really critical. What they want to see, apparently, is a nice, neat set of plans that all look alike. It just doesn't make sense.

Unfortunately, situations like this are not unusual. Some overzealous staff person or corporate group designs a series of forms that are completely out of phase with the realities of the business. The resulting paperwork chews up great blocks of precious time without producing anything more than a lot of accounting schedules and some kind of written description of what would have been done anyway.

Lack of Alternatives

Given the dynamics of most business situations, it is surprising to find that many planners have tunnel vision in thinking about how the business should be run. Many plans are nothing more than repetitions of prior programs, and hardly worth the paper they are written on. This is the reason so many industrial companies are chronically behind the competition and plagued with poor results. The tendency to base current plans on past practice was forced into the open in one company when each planner was asked by top management to outline alternative strategies for developing his or her assigned market area and to summarize the commitments required (financial, staff, facilities) and the payoff expected (sales, profits, ROI). The request drew a complete blank. The planners were so locked into their accustomed way of thinking about selling their products that they could not conceive of a different approach that made any commercial sense at all.

This planning problem stems from a deficiency that has plagued industrial businesses seemingly forever. Far too many managers have let their businesses "die on the vine" or missed major opportunities because they thought only about selling and promoting their products and technologies instead of serving the marketplace. Levitt called this failing "Marketing Myopia" in his classic *Harvard Business Review* article.[1] It is exceedingly difficult to think about abandoning traditional products, technologies, and basic business beliefs to preserve or secure a stronger position in markets. However, the tendency to concentrate on existing products and technologies without sufficient regard for what is going on in the marketplace is a critical weakness. William Brickner, the CEO of Diamond Shamrock, put the importance of this point into focus when he responded to a question about the loss of vitality in American industry with this comment:

[1]Theodore Levitt, "Marketing Myopia," *Harvard Business Review,* July–August 1960, p. 176.

> To my mind, one central reason is this—our strategies have become too rigid. In trying to make our companies more manageable, we've constructed formula after formula which tells us how to run our businesses, and too often we get so tied up in the formula, we forget the real world. We're like a football team that sticks to its game plan late in the fourth quarter—even though it's losing 21–0.

Insufficient or less-than-candid analysis is a prime cause of unimaginative planning. Many planners either misjudge or fail to understand the underlying economics of the business or the changes in the marketplace (competitive moves, shifts in usage or demand patterns) that call for new strategies. Many planners also appear reluctant to face up to unpleasant truths about their competitive situation, such as high price, low product quality, or poor service, that place the company in an untenable position. Without a thorough, candid appraisal of the business climate, the need for fresh ways of running the business goes unrecognized. Thus, instead of getting a choice among alternatives, top management all too frequently has to settle for a single recommendation that usually calls for the continuation of the same old strategies.

SOME SUCCESSFUL PRACTICES

Despite the pitfalls in the path of formal planning, many companies have successfully built formal planning into their management process. Without exception, these companies concentrate on developing market-driven plans that are part and parcel of the management process of each product-market business. They have reached this level of sophistication primarily because of three factors:

1. Better direction from the top
2. Planning based on cold, hard facts
3. Superior programming for implementation

Let's examine each of these vital factors in some detail to see how they can lead to better ways of doing things.

Good Direction

The business planning done in leader companies produces results because it is carried out with full recognition of the multiplicity of products, markets, and channels, and of the need for a total business rather than a sales or merchandising orientation. The president of an automotive parts company demonstrated the importance of this point with the following comment:

> It took me three years to realize that our marketing people couldn't come up with the kind of plans I wanted for our products and markets unless I worked closely with them. They have always been able to develop a picture of where our markets are heading, identify the opportunities that exist, and interpret what we have to do

> to build the business. But so many considerations and options require a general management perspective that marketing can't be expected to come up with recommendations that make sense from my point of view. Unless I set the basic direction and targets for our business, specify who is to plan what, see to it that engineering, manufacturing, and sales really work with marketing to provide what is needed, and then challenge and contribute any ideas I can on how our business can be developed, the whole planning effort is nothing more than a paperwork exercise.

This comment underscores several ways in which top management must participate in the planning process to make it pay off. It must define objectives and guidelines, as well as planning units; follow a practical approach; define expected content; ensure coordination; and contribute ideas.

CORPORATE OBJECTIVES AND GUIDELINES. "If only top management would tell me what they want!" is a common complaint among division and middle managers with major planning responsibilities. Perhaps some of them expect too much. Perhaps some would like top management to spell everything out for them in detail. But they are right in asking for guidelines that spell out the rules of the game. It is unquestionably a necessity for anyone who holds a key planning responsibility to know in specific terms how fast top management wants the business to grow, what products and markets should be emphasized, what kinds of businesses should be avoided, and what profit returns are acceptable.

Guidelines like these are essential to provide a directional framework for managers actually doing the planning in the various business units. The key here is to make sure that the criteria are rational and in line with the realities of the business. Guidelines should provide focus and direction without putting anyone in a strait jacket (see the box). Continuing emphasis on guidelines and targets tends to force the strategic thinking and planning in each business unit into areas of business that have the potential to accomplish corporate objectives and out of areas where this possibility does not exist.

PLANNING UNITS. As we have said, it is usually unrealistic to develop plans for an industrial division or product business as a whole. It makes more sense to find a way of segmenting the business according to some combination of product, market, customer, supplier, or application. These segments should be the building blocks for planning rather than the large operating units that are typically shown on corporate organization charts. The slogan "small is beautiful" is a most appropriate reminder to business planners. It is much easier to develop strategies for discrete product-market segments than for some big organization unit that houses multiple product-market businesses with quite different customers, competitors, and product requirements.

Sometimes these planning units cross organizational boundaries, as when products in several divisions combine to serve a particular market. A multinational company in the electrical products field combined the utility products produced in three separate divisions into one strategic planning unit so that a comprehensive plan could be developed for achieving a larger position in the power utility market. It is not unusual for companies that are successful at strategic planning to break five or six major organization units

GIVING DIRECTION THE RIGHT WAY

This letter from the president of a machine tool manufacturer to the company's division managers set the stage for effective planning:

> As you know, our fundamental purpose is to earn a return for our shareholders that is more attractive than they could expect from other investments with similar risks. To do this means we must consistently compound our earnings at a rate that is 5 to 7 percent higher than inflation and achieve a return on stockholder equity in excess of 22 percent. For the corporation to achieve this kind of performance means that each operating unit must compound its earnings growth at the same rate and achieve an after-tax return on assets of at least 20 percent. In most cases we will need to improve our after-tax return on sales to 7 percent or better to achieve the target return on net assets.
>
> Sustained performance at these levels will place our company in the upper quartile of all *Fortune* 500 companies, which is what we need to do to generate attractive gains for our shareholders. These goals are mathematically compatible given our capital structure, debt limitations, and dividend requirements. Even more important, they are achievable. In fact, the leader companies in our industry have done better over the past several years.
>
> It should be obvious that we need to refocus several parts of our business to achieve the profit goals outlined in the second paragraph. As you commence your planning assignments, be sure to keep the following ground rules in mind.
>
> 1. We want to reduce our dependence on the automotive industry specifically and capital goods spending in general so that we can achieve a more stable earnings pattern.
> 2. We want to shift our focus from building and selling traditional products to serving selected markets (e.g., aerospace, oil field, electronics, office equipment), which we believe have more attractive growth prospects than the economy overall.
> 3. We want to grow our business in these target markets at the expense of our position in our traditional businesses and we want to recover capital that is marginally employed in any of our current operations.
> 4. We want to set up all of our service and repair operations as discrete profit centers and grow these businesses faster than our total business; we will enter new service and repair areas to do so.
> 5. We want to operate an increasing percentage of our business in a nonunion environment and we will incur the cost penalties and supply the capital required to do so.
> 6. We don't want to put new capital into any product-market business that does not offer the possibility of achieving our profit goals within the next two to three years.
> 7. We will accept a negative cash flow to support growth as long as earnings projections grow faster than 20 percent each year and there are no shortfalls from plan.

down into 50 or more discrete chunks for strategic planning purposes. Reliance Electric is a case in point. Although the company is managed around five major organization units (electrical products, mechanical products, Toledo scale, telecommunications, and Federal Pacific), the business is planned and controlled around more than 100 separate product centers, each with its own plan.

PRACTICAL APPROACHES. To avoid overemphasis on form or systems, top management should insist on a straightforward planning approach. Although any approach to planning obviously needs to be tailored to the particular characteristics and requirements of the situation, it is essential to keep several fundamental points in mind:

1. In most mature industrial operations, past trends are the most likely predictors of the future. Following this line of reasoning, the planning for each product-market business should start with a straight-line extrapolation of sales and profit trends over five years. In most cases, this projection will provide a realistic picture of what future results are likely to be, assuming no change in the business cycle or direction of the business. If the results of this first projection appear to be satisfactory, the whole purpose of planning should be to ensure that they are achieved. If the results are unsatisfactory, the focus should shift to doing whatever is necessary to improve them.
2. Only four factors can cause future results to depart from the projection of past trends: (a) a change in the rate of growth of the total market, (b) a change in the definition or scope of the market served, (c) a change in market share position, and (d) a change in the cost or profit structure of the business. The extent to which management intends to cause improvements in any one or a combination of these factors so that planned results depart from the initial trend projection can and should be quantified. It is essential to know how much change is required in any of these areas as a basis for thinking through the programs, actions, and decisions that serve as the foundation for the plan.
3. The great bulk of the planning effort should revolve around cross-functional discussions covering such points as (a) how the business has performed to date; (b) what forces are at work that will affect its future; (c) what kinds of improvements in market growth, market share, or the basic cost-profit structure can realistically be achieved; and (d) what requirements and commitments are needed from each functional group to make the right things happen. This give-and-take cross-functional discussion should be the heart of the planning process. It promotes a team effort, ensures that problems and alternatives are considered in light of overall business needs, and provides the basis for making commitments that will lead to successful implementation.
4. The agreed-upon programs, actions, and decisions that will lead to improved results, as well as the rationale for assuming success, should be defined in a few convincing sentences. Anything more generally means that the planners are trying to get by with verbiage instead of good ideas.
5. Facts, not emotions, should control all decisions. No "sacred cows" should be allowed, and everyone should understand there is no single way to run the business. If overall growth and profit targets cannot be achieved in a reasonable time frame with the current business structure, the focus should be on how it can be changed. If the

business cannot be restructured to achieve growth and profit targets, management should focus its efforts on the best way to recover the capital employed.

There is nothing sophisticated about these points, but keeping them in mind prevents devoting a lot of time and effort to generating a massive flow of paperwork and a lot of useless "pie in the sky" plans.

EXPECTED CONTENT. In companies with many divisions or business units, the chances are great for a wide variety of interpretations if top management does not provide direction as to the end products expected. The trick is to provide direction without locking anyone into a straitjacket. The following memorandum sent to all operating managers by the president of a multidivision company serving the oil field industry illustrates how direction can be provided without getting everyone strapped into an elaborate set of forms and procedures.

> As we move toward our plan review dates, it is important to agree on what your end products should look like. I think you can summarize everything I want to see on a few slides.
>
> 1. Define in a paragraph or two what it is your division is seeking to do in a way that provides the rationale for the growth and profit goals you have set. In other words, state the business mission you have defined for your division and the strengths you intend to build on to accelerate profit growth.
> 2. Show a five year history of sales, market share, earnings before taxes, return on sales, return on net assets and cash flow and compare with our corporate targets. Do this for your division overall and for each product-market segment for which you have prepared a strategic plan.
> 3. Show three year projections of sales, market share, earnings before taxes, return on sales, return on net assets and cash flow for your division overall and for each product-market segment.
> 4. List the key strategic decisions, commitments and programs required for your division and for each product-market business. If major capital or expense commitments are required, be sure to highlight these and indicate the probable timing. Also, be sure to comment on your priorities in the event that corporate resources cannot fund everything you want to do.
> 5. Describe what strategic alternatives you could pursue to accelerate your profit growth, assuming no constraints on capital or short-term profit requirements.
>
> Be sure to have the backup detail to respond to questions that are sure to be raised during your presentation. You will undoubtedly want to have your whole management team with you so that questions can be directed to those most directly responsible.

In another successful company, top management chose to be even more definitive and provided the form shown in Exhibit 13-2, which was to be completed for each product-market business. As you can see, it covers many of the same points outlined in the president's letter to his operating managers. The choice of a form or a letter is a matter of

EXHIBIT 13-2

PLANNING SUMMARY FORM

STRATEGIC SUMMARY

1. Product and/or Service

2. Customers

3. End Use

4. Rank	Direct Competitors	Yr. before Last: Market Share	Last Year (CY____): Sales, This Market	Last Year (CY____): Market Share
1.				
2.				
3.				
4.				
5.				
6.				
7.				
8.				
9.				
Total Direct Market		100%	$ K	100%

5. Competitive Advantages — VERSUS LARGEST COMPETITOR

6. Competitive Disadvantages — VERSUS LARGEST COMPETITOR

7. Market Alternatives (Competing Techniques)

8. Factors Affecting Future Market Growth

9. Summary of Strategy — SIMPLE DECLARATIVE STATEMENTS OF WHAT IS TO BE DONE AND HOW IT WILL BE DONE, THEN AMPLIFY AS NECESSARY, INDICATING KEY IMPLEMENTATIONAL EMPHASIS AND ACTIONS.

TYPE			Build
			Hold
			Harvest
			Withdraw
			Explore
DIRECTION			Base
			Market Seg.
			Output Diff.
			Mark't Devel.
			Outp't Devel.
POSTURE			Leader
			Me Too
			Performance
			Value
			Price
			Economy
			Prestige

10. History/Forecast									
Market									
Share of Market, %									
Sales									
Operating Profit, % to Sales									

Date

Source: Regency Electronics Co.

style, as long as the content required is appropriately defined. The end products required may vary from company to company, but the objective should always be to avoid a lot of details, forms, and schedules and concentrate instead on content that brings the strategic issues and options into sharper focus.

COORDINATION. Even the most carefully conceived marketing organization structure will fail unless marketing planners work effectively with the other functions that influence performance in the marketplace. To do this, they must command the respect of their functional counterparts. And all concerned must have a clear understanding of how they are expected to work together.

A manufacturer in the building products field learned this lesson the hard way. The company set up a product management group in its marketing organization to spearhead business planning for each product area. During the first two years of the group's existence, the plans developed fell far short of everyone's expectations, and there was much friction between the product management group and other functional managers. One of the product managers put his finger on the problem when he pointed out the many functions other than marketing and sales he had to work with to do a good planning job. Much of the difficulty he encountered, he said, stemmed from misunderstanding on the part of many functional managers about the role product managers should play in the planning process. Even the product managers themselves, he added, were unsure about their responsibilities.

Recognizing the need to put the product group on a stronger footing for dealing with functions outside marketing, the president took three steps. He decided first to replace four of the product managers, who were basically sales-oriented, with people who had stronger technical backgrounds and a better grasp of the business as a whole. He then eliminated the position of group product manager and moved the product managers up to a level on an organizational par with their major contacts in other functional areas, thus enabling them to communicate more effectively. Even more important, since the product managers reported directly to the marketing vice president, they could stay in close touch with top management. Third, he held a series of meetings with the executives of all major functions to explain what the product managers were trying to accomplish and how the different functions should work with them. At these meetings, the president made it clear that he was looking to the product managers to play a lead role in developing plans geared to the characteristics and requirements of the marketplace. He also left no doubt that he expected all functions to cooperate with them. This no-nonsense statement on their role cleared away any misconceptions blocking effective interaction between the product managers and other functions and paved the way for a much more productive planning effort.

IDEAS AND ALTERNATIVES. If top management truly wants to find ways of improving profits and growth, it must actively participate in the development of strategies by challenging their underlying assumptions and by contributing alternative ideas. Most strategic decisions, particularly those that involve a change in direction, require the experience, perspective, and "feel" of top management—not just its blessing. To be sure, many top executives try to do this; but the way they do it often stifles rather than encourages new ideas. They must take pains to avoid the atmosphere of an inquisition and instead encourage an open exchange of ideas and opinions. In such an environment one idea leads to another, and the management team soon finds itself exploring new and imaginative ways of developing the business.

An interfunctional give-and-take discussion of this sort led one heavy machinery manufacturer to adopt a new marketing strategy that gave its parts operation a chance for survival. In this company, as in many others, parts sales had traditionally been a major source of profits. Now management was concerned because "parts pirates" (local parts producers) were cutting sharply into its business. Asked to develop a marketing strategy that would reverse the trend, the parts manager first came up with a plan that called for adding three salespeople and cutting prices on a large number of parts. As he acknowledged, the plan was essentially no more than a holding action. During the planning review session, in which all functions took part, the company president encouraged everyone to take an entrepreneurial look at the parts business and to try to think of ways to preserve or even enlarge it. Predictably, fresh ideas were hard to come by in a business that had been run the same way for years. But eventually three ideas emerged that were considered worthwhile: (1) build a service organization and sell contracts for maintenance service instead of just parts; (2) decentralize the parts business and set up local parts and repair shops to compete head to head with local competitors; and (3) start to buy and sell parts for other manufacturers' equipment in order to spread overhead costs. The parts manager was naturally somewhat reluctant to do any of these things, since they would revolutionize his end of the business. But with top management backing and encouragement and a knowledge of the business, he did the required analytical work and came back with two possible strategies based on the first two ideas that offered a much more attractive outlook.

This process does not always lead to a viable strategy, since it is not always possible to overcome the scarcity of fresh ideas characteristic of a business that has been run the same way for years. Moreover, alternative strategies are not always visible on a first pass. But the more successful companies insist that all plans include alternative strategies and avoid getting locked into a self-defeating "business as usual" pattern of thinking. Free generation of ideas among marketing, top management, and other functions is really the heart of the planning process, for it is during these discussions that marketing presents the requirements of the marketplace and the other functions discuss feasible ways of responding to them. A discussion to generate strategies must be driven by an intimate knowledge of trends in the business brought about by changing customer requirements, competitive actions, and emerging technologies. With all the opportunities and constraints out in the open, top management has a good basis for deciding how to allocate corporate resources. Once the best combination of ideas is agreed on, the various functions are in a position to make commitments on the timing and costs of the actions that underlie the marketing plan. Leading company executives insist this is the best vehicle for triggering fresh ideas and ensuring interfunctional coordination.

Planning Based on Cold, Hard Facts

Companies that excel in strategic planning never let emotions or wishful thinking influence their plans and decisions. Their managements are well aware of several truisms that greatly influence the outlook for most industrial companies.

To begin with, strategic thinking must always start with the market. This is particularly true now, when market growth is no longer an automatic "given" in most industrial situations. In the 1960s and early 1970s, it was not unrealistic to think in terms of 4 to 5 percent real growth for most businesses, since GNP was growing close to that rate in real terms. Since 1973, however, the rate of real growth and GNP has declined significantly. Most economists are now projecting a prolonged phase of lower economic growth. Multinational competition has increased, and an increasing number of industrial markets are likely to be stagnant or slow growing. This does not mean that growth is impossible or should be forgotten as an objective in the industrial world. It does mean that product-market strategies must be realistically geared to four "facts of life":

1. Rapid growth for any industrial product tends to be short term because new products and new competitors will generally find their way into attractive growth markets. A "boom market" can mislead management in its strategic thinking and planning. The importance of market share is often overlooked because sales are growing rapidly with the market. The need for fully competitive costs and products is often obscured because a growth market will absorb marginal producers and products. But the euphoria of a growth market will not continue forever, and marginal producers and products will fail as the market moves into a mature stage.
2. Rapid growth usually does not return to a mature industry; although it is possible for a mature or declining market to experience short growth spurts, strategy should be guided by the market's long-term prospects. There are exceptions to this generalization, however. When rapid growth does return to a mature industry, it is because of some structural change in the underlying technology or economy. For example, from 1950 to the mid-1960s the industrial scale market was essentially saturated and showed very limited unit growth. In the mid-1960s, however, the technology shifted from mechanical to electronic. The significant advantages of electronic scales motivated many customers to replace mechanical scales that were still perfectly usable. The combination of a large number of replacement sales plus higher unit volume triggered a growth rate in the market that was significant for the next ten years. Similarly, the market for automatic screw machines has been flat to declining for the past ten years. However, automatic screw machines are the most efficient means known to produce small arms munitions. If a major war should break out (God forbid), the market demand for these machines would grow dramatically.
3. Competition tends to be more intense in low-growth markets because a company in a high-growth environment can increase its sales without taking market share from its competitors. When a market is flat or declining, however, growth occurs only at the expense of others. For this reason, a division in a stagnant market can be a greater managerial challenge than one in a high-growth market.
4. Changes in products, technology, and distribution continue to occur in stagnant industries. For example, the technology for producing steel and automobiles has improved dramatically during the past decade despite greatly increased competition and unfavorable market trends. Stagnant demand, therefore, does not mean stagnant technology.

Given these "facts of life," the key to developing a successful product-market strategy is to ensure that it is developed around some genuine competitive advantage gained by a distinctive approach, such as offering products with distinctive performance or cost characteristics, using alternative sales and distribution channels and/or manufacturing processing, offering superior postsale service, or achieving an advantageous cost structure. Whatever the approach, the objective is always to establish a clear and favorable differentiation from competitors. Without such an advantage, it is unlikely that any strategy will provide the basis for generating above-average profit growth over the long term. Product performance, price, and service are the basics of any industrial business, and a disadvantage in any one of these areas simply cannot be offset by hard work or brilliant management. This means that in situations where disadvantages in any of these areas exist, the product-market strategy must focus on ways to correct or overcome them.

Companies that compete most successfully in the industrial world develop their strategies around three approaches, all designed to achieve and sustain a competitive advantage.

1. They concentrate on growth segments within the markets they serve. Even the most stagnant markets generally offer a segment—a particular customer group, product characteristic, or type of distribution—capable of supporting better than average rates of growth. For example, electronic test, medical, and office equipment markets have sustained attractive growth rates during the current recessionary period.
2. They emphasize high quality and product innovation. Innovations, especially those that are proprietary, are difficult and expensive for competitors to imitate. They keep a product from becoming a commodity and thus allow the company to compete on a basis other than price. Toledo Scale took the lead in moving the very mature and slow-growing weighing industry into electronics and picked up significant market share and profits by introducing sophisticated computing scales for parts counting and other industrial applications.
3. They continuously strive for operating efficiencies by specializing and automating to reduce unit costs, by consolidating products and facilities if demand increases to take advantage of scale, and by seeking broader and more efficient distribution to lower costs. In short, they recognize the need to drive toward the lowest possible cost base to be an effective competitor over the long term.

Many managers talk a good game about making a factual assessment of the performance, competitive standing, and outlook for their business, but few really do it in a tough-minded way. Instead, too much emphasis is generally placed on verbal explanations of why sales have not materialized, why profit returns are low, or why competitors seem to have an edge. The objective should be to strip away all the rhetoric and rationalizations and simply look at the cold, hard facts. There are several ways to make this factual assessment: flow charts, life cycle analysis, and historical pattern analysis.

FLOW CHARTS. A flow chart should show the major steps involved in serving the customer, from sourcing the raw material to providing postpurchase service. Once this flow chart is developed, it is much easier to pinpoint competitive strengths and weaknesses. Exhibit 13-3 shows how this was done for a manufacturer of industrial scales and weighing systems.

As you can see, these flow charts present a much sharper picture of the company's

EXHIBIT 13-3

FLOW CHART ANALYSIS OF STRENGTHS AND WEAKNESSES

A. Identifying points of leverage

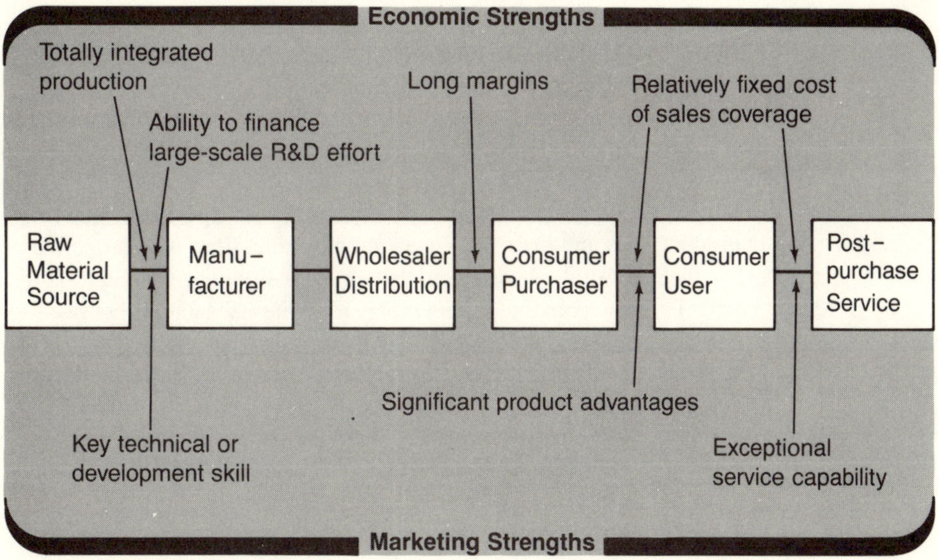

B. Identifying points of vulnerability

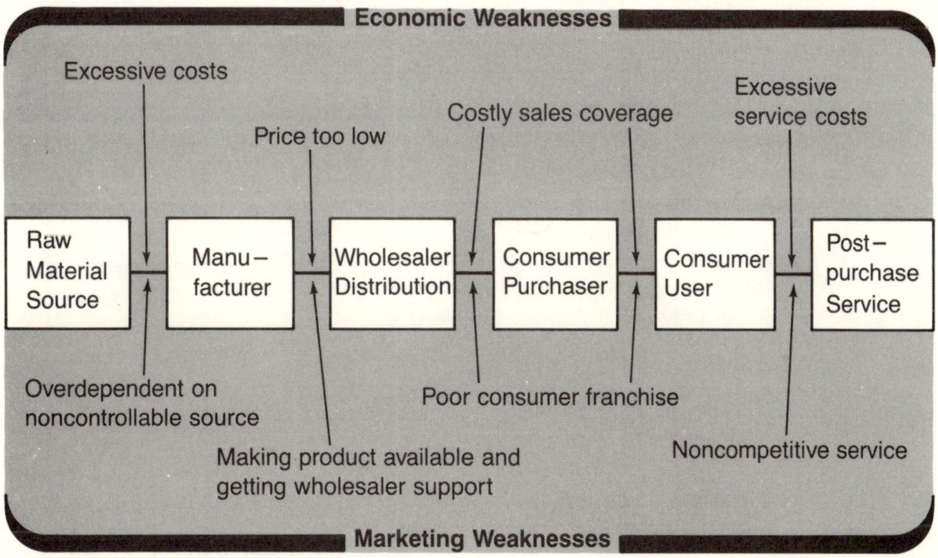

Source: B. C. Ames, "Marketing Planning," *Harvard Business Review,* September–October 1968, p. 107.

competitive strengths and weaknesses than a simple listing of the same points. They can also be used to gain management understanding and agreement on how the business flows, where major assets are committed, and how the company is positioned in the market against its competitors so that better questions can be raised about the real advantages of perceived strengths and the seriousness of perceived weaknesses.

LIFE CYCLE ANALYSIS. Another useful way to look at the facts is to relate the current competitive position of each product-market business to its position on a life cycle curve. Understanding this relationship is crucial, since it enables management to see which businesses offer real growth potential and which do not. Exhibit 13-4 shows how a manufacturer of machine tools made such an analysis of its major product lines. As you can see, this chart suggests that the company has the strongest competitive position in its mature product lines and very little strength in product lines with attractive growth prospects. The picture can be made even clearer by positioning competitor products on the same chart. There are obviously a number of additional factors that need to be considered before conclusions can be drawn; however, this chart alone provides a useful foundation for thinking through the strategic alternatives open to management.

EXHIBIT 13-4

LIFE CYCLE PORTFOLIO ANALYSIS

Competitive Position	EMERGENCE	GROWTH	MATURITY-1	MATURITY-2	DECLINE
Excellent				Automatic screw machines	
Good				Dedicated transfer lines	
Average				Standard drill press	
Poor	Computer controls	Robotics factory automation			

Industry Life Cycle Stage (Prospects)

Source: Framework developed by H. Igor Ansoff in personal discussions.

HISTORICAL PATTERNS. Still a third way to look at the facts is to simply plot historical growth and profit patterns for each product or market business on a grid developed around corporate growth and profit targets. Plotting average performance over some period of time or even last year's results shows how well each product-market segment has performed against corporate targets and how much improvement is required to bring the business up to par. Exhibit 13-5 shows such a grid. In this example, the two axes of the grid reflect the company's return on assets and compounded growth rate targets (17.5 percent return on average net assets and 14 percent growth). As you can see, the grid is divided into four quadrants: high profit–low growth, high profit–high growth, low profit–low growth, and low profit–high growth. The ultimate aim, of course, should be to move all the product-market businesses into the upper righthand quadrant—the high profit–high growth category. Businesses in the lower left quadrant—low profit–low growth—would obviously be under pressure for significant improvement as strategic plans are developed. Arrows can be used, as shown, to indicate the direction management intends to go with any particular product.

A SUCCESSFUL EXAMPLE. These analyses, or any others like them, are only useful if they contribute to management's understanding of the business and ability to make intelligent strategic decisions or plans. Let's look at how one outstanding company, which we will call company A, built a marketing strategy for its major product line on just this sort of understanding.

After a thorough analysis of demand and share trends, the planners in this company recognized that they were operating in a slow-growth business, offering a commodity product for which demand was highly inelastic. They therefore concluded that (a) it would not make sense to sacrifice short-term profits to build a larger share position, since the value of a share point would not increase enough to pay off such an investment, and (b) although price is an important consideration in market share, it would not influence total demand. They also uncovered an important trend: Company A was losing market position to the strong second-place factor in the industry, company B. Since no other important shifts in market share had occurred, company A concluded that its marketing strategy should be aimed first and foremost at reversing its losses to company B. Next, the planners at company A compared their own profit structure with that of company B to find the weaknesses and strengths of the two companies. Their analysis produced the information shown in Table 13.1.

Admittedly, obtaining information of this sort about competitors is tough. No one is going to hand it to you, and it is not likely to be available in published material. But, as discussed in Chapter 4, bits of data on competitor sales and capacity levels can be pieced together from annual reports, newspaper articles, and trade and government publications. By combining such data with one's own experience, conservative assumptions can be made about competitor costs and efficiency to complete the picture.

By the time the planners in company A had completed this comparative analysis, they were in a position to predict what company B's strategy was likely to be. Assuming that B knew its own market and economic position, they thought it would seek further share gains by competing on price. Specifically, they expected B to:

EXHIBIT 13-5

BUSINESS SEGMENT PROFIT/GROWTH GRID (ROANA and NSB‡ Growth)*

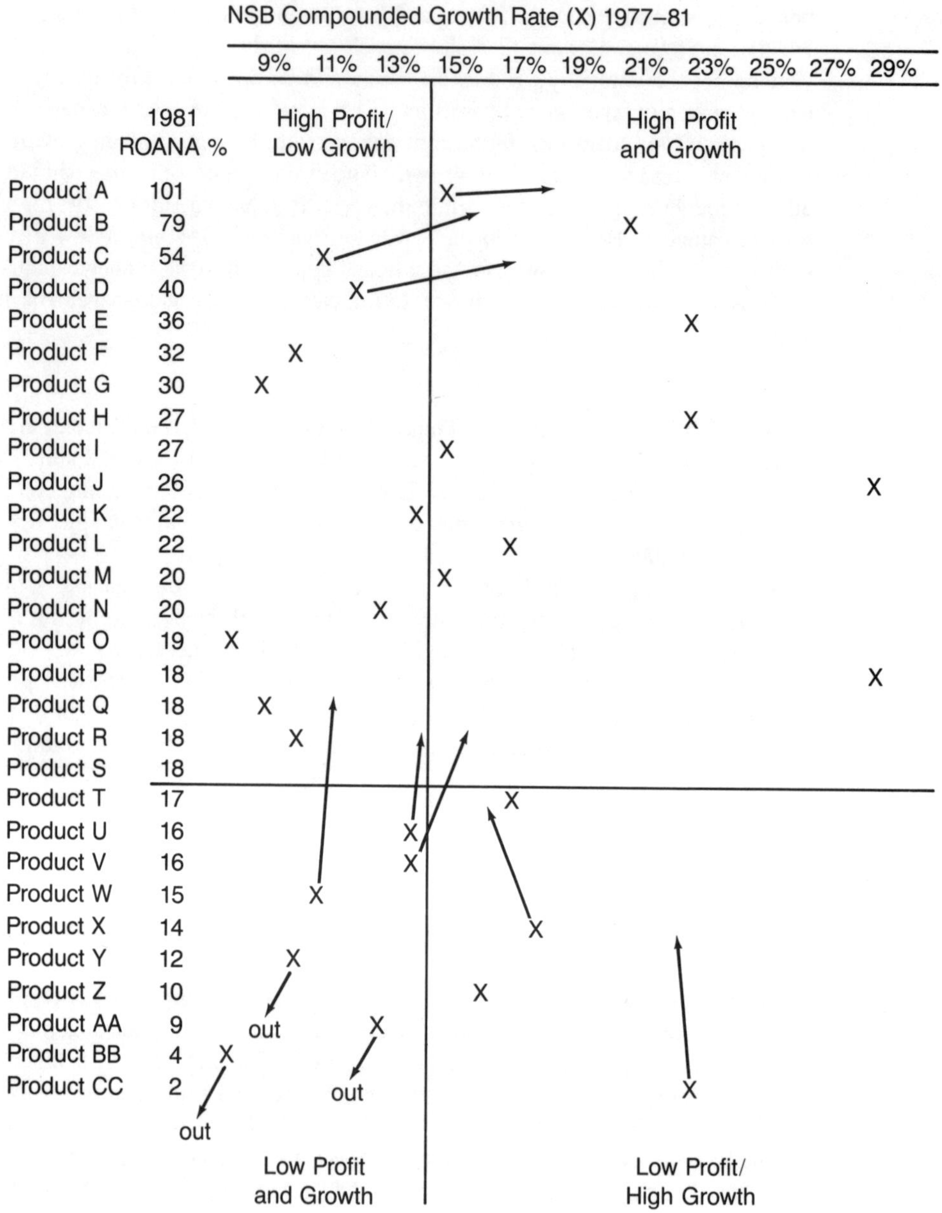

*ROANA = Return on Average Net Assets
‡NSB = Net Sales Billed

TABLE 13.1

PROFIT STRUCTURE ANALYSIS

Economic Indicators	*Companies* *A*	*B*	*Conclusions*
Current dollar sales	$403	$146	A's sales volume is roughly twice B's.
Breakeven point	$217	$121	B's breakeven point is lower, but B is operating much closer to breakeven than A.
Contribution margin rate (sales dollars less variable costs)	48%	45%	Contribution margin rates are about the same.
Contribution loss from 5 percentage point drop in unit margin	$20	$7.3	However, because of differences in dollar volume, company A stands to lose far more marginal income than B by lowering unit margin.
Volume gain to offset 5 percentage point drop in unit margin	$46.5	$18.2	Thus, the volume needed to offset a 5 percentage point drop in unit margin would be much greater for company A.
Equivalent share point gain	7.0	2.8	

Cut prices on the products competitive with company A's highest volume products to upset price stability and to force company A to retaliate or give up volume.

Add new industrial distributors by giving larger discounts, and go after company A's distributors in prime markets.

Emphasize development of lower-cost products, thereby gaining more flexibility to compete on a price basis.

Given these assumptions, the planners in company A decided that their counterstrategy should be to avoid going for volume through pricing or by adding to unit costs. The key points of the strategy were to:

Hold a firm price line with distributors, even at the risk of losing share in the most price-sensitive markets.

Build the marketing program around activities (services) whose costs do not vary with volume, such as upgrading and enlarging the sales force, strengthening distributor programs, and improving the physical distribution and warehousing network.

A superficial review of the situation would undoubtedly have led the planners to come up with quite a different strategy. In view of the high contribution rate and apparent profit leverage on volume, the most obvious strategy would have been to cut price to counteract any aggressive pricing actions by company B. Instead, company A planners decided to avoid price concessions or any actions that would raise unit costs. They recommended concentrating on marketing programs with costs that could be amortized over their much larger unit volume and on other programs that would reduce their cost base. Management agreed, reasoning that this strategy would enable the company to lead from strength rather than play into the hands of its major competitor.

The details of company A's strategy may be open to dispute. In themselves, however, they are not important. The purpose of the example is to show how a penetrating analysis of market and economic facts can provide a reasoned basis for strategy development. This is the process by which sophisticated planners gain significant advantages over competitors, and it is easy to see the three reasons why:

1. Planners can help focus management attention on actions that really count in the marketplace and make sure that these are based on facts and judgment, not hunch or opinion.
2. They can adopt an aggressive posture instead of having to rely on retaliation or defensive maneuvers.
3. They can minimize the impact of surprise competitive moves by developing contingency plans.

Superior Programming

There is no single best strategy that is exactly right for a situation or that will guarantee success. Properly executed, quite different strategies for the same product-market business can be equally successful. What this says is that execution is a crucial ingredient in the success of any strategy. "Weak leadership can wreck the soundest strategy; forceful execution of even a poor plan can often bring victory." So wrote the Chinese general and philosopher Sun Zi in 514 B.C. Today, 25 centuries later, that axiom still holds in business.

Successful execution depends on programming, which simply means identifying the sequence of steps and events that must occur to achieve planned objectives and then following through to ensure that these steps and events take place on schedule. Everybody goes through the motions of programming, but leader companies follow three ground rules that enable them to do a superior job of strategy implementation.

1. Management will approve no major program or project that is not inextricably linked to a product-market strategy. This approach may sound a little narrow-minded, but it makes eminent good sense, for the linkage keeps the functional areas of a business working together for a common purpose and prevents them from being sidetracked to functionally interesting activities that lack commercial relevance. There is really no way to evaluate a program's usefulness without the background of a product-market strategy.

2. Management makes some sort of organizational provision for follow-through on major programs, particularly those that cut across functional lines. In some cases, managements have enlarged the role of product managers. In others, they have set up a task

force with responsibility for following a program to completion. One industrial controls producer took the first approach to implement a complete redesign of the product line to improve performance characteristics and to lower cost. Even though the bulk of the actual work had to be done by engineering and manufacturing, the president pulled the responsible product manager out of the marketing department and made him fully accountable for coordinating and pushing the program through. As the president told us:

> This program can make or break us in the marketplace. It's so vital to us I'd watch over it myself if I could let some other things slip. Since I can't, I want someone to do it for me, and the product manager is the logical one to do it. I know I'm stretching his role somewhat in giving him this assignment, and I know some noses are going to be out of joint in engineering and manufacturing, but the job is too important not to have a full-time program manager.

Whatever the approach, the objective is always to ensure interfunctional coordination for all major programs and to overcome any obstacles to successful completion.

3. Leader companies see to it that the detailed steps involved in major programs are mapped out in such a way that performance can be measured against these individual steps. For some time, companies in the aerospace, military electronics, construction, and other industries have been using network scheduling techniques to control large and complex projects. Well-managed industrial companies apply similar techniques to ensure interfunctional coordination on a wide variety of programs that affect market performance, since they permit managers to flag potential problem areas and initiate corrective action before the program slips or gets off track.

In one company, the program for introducing a new line of flow meters was broken down into 25 steps over an 18-month time span. The first step was a kick-off meeting with R&D, engineering, manufacturing, and marketing to define performance and cost requirements. Subsequent steps tracked the new product idea through development, manufacture, and market launching. Each week, management received a report showing whether scheduled steps had been completed and if not, where the bottleneck was. This feedback made it much easier to trace problems to their source for collective action. Said the president: "The program is too important to us to rely for control on typical accounting reports. They simply tell us after the fact whether we won or lost. They're no help when it comes to making sure the program doesn't collapse." It would be absurd to structure every program in so much detail. But detailed planning is essential for effective control over major programs that involve many functions and require tight scheduling and careful adherence in order to achieve profit and market objectives.

SUMMARY

Formal business planning can help managers cope with the complexity and velocity of change in today's business world. Yet few companies are completely satisfied with their results, especially when considering the time and effort involved in drafting a comprehensive business plan.

When planning fails to produce satisfactory

results, the problem can usually be traced to (1) failing to fit the concept to the industrial context, (2) confusing the various types of planning, (3) overemphasizing the system at the expense of content, and (4) failing to develop alternative strategies. Companies that have built formal planning into the management process have succeeded because of better management from the top, planning based on hard facts, and superior programming for implementing the plan.

Formal business planning can undoubtedly make a real contribution to the performance of any industrial company, just as it has in consumer goods companies. But if it is to have a real impact, it has to be adapted to the particular requirements of the business. The focus must be on achieving substantive improvements in thinking and actions through tough-minded analysis, continual interchange between marketing and technical executives, and top management inputs.

14

Evaluating Strategies and Plans

Fred Cook was brimming with confidence as he began his presentation to the corporate president and his staff. He had been appointed product manager for the company's line of programmable controllers last fall and had worked hard for six months to put a plan together. He was especially pleased because the general manager of the division had expressed confidence in the plan and had asked him to make the presentation.

During his first month as product manager, Fred had seen that previous sales and marketing efforts had been badly misdirected. Not nearly enough emphasis had been given to several large target accounts, and the export market had been completely neglected. It didn't take him long to work out an aggressive plan that would increase sales volume by 40 percent the first year and at least 25 percent a year for each of the following four years. As he enthusiastically explained the plan for improving the export business, he noted that the corporate president was frowning and obviously not following the presentation. Fred was explaining why growth potential in the export market was so significant when the president suddenly interrupted: "I haven't any interest in wasting more time reviewing a lot of optimistic sales projections. This business has lost money each of the last four years and more volume is not the answer. The cost structure is way out of line, and my guess is we will have to write off a couple of million dollars' worth of obsolete inventory at the end of this year. The only thing I want to see is a total business plan that will help us decide whether we should stay in this business or get out."

After a few seconds of stunned silence, Fred's general manager said he could get together the kind of plan the president wanted, but he would need help from the corporate controller and the director of corporate planning. They would have to start all over again, thought Fred; and six months of hard work had gone down the drain.

What is wrong with Fred's plan?

What should a total business plan encompass?

Is it wise to try to salvage Fred's plan by incorporating it into a larger plan? Why or why not?

In the previous chapter we talked about the importance of planning in the industrial world and emphasized the need to develop business strategies and plans that commit all key operating functions to courses of action that will effectively serve the market. We also discussed the need for an integrated business plan for industrial products, since success or failure in the market generally depends more on how functions like manufacturing, engineering, and distribution perform than on what goes on within the marketing department itself. For this reason, the industrial company's planning should encompass the full range of business activities. The marketing function should take the lead in drawing the plan together, but the end product should be a total business plan rather than a stand-alone marketing plan like those found in the consumer products world.

Most industrial companies recognize the importance of planning and prepare both longer-term strategic plans and annual operating plans. But despite all the time and effort that goes into planning, there are wide variations in the quality of the end products. Some are very useful instruments that provide the basis for directing and controlling the business. Unfortunately, many others lack the substance to be a useful management tool. Of course, no one can guarantee the success of any plan, and there is no readymade checklist that will show absolutely whether a plan is good or bad. There are, however, several good articles that outline in some detail what the content of a plan should be and what considerations should be covered.[1,2] More important, there is a logical thought process to be followed that will greatly assist management in deciding whether a plan is a solid vehicle for moving the business ahead or just a lot of words and numbers without real substance. This chapter describes how to use this thought process to decide whether proposed plans are soundly conceived and worth the commitment of resources to carry them out, or whether they should go back to the drawing board for more work. There is nothing sophisticated about this thought process. It is based on common sense and a basic understanding of the requirements for business success in industrial markets. We have organized our discussion of this thought process under three broad questions:

1. Is the plan structured correctly?
2. Is there anything about the plan that detracts from its credibility?
3. Is management's attitude and approach to planning sound?

Although these broad questions may be obvious, the answers are often obscure, and it frequently takes a lot of digging and detailed questioning to bring them into focus.

STRUCTURAL CONSIDERATIONS

To start with, the plan should be a complete and self-explanatory document. This means that even without prior knowledge of the business, anyone should be able to read the plan

[1] B. C. Ames, "Keys to Successful Product Planning," *Business Horizons*, Summer 1960, p. 49.
[2] E. Raymond Corey, "Key Options in Market Selection and Product Planning," *Harvard Business Review*, September–October 1975, p. 12.

and decide whether it makes sense. That is, they would understand the direction management has in mind for the business, why this direction was selected, and how the company intends to pursue this route. A plan that is understandable and reads well is not necessarily sound, but unless it has these attributes, it simply isn't worth further review. Far too much time will be wasted trying to figure out what the plan really means, what management intends to do, and whether proposed actions are worthwhile.

Strategy Statement

To provide this understanding, the plan should be prefaced by a brief strategy statement that explains in one or two paragraphs what management is trying to do with the business and the basis for believing that the plan can be accomplished. Here is an example of a well-worded statement taken from a plan to build a business in the telecommunications equipment market:

> Our continuing objective is to build a $300 million business in the telecommunications equipment market within the next three years. We intend to concentrate our efforts on the equipment area involved in the "subscriber loop" where we have a significant technical base. We do not intend to get into switching or toll transmission, nor do we intend to get into the interconnect business. We will sell only through commonly accepted channels to Bell System and independent companies.
>
> We will achieve this objective by introducing several new products with significant cost and/or performance advantages that will help telephone operating companies hold down or cut back their labor costs and prolong the useful life of their existing plant and equipment. These new products will account for 50 percent of our volume growth each year through 1987. We will also have to acquire several new products and pools of technology that we do not now have to serve this market.
>
> Accomplishing this plan will enable us to sustain a real growth rate of better than 10 percent a year, bring our after-tax ROS to 10 percent and our after-tax ROA to 25 percent.

A clear directional statement like this is the hallmark of any good business plan. It states a precise objective and a time frame for reaching it. It defines the market segments the business has targeted and explains the competitive basis for believing the business can be enlarged. It defines the focus of management attention—both what will be done and what will not be done. It states the type of action management intends to take, and it states the expected financial results. In short, it provides an initial perspective on whether those responsible for the plan have a concept for running the business that makes sense.

One point about defining a concept for the business is worth emphasizing. It is equally important to define what you do *not* want to do as it is to define what you *do* want to do. Defining what you do not want to do is like getting a "no" answer in "20 Questions." Even though a "no" answer is negative information, it provides an insight to the ultimate solution. Similarly, a statement defining what you do not want to do in a business helps bring the strategic direction you do want to take into sharper focus. Note how the telecommunication strategy statement achieved precision by naming the business in which the company would not engage.

A statement like the following is in direct contrast to the statement we just examined:

> We intend to grow our business in motor controls at the fastest possible rate and maximize profits. We intend to broaden our customer base and gain market share. This will require competitive products and an especially strong selling effort.

As you can see, this statement doesn't really describe any kind of business concept or focus. It doesn't establish any parameters on the size or scope of the overriding business objective; it makes no attempt to define a strategy for accomplishing this objective; and it says nothing about the financial implications. The lack of thought in this statement is highlighted by stating the converse—a test frequently used to determine whether a politician has said something of substance or simply spewed out a lot of rhetoric. If a statement does not make sense when the converse is stated, it probably isn't worth saying. Does it make sense to think in terms of growing the business at the "slowest possible rate," to make "minimum profits," or offer "noncompetitive products" supported with a "very weak selling effort"? The words "fastest rate," "maximum profits," "competitive products," and "strong selling effort" don't mean much more.

Recommended Programs and Control

The body of the plan should outline a series of actions and programs linked to the business concept or objective. Given the strategy statement for telecommunications, you would expect to see recommended actions and programs designed to develop new or improved products for the "subscriber loop" market and thus improve profit margins to the 10 percent level. If planned actions and programs do not fit this pattern, the logic has to be faulty and something is fundamentally wrong with the plan.

All the recommended actions and programs should be defined in sufficient detail to provide the basis for effective management control. For example, do the key programs proposed to improve performance in one area or another show the major steps to be taken, the costs involved, the timetable for accomplishment, and who is responsible for each step, so that appropriate corrective action can be taken if something slips? Are there any parts of the plan where actual performance cannot be measured so there is no basis for control? For example, many companies are saddled with information systems that do not provide the basis for tracking costs and profits for individual products or markets. There may be other gaps like this in the company's information system. If this is the case, plans to improve sales and profits for these individual product or market segments—or for anything else where actual results cannot be determined—cannot be controlled. Since it doesn't make sense to plan something you can't control, any part of a plan that falls into this category should be discounted. Ensuring sufficient detail to provide control is crucial. If the characteristics essential for control do not exist, the plan does not have much value as a practical management tool and will more than likely end up simply gathering dust in someone's drawer.

Summary Projections

Finally, the plan should be summarized in a series of cost and profit projections that are also consistent with the business strategy or concept statement. In the case of the telecommunications plan, these projections should reflect a growth pattern that heads toward a $300 million business in three years. Profit results should show 10 percent after-tax ROS and 25 percent after the ROA. If the projections show a different picture, something needs to be corrected before the plan is subjected to detailed review.

Structure Overview

Step one in reviewing any industrial marketing or business plan should be to examine the plan document for completeness and logic. Is it understandable, and does it make sense? Is there a brief summary statement that explains clearly what management is trying to do with the business? Does this statement sound reasonable, and is it supported by recommended actions and programs that will move the company closer to its goal? Are recommended actions and programs sufficiently detailed? Do sales, cost, and profit projections make sense in light of what management wants to do and the actions and programs that are proposed?

This first step in the review process does not entail any kind of in-depth questioning or analysis. It shouldn't. There is no use wasting time getting into detail if the basics are not right. Any plan that cannot pass this superficial examination of its structure and content should be reworked before more management time is wasted reviewing a document that is inherently unsound.

CREDIBILITY ISSUES

Assuming the plan is structurally sound, the next step should be to look for weaknesses or inconsistencies that detract from the plan's credibility. A lot of things can detract from credibility. The best way to make sure all the bases have been covered is to follow five lines of questioning: (1) Is the fact base sound? (2) Do the sales, cost, and profit projections make sense? (3) Are key physical ratios reasonable? (4) Does the risk-reward ratio make sense? (5) Has adequate allowance been made for contingencies?

Fact Base

A solid fact base is crucial to good business planning. It is the foundation for management's evaluation of the product, market, and competition, as well as cost and profit projections. Few will disagree with the importance of solid facts in good planning, but it is essential to understand that what are often presented as facts are not really facts at all. When the truth comes out, many of these statements of fact turn out to be:[3]

[3]These comments on facts are based largely on a memo written by Hal Geneen when he was CEO of ITT.

1. "Apparent facts" that have grown up with the business and never really been challenged. For example, "our product costs more, but it performs better," or "our distributors will revolt if we attempt to sell direct." Are these really facts, or simply folklore that may not hold up under objective scrutiny?

2. "Assumed facts" that are necessary assumptions about the future, but not facts—for example, GNP will grow or inflation will run at a certain rate, costs will increase by a certain amount, competitors will react in a certain way. Statements of this kind should be clearly labeled as assumptions and not presented as facts.

3. "Reported facts" that tend to be given unwarranted validity simply because they have been published by some association or industry "expert." Published data should never be accepted as fact until the source and method of collecting the data has been identified and found to be satisfactory.

4. "Hoped for facts" that represent situations management would like to believe but do not reflect an accurate picture of the situation. "We are the most profitable company," or "we have the best sales force" are typical examples of "hoped for facts."

5. "Half true facts" that have a certain element of validity but not the certainty of an incontrovertible fact. "The market has grown at an average rate of 10 percent a year over the past five years" may be a true statement. But it is misleading if five years ago the market had dipped to an unusually low level and much of the 10 percent growth was simply a catchup to where the market should have been.

In many situations, these distinctions between facts that are real and facts that are not real may not be too important. But in business planning, the distinctions are vital. The whole plan is worthless if it is based on anything except real facts. And there is no way to make sure that proposed actions and programs are based on nothing but incontrovertible facts except through hard-nosed questioning that challenges some of the facts and places the burden of proof on those presenting the plan.

Sales, Cost, Profit Projections

How do you tell whether the sales, cost, or profit projections in a plan are sound? What do you look for in making this kind of evaluation? You do not have to be a financial wizard, but you do have to have a solid understanding of cost and margin relationships and how they change or should change as volume moves up or down. Exhibit 14-1 shows several red flag indicators of weakness in the sales, cost, and profit projections that management should look for whenever a plan is being evaluated.

1. Watch out for sales projections that call for a faster rate of market growth than historical patterns show or that require a significant gain in market share. Market growth

EXHIBIT 14-1

RED FLAG INDICATORS

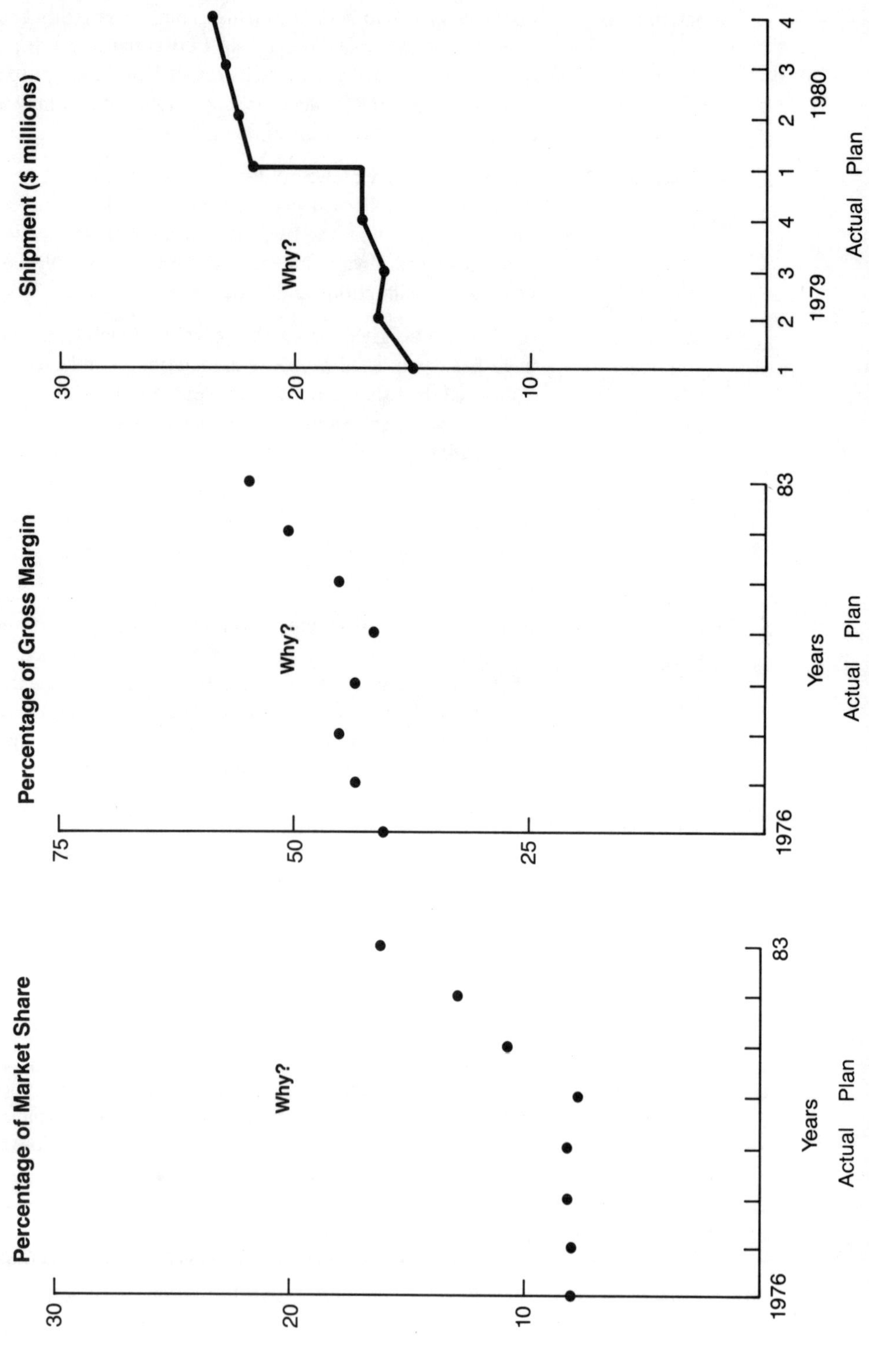

rates or share positions may increase in the industrial world, but not easily and generally not quickly. Every perceived opportunity for market gain is usually accompanied by some risk or threat that could cause a decline. In most cases, vulnerabilities or threats are overlooked and only opportunities are emphasized. When the success of a plan depends on accelerated sales growth, especially with market share improvement, it is essential to dig into the reasons why the change is projected and ensure that they are valid. It is generally much safer to bet on a business plan geared to a conservative sales forecast—and then "scramble" to exceed the plan if the market opportunity develops—than it is to bet on a plan with a higher sales forecast that requires a cutback in costs and operations if the market opportunity does not occur.

2. If cost and profit projections show sharp improvement from past patterns, look for the reasons for this change. Cost and profit patterns do not typically improve unless someone does something to make it happen. Who is going to do what? When? What is the evidence that it can be done and will yield the desired result? Watch out for long-term "hockey-stick" projections (three to five years out) that are much more favorable than projections for next year. It is difficult to hold anyone accountable for long-term improvements, and they usually represent wishful thinking rather than any concrete plan.

3. Be wary of an abrupt change in the operating rate that causes profits to improve sharply over a prior period. Planners frequently overlook the practical problems involved in stepping up production and jump the business from one operating level to another without allowing sufficient time for manufacturing to gear its operations to a higher level. This oversight shows up most frequently when a much higher operating level for the year is planned and then spread evenly over the 12-month period. As a result, first-quarter profit projections tend to be overstated.

4. Be sure that gross margins are adequate to cover all related expenses and generate satisfactory profit margin. Of course, gross margins vary widely across businesses, but it pays to be suspicious of the profit potential of any industrial business with a gross margin that is much less than 50 percent. Gross margin equals sales dollars less all manufacturing costs to cover the product from raw material to finished stock. It does not include costs of distribution, product development, corporate charges, or sales and administration. In some cases, particularly where the business is based on the sale of a relatively few high-ticket products or systems, sales, marketing, and administrative expenses are sufficiently low to permit a satisfactory profit level with a lower gross margin. Nevertheless, a gross margin under 50 percent should be viewed as a "red flag." It is essential to find out why gross margin is lower and whether it makes sense.

5. Check to see that anticipated cost increases for labor and materials are adequately reflected in economic projections. In today's inflationary climate, it is all too easy to underestimate cost increases for these items in a way that leads to unrealistic profit projections. The only way to avoid this possibility is to ask very specific questions about the allowances for cost increases that have been factored into profit projections. For example, ask purchasing what price increase is expected on steel, castings, bearings, or other important items, and when. Ask employee relations management what kind of wage or benefit increases are anticipated for both hourly and salaried workers, and when. Ask insurance management how much allowance has been made for increasing costs of medical, disability, and liability insurance, and why. Then ask the controller if all these allowances have been correctly factored into the plan.

6. Examine expense levels for key areas to ensure that they are correct in light of prior spending patterns and the job that needs to be done. In some cases, planned expenses may be too low. Some managers may cut back on expenditures that should be made in critical areas such as new product or market development in a way that makes their current profit look good but is harmful to the long-term health of the business. In other cases, planned expense levels may be too high. Sloppy planning habits lead many managers to increase their budgets automatically for advertising, promotion, sales, and other areas that can move up or down very easily, without regard for what is really required to support the plan.

Industry comparisons that will help determine whether a particular expense level is too low or too high are generally available through competitor reports, trade association data, or industry publications. If sales, advertising, or product development expense is out of line with published industry data, it is important to ask why. An easy and frequent answer to this question is that the comparisons are not valid ("apples and oranges" is a common claim). Don't settle for this answer. There may well be differences in what different companies include in various expense categories, but if the ratios are significantly different there is a good chance something is fundamentally wrong.

7. Be sure that profit on incremental volume is satisfactory. In any business that has a sound economic structure, higher volume should generate higher profit margins and hence significantly higher earnings, since it should be possible to achieve leverage on the fixed cost component. Unfortunately, most costs tend to be far too variable as volume increases and far too fixed when volume declines. As a result, the profit gain from added volume does not vary as directly with volume as it should. It is not unfair in most industrial companies to look for something like a 30 percent increment in profit on incremental volume and to insist on a clear explanation whenever this is not projected. Conversely, if volume should decline, it is not unfair to ask why the same profit margins cannot be maintained and why profit dollars should be any lower than they were when the business grew through this volume to a higher level.

Key Performance Ratios

Three performance ratios deserve examination in the evaluation of any industrial plan, since they are indicators of how efficiently the business is being managed. These ratios may vary in importance, depending on the situation, but it is doubtful that any business can be healthy if they are out of line with industry standards or key competitors.

PRODUCTIVITY. The first ratio to consider is some measure of productivity. This is simply some measure of output versus input that can be tracked over time and compared with other businesses. With labor costs increasing in most situations, this ratio is especially important because improved productivity is essential to maintain or improve profit margins. There is no single measure of productivity that applies in every situation, but ratios like sales, shipments, or production units per employee, value added per employee (sales minus direct material cost), or total labor cost per unit shipped will indicate the direction of the trend. Obviously, any of these ratios have to be adjusted for inflation and different degrees of vertical integration to ensure meaningful comparisons. If productivity gains are not shown in the plan and supported by concrete actions and pro-

PRODUCTIVITY MEASURES AT TRW

TRW has developed what is probably the most sophisticated approach to productivity measurement. It actually evaluates its key operations against these six productivity performance measures:

1. Sales per employee (constant dollars)
2. Sales divided by total deflated employee compensation costs
3. Value added—sales minus direct material costs—per employee
4. Sales divided by deflated materials cost
5. Sales per unit of energy consumed
6. Sales divided by plant and equipment replacement costs, less depreciation

grams to achieve improvement, there is good reason to challenge the cost and profit structure.

Many well-managed companies are currently devoting much more management time and attention to productivity improvement in an effort to become more competitive. A recent article in *Business Week*[4] outlined many sophisticated measures of productivity that are employed by such companies as General Electric, Westinghouse, United Technologies, and TRW (see the box).

CAPITAL USE. The second performance indicator has to do with how efficiently working capital is being used. In today's inflationary environment, enormous amounts of capital can be tied up very inefficiently if these ratios are out of line, and profit performance can suffer greatly as a result. Moreover, it is easy to develop a plan for increased sales that may do the company more harm than good if the costs of added working capital requirements are not adequately considered. These ratios also vary widely from business to business, but comparisons can be made with industry and competitive data. There is also a cross check against these ratios that applies in most industrial manufacturing companies. In most manufacturing industries, the investment in inventories and receivables should not exceed 35 cents for each dollar of sales. This rule of thumb may not always be applicable, but questions should be raised about the working capital investment when this figure is exceeded.

PRODUCERS TO SUPPORTERS. A third indicator to examine is the ratio of what might be called "results producers" to "supporters" in the organization. This ratio does not reflect a traditional way of looking at a business, nor does it tie in with common definitions of work assignments. It is, nevertheless, a useful indicator of any operation's cost structure and profit-making capability. Anyone that contributes directly to results should be included in the category of "results producers." This would include all direct hourly workers, all sales personnel with specific sales assignments, all engineers involved in designing products or responding to customer requests for special features, service technicians that install and/or maintain the equipment, and anyone else who performs a function directly linked to a company's design, manufacture, sales, and service capabilities. All

[4]"The New Broader Gauges of Productivity," *Business Week*, April 19, 1982.

other personnel in the organization fall into the category of "supporters." They provide support services to the "results producers." This group includes all full-time managers, all staff personnel, all secretarial and clerical help, and anyone else in the organization who does not actually design, make, sell, or service the company's products.

As a general rule, the ratio of "supporters" to "results producers" should be something close to 1 to 3. Whenever the ratio gets close to or exceeds 1 to 1, it is very difficult for any organization involved in traditional industrial manufacturing and sales activities to generate a satisfactory profit. Not enough people are producing, and support costs are too high. Obviously, this ratio does not hold in process or highly automated businesses where large capital investments supplant many direct workers and a large number of highly skilled manufacturing or process engineers are required to operate and maintain the equipment. With this exception, however, it is a good indicator to check whenever a marketing or business plan continues to show marginal profits on a growing sales base.

These ratios, of course, vary widely with different businesses, and what are correct ratios for one situation may not be correct for another. Moreover, there will always be arguments over definitions and the appropriateness of a particular ratio in a given situation. Despite these difficulties, ratios can be developed for any situation, and they can help determine whether or not the cost-profit structure is sound. It should not take long to determine what is a fair measure of performance for any particular situation. And certainly the value of each increment of improvement (each day's reduction in receivables, each added thousand dollars of sales per employee) can be calculated to determine whether profit improvements can or should be made and whether enough emphasis has been placed on these improvements in the plan.

Risk-Reward Ratio

Some wise person has been quoted as saying, "Risk and opportunity always go hand in hand." This point is important to keep in mind in reviewing any business plan. It should be obvious that every plan involves some degree of risk, since no one can predict future events with absolute certainty. However, the degree of risk varies widely from plan to plan, and it is essential to ensure that the opportunity for reward is commensurate with the degree of risk involved. Let's examine the contents of some different plans to see how the degree of risk varies and what some of the factors are that cause these differences.

EXAMPLE A. In the spring of the planning year, marketing management for a manufacturer of electronic communication equipment submitted a plan to double sales volume for one of its new and high-growth product lines. Doing so required a plant addition involving a $2 million investment and an equal investment for added working capital. The company's sales of this product had doubled during the previous four years, and the total market was projected to more than double during the next five years. This total market projection was not out of line with past growth trends and was supported by a growing customer base that perceived real economic advantages in the company's product. Product cost estimates had proved valid, and projected profit returns on sales and investment were well in excess of the company's accepted hurdle rates. Payback on the new plant addition was planned in 2.4 years.

EXAMPLE B. The marketing and sales executives in a machine tool company presented a plan to take the company into robotics. The plan emphasized the growing interest in robotics in both foreign and domestic markets and projected a dramatic increase in sales during the next decade. The company's product development group had developed a modular concept for a line of robots that appeared to offer opportunities for major cost savings in the manufacturing process. Product development also claimed that the line would have better speed, range, and load-carrying capability than any other competitive offering. Pictures of a design or "breadboard" prototype were presented to prove the feasibility of product development claims. Continuation of the program required additional funding of $2.7 million for further product development activities and a joint venture with another independent research firm to ensure the control capability that would be necessary. Management of the product development group was committed to having a prototype for the machine tool show in the fall of the following year, and marketing expected to capitalize on the introduction of the new robot with an integrated sales and promotion program to major potential users. The company had available manufacturing capacity to meet projected sales requirements, and no immediate investment was required for new plant or equipment. Total costs of pursuing the plan were about $5 million, with product development and market development expenses accounting for the great bulk of this sum. A payback period of 4.5 years was projected; profits beyond that point were expected to grow at a much faster rate than anything the company had ever experienced.

IMPLICATIONS. It doesn't take much insight to see that the potential risk-reward ratio in example A is much more attractive than that in example B. Both situations are based on a set of exciting market characteristics and appear to offer attractive growth opportunities. However, the plan in example A is based on a proved product with an attractive sales and profit history; the plan in example B is based solely on claims of what the product development group can do against a formidable array of competitors already in the market. Moreover, the payback period in example A is much shorter term, and the company's exposure to potential loss is much less.

All these points are relatively easy to see when the examples are succinctly described on paper. They are not nearly as easy to see in a real life situation, especially when the plan is presented by enthusiastic and articulate marketing and engineering managers who have the utmost confidence in their own abilities. For this reason, it is always worthwhile to ask two specific questions: (1) "What is the risk-reward ratio?" and (2) "What happens if customers or competitors react differently than anticipated?"

Obviously, the degree of acceptable risk, irrespective of potential rewards, varies from company to company, depending on its size and financial condition. However, an attractive risk-reward ratio is an important ingredient to check out in any business plan. In a high-risk situation, the potential reward should be several times (6 to 10) the dollars placed at risk in a relatively short time frame. In situations where the risk is less, the company can settle for reduced reward opportunities because of the greater certainty of achieving planned results. In any event, a plan should never be approved unless those proposing it can respond to questions about the risk-reward ratio in a way that demonstrates they have given it serious consideration as their plan was developed.

Allowances for Contingencies

Many explanations of business planning compare the plan to a roadmap, and for the most part this analogy is correct. Like a roadmap, the plan shows where you want to go and how you should get there. However, you can be a great deal surer you will get where you want to go when you are following a roadmap than when you follow a business plan, no matter how brilliantly the plan may have been conceived and prepared. Unexpected road construction or detours might thwart the driver's plan to follow exactly the route planned. But these difficulties are minor compared to the roadblocks any business plan is likely to encounter. Unforeseen changes in the economic climate, competitor actions, customer or user requirements, or internal performance or capabilities all represent uncertainties that are an order of magnitude more severe than those facing a driver following a map.

Unless adequate allowances are made for these contingencies when the plan is developed, it is almost certain to be too optimistic. It is not prudent to accept any business plan when successful execution requires all the pieces to fall into place exactly as planned. There must be some margin for error. How much depends on the penalties involved if the plan is not successful. When the penalties are very severe, the plan should not be accepted unless there is a high probability of success even if Murphy's law prevails. (Murphy's law holds that everything that can possibly go wrong will go wrong.) In most cases, it is not necessary to be quite so pessimistic as long as reasonable allowances for contingencies have been factored into the plan.

The best way to make this determination is to ask a series of "what if" questions. What happens to planned results if:

Sales volume is 5, 10, or 20 percent below forecast?

Critical costs are above estimates by some significant number?

Deadlines for important project completions are missed?

Material shortages or unusually slow deliveries occur?

Competitors cut prices by a significant amount?

Naturally, the questions will vary with each situation, but the technique is always the same. Simply look for the key variables and ask what happens if any of them go wrong. Inadequate answers probably indicate that insufficient thought was given to the possibility of things going wrong as the plan was developed.

MANAGEMENT APPROACH AND ATTITUDE

Two final points must be considered to complete the evaluation. First, it is important to determine whether the plan is integrated and truly reflects the thinking and requirements of all key areas of the business, or whether it is simply a sales and marketing proposal that none of the other business functions know anything about. It is equally important to determine that the entire management team really believes in and is committed to achieving plan results.

Functional Integration

One of the most common and serious deficiencies of industrial marketing plans is that they are just that—marketing plans. They have been drawn together by sales and marketing management and have not been properly integrated with the plans of other key functional departments. This is the key reason so many so-called industrial marketing plans have so little meaning and make so little contribution to the management and decision-making process. When marketing plans are developed in a vacuum, sales forecasts are discounted or "second guessed" by manufacturing, and inventory levels inevitably get out of line. Product development activities tend to be far too technically directed and thus out of phase with market trends. The sales force operates with an unhealthy emphasis on volume, and too little thought is given to focusing on selected customers or market segments that could make the business stronger and more profitable.

It is not difficult to determine whether a plan is really an integrated instrument to help manage the business. The first clue is what the plan is called. If it is called a "marketing plan," it probably is just that, and it probably has all the shortcomings identified above. The second clue is how it is presented. If it is written and presented solely by marketing management, it is a fair bet that other functional departments have not been adequately involved. Another way of checking is to ensure that all functional departments are represented when the plan is presented and by asking some objective questions. For example, ask manufacturing people if they agree with the sales forecast and if their inventory and production plans are actually geared to it. Ask if the planned mix of sales is compatible with existing production capabilities or if this factor was even considered when the sales plan was developed. Ask the controller if his or her department has determined the relative profitability of alternative sales strategies and if this information was considered as sales plans were drawn together. Ask engineering people to identify their planned project priorities and show how engineering time will be allocated to these projects. Then ask marketing people to explain how these priorities and allocations tie into their assessment of marketing needs and opportunities.

The answers to these kinds of questions will clearly and quickly indicate if the plan is based on a true team effort with cross-functional input. If it is not, it is not worth much and should be rejected.

Management Commitment

Management commitment to a plan is a difficult concept to define and probably the most difficult area to probe. At the same time, it is in many respects the most important area to know about. A deep-rooted sense of commitment is the reason some managers or groups overcome all the things that go wrong and still achieve planned results. It is the same ingredient that enables a team to win against tough competition even though the best players are injured or all the breaks in the game go against them.

Without attempting to be a psychologist, there are several things you can look for to determine whether this sense of commitment exists. What has been the track record of those submitting the plan? It is a positive sign if they have a history of fulfilling commitments. Conversely, if the group has not met its commitments in the past, it is essential to find out what has changed that makes their commitment to the current plan any more meaningful. Is there evidence that individuals understand how a failure to meet their personal or functional commitments would jeopardize the ability of the whole group to accomplish the plan? Is there any indication that anyone in the group feels that any function has overcommitted or that they have been pressured into making commitments that are unrealistic?

It is unlikely that people will admit they are not committed to a plan they developed and recommend. But questions directed to each functional area about the certainty or difficulty of achieving its part of the plan help everyone see what must be done to accomplish the plan. Such questioning helps to establish the importance of each individual's personal commitments not only to the plan, but to the rest of the organization. In a sense, it helps to develop a form of peer pressure, which is just as important in the execution of the business plan as it is in other walks of life. No one enjoys being in the position of having let teammates down.

None of the questions raised in this discussion should be difficult to answer if the plan has been properly put together and coordinated across all key functions of the business. Management should be able to answer crisply and directly. Excessively long, vague, or indirect answers are a good indication that the plan is not solid and should not be approved.

SUMMARY

After reading this chapter, some product or marketing managers may conclude that many of the points discussed have little to do with their marketing planning responsibilities. They may argue that the marketing function should not be concerned with such things as inventory turns, productivity measures, or expense levels in other functional areas. Those who think this way are wrong. Industrial marketing managers have a broad responsibility for making sure the total business is geared to meet market requirements and achieve maximum profit growth. This means they must be aware of and concerned about any activity in any functional area of the business that impacts the company's cost-profit structure and ability to compete. To do their job properly, they must be aware of and concerned about the total dynamics of the business and ensure that all the points covered here—structural issues, credibility issues, and management's attitude—have been properly considered in the evaluation of their plans. Otherwise, they will not provide the business leadership they should for their assigned product or market areas. Brilliant management or marketing skills alone are never sufficient to offset fundamental deficiencies in the cost-profit structure of a business, and any such deficiency must be challenged in a business plan review.

V

STRUCTURING AND MANAGING THE ORGANIZATION

15

Organization Alternatives

David Foster, vice president of sales and marketing for Newtown Tool Company, was nervous as he walked toward the headquarters conference room for his first staff meeting with the company's new president. The new president, who had a reputation for being a tough-minded executive, had been brought in by the board of directors to provide stronger marketing leadership.

Newtown Tool had been in business for over 70 years and was widely recognized as the market leader, with the most complete line of cutting tools in American industry. David had started with the company as a new sales engineer 24 years earlier and progressed through a number of sales management assignments before being promoted to his present position in 1976. He was recognized as the top sales executive in the company and was frequently called upon to negotiate large orders with both key distributors and direct accounts.

The staff meeting got underway. The president expressed himself as enthusiastic about the company's opportunities for achieving further profit growth if management did the right marketing job. He then asked for a brief report from the head of each functional department. The manufacturing vice president described the company's three plant facilities and pointed out the need for additional capacity, probably within the next two years. The technical director explained several projects underway to develop new products. David was explaining the attractive sales gains made by the company over the past five years and describing the strong position the company enjoyed with many of its major accounts when the president interrupted:

"You sound more like a sales manager than my vice president of marketing. What I want to know from you is: (1) How the market is segmented by end users and the relative profitability of each of these segments. (2) What the cost and profit structure looks like for our major product lines and which line is the most profitable. (3) How much money we make on direct sales versus sales through distributors and the volume trends for these two channels over the past five years."

David hesitated; he did not have the information to answer the questions then and there. The new president's response did not reflect a lot of sympathy:

"Let me make a couple of points just to set the record straight and to make sure all of you understand my point of view. First, the questions I've asked you are questions that any good marketing executive should be able to answer without batting an eye. Second, I don't expect you to personally develop and maintain all the knowledge required to answer these questions. However, you need to think through the kind of organization assistance you need to ensure that this information is always at your fingertips, since I don't want to spend a lot of time deciphering vague or general answers."

After the meeting, the new president apologized for being so abrupt, and said he would be glad to talk with David anytime about organization alternatives.

What factors in the company should determine the approach used to structure the organization?

What should be the objective of organizational structure?

What problems could conceivably result from overstructuring?

This chapter discusses alternative ways to organize the marketing function within a company. Organization alternatives is an important subject to consider, but it is also one that must be kept in proper perspective. Management in many companies tends to devote too much time and emphasis on alternative ways to perfect or strengthen the organization, and the danger of overorganizing or overstructuring is very real. As we stressed in Chapter 1, structure is one of the trappings of marketing frequently pointed to by management as an indicator of its commitment to marketing. However, by itself an organization structure is nothing more than lines and boxes on a chart; it does not in any sense ensure solid marketing performance or leadership. It is all too easy for managers to delude themselves into thinking they have an outstanding marketing company because they have a large or highly structured marketing organization.

Organizations, particularly those that are highly structured, are anathema. One could easily argue that the whole world would be a much better place if the need for large-scale organizations, with their layers of staff and formal procedures for almost everything, did not exist. They make it easy for groups to "syndicate the risk" so that no one can be held accountable for anything. They cover up incompetence and enable those at higher levels to pass the blame for anything that goes wrong down the line. They lead to rigidity and a lack of sensitivity and response to changed or changing conditions that often determine whether the organization succeeds or fails. In short, they are breeding grounds for bureaucracy that tend to interfere with or even thwart the achievement of the organization's very reason for being.

Here is a quote from a recent article in *The Atlantic Monthly* that clearly illustrates how overemphasis on organization and structure has placed much of American industry at a competitive disadvantage.[1]

> The sudden proliferation of staff positions within American firms is particularly striking by comparison with firms in other nations. In the typical Japanese factory, for example, foremen report directly to plant managers. The foreman in the typical American factory must report through three additional layers of management. Until very recently, Ford Motor Company had five more levels of managers between the factory worker and the company chairman than did Toyota.
>
> Bureaucratic layering of this sort is costly, and not only because of the extra salaries and benefits that must be paid. Layers of staff also make the firm more rigid, less able to make quick decisions or adjust rapidly to new opportunities and problems. In the traditional scientifically managed, high-volume enterprise, novel situations are regarded as exceptions, requiring new rules and procedures and the judgments of senior managers. But novel situations are a continuing feature of the new competitive environment in which American companies now find themselves.
>
> The typical sequence now runs something like this: A salesman hears from a customer that the firm's latest bench drill cannot accommodate bits for drilling a recently developed hard plastic. The customer suggests a modified coupling adapter

[1]Robert B. Reich, "The Last American Frontier," *The Atlantic Monthly,* March 1983.

and an additional speed setting. The salesman thinks the customer's suggestion makes sense, but he has no authority to pursue it directly. Following procedures, the salesman passes the idea on to the sales manager, who finds it promising and drafts a memo to the marketing vice president. The marketing vice president also likes the idea, so he raises it in an executive meeting of all the vice presidents. The executive committee agrees to modify the drill. The senior product manager then asks the head of the research department to form a task force to evaluate the product opportunity and design a new coupling and variable-speed mechanism.

The task force consists of representatives from sales, marketing, accounting, and engineering. The engineers are interested in the elegance of the design. The manufacturing department insists on modifications requiring only minor retooling. The salespeople want a drill that will do what customers need it to do. The finance people worry about the costs of producing it. The marketing people want a design that can be advertised and distributed efficiently, and sold at a competitive price. The meetings are difficult, because each task force member wants to claim credit for future success but avoid blame for any possible failure. After months of meetings, the research manager presents the group's findings to the executive committee. The committee approves the new design. Each department then works out a detailed plan for its role in bringing out the new product, and the modified drill goes into production.

If there are no production problems, the customer receives word that he can order a drill for working hard plastics two years after he first discussed it with the salesman. In the meantime, a Japanese or West German firm with a more flexible, teamlike approach has already designed, produced, and delivered a hard-plastics drill.

All this is not to suggest that organizations are unnecessary institutions or that the business world can do without them. A carefully thought through organization structure is the only logical vehicle for directing and coordinating the diverse but related activities of large numbers of people toward common goals. Moreover, with increasing emphasis on expanding products and markets all around the world, it is clear that the need for organizations that work effectively is not likely to decline. What we are suggesting, however, is that management must recognize how easy it is for any organization to become bureaucratic, particularly as it grows larger. While bureaucracy is a problem for any organization, it is devastating to sales and marketing activities where crisp, responsive decisions and actions are crucial to meet customer and market needs. Recognizing bureaucratic symptoms, such as those in the example just described, is a continuing management responsibility. Even more important is the need to assess constantly how the organization is functioning and to think through alternative ways the organization and decision-making process can be streamlined to avoid the development of bureaucracy.

Given this perspective on organization structures, let's examine alternative ways of organizing marketing activities and the considerations that would lead to the selection of one alternative over another.

ALTERNATIVE STRUCTURES

The correct structure for any business function or operating unit is always a lively subject for discussion since there are so many different approaches that could be followed and so many different "expert" ideas of what is right or wrong. Looked at in fundamental terms, the organization structure for any business unit is simply a framework for carrying out the key activities essential to the success of the operation. Designing this framework requires careful thought, since there is always a variety of ways it can be structured, and major penalties to be paid if it is designed incorrectly. It is probably unrealistic to think in terms of a perfect solution to any organization question, since there is not likely to be a perfect match between people's skills and capabilities and job requirements. For this reason, compromises and tradeoffs are almost always involved in developing any organization plan. The objective should be to seek the right balance between an organization approach that theoretically makes the most sense and one that is practically possible given the realities of the situation—existing skills and capabilities, time or cost constraints, or profit pressures.

There are probably more inherent difficulties in organizing the marketing department effectively than there are in organizing most other functional areas. To start with, all marketing activities must be structured in a way that will ensure leadership and direction to all the other functional disciplines, the very essence of the marketing concept. In other words, there is very little chance of having a successful marketing effort if the functions outside marketing go their own way without looking to the marketing organization for leadership. Also, a large number and wide variety of activities may be a part of the marketing department, including both headquarters marketing (market research, market planning and development, sales planning) and direct sales activities performed in many remote locations. This means the strategy, plans, and programs developed in the marketing support groups must be translated into action in widely separated geographic areas and frequently through diverse channels to distinct market segments and customer groups. Finally, many people in the marketing group have highly specialized skills that contribute significantly to the company's success. Since these skills are not easy to find and hold on to, management must take care not to drive them off or put them into a position where they cannot contribute. Given these conditions, it is clear that careful thinking and analysis is required to determine how the organization can be structured to overcome these difficulties and meet marketing requirements.[2]

The Four Basic Structures

Although it is unlikely that you can find any two marketing organizations in the industrial world that are exactly alike, there are really only four basic alternatives to consider. The marketing organization can be structured around:

[2]These points were outlined by Arnold Corbin in "Organization for Marketing," *Handbook of Modern Marketing* (New York: McGraw-Hill, 1970).

The key marketing *functions* (sales, sales order entry, market research, advertising, distributor development)

Major *product lines* or product groups (A-C motors, D-C motors, drive systems, controls)

Primary or *target markets* (end use, industry, geographic)

Some combination of these three approaches.

As a general rule, there are several alternative structures to choose from within each of these four basic alternatives.

Exhibit 15-1 illustrates a traditional marketing organization structured around the key marketing functions. It is commonly used in single-product, single-market companies where all marketing efforts are directed toward strengthening the sales, market, and product position of the product. There is nothing very complicated about this structure, and not a lot of choices to make once the key marketing functions are defined. All are simply grouped under the marketing department head. In addition to the advantage of simplicity, it probably provides the best basis for control, since decision making can be centralized. However, it has proved to be an awkward approach for managing the complexities of the marketing function when multiple products or markets are involved.

When companies add new product lines or move into new markets, organizational problems become far more difficult because the potential for conflict between products or markets exists (e.g., which product or market gets priority for capital, sales effort, manufacturing capacity, etc.). This means the organization must be structured to ensure that each important product or market segment gets its fair share of time and attention from each of the key activities that affect that segment. There are several ways this can be accomplished, but the most common approach generally involves some form of organization developed around individual products or markets. Exhibit 15-2 shows one example of how an industrial marketing organization might be structured completely around products or markets. This type of structure may be useful when a company has several different product businesses and management wants to centralize the overall marketing responsibility. Several multibusiness companies have followed this approach with varying degrees of success. There is always some question about the ability of one marketing executive to provide effective marketing leadership for a group of diverse businesses with quite different requirements. More important, the structure tends to be top-heavy with managers and too costly, since each of the key functional marketing activities is set up separately for each product or market division.

Exhibit 15-3 shows an arrangement that provides sales specialization by product, which is usually a more cost-effective structure. Here, the headquarters market support functions are centralized and responsible for work on all products. The selling organization, on the other hand, is structured around separate product sales groups responsible for sales of a single product line. There are two weaknesses in this arrangement. First, the responsibility for planning for all products falls on the shoulders of the department head. In this case, a marketing planning manager is shown to help share the burden. But it is difficult and unfair to hold this position accountable for much of anything, since the

EXHIBIT 15-1

SIMPLE FUNCTIONAL ORGANIZATION

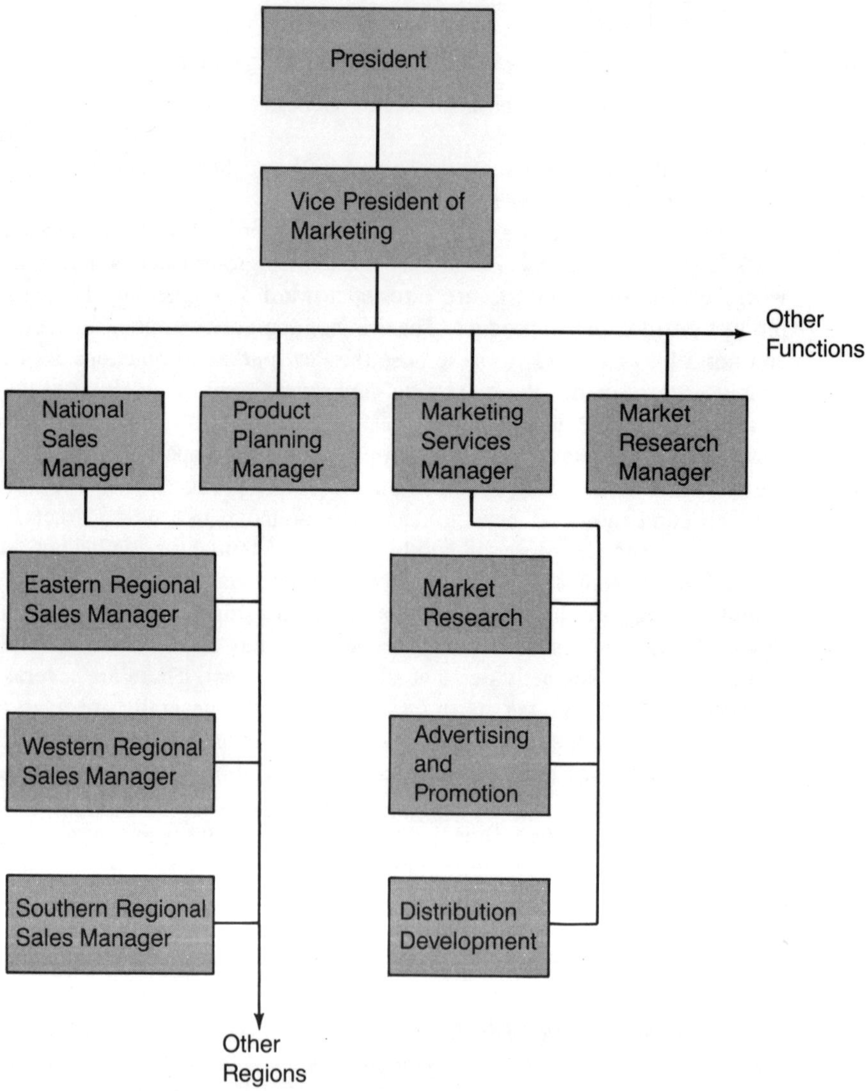

planner typically has nothing to do with implementation. Also, there is no provision made for easy interaction and coordination with manufacturing, engineering, and other functions that affect product performance in the marketplace.

Exhibit 15-4 shows another marketing organization structured around product or market managers. This approach is usually followed when different but related products are

EXHIBIT 15-2

PURE PRODUCT OR MARKET ORGANIZATION

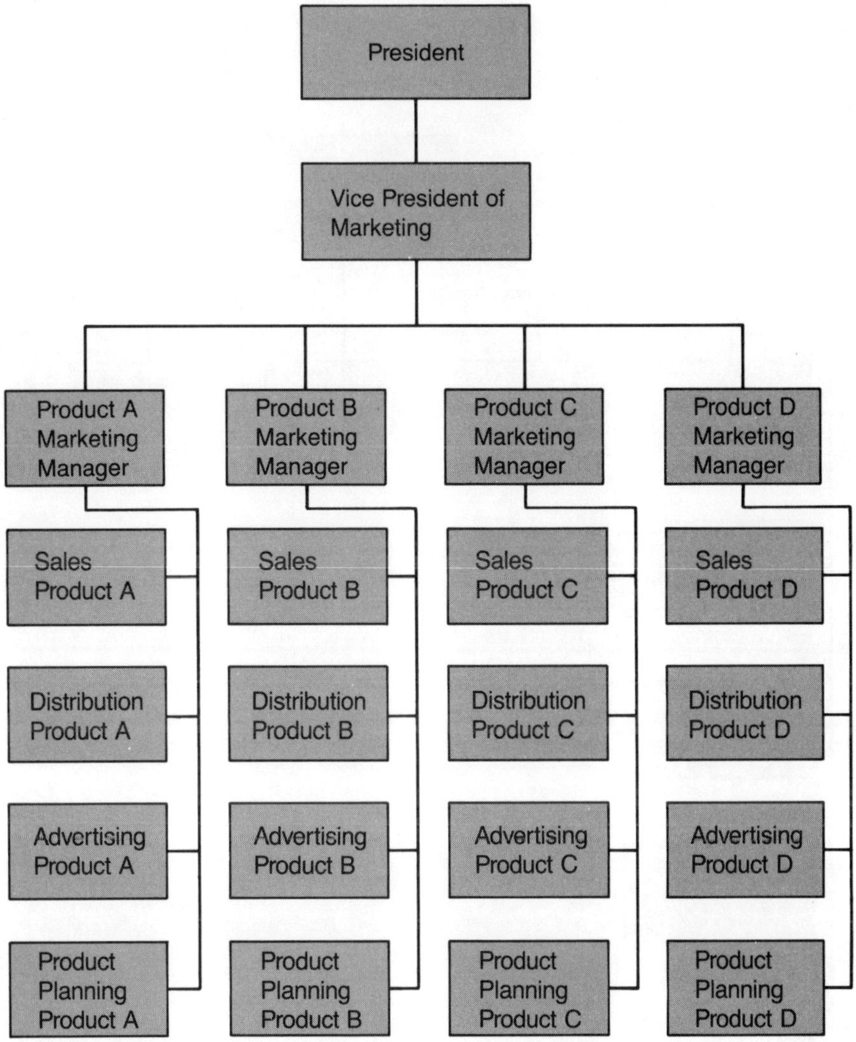

Note: Structure would be developed around marketing as well.

EXHIBIT 15-3

PRODUCT OR MARKET SALES ORGANIZATION

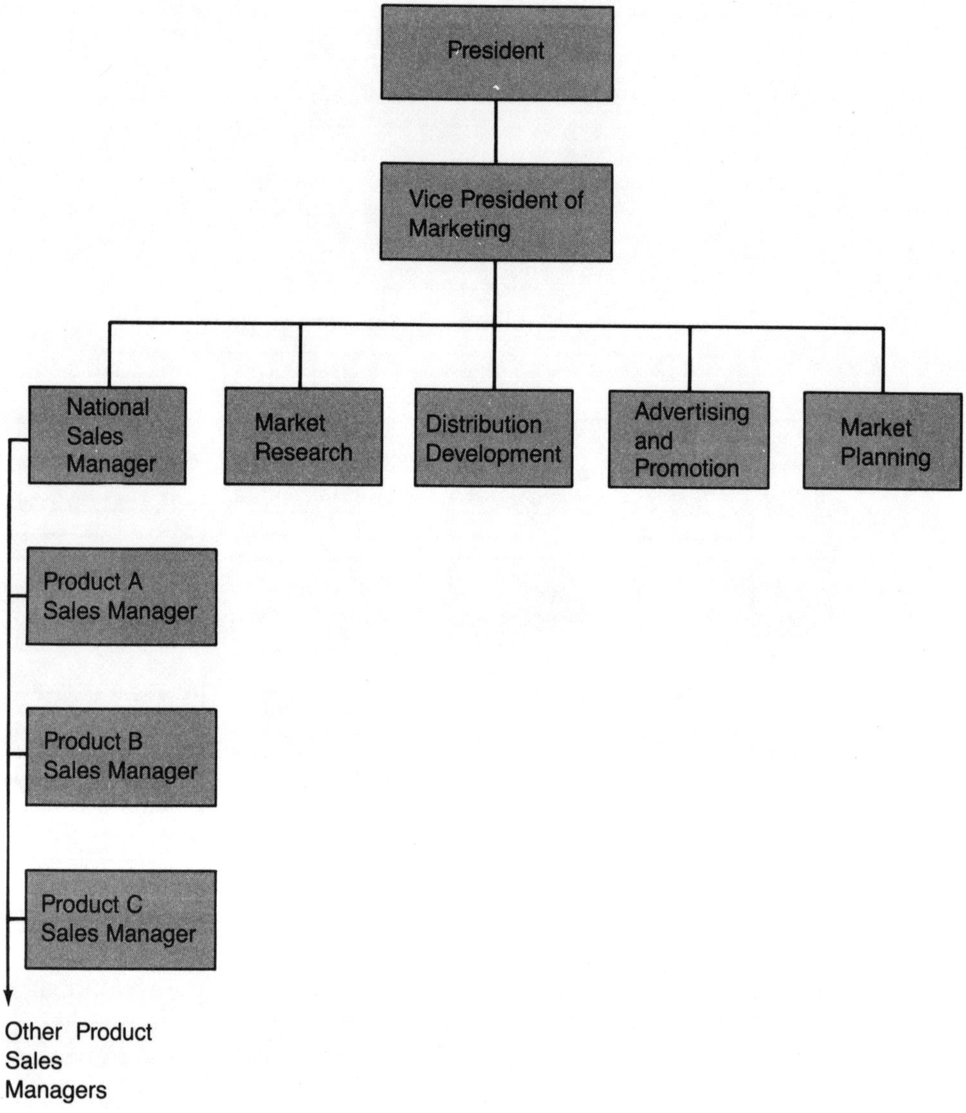

Note: Sales management assignments could be set up around markets as well.

EXHIBIT 15-4

TYPICAL PRODUCT OR MARKET ORGANIZATION

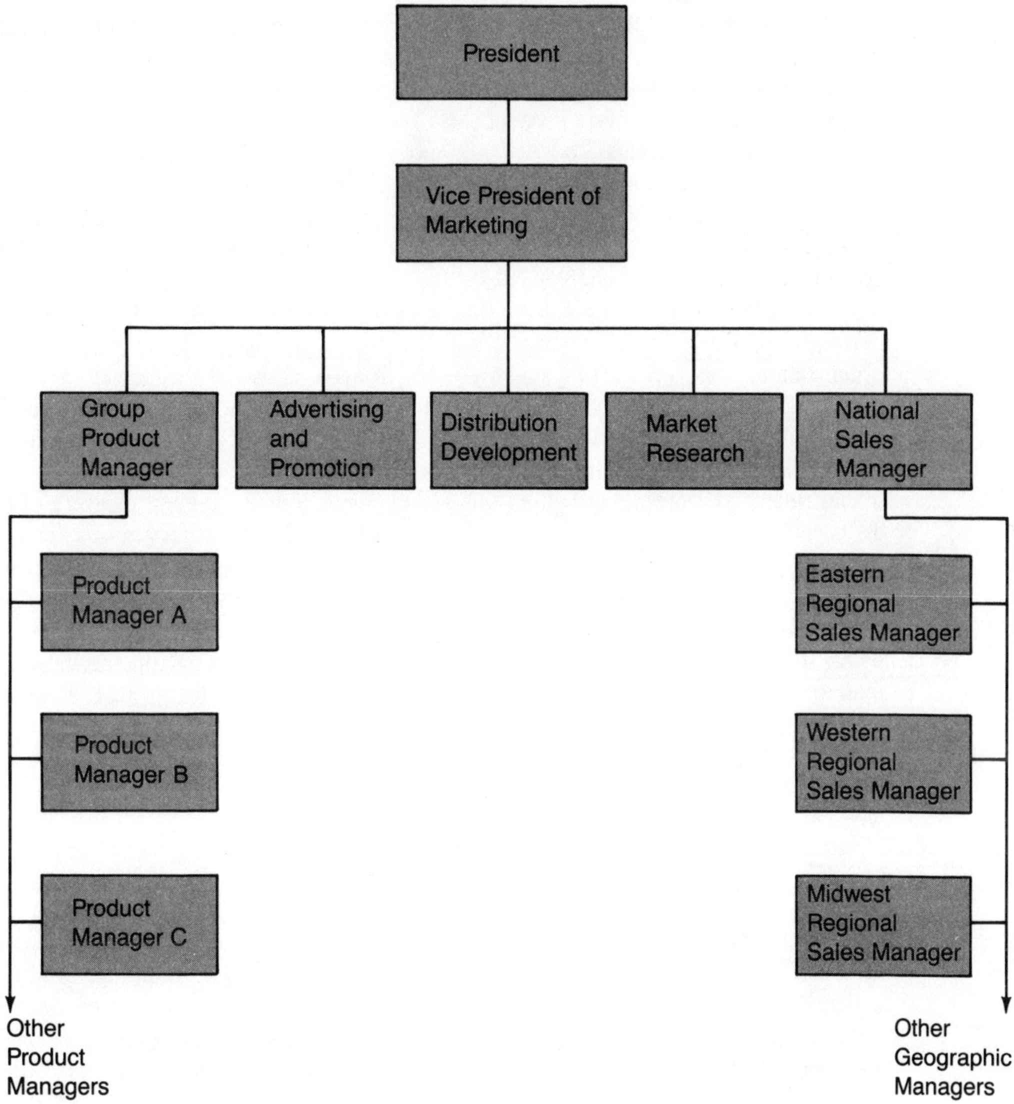

Note: Product assignment could be end use or industry markets as well.

sold to a common set of customers that can be served by a single sales organization. Manufacturing and engineering activities tend to be scrambled, not separated for each product area. It is an approach used successfully by a growing number of multiproduct industrial companies to achieve stronger management for each product-market business. The product manager serves as the marketing head for a product and makes sure it gets a fair share of attention from sales, manufacturing, engineering, and all other functions that affect the product.

The selling organization is generally structured around geographic areas, with salespeople handling all products. Product sales specialists can be assigned to different areas if more specialized product knowledge is required. Obviously, the same approach could be used to structure around markets if a company had a single line of products flowing into multiple markets and wanted the planning emphasis on markets rather than products. Because of the importance of this organization concept, we will discuss it in much greater detail in the next chapter.

As you look at Exhibit 15-4, note that it shows the product (or market managers) reporting to a group product manager, who in turn reports to the head of the marketing organization. This is the arrangement you see in most industrial companies, but it is not necessarily correct. The product manager function tends to be downgraded when it reports through a group product manager. Moreover, a strong case can be made for positioning product or market managers in the organization so they report directly to general management. The reasoning behind this arrangement contains a good measure of logic. To be effective in the industrial world, product or market managers must extend their thinking, planning, and influence across all functions of the business. In carrying out this role, product or market managers in effect serve as extensions of general management, performing many of the tasks general management would perform if it had the time. This being so, it is advantageous for them to report directly to general management rather than to the head of marketing. The relationship between the product or market managers and general management is clearer and not filtered by a third party. And working relationships with functions other than marketing tend to be much smoother when product or market managers have a direct reporting link to general management.

INTERNATIONAL MARKETING

Additional organization issues are raised when a company moves into the international arena. If a company simply exports into foreign markets, sales, shipping, billing, and collection arrangements are typically handled by an export department. Although export opportunities are significant in many industrial companies and involve a lot of specialized work because of the problems inherent in doing business with many different countries, the organization issues are not that difficult. Generally, export activities are best handled under the leadership of an export manager. The key questions are what activities need to be covered, and where the export group should be positioned in the company's overall structure. Many industrial companies have assigned responsibility for export to the marketing department, with the export manager reporting directly to the head of marketing. This arrangement works out well, since it places the responsibility for balancing priorities and requirements between domestic and foreign markets with one individual and provides for a close association between domestic and export sales efforts.

In recent years, many companies have found that import restrictions and other barriers designed to enhance nationalistic interests make it difficult to rely solely on export activities to achieve their growth and profit objectives. For this reason, they have taken various steps to secure an ownership position in operations set up to manufacture, assemble, sell, and service their products within these countries. When an industrial company takes this step and establishes an operation to manufacture and sell in foreign countries, the complexity of organizational considerations is greatly increased. One or some combination of the basic organization alternatives discussed above (structuring around functions, products, or markets) will more than likely be an appropriate framework for setting up the marketing department. However, now the whole question of how to support, control, and coordinate product line businesses in foreign countries where market requirements, competitors, and the rules and methods of doing business are quite different becomes a very important consideration.

The question of support is crucial, particularly as it relates to marketing. Many foreign subsidiaries of highly successful companies fail to meet expectations or even "die on the vine" because they do not receive sufficient technical and marketing support from the domestic organization. There is simply no way to be competitive in most markets around the world without top-flight technology and marketing, and the organization arrangement must ensure that these capabilities are available. Product control and coordination are also important, especially when the company manufactures and sells in different countries. Here, it is essential to ensure adherence to such things as quality standards, design features, and pricing strategy so that the product line does not drift out of control. This is particularly important in today's environment, when there are frequently economic reasons for sourcing parts or products in one country to sell in another. Moreover, many major customers frequently have operations in different countries and want to be sure that the product and service they buy from the same suppliers in these countries are priced and perform the same as in the home market.

Two basic approaches can be followed in structuring international operations. One approach, which many companies have employed, is to set up separate international units at the corporate level that parallel the structure used to manage domestic operations. Exhibit 15-5 shows how this arrangement looks. This approach works best when the foreign operations are sufficiently large to be relatively independent and do not require much support from their domestic counterparts. However, if foreign operations are dependent on the domestic home base for product and marketing assistance, control and coordination problems can occur because there is no provision, on paper at least, for integration until you get to the very top of the organization chart. To overcome this problem, some companies have assigned worldwide responsibility for each product business to the domestic operation. If there is only one or possibly two product businesses with operations abroad, this approach could well be the best choice, since international activities are relatively self-contained.

The problem becomes more difficult in multibusiness companies with several operations in various countries. Here, considerations of whether and how to provide centralized financial management, purchasing, legal services, and industrial relations and how

EXHIBIT 15-5 ***ONE APPROACH TO INTERNATIONAL MANAGEMENT***

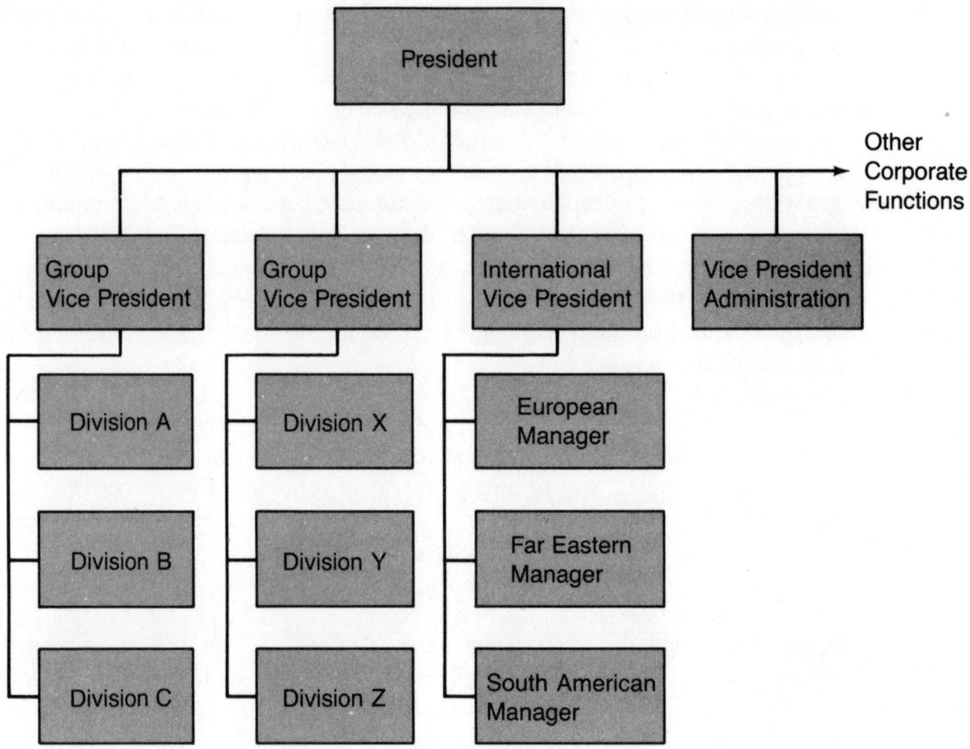

to ensure administrative consistency across all operations in the same country add to the complexity of setting up an appropriate organization. Exhibit 15-6 shows how a large electrical products company employed a matrix approach to ensure that the company's foreign operations received the proper support from domestic divisions and that division operations within various countries were managed in a way that ensured administrative consistency and achievement of total corporate growth and profit objectives.

Under this concept, domestic division management is held accountable for total product profit performance on a worldwide basis and has direct responsibility for approving growth and profit plans, product market strategy, product development, and acquisition proposals from its counterpart operation in each foreign country. The general manager of each foreign operation is held responsible for developing operating plans, for achieving operating results, and for market evaluation and development that will lead to additional profit growth in that country. Finally, a country management group is established and assigned responsibility for the total growth and profitability of all operations in the country and for providing financial management and other staff support to all operating units in a

EXHIBIT 15-6

A MATRIX APPROACH TO INTERNATIONAL MANAGEMENT

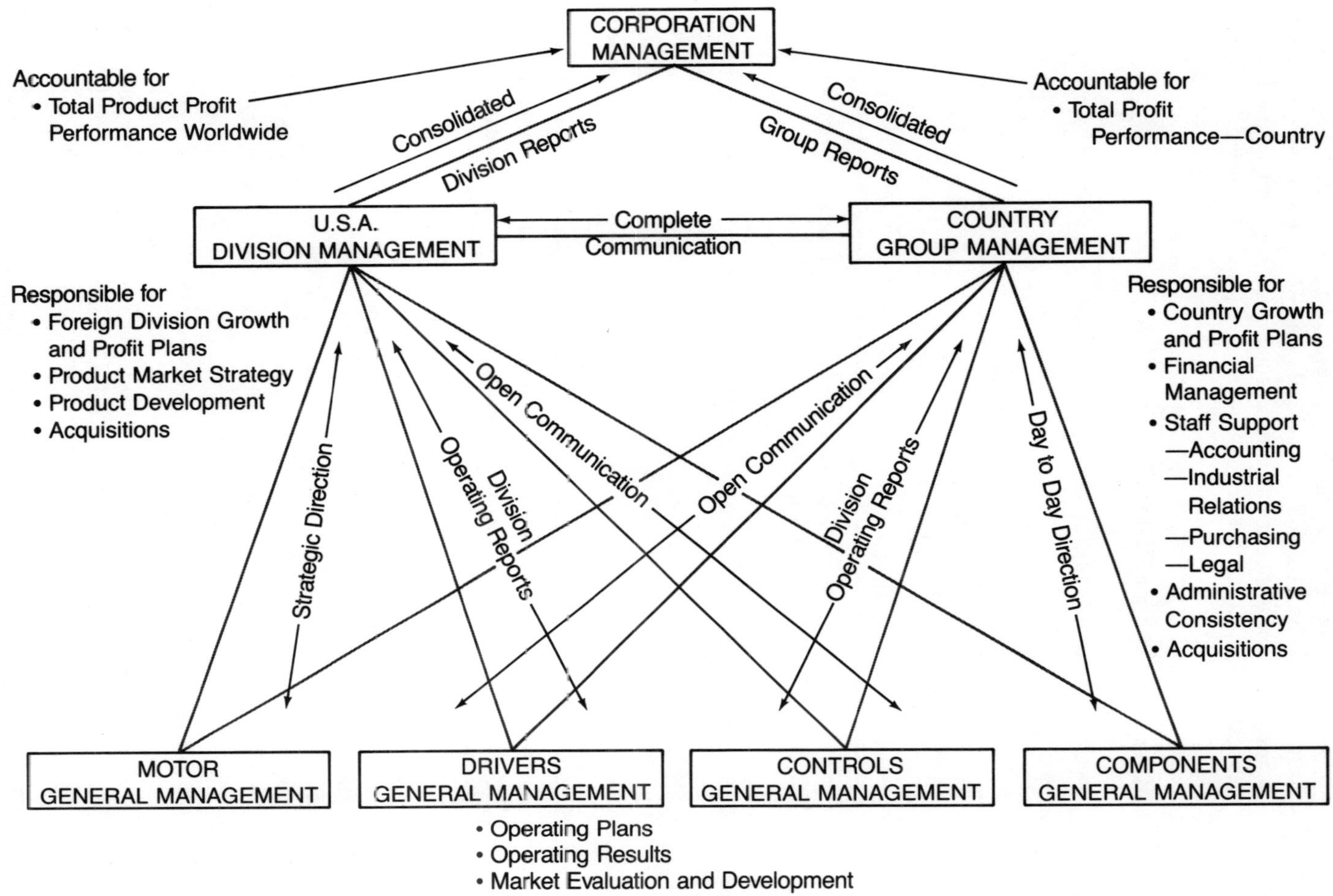

way that will ensure administrative consistency. The foreign division manager reports on a matrix basis to both the domestic general manager and the country manager. And both domestic division management and the country manager report directly to corporate management so that conflict situations can be resolved as required.

SELECTING AN ALTERNATIVE

The final choice of an organization approach should be influenced by several key considerations:[3]

1. The requirements for competitive success
2. Basic marketing plans and strategies
3. Realities of the present situation
4. Management philosophy
5. Principles of organization

Let's examine each of these points separately and see how they influence the ultimate choice of a marketing organization.

Requirements for Competitive Success

Every company has a wide range of requirements it must meet to participate successfully in a particular business. Certain manufacturing facilities are required, certain staff skills are important, certain technical skills are essential, certain financial measurements must be met, and so on. However, some requirements are central to the success of any business. For example, styling and distribution are central requirements in the automobile industry; cost control and selling a mix of products are central requirements in any chemical operation; and price, distribution, and product performance are central requirements in the electronic component business.

How does an understanding of these requirements relate to the marketing organization plan? The answer is clear if you think about it. Understanding these requirements helps to point up the range of activities that must be carried on in a successful marketing organization and how the marketing department should interact with other key functions of the business unit. More important, it should indicate which of these activities are pivotal so they can be given proper emphasis, and it should provide insights into what arrangement would be most appropriate to ensure that they are carried out effectively.

Marketing Strategies and Plans

Common sense suggests that anticipation of the future should be an important input in evaluating organization alternatives. Plans for the strategic selection of certain products or markets for emphasis can affect the selection of an organization approach. For exam-

[3]The discussion of these points is taken from material developed by D. Ronald Daniel, a director of McKinsey and Company, Inc.

ple, a company with major expansion plans in certain products or markets probably has a need to shift from a functional marketing organization that covers all products and markets to separate product or market groups for each priority area. This kind of a shift is essential to ensure the focus and emphasis required for each target product or market business. Conversely, when the market softens or business in target industries turns down, it may be appropriate to shift away from separate product or market groups to a more centralized arrangement as a means of achieving tighter control and cutting back costs.

Realities of the Present Situation

Two practical considerations are most important in deciding on the merits of one organization alternative versus another. The first is existing staff resources, which is always a consideration since it is generally impractical to think in terms of staffing any organization with a completely new group of people. And it would not make sense to adopt an organization approach completely unsuited to the background and experience of the people in the existing marketing group. So most organizations must be tailored somewhat to the capability of the people that will make them work. More than one company has had a disastrous experience trying to make some appealing organization concept work that was far too sophisticated for its existing group of people.

On the other hand, it doesn't make sense to turn away from an attractive organization alternative simply because people are not available. The best approach is probably to develop a target structure and then move toward it as new people are hired. Doing this may take two to three years, but it can be done effectively as long as everyone knows what the target structure is and interim changes are designed to move the organization in a consistent direction.

The second important practical consideration relates to cost and affordability. There are a lot of organization approaches that would be nice to have, but they simply are not affordable. For example, it would be nice to have sales specialists for every product line or product and market managers for every conceivable product or segment of the business. However, the cost-benefit relationship is simply not attractive. That does not mean management should never be willing to invest in an organization and people to build for the future. Nevertheless, the bottom line for business is profit, and the cost of one organization alternative versus another must always be considered.

Management Philosophy

Whenever organization alternatives are weighed, attention must be given to the philosophy that reflects top management's thoughts, values, and attitudes on how the organization should be managed. You simply cannot make a structure work if it requires a different management style or philosophy than actually exists. Management philosophy, which always emanates from the top, determines whether the organization will be run as a "tight ship" or whether a "free wheeling" approach will be followed. It defines the degree of toughness or paternalism that will characterize the organization. It indicates the level at which key decisions will be made and the degree of authority that will be granted.

Many managers have different ideas on these points, and there is no one set of ideas that is absolutely correct. As you can appreciate, all these factors have an important bearing on organization planning. It is essential to understand how management thinks and to understand how and why an organization functions as it does. For example, it would be difficult to use any kind of a decentralized organization approach around products or markets if top management insisted on maintaining a tight rein on all decision-making authority.

Principles of Organization

Finally, some time-honored principles of organization should be considered. All kinds of principles have been developed over the years. Although some are valid, many are too rigid to be useful in today's complex business environment. Nevertheless, it is useful to understand what points were important to some of the early experts on organization theory. The boxes on page 333 present two examples from the literature that have stood the test of time.

Principles like these are frequently used by senior managers in real life situations to guide organization thinking in their operations. Here is a memo from a company president to his staff that makes it very clear he wants all the parts of the company to be structured according to his principles:

> To: All Operating Managers
>
> From: President
>
> I have a strong belief that each of our three large operating units has way too many salaried and management people in their overhead structure. I believe that many of these people are marginal performers and that many of them are way overpaid for what they do. I would much rather see us have a far more streamlined organization with fewer people earning a lot more money. Please be prepared to address this point during your next organization review. In addressing this point, remember a few principles that make sense to me in structuring and staffing any organization.
>
> - No assistants or assistants to: there is no room for "gophers" anywhere.
> - No one-over-one, one-over-two, or one-over-three situations in any organization. If a manager isn't managing at least five people his job isn't structured right.
> - No marginal performers at any level.
> - No unnecessary duplication of division staff in plant operations (i.e., division controller–plant controller, division engineer–plant engineer).
> - No more than five layers between division managers and production workers.
> - No secretaries supporting less than 3 to 4 managers.
> - Everyone in the organization accountable for some measurable result.
>
> Please be prepared to discuss any exceptions to these principles that exist in your organization during our next review session.

There are many different ideas on how these principles should be used in organization planning. Some experts believe that any organization should be rigidly structured around

PRINCIPLES OF ORGANIZATION

James O. McKinsey

1. In every business there should be centralized control accompanied by proper delegation of authority.
2. Responsibility and authority should go hand in hand.
3. Activities should be classified so that specialists will be developed.
4. The number of subordinates reporting to each executive should be limited.
5. Proper means should be provided for effective coordination of activities.
6. The distinction between line and functional control should be recognized.
7. The personal element must be recognized.

Source: McKinsey and Company, Inc.

PRINCIPLES OF ORGANIZATION

Harold Stieglitz

Objectives

1. The objectives of the enterprise and its component elements should be clearly defined and stated in writing. The organization should be kept simple and flexible.

Activities and Grouping of Activities

2. The responsibilities assigned to a position should be confined as far as possible to the performance of a single leading function.
3. Functions should be assigned to organizational units on the basis of homogeneity of objective to achieve most efficient and economic operation.

Authority

4. There should be clear lines of authority running from the top to the bottom of the organization and accountability from bottom to top.
5. The responsibility and authority of each position should be clearly defined in writing.
6. Accountability should always be coupled with corresponding authority.
7. Authority to take or initiate action should be delegated as close to the scene of action as possible.
8. The number of levels of authority should be kept to a minimum.

Relationships

9. There is a limit to the number of positions that can be effectively supervised by a single individual.
10. Everyone in the organization should report to only one supervisor.
11. The accountability of higher authority for the acts of its subordinates is absolute.

Source: Organizational Planning (New York: National Industrial Conference Board, 1962).

them. Certainly the company president expressed a strong point of view. Probably the most balanced approach is to use them as a checklist to ensure that a particular organization has not been inadvertently structured in a way that flies in the face of what those with experience regard as good practice. On the other hand, there may be very good reasons for departing from some of these principles, and the structure should not be modified or discarded simply to comply.

In other words, the principles should be used as guidelines, not controlling considerations in any organization plan. By definition guidelines are just that, and they can be violated if it makes sense to do so. For example, the old saw that authority should be consistent with responsibility does not hold true in the case of a traditional product management arrangement in which the product manager has all kinds of responsibility without commensurate authority. Also, some quantitative limit on the span of control, such as 4, 5, or 7 people reporting to a superior, is not a rule that should be followed rigidly. There are plenty of industrial sales and service organizations that have as many as 15 or even 20 individuals reporting to a supervisor who carries the responsibility very effectively. The number of individuals reporting to a superior depends entirely on what is required in the way of supervision, not solely on some principle of organization.

WHEN TO MAKE A CHANGE

The need to change or restructure the marketing organization depends on two factors. First, how effectively the current organization operates. Second, how adequately it provides the focus necessary to capitalize on future product and market opportunities. Deciding that the market organization is or is not functioning effectively right now is obviously a judgment call, but there are several questions you can ask to help make this judgment.

1. Is the organization responsive to customer needs, competitive actions, and/or shifting market requirements? Is it easy for customers to do business with the organization? Are quoted delivery dates met? Are customer inquiries or requests for quotes on special items handled promptly?
2. Does the organization produce creative business strategies and solid business plans that result in a competitive advantage for each of its priority products and markets?
3. Does the organization fulfill its role as the lead function of the business and ensure that all key functions are properly geared to serve the company's target markets? Are the communication links with manufacturing, engineering, and finance clearly defined?
4. Does the organization provide the necessary focus or emphasis on priority product-market segments? If the marketing strategy is focused on products or markets A, B, and C, is the organization structured to facilitate the same focus?
5. Does the organization achieve planned market performance and profit objectives? Are prompt corrective actions taken when actual performance falls behind plan? Is it clear who is accountable for results in each segment of the business and for each major program?

If the answer to any of these questions is negative, some kind of change is required. It may well be that a structural change in the organization to provide for better planning, closer coordination with other functions, stronger sales management, or some other such improvement is the answer. However, it is also essential to determine whether the problem really stems from a fault in the structure or in the people involved. Performance evaluation is especially important. No organization structure will ever work effectively with inadequate performers. Nor are inadequate performers likely to work any more effectively under a new or changed alternative structure. A lot of time can be wasted shuffling boxes on a chart or putting names in different boxes if management does not face up to fundamental weaknesses in the people involved.

Looking to the future, the key questions to ask are these: What are the product-market areas selected for emphasis? How do we ensure the strong management and entrepreneurial drive to capture the business in these areas? If major opportunity areas are not specifically assigned in a way that brings these skills to the forefront, some organization change is in order. The change may be as simple as giving some individuals dual role assignments (such as, continue as regional sales manager and also be responsible for planning growth in the marine market). Conversely, the change may require a major restructuring of the organization to provide stronger product or market management. Although different approaches may be used to achieve proper product-market assignments, the objective should always be the same: to ensure that someone feels the burden of responsibility for profit growth in each product-market area. Otherwise, these areas will be fun and interesting to talk about, but nothing much will happen to advance the company's position.

One final caveat on organization can be best illustrated with a quote from history:

> We trained hard—but it seemed that every time we were beginning to form up into teams, we would be reorganized. I was to learn later in life that we tend to meet any new situation by reorganizing. And what a wonderful method it can be for creating the illusion of progress while producing confusion, inefficiency and demoralization.[4]

What was true in A.D. 66 holds true today. A change in the organization structure, by itself, is never the answer to more effective marketing. Unfortunately, in far too many cases managements tend to tinker with the organization whenever they run into trouble in the marketplace instead of searching for and facing the causes of problems. It is unquestionably important to think through how the marketing organization should be structured in light of market requirements and what jobs have to be done. It is also true that periodic adjustments are necessary to keep the structure geared to the changing requirements of the marketplace. But organization changes by themselves will not make a significant difference in marketing performance.

In the next chapter, we'll dig deeper into the problems and considerations that come into play as we move from the straightforward functional approach to marketing organization toward a product or market management structure.

[4]From *Petronii Arbitri Satyricon,* A.D. 66, attributed to Gaius Petronius.

SUMMARY

Certain organization alternatives and considerations are important as a backdrop for reviewing, planning, or altering any marketing organization. The four basic ways of organizing marketing are by key marketing function, by major product lines or groups, by primary or target market, or some combination of these three. When a company moves into the international arena, the alternatives are to set up parallel international units at the corporate level or to assign worldwide responsibility for each product business to the domestic organization. Which structure is selected depends on the company's requirements, plans for the future, and present situation.

16

Product-Market Management

After several discussions with his vice president of marketing, Al Waters, president of Electronic Systems, Inc., decided that the company should restructure its marketing organization around product managers. The business was growing very rapidly, and he was concerned about things slipping "between the cracks." Electronic's major competitor appeared to be gaining market share, and he had heard the vice president of marketing for that company describe in glowing terms how its product managers worked. He knew his people were not enthusiastic about product managers, but he pushed ahead anyway and actually hired two people from the competitor to fill product management positions. Two other product managers were appointed from the company's sales force. Waters had agreed to review periodically with his staff how the product manager idea was working, and a meeting had been scheduled for this purpose. Unfortunately, Waters could not attend the meeting because of prior commitments, and asked one of his administrative assistants to substitute for him.

Jack Sanford, vice president of manufacturing, and Robert Dixon, vice president of engineering, were the most negative in their reactions to the product management group. They had the same basic complaint: They were convinced the product managers were interfering with their ability to do their jobs. Although four product managers had been appointed to manage the company's four major product lines, the two who had been brought in from the outside were the ones who had received the most notice. Jack claimed, "They don't really know anything about our company's business and yet they try to tell me how and in what quantities to manufacture." Bob Dixon was "damned sick and tired" of having young "hot-shot" MBAs telling him how much should be spent for development projects and which projects should get top priority.

It didn't take long for a heated argument to start. The two new product managers reacted defensively, claiming that they had to be involved in setting priorities in both the manufacturing and engineering areas or they couldn't do their jobs. One of the product managers made the point that he had been told by the president of the company to think and act like a general manager. The two critics responded with the same words: "Your job is to plan and coordinate, not to be a general manager. We get along fine with the other product managers, but you two will wreck our whole operation if you keep trying to tell people what to do."

Is Waters' rationale for restructuring around product managers sound?

What mistakes did Waters make in introducing product managers into the company?

Is it possible to manage a product line without participating in manufacturing and engineering decisions? How much authority does a product manager need?

The product or market management concept is not a new organization alternative. It has been employed successfully in many large, complex multiproduct corporations to achieve the vigorous product or market leadership that top executives of smaller, more tightly knit companies provide through a centralized organization. Both positions have been used successfully throughout industry to provide the necessary market orientation and to ensure sound planning for various product-market segments. And the purpose of both has always been the same: to safeguard the commercial health of the business by ensuring that the necessary plans, decisions, and commitments made throughout the company effectively meet the changing needs of the marketplace.

Product managers are most appropriate when a company has multiple products flowing into a common market through the same channels and to the same customer groups. Market managers get the nod in the reverse situation – when the company needs to develop different markets for its products and the focus is on developing the market rather than on taking the product to market. In the discussion and examples that follow, any of the comments we make or examples we cite about product managers apply to market managers, and vice versa.

Despite its widespread application, the product or market management concept is not an easy one to make work, and many companies have been disappointed with the results. For example, a marketing vice president in a basic metals company complained: "We moved to a product management setup because we thought we could improve our profits if we had product managers with full-time responsibility for planning to improve the overall mix of products moving through our plants. But it's beginning to look as though we were kidding ourselves. Our product management group costs us $500,000 a year, but I can't honestly say our product mix is any more profitable today than it was before they were around. Our product managers have put all kinds of plans together, but not one of them has really done the job we wanted." Assuming the concept is sound, why is the record so mixed? Our analysis of the experience of a wide range of companies suggests that product or market management pays off only under very special circumstances and only when very specific organizational requirements are met (see the box, page 346). In this chapter we discuss who should use product and/or market managers and how they can be used most effectively.

WHEN SHOULD THE CONCEPT BE EMPLOYED?

The job of product or market manager was created to fill a critical need in large, multiproduct companies where manufacturing, engineering, and sales had responsibility for all products. In these situations, the task of managing all the factors bearing on the success of each of many products had proved too much for any one executive to handle. And it was unrealistic to expect functional department heads to balance and coordinate the interests of many products in the best interests of the company. It was to fill this void that the product or market manager form of organization was created.

HOW THE CONCEPT WORKS

The experience of a leading electronics manufacturer shows how a strong product manager can positively affect a business.

For years, this company had dabbled in the nuclear instrumentation field with little success. Its sales growth had lagged behind the competition, and profits were too slim to support the development effort needed to keep pace with the field. Understandably, management had its doubts about this business, but problems in other product areas were always more important. For some time, the instrumentation business was allowed to drift. Many managers had an interest in it, but no one had specific responsibility for results. Eventually, under pressure of mounting problems, management decided to reorganize its marketing department along product management lines. One product manager was assigned full-time to the company's nuclear instrumentation line. The charter: to develop a plan for getting some market momentum behind the line—or a plan for withdrawing from the business.

Within three months, the product manager was convinced that the potential of the nuclear instrumentation line alone was too limited to justify the company's continued interest. But he had also identified a real opportunity to expand into the much broader and more attractive controls field. Accordingly, the plan he submitted called for adding technical staff and acquiring a small foreign manufacturer to obtain the broader base of products the company would need to compete in the controls area. His plan was adopted, and today his product line is the fastest-growing and most promising segment of the company's entire business.

It doesn't follow, however, that just because a company has multiple products and many product problems, product or market management is the answer. In companies where each product-market group really represents a distinct business large enough—or potentially large enough—to support its own production and marketing operations, it may make more sense to divisionalize the company and set up separate and self-sustaining units for each major product or market group. In other companies, it may be better to set up separate marketing groups for each product and/or market and keep the manufacturing operations centralized. This makes more organizational sense when complete divisionalization is not feasible, but sales, distribution, and marketing requirements are significantly different for each product. In still other companies it may be advantageous to have separate sales operations for each product-market group, with marketing and manufacturing activities maintained centrally. This is a more logical approach when separate customer groups must be served, when the business of each product is too small for divisionalization, or when the only place product specialization is important or practical is in the sales area.

The product or market manager concept should be used only when these alternatives are impractical or undesirable. Usually this situation exists when the product businesses involved are small, when functional activities (manufacturing, engineering, sales) are common or scrambled for all products, and when divisionalization or separate marketing groups do not make economic sense. Likewise, when there is a common set of customers for all products, setting up separate product-market sales forces is usually costly and awkward; it is more sensible to have a single sales manager representing all the company's products to this common customer group. In short, only in multiproduct companies where physically separated operating divisions, marketing groups, or sales units are not practical is product or market management the preferred organizational alternative. In these cases, the product or market manager provides a means of ensuring individual attention for all major products or markets without separating off any part of the line operations.

The only difference between the product manager and the market manager is the marketing circumstances that make one approach more effective than the other. The product manager approach is more appropriate for companies with a number of different products that have to be produced and marketed through the same manufacturing, marketing, or sales divisions. If a company has an essentially homogeneous, or at least closely related, line of products that appeal to different segments of the market, the market manager approach may make more sense, since it may put appropriate focus on each of the marketing opportunities.

MAKING THE CONCEPT WORK

Because the product or market manager concept is an organization anomaly (that is, responsibility is not matched with authority), it is a difficult one to make work. Special management care and attention is required for successful implementation. Let's examine some of the problems encountered when the concept is employed and how these problems can be avoided.

Often the product-market manager concept never gets off the ground in a company because managers are simply appointed and their jobs set up on the basis of what someone has heard about what some other company has done. No one takes the time to think through the specific requirements for the company involved.

The frustrating experience of a large electronics company dramatically illustrates the importance of careful attention to organizational needs. Four product managers were appointed; no other organizational changes or staff additions were made. They were expected to resolve an Augean stable load of problems that had plagued the company for a long period of time. For example, inventories and manufacturing costs were way out of line; there was serious slippage on engineering projects; and the sales organization had let the backlog drop below the safety level. These were all difficult problems, rooted deep in the line operations of the company. To think that the new product managers, by themselves, could solve these problems was totally unrealistic.

Not only did top management place superhuman requirements on the new product managers, it also failed to provide the kind of training that might have helped them grow in their jobs. The experience of these managers had been, for the most part, in sales. It was understandably difficult for them to flag potential problems in manufacturing and engineering, and next to impossible for them to develop appropriate programs of action or to persuade line executives to respect their recommendations. Instead of helping and supporting the new product managers, management blamed them for everything that went wrong. This, in turn, weakened the one weapon they had—the respect of line executives for their competence. Consequently, the product managers were unable to begin to develop the cooperative relationships they needed with the various functional executives.

The product managers unenthusiastically compared their position to "walking blindfolded on a treadmill." They recognized that it was impossible to handle all the problems management expected them to deal with. They lived in jittery anticipation that management might blame them for almost anything that went wrong. Within a short time, three of the four were replaced, and there was a general feeling of dissatisfaction with the whole idea.

A closer look at the experience of this company suggests the organizational requirements that must be met if the product or market manager is to have a chance at success. It becomes apparent that all concerned must clearly understand the role and responsibilities of the product or market manager, that the managers must have access to line management, that the managers themselves must be chosen carefully, that they must receive adequate training and orientation, and that appropriate standards of performance must be applied when judging their success.

Clear Responsibilities

There are many different points of view on what the product or market manager's role really is. Some say the activity should be limited to product or market planning. Others argue that this is far too restrictive, since many other factors contribute to the success of a product. Many say the product or market manager should have full profit responsibility and final authority over many important decisions—for example, pricing, inventory levels, and product improvements. An equal number contend that he or she should not have final decision-making responsibility in any of these areas, since these are properly line decisions. Obviously, the product or market manager's responsibilities differ from one company to another and should be tailored to the particular needs of each product at a particular point in time. However, the biggest risk in all situations is that the responsibilities are defined in a way that blocks the manager from fulfilling a business management role. As a general rule, therefore, the manager's responsibilities should be defined as broadly as possible even though he or she lacks the line authority to carry out these responsibilities alone.

Because the job can vary so from company to company—and because the scope is potentially so broad—the objectives, responsibilities, and working relationships should be committed to writing as a basis for gaining agreement and understanding. Exhibit 16-1 is an example of a product manager's position statement that shows the kind of detail required. Note that in addition to describing the product manager's responsibilities in specific and "how to" terms, this position description defines his or her relationships with other key functions in substantial detail. This emphasis on relationships is key, since the product manager does not have line control over any of these functions, yet his or her success depends on how effectively he or she works with and through them to achieve business objectives.

When management is reluctant to give its product managers enough responsibility or appropriate status in the organization, the job frequently degenerates into a low-level

EXHIBIT 16-1

A PRODUCT MANAGER'S STATEMENT

GENERAL POSITION DESCRIPTION FOR PRODUCT-MARKET MANAGER

Any position description for a manager handling an assignment for a single or a group of products or markets should be specific for that particular assignment at that particular time. Therefore, this position description outlines only the general objectives, responsibilities, and relationships of our product managers. Specific objectives and priorities should be defined each year (or more frequently if necessary) for each product management assignment.

General Objectives

All product-market managers share a common objective to generate maximum profit growth and return on the assets employed in their assigned area of the business. To achieve this objective each product-market manager is expected to think, plan, and operate like an overall business manager, even though he or she does not have commensurate authority. This means he or she must:

1. Quickly develop a clear understanding of the business economics for his or her product-market. As a minimum he or she should know: (1) the value of assets committed to the product-market business and where they are employed, (2) which costs vary how much with volume, (3) what the major cost and expense elements are and (4) what actions have the greatest impact on costs and profits, and how these economics compare with competitors. To get this basic economic understanding of the business, the product-market manager should feel free to discuss any aspect of the business with executives at any level in any functional area—and he or she should challenge any statement that doesn't seem to make sense.
2. Always be sure the cost-profit structure for each product-market or added increment of volume or market share is sound and never be misled by so-called full line, volume, or market share benefits.
3. Avoid being misled by standard or accepted accounting procedures or pricing formulas that may produce wrong information, leading to incorrect operating or economic decisions.
4. Insist on having a monthly net profitability analysis (including all allocations for each product-market segment) and make certain that allocation assignments are reasonable.
5. Pinpoint the poor profit performers with low gross margins (i.e., 40 percent or lower), and, after making sure that the financial data and results are really correct, initiate action to:
   a. Raise the selling price.
   b. Improve the cost structure (both direct and indirect costs; short and longer term actions).

Source: Much of this position description was developed for use at Reliance Electric by E. G. Orahood, executive vice president.

EXHIBIT 16-1

(cont'd)

c. Withdraw from the market. *Note:* In some cases a large price increase can be the first step to withdrawal or it can be the means of achieving a satisfactory profit on a lower level of volume.
d. Come up with other possible solutions.

6. Pinpoint the good profit performers with high gross margins (i.e., 50 percent or better), and, after checking to make sure the numbers are accurate, initiate action to:

    a. Make certain that competitors do not undermine the present market share position with a lower price strategy.
    b. Increase selling and promotional emphasis to gain immediate market share while maintaining high profit margins, and step up development activities to ensure a continued strong market and profit position for the longer term. *Note:* Opportunities often exist in geographic markets or channels where market share is below average.

7. Plan and control new product development activities and initiate improvements to maintain competitive leadership. All major investment recommendations for new or redesigned products must be supported with a marketing and total business plan. Detailed budgets including engineering hours, expenses, and capital must be established for these plans so they can be tracked and charged against the correct products.
8. Develop both an annual business plan and an updated five year plan for his or her assigned product area. To be meaningful and realistic, these plans must consider the limits of resources available. Typical resources (all of which have limits) are:

    a. Plant, machinery, workforce (additional capacity available by increasing the workforce or shift supervision).
    b. Engineering hours.
    c. Engineering talent and capability.
    d. Sales hours.
    e. Sales talent and specialization.
    f. Expense dollars.

Responsibility and Authority

Given the objectives described above, it is clear that the product-market manager is charged with the same (or part of the same) basic responsibility of the general manager. The product-market manager has direct responsibility for pricing and for the level of finished goods inventory (at factory and distribution locations) for his or her products. Although the product manager does not have direct line control over many of the people influencing the profit results, he or she must cover all areas and initiate action when he or she is not getting the proper results or responses from other disciplines. This includes taking conflicts that cannot be resolved to general management for resolution.

EXHIBIT 16-1 *(cont'd)*

Relationships

The product-market manager must work closely with the following departments to achieve desired results:

1. *Sales:* To implement specific product sales programs, to ensure proper sales emphasis on assigned products, to obtain continuous and meaningful feedback from the marketplace, i.e.: (1) Competitive activity: e.g., product, price, strategies, capacity, economic structure. To ensure an adequate "Profit Return" on all expense dollars charged against his or her product by sales (for direct sales, activities, order entry, etc.). To work with Sales Managers to: (1) Evaluate distributor performance. (2) Establish target accounts. (3) Ensure that competent salespeople are assigned on all key accounts. (4) Achieve market penetration in specific channels, locations, or accounts.
2. *Engineering and Development:* To ensure market input in setting priorities, to evaluate and plan new product development alternatives, to improve costs or performance of existing products, to correct defects in existing products.
3. *Financial:* To ensure understanding of business economics, to obtain current and meaningful reports on the cost structure and profitability of his or her assigned products, to ensure allocations made against his or her assigned products are reasonable and fair, to obtain reports on total assets assigned to his or her particular products, to monitor results achieved on new product development or redesign and check against predicted return.
4. *Advertising and Sales Promotion:* To develop a specific promotional plan for the upcoming fiscal year and determine the budget dollars to be charged against the products, to define clearly the objectives of such a plan and the return expected, to monitor results and to take quick action to cancel continuing promotional efforts if results are not being achieved. *Note:* Industrial advertising and promotion can be a "sink hole." Spending proposals often follow historical precedent without concrete plans to achieve specific results on dollars expended. For this reason, the product manager is directly responsible for ensuring that he or she obtains definite measurable results for his or her dollars.
5. *Marketing Research:* To obtain realistic potentials for his or her products by trading areas, channels, and sales locations, to obtain feedback data to indicate degree of market penetration by sales location and by individual salesperson, to obtain regular reports showing status on each specific product.
6. *Manufacturing:* To understand plant capacities and manufacturing costs for each product, to understand specific economics (for his or her own operations and competitors) of: (a) standards versus specials; (b) different lot sizes; (c) spare parts manufacturing.
7. *Order entry and sales service:* To monitor and obtain continuous feedback from the field for the following functions: (a) ensure prompt and correct entry of order; (b) ensure correct and factual scheduling of order to meet customers' needs; (c) ensure that schedules are met and that correct items are shipped.

clerical assignment. The contrasting experiences of two market managers from competing companies illustrate this dramatically. In the one case, the market manager played a very strong role in planning for and managing the company's business in her assigned market. She constantly analyzed market conditions and requirements and made sure that programs were developed and implemented to capitalize on major market opportunities. She pinpointed selected areas for distribution-building programs and obtained approval to increase warehouse stocks for faster delivery. To keep costs down, she got the manufacturing and development departments to program a 10 percent cost reduction in a line of distributor products. Once a year she worked up and presented a written business plan for enlarging the company's position in her market to top management. As soon as this was approved, she began working with all departments to ensure that their plans were tied into the overall plan for her market. She then followed up with appropriate line executives to see that programs and decisions affecting her market were implemented and carried out effectively.

She was, in fact, the business manager for her market area. By contrast, her counterpart's job was structured so that he was a combination fact-gatherer for higher-level management and correspondence clerk for his assigned market area. He collected information, which he passed on to line executives so they could make plans or decisions. He was not expected and made no effort to draw together an overall plan for his market. He spent much time dealing with routine sales correspondence that should have been handled in the field. And he never followed up on programs that affected his market business to see that they were carried out properly. As a result, both management and market manager rapidly became disillusioned with the whole idea.

Proper Position in the Organization

As we have emphasized, the concept of product or market managers is an organizational anomaly in that it violates a longstanding organization principle; that is, responsibility should always be matched by equivalent authority. The product or market manager is not a line executive in the classic sense, for he or she has little or no actual authority. Nor is he or she staff in the traditional sense, since his or her responsibilities usually go far beyond analysis and recommendations. He or she usually has the unqualified responsibility for seeing that everything related to the product or market gets done well and on time and that satisfactory profit growth is achieved.

The manager's success depends largely on how well he or she is able to develop and maintain a host of complex working relationships with other executives throughout the organization. It is extremely important, therefore, to keep the channels as clear as possible. It is even more important to recognize that each product manager's assignment must be tailored to enable him or her to focus on the particular activities that are vital to the product's growth and profitability, regardless of what they are or where they fit in the organization. In effect, the product manager serves as a hub or nerve center to ensure interfunctional coordination with all the functions and activities that affect the product business (see Exhibit 16-2). In this position, the product manager must ensure that the communication flow between functions is clear and accurate and that all the various efforts for the product line are synchronized.

EXHIBIT 16-2

THE PRODUCT MANAGER AS HUB

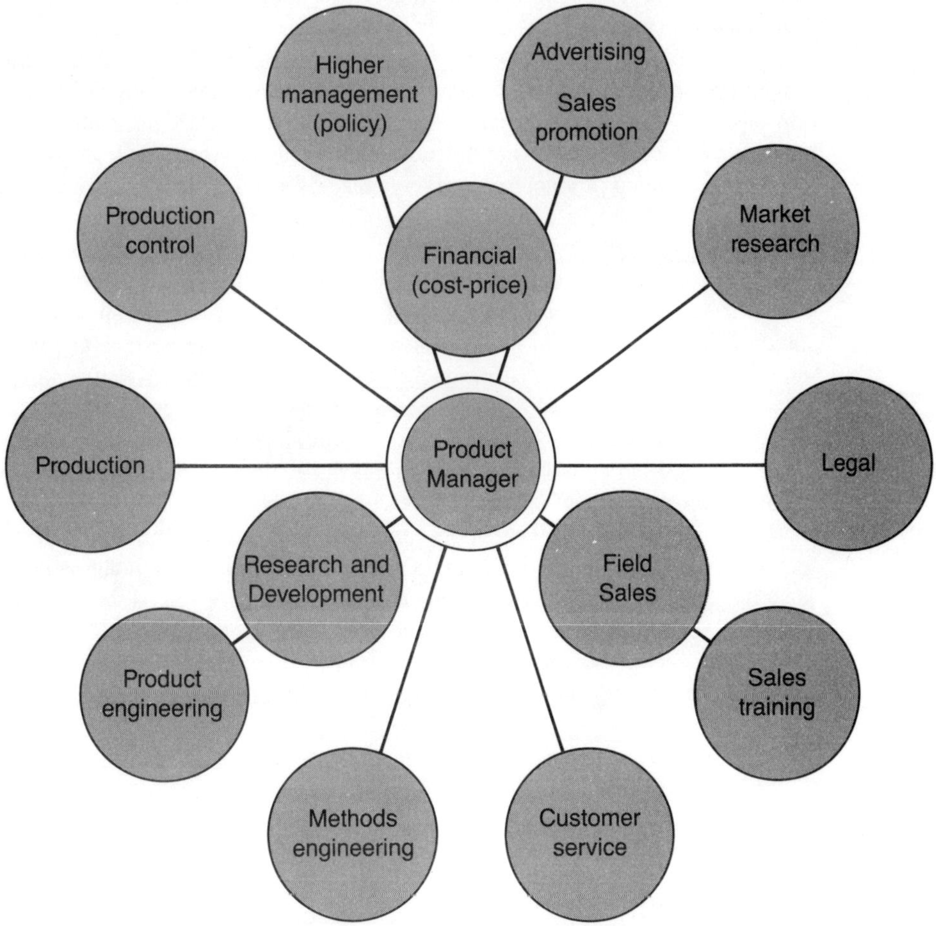

Source: Karl H. Tietjen, "The Industrial Product Manager," *Handbook of Modern Marketing* (New York: McGraw-Hill, 1970).

A product manager in the plastics field found the organizational barriers in his company crippling. In sharp contrast to the hub concept, he was organizationally cut off from direct contact with product scheduling or product development. Top management, applying a generalized concept of the job, had restricted the product manager's assignment to the marketing area. Yet the profit for his product depended heavily on maintaining uninterrupted production, even at a sacrifice in unit margins. And product improvements were the major weapon for entering new markets and capturing the new business that would strengthen his competitive position. He rightfully complained: "These activities are the heart of this business. Unless I get into these areas with both feet, my role as product manager is a joke." Management must make sure its product and market managers are positioned in the organization structure to have the status and access to key decision makers required to carry out their assignments. It is essential to avoid burying them beneath layers of organizational levels if they are to function effectively. In fact, many companies have moved their product and/or market managers out of the marketing department to a position reporting directly to the general manager so that they are not restricted by organizational lines. Although this is not the most common arrangement, it underscores the importance of positioning product and market managers as high in the organization as practical.

The Right Qualifications

The product-market manager concept simply will not work with anything less than outstanding people on the job. Product or market managers, more than anyone else, should influence the destinies of their product or market. All the line executives in the company have functional responsibilities that span all products or markets; product or market managers are the only ones with a full-time commitment to a particular product or market. Moreover, with no authority to order things done, they must convince line executives to act on the programs and ideas they develop. They can do this only if they are the most informed people in the company about the product, how it is manufactured, its underlying technology, and the needs of the marketplace. They must have imaginative yet practical ideas for meeting these market needs that are practically linked to the dynamics of the business, plus the personal skills to get their ideas accepted.

Managements often lose sight of these points in setting up or making product-market manager assignments and make mistakes like the following:

> In one company, four of the five incumbents were made product managers after they failed to make the grade in the field selling force.
>
> In another company, the market manager's compensation range was locked into the salary structure at such a low level that it was impossible to attract the caliber of person needed to do the job.
>
> In still another company, the pattern was to use the product manager position as a training ground for promising younger people to groom them for district sales management assignments.

The results were the same in all these cases: Those appointed to product or market manager positions did not have sufficient experience and business skills to do the job. In such situations, there is little justification for blaming the concept.

On the other hand, the difficulty of finding qualified people to fill product or market positions cannot be passed over lightly. One president put this problem in perspective when he said: "I have no doubt about the usefulness of the product manager concept. However, I do have doubts about our ability to find the paragons who can effectively fill these jobs. We have a hard enough time finding good general managers; now we must uncover people with comparable ability or potential at a starting salary level we can afford to pay." Actually, this overstates the case. A good product or market manager does not have to be an expert in everything that relates to the product. To start with, he or she has to have a solid appreciation of the product and how it is manufactured, what is important for success in the marketplace, and good business sense. The rest can be mastered as part of on-the-job training. Many companies have found that product or market manager jobs are the best possible proving ground for general management assignments. Every product or market manager is not going to graduate to general manager, but he or she has to have many of the requisite capabilities.

In short, then, those companies that have achieved outstanding results from their product or market managers have succeeded largely because they staffed the job with qualified people. A definition of "qualified" includes multiple abilities. The product or market manager must have—or must develop—superior product or market knowledge, management skills, and planning abilities. Even more important are other skills that are frequently overlooked. A demonstrated sense of business judgment, the personal skills to operate effectively on a staff basis, the faculty to deal effectively with a full range of business problems, and the verbal ability to articulate a point of view and persuade others to see it are also requisites for any product or market manager.

One company in the electronics industry recently achieved a major turnaround in its business chiefly as a result of settling for nothing less than recognized leaders in their fields for each of its product manager positions. This required changing the salary structure so that these managers were paid on a par with the number two person in the marketing department, and in certain cases even providing stock options to attract the very best people for these jobs. This increased costs, but management today is convinced that the company's markedly improved performance is attributable to this action and that it has been well worth the added investment. In another company, concerned about lagging growth in its major market, management drafted the person generally considered to be "the best commercial brain in the company" for the market manager position. This move made good sense, because the market area contributed nearly 50 percent of the company's profits.

Often, the established compensation range is not adequate to attract the caliber of manager needed. Consequently, there is an understandable tendency to settle for second best. But the odds are heavy against any company that does not stick to the standards established here. For effective product management depends, more than on anything else, on the skills of the individuals appointed to the jobs.

Adequate Training and Orientation

It should be obvious that the role of product or market manager is unique, and few come to it fully experienced. As a result, management must be prepared to provide for the thorough orientation and training of people appointed to product or market management positions. Those companies that have taken the time and effort to indoctrinate and train their product and market managers properly have received a real payoff in improved performance.

One such company has a three-part program for new product and market managers. In the first part of the program, the new product or market manager is given a list of specific first steps to be taken when beginning the assignment. The following six tasks (excerpted from the company's written program) illustrate the kind of startup activities the much longer list covers:

1. Study carefully all available descriptive literature about your position. Pay particular attention to the position description, especially that part which defines the role and relationships. It is up to you to become thoroughly familiar with the major responsibilities of the position. Obtain a clear understanding of your working relationships with other executives in the company. Use the "role and relationships" description as a basis for discussions with other executives to ensure complete understanding and agreement on the way you will work together.
2. Talk to the vice president of marketing about how you should manage your assigned product line. Since your role is an extension of the role of the vice president of marketing, you should become familiar with his ideas on: major problems related to the product line, significant opportunities for strengthening market position, overall marketing strategy, and internal strengths and weaknesses affecting the marketing of the product line.
3. Talk to the vice presidents of manufacturing, engineering, and finance about your product business. Be sure you establish a communication link with all these departments. Also, be sure you get a picture of their ideas for strengthening your product business. Finally, listen to any caveats they might have about things to avoid as you take on your new assignment.
4. Become familiar with the company's marketing planning and control process. Study the principles, elements, and steps in planning described in the planning guide (see description of second part of the company's program). Discuss with the planning director the technique, format, and timing involved in developing a product marketing plan.
5. Take steps to ensure that you will have adequate information available to you and that you know how to use it. Read the memorandum "Interpreting Control Reports to Pinpoint Trouble Spots" (see description of third part of the company's program), using it as a guide to discuss your needs with market research and the controller.
6. Develop a first-cut business plan for your product or market area. Review it with and obtain the endorsement of the vice president of marketing. Discuss it also with other key executives to ensure their understanding of the plan as the standard of executing programs and measuring performance during the ensuing period.

The new product or market manager who has a series of specific task assignments, beginning the first day of the job, stands a much better chance of getting the right start than the person who is left on his or her own to figure out how to get underway.

In the second part of the program, each product or market manager is coached in the fundamentals of planning. Here special emphasis is put on showing the manager:

What constitutes a plan, and what areas deserve major attention

How it should be developed and tied together with other departments' plans

How it relates to budgeting and other operating procedures

How it fits into the management process, including how it should be used once it is completed and approved

When and how it should be modified

In the third and final part of the program, a working guide aimed at helping the product or market manager carry out the role is developed and continuously updated. This guide focuses on the "how to" aspects of the product or market manager's job and covers explanations of such basic activities as these:

Developing the product strategy and plans

Recommending capital appropriations

Keeping abreast of the economics of the product's business

Working with engineering and manufacturing to interpret market requirements and develop the cost impact of manufacturing on product design alternatives

Interpreting sales and financial reports to pinpoint trouble spots and areas where attention is needed

Such a guide serves as a useful reference document for new and experienced product or market managers alike. As new ideas or improved procedures are developed, the manager is given the extracurricular assignment of developing a new guideline. The objective is to develop a handbook that will give the product or market manager a running start in mastering most of the knotty tasks within his or her sphere of responsibility.

Properly done, any one of the three parts to this program unquestionably requires some time and effort. And it would be wrong to think that every company should have a program this extensive. However, the example shatters the idea that training a product or market manager is impossible. Many companies could achieve a much higher level of performance by taking a cue from this program.

Appropriate Performance Measures

Because of the wide variations that exist in product or market manager assignments, it is difficult to agree on standards of performance that will provide a basis for evaluating how well the job is being carried out. Although product profitability and share of market performance are indicators that cannot be overlooked indefinitely (since, after all, the primary role of the product or market manager is to provide the specialized attention needed to improve these), it is not fair to hold product or market managers accountable for these factors on a short-term basis. Too many influences beyond their control contribute to profit and market share changes.

The following criteria are a fairer and much more realistic basis for evaluating how a product manager is performing over the short term:

1. Is he or she on top of varying market conditions and requirements so that he or she is able to interpret accurately the changing needs of the product or market business?
2. Does he or she draw together complete and imaginative plans for the product or market assignment that are acceptable to top management?
3. Do his or her plans include concrete programs for effecting required improvement in the product or market business?
4. Does he or she follow up and, if necessary, modify approved plans to see that product or market objectives are achieved?
5. Is he or she generally regarded by other functional executives as the most knowledgeable about product or market requirements for the area, and do they look to him or her for ideas on what they should do to meet product or market needs?

Ultimately, however, it is results that count. If results are not satisfactory after a product or market manager has been on the job for two years or more, the person probably should be replaced. The ability to plan, communicate, and follow up are certainly attributes. But in the final analysis profit growth is the hallmark of successful product or market management, and the product or market manager has to be measured against this standard.

WHEN BOTH PRODUCT AND MARKET MANAGERS ARE REQUIRED

As long as a company has a series of products that funnel into one market or a single product line that flows out into several markets, a single product manager or market manager can handle this responsibility. As Exhibit 16-3 shows, it is relatively easy to carve out a discrete area of responsibility for such a manager under these fairly simple product or market conditions. But because product and market proliferation have increased greatly in a large and growing number of industrial companies, many find themselves selling multiple products in multiple markets, with no neat product-market match. Rather, they have to cope with a crisscross of products and markets, which dramatically increases the complexity of the planning and management job to be done, as Exhibit 16-3 shows.

Under these circumstances, planning from only one perspective—product or market—tends to be self-defeating. Neither one nor the other can be downgraded or disregarded in the planning process without severe penalty. If product managers are chosen, each one is likely to concentrate on selling his or her assigned products, rather than on determining what it takes to serve the markets more effectively. In so doing, the managers will probably miss important opportunities in related products and services. Even more important, without sufficient focus on the market, the chances are good that the product lines will lag behind competitive offerings or even become obsolete, as the managers find themselves unable to keep up with changing user needs. If market managers are selected, each will tend to focus on meeting the requirements of his or her assigned market without regard for the impact that these actions or recommendations may have on the company's ability to meet the needs of other market areas with the same product line. Thus, if a company has exceptionally strong or persuasive managers covering one or two market

EXHIBIT 16-3

THREE PRODUCT-MARKET BUSINESS SITUATIONS

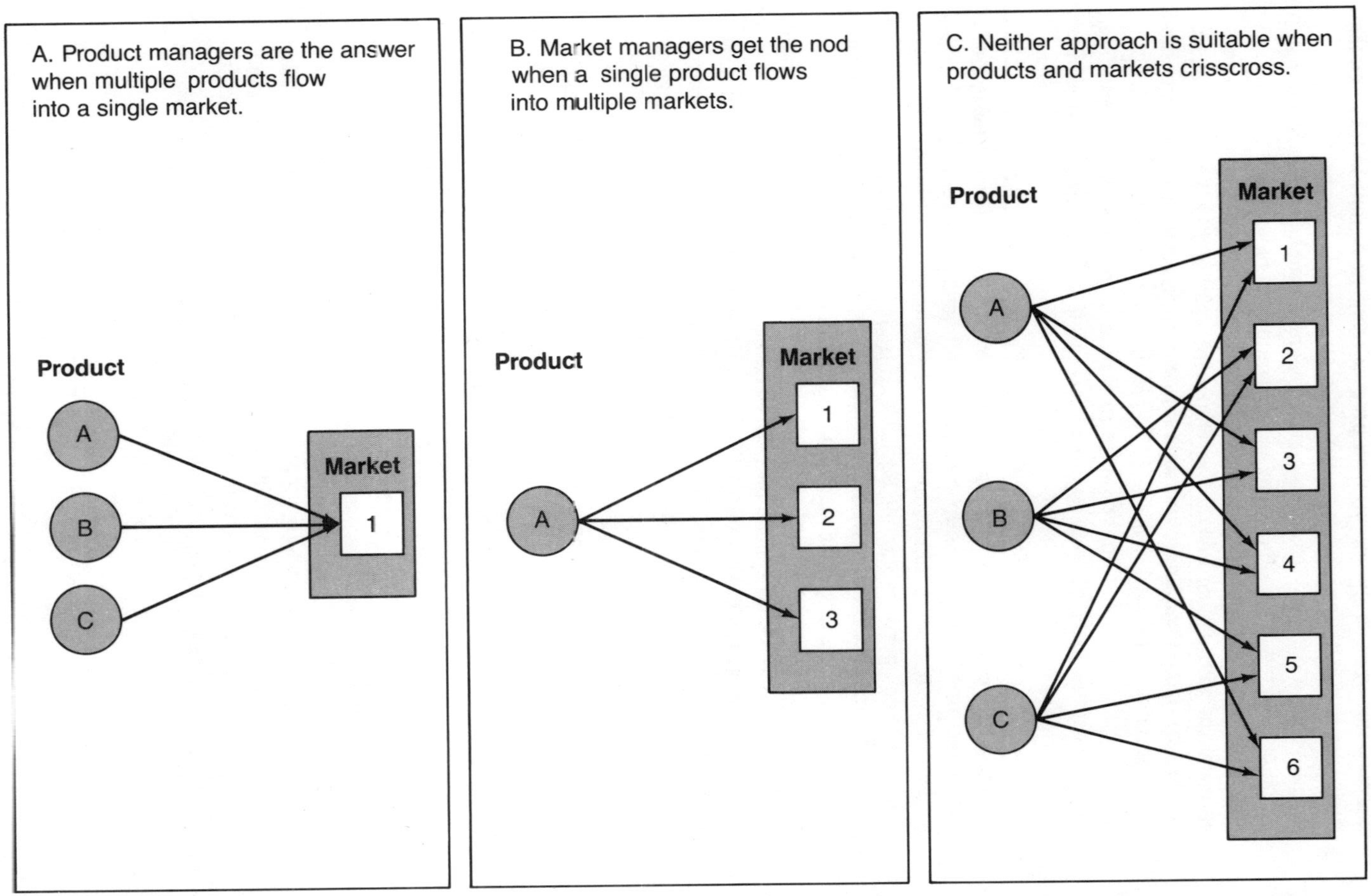

Source: B. Charles Ames, "Payoff from Product Management," *Harvard Business Review,* November–December 1963.

areas, it can very easily end up with product plans or actions in these markets that seriously jeopardize the company's position in other market areas.

How does a company ensure the right planning emphasis and balance in this kind of situation? A growing number of industrial companies have found that the only solution to this dilemma is to stop trying to decide between product or market managers and instead to use them both. Under this dual arrangement, market managers have an external focus toward the market and are responsible for determining what the company should do to be more responsive to market needs. The product manager's job is to seek a balanced response to the needs and opportunities in certain markets without jeopardizing the company's position in others and without placing an unfair burden on manufacturing and engineering.

This dual approach positions the center of gravity for a particular product or market business between these two managers. In so doing, it provides the basis for achieving (a) the market orientation that is so essential to competitive success in any business and (b) a system of checks and balances to ensure that unbridled enthusiasm for market response does not wreak havoc within the business. It is clear that a matrix management approach conceived this way offers a means of coping with the complex product-market situation that exists in many large-scale companies. However, when product and market managers are set up to work parallel with each other, the potential for conflict is automatically created. After all, the fundamental purpose of either of these two jobs is to fight for time and attention from engineering, manufacturing, and sales for their assigned products or markets. The potential for conflict is brought out sharply when both product managers and market managers are present in an organization. Let us look at the inner workings of this conflict more closely.

Since the market managers' primary responsibility is to identify and meet their market's needs, they will quite naturally seek modifications in the existing product or service package without regard for any other market or the functional difficulties they may create. And since the product managers are responsible for keeping their product lines responsive to the needs of all the company's markets in terms of costs, design or performance characteristics, pricing policy, service and warranty arrangements, and so on, they cannot bend indiscriminately to the requirements any one market manager perceives. But although it is inevitable, the conflict arising from the interaction of product managers and market managers should not be viewed as negative. In fact, this kind of conflict is specifically what the dual management concept is designed to produce, and it should be regarded as a positive force. If it is properly managed, the conflict should help uncover a multiplicity of market opportunities that would otherwise go unnoticed, and at the same time provide a mechanism for sorting through these opportunities so that the company's overall interests are best served.

Examples

Here are two examples of how this dual management approach has been employed.

THE ENGINE MANUFACTURER. An engine manufacturer found that its three product lines were losing ground in terms of both market and profit growth after a period of rapid expansion. Management saw the need for market managers because the products were sold in three separate markets, each with its own distinct characteristics and requirements. At the same time, there was a clear need for greater management attention to key products.

After a lot of give-and-take discussion, the president concluded that both product and market managers were necessary. Within a few months, the market managers had developed a host of ideas for modifications in the existing product and service packages as well as several promising ideas for new product entries. The product managers then screened these ideas, and the two groups, working together, were able to help the company develop a stronger product-market strategy that nearly doubled volume and earnings per share.

THE TEXTILE COMPANY. A textile fibers company, confronted with a similar situation, actually made the shift from product managers to market managers as the key planning unit. This company sold three basic fibers in several end-use markets with different characteristics and requirements, and management reasoned that a market focus on planning was more appropriate than a product focus. A chaotic situation arose, however, when plant and development managers discovered they could not possibly respond to all the requests coming to them from the market managers. As one plant manager put it: "Our production costs on product X have gone up by 12 percent because of all the short-term requests for additional stocking requirements. Also, we are running out of capacity for one of our most profitable products, and no plans are being formulated to add new capacity. It is a fine thing to be responsive to market needs, but someone had better watch out for product costs and capacity, or we will have a plant full of unprofitable business and will lose the chance to sell more of our profitable items."

Management then reinstated a product management group to work with the market managers. The product managers quickly took hold of the product planning problems that had led to the chaotic situation in plant and development operations. At the same time, the market managers provided the end-user orientation so essential to success in the marketplace. As a result of product and market manager cooperation, the company struck a better balance between control of its manufacturing process and market response and achieved a short-term profit pickup of several hundred thousand dollars and a much stronger market share position.

Who Does What

If management decides that this dual approach is appropriate, the next step is to decide how the roles of the two types of managers should be defined and how they should work together. By and large, product managers should be held accountable for all aspects of product line management, including long-term profitability. Market managers, on the other hand, should be held accountable for the long-term growth and profitability of their assigned markets. More specifically, the two roles can be defined as follows.

Market managers should concentrate on:

Developing a comprehensive understanding of customer and end-user operations and economics and specifying ways that the existing product or service package can be improved to provide a competitive edge.

Identifying related products and/or services that represent attractive opportunities for profitably enlarging the company's participation in the market through either internal development or acquisition.

Drawing together at regular intervals an organized summary of the most attractive opportunities in the marketplace, specifying what must be done internally to capitalize on them, and recommending a first-cut strategy for the business.

Developing a reputation for industry expertise among key customer and end-user groups and bringing this know-how to bear on the negotiation of major orders and on the training and development of field personnel.

Product managers should focus on:

Protecting the pricing integrity of their product—that is, seeing to it that the pricing policies and practices in one market do not jeopardize the company's position or profit structure in another.

Maintaining product leadership by making certain that product design, cost, and performance characteristics not only are broadly responsive to customer needs in all markets, but also are not inadvertently altered to meet the needs of one market at the expense of the company's position in another.

Ensuring that the product is responsive to market needs while at the same time avoiding changes that will clutter the engineering and production process with a proliferation of small-lot, custom, or special orders; in effect, they temper market managers' enthusiastic customer orientation with sober judgments on operating capability and economics.

Ensuring that production scheduling and capacity are intelligently planned to meet profitably the current and anticipated aggregate demand of various markets.

Providing the in-depth technical and/or product knowledge required to support selling efforts on major and complex applications.

The broad activities just cited are always the core of the job for both market and product managers. However, the makeup and importance of the company's various products and markets should determine exactly how the jobs are structured. Product managers invariably function on a full-time basis but may, of course, be given responsibility for more than one product. There is little latitude in structuring this position. The market manager's job, however, is quite a different matter. It may be structured in three different ways, depending on the number, importance, and geographic spread of the markets involved.

1. Most companies assign the market manager a full-time staff role, dividing the product and market planning job into two parts and setting up the two groups—product managers and market managers—in parallel, as shown in Exhibit 16-4(a). This first approach is popular because it is a natural evolution from either product or market managers and is the easiest to introduce. This is the approach when all the markets are equally important

to the company and the number to be covered is relatively small—say, four to eight. Under these circumstances, it is practical to have a full-time staff planner for each one.

2. Some companies give the market manager line sales responsibility as well as the staff planning assignment, as shown in Exhibit 16-4(b). This means that the market manager has direct responsibility for a group of salespeople who specialize in selling to the accounts that make up that market. Theoretically this second approach is best, since it gives one person combined responsibility for both planning and execution within each market area and thus makes it possible to hold him or her fairly accountable for results. It also ensures that he or she has firsthand knowledge of customer and market requirements and helps avoid ivory tower planning. But practically, its application is limited because it is often difficult to justify the degree of sales specialization inherent in this kind of arrangement. Although most companies can point to a cluster of accounts in certain geographic areas for which they could economically justify a specialist salesperson, to get national coverage they must inevitably turn to the general sales representative who sells all products to all markets. Accordingly, in most cases it simply is not feasible to work out an arrangement where the sales force can be divided neatly under several market managers.

3. Still other companies have used the market manager as a part-time planner. These companies add market planning assignments to the responsibility of senior salespeople, sales managers, or application engineers who have some expertise in a given end-use market. This compromise approach is normally followed by companies that deal in such a large number of markets they simply cannot afford to provide full-time market manager coverage for each one. For example, one company identified over 30 markets that needed to be brought into focus. Even after considering various ways these markets might be combined into planning assignments, the number of full-time market managers required could not be justified. Consequently, the company gave market planning assignments to selected salespeople who had special experience or a concentration of accounts in key markets.

Although these approaches to the market manager's job are described separately, they can be combined as necessary to meet the needs and structure of the marketplace. For example, one company was able to give two of its market managers line sales responsibility because there were groups of specialist salespeople that could logically be assigned to them. The company could also justify two additional part-time market manager assignments with the thought in mind that these positions could be upgraded to full-time assignments if the markets developed to any great extent.

System Changes

Management must change the information and planning systems to reflect the existence and needs of both managers. Product managers need detailed operating information (engineering standards, production schedules, and cost breakdowns) to perform their jobs effectively. Market managers must have access to cost information for all products sold in their markets and to detailed market and customer information. Ultimately, both managers should have profit and loss statements for their respective areas as a benchmark for evaluating performance.

EXHIBIT 16-4 ***TWO APPROACHES TO MEET THE NEEDS OF THE MARKETPLACE***

A. Market manager in staff capacity only . . .

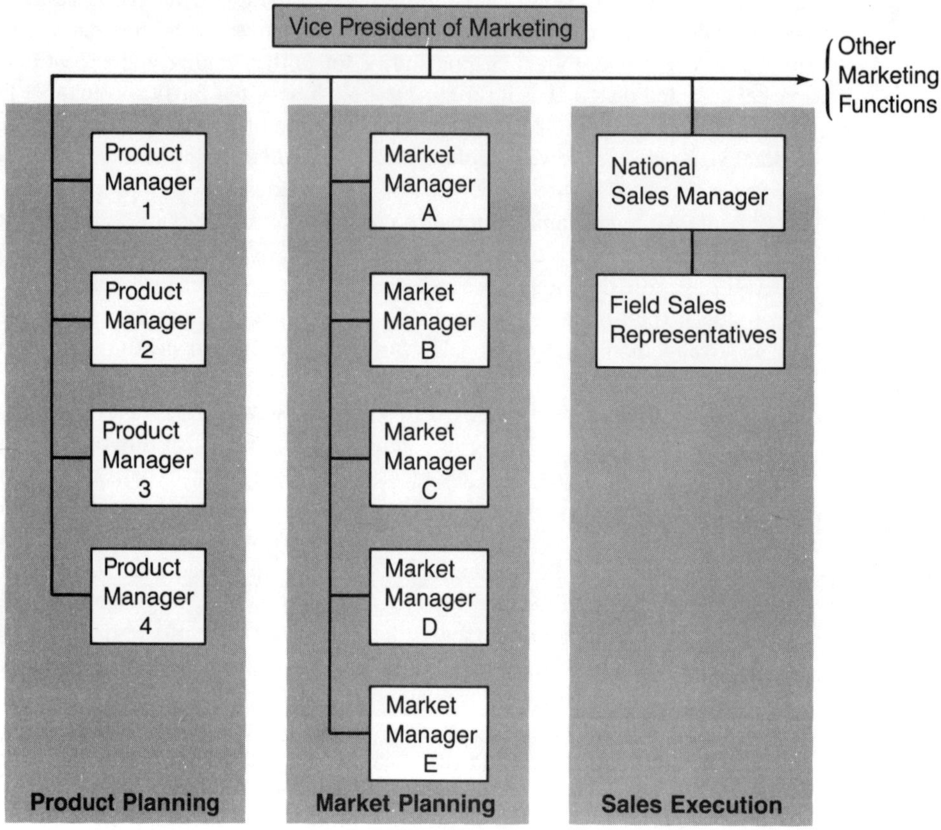

Source: Harvard Business Review, March–April 1971.

In many cases, the kind of cost, operating, and market information required for intelligent product and market planning either is not available or is in a form that is unusable. Correcting this situation may require a major effort (special research projects, restructuring of accounting information). Even with a modified information system, product and market managers also need a close working relationship with engineering, manufacturing, and finance so that they can secure the assistance necessary to interpret much of this information in the correct manner. Regardless of the effort involved, the information and assistance must be provided, or the concept does not stand a chance of getting off the ground.

On the planning side, two changes are necessary. One is a change in the way strategic plans are developed. Market managers should be given the responsibility for developing

B. . . . and with combined line and staff responsibility

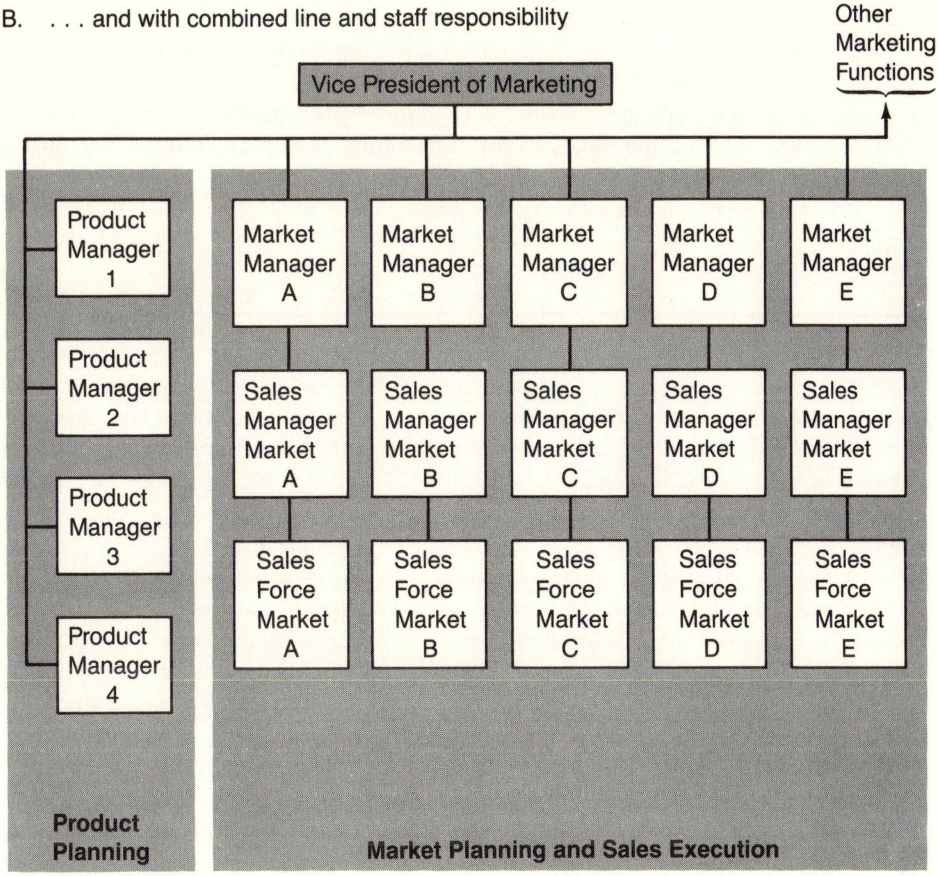

an overview of their market and a no-holds-barred set of recommendations for capitalizing on the opportunities they see. They should then review their ideas with the product managers concerned with their markets to determine what is feasible and what is not, as well as to gain agreement on a point of view that can be presented to other functional managers. From this point on, the process follows a normal planning pattern, with all functional managers collaborating to come up with a final recommendation for top management. The other change in planning has to do with the way top management reviews and responds to strategic recommendations. Basically, the planning system must be adjusted to cope with increased planning inputs. If the dual approach is successful, it should generate a vastly increased number of options and recommendations for building the business in various product and market segments.

One company generated some 20 different strategic options for building just one product-market business with different levels of resource commitment and payoff expectations. To cope with this avalanche of ideas, top managers had to draw extensively on their central planning staff and set aside substantial blocks of their own time to decide which options to accept and which to reject. This may be a unique situation, but bear in mind that the fundamental purpose of this dual management approach is to generate more ideas and recommendations for accelerating growth and profits. Top management must properly evaluate and respond to this flow of ideas to avoid frustration and discouragement in the product and market groups that could cripple the concept.

SUMMARY

There are no ready-made rules to guarantee effective product or market management, but certain specific steps can be taken to avoid the common pitfalls. First, weigh the concept against other organization alternatives to make sure that it offers the best means of fulfilling the needs of the operation. Above all, make certain it is not being installed simply because it has worked for a competitor or some other company. After the pros and cons of each alternative have been considered, the case for product management may not be as clear-cut as it seemed at first glance. And since it is a difficult concept to make work, it should be chosen only when it is demonstrably the best alternative.

Even in those situations where all conditions are favorable, whether or not a product or market manager is successful depends largely on whether or not top management creates the proper environment. In the last analysis, all this requires is attention to fundamentals: starting with the right people, carefully defining their planning responsibilities, structuring their jobs properly, providing the necessary guidance and direction, and applying appropriate performance measures.

Using both product and market managers provides a basis for achieving the kind of product and market planning necessary in most multibusiness companies. The concept unquestionably means added staff, added expense, and greater complexity in the management process. And making the concept work will probably add problems for most companies. But if a company with a crisscross of products and markets balks at attempting this organization approach simply because it sounds too complex or because it will add to marketing overhead, it is missing a real bet. For it has been the experience of those who have tried it that this concept can provide a significant payoff in increased market opportunities, stronger competitive actions, and profits that far outweigh either the added costs involved or the difficulties of making it work.

17

Guidelines for Effective Implementation

Frank Wilson had just finished two years as division vice president of marketing. During this time, he and selected members of his management team had attended several management development courses and read numerous books and articles on the broad subject of management. Despite these efforts to improve their management skills, their performance had been less than satisfactory. The following deficiencies had been emphasized in Frank's latest management review.

Sales were close to plan, but profits were far from expectations.

New product introductions were lagging.

Costs and expenses were over budget.

The organization did not seem to have either the managerial capabilities or sense of urgency to correct these problems.

Frank was particularly concerned about one comment made by the boss during the review meeting:

> One problem you have, Frank, is that you haven't focused on the substance of what it takes to be a good manager and get things done. My advice to you is to stop going to so many management seminars and start to work on the fundamental management problems that exist in your organization. You've allowed politics to come into the picture, you've too many mediocre people in key jobs, and too many people spend too much time in committees that never seem to get anything done.

Later he sought advice from John McSweeney, who had retired from the company but had been a very successful marketing executive when the company had performed at its peak. After listening to Frank, John made the following comment:

> Frank, I'm afraid you and your management team have gotten too enamored with a lot of management trappings and have failed to do the hard work required to be effective. Being a good manager is a tough job and requires many tough decisions. It sounds to me like you have listened to a lot of people tell you about good management methods, but you haven't made the effort to make sure they are followed in your organization.

What *does* it take to be a good manager?

How can Frank keep politics from disrupting the organization?

If Frank is to replace his "mediocre" people, what qualities should he seek in job candidates?

What personal qualities suggest that an employee is worth developing for the future?

Industrial marketing has little chance for success without effective management throughout the organization. To some extent, this point applies to consumer marketing as well. Consumer marketing, however, is more of a discrete function that can often succeed despite weak management, if enough creative genius and money are poured into the key marketing activities. Conversely, marketing in the industrial world is more of a philosophy designed to guide the way the business is managed. This in turn dictates the need for very strong management at all levels, since this marketing philosophy must permeate the entire organization if it is to serve as the cutting edge of the business.

Business reference libraries are full of good articles and books about management theory, techniques, and requirements; management seminars and management programs abound in universities and graduate schools. We do not in any sense intend to duplicate or compete with these efforts in this book. We do believe, however, that many of the management principles emphasized in the literature and in management programs seem to be too easily forgotten. In fact, we submit that many of the problems facing American business today are the direct result of ineffective management that has strayed from some basic principles that should be the very foundation of the management process in any organization.

The purpose of this chapter is to reaffirm briefly these principles without attempting to review all the points one could make about what it takes to be an effective manager. To do this, we have attempted to distill from the literature and our own experience a number of practical guidelines we believe any manager must follow to be effective. As far as we know, these guidelines have never been explicitly defined in other books or articles. At least we have never seen them. Nor do we believe they have been taught or covered explicitly in any school for managers. We believe firmly that real understanding of, and commitment to, these guidelines must be chiseled into one's makeup through real life experience in management situations until they become as deeply ingrained as any other fundamental beliefs that affect the way we intuitively think and act.

For purposes of organization, we have divided the ground rules into three groups that we believe represent the core responsibilities of every manager's job:

1. *Planning and implementation.* Determining specifically what needs to be done and how it will be accomplished and then following up to ensure that everyone understands his or her role and does his or her part to accomplish results.
2. *Organization and staffing.* Determining the number and kinds of people needed to accomplish the objectives of the organization and dividing the tasks among them.
3. *People development.* Determining and carrying out the actions necessary to ensure a continuous upgrading of skills within the organization and an infusion of new people required to continually strengthen the organization's capabilities.

Obviously, a variety of activities can fall under these core responsibilities, and the activities undoubtedly vary in importance from situation to situation. In our judgment, however, these three core responsibilities are always the heart of any manager's job whenever and wherever the management of people and tasks to accomplish certain objectives is required. Let's look first at some important ground rules that underlie the manager's planning and implementation responsibilities.

PLANNING AND IMPLEMENTATION

Ground Rule 1

Good planning is the key to successful results for any business operation. Operating without a plan is like flying blind or playing Russian roulette; far too much is left to chance. To be of any value, the business plan must be down on paper. If it is not in writing, it is fair to assume that a quality plan simply does not exist, no matter how enthusiastically a proposition might be described. The discipline of committing a plan to writing is the only way to eliminate the holes and vagaries that are virtually certain to be present when a plan is "ad libbed." Although management should insist on written plans, it is essential to avoid becoming so enamored of flowery prose or format that substance is lost. Any plan, regardless of its complexity, can be put down in a few paragraphs. Good planning requires good thinking and substance; eloquence and form are not substitutes.

It is also essential to understand that planning alone never accomplished anything; somebody has to do something to get results. The danger of becoming so enamored with planning that nothing gets done is very real. As a general rule, most of the benefits from planning typically accrue from the first 30 to 50 percent of the effort. The remaining time and effort devoted to planning simply make people more comfortable and enable them to avoid getting on with what really needs to be done. Failure to achieve planned results means that the plan was no good to begin with, or that execution was bad. Either way, it is the manager's responsibility. Although it is unrealistic to expect that every plan will be achieved, the organization's success depends ultimately on its ability to achieve planned results. Any manager who repeatedly fails to create good plans or fails to overcome the difficulties that stand in the way must be moved aside so that someone who has these abilities can be given a chance.

A key point to remember is that the management task is much more difficult when the responsibility for planning and execution is divided between two people or groups. If planned results are not achieved, the person or group responsible for execution can argue that they did a good job but the plan was not sound. Conversely, the person or group responsible for planning will ultimately argue that the plan was sound but execution was weak. The manager in this case is caught in the middle, and assuming both parties or groups report to the manager, he or she is the person who will be held accountable. For this reason, the smart manager always tries to assign a combined responsibility for planning and execution to an individual or group and also seeks to push this responsibility as far down in the organization as possible.

Ground Rule 2

Every manager must be tough-minded in identifying issues, and evaluating problems or proposals. A manager should approach an evaluation of any situation with an open mind, but always maintain a questioning or challenging point of view. Pat solutions or easy answers are seldom correct. And solutions or answers based solely on experience or "gut feel" are most often wrong.

For this reason, management should insist that all complex issues, analyses, and recommendations be committed to writing and supported by hard facts. This doesn't mean that every idea spawned by the organization has to be committed to writing; there is no need for a paper avalanche. However, as stated earlier, committing one's thoughts to writing is the only way to ensure good thinking. It helps to avoid the faulty thinking that so often occurs when someone "fires from the hip." Anyone who cannot get his or her thoughts into writing in a way that makes sense to the reader hasn't really thought through what he or she wants to say or do.

Ground Rule 3

Once a plan is approved, it is the manager's job to ensure that everyone in the organization has a deep-rooted sense of commitment to achieve results. This is a crucial point, since the failure of some to meet their commitments is the chief reasons so many plans are unsuccessful. Most commitments are broken because of an attitude of always finding an excuse or a rationale for not doing something that was supposed to be done. For this reason, management should insist that all commitments be met once they are made and be critical of anyone who does not meet them. These people must understand that they have fallen down on their jobs and damaged the entire group's credibility and ability to perform. It makes no difference whether the commitment seems trivial (to return a telephone call or pass on certain information by a certain time) or crucial (to meet a project completion or delivery date). Once made, the commitment must be met.

Unless management rigorously enforces this attitude, commitments will be broken, planned results will not be achieved, and the organization's credibility will suffer. Credibility is a precious asset, both for the manager and the organization. Without it, neither the manager nor the organization can be effective (see the box).

Ground Rule 4

One of the most difficult tasks of any manager is to keep priorities straight. It is very easy for managers to duck current problems or issues that are often unpleasant to face by shifting their thoughts to longer-range problems or new opportunities. Falling into this trap is a mistake that is certain to lead any manager into major difficulties. To avoid it, managers should always follow these priorities:

1. Stay on top of day-to-day activities to minimize surprises that can wreck the business, and keep senior management informed of all developments, good or bad.

HOW IS COMMITMENT LIKE HAM AND EGGS?

In the business world the word *commitment* is not one to take lightly. The truth of this point was driven home in the following situation:

The president of a U.S. based telecommunications company had reached an agreement with a bank in England to buy a company—from an estate for which the bank was a trustee—for a price based on planned earnings for the year. The president and his team spent the better part of two days visiting top mangement of the English company and touring the operation. The products, facilities, manufacturing methods, and technology all seemed to be satisfactory. Sales and profit, however, were about 10 percent below plan for the year to date, and since there were only four months remaining in the year, the president naturally was concerned whether earnings to justify the sale price would be achieved. Management of the English concern assured the president that they could make up the gap that now existed, but he was not entirely satisfied.

At a final meeting between both management groups, the president continued to have nagging doubts about the English firm's ability to achieve its planned earnings. Because the matter was so important, he asked the same question several times at different times during the meeting. "Are you guys really committed to actually achieving your sales and earnings plan?" Each time he emphasized the word *commitment,* and each time he was assured that the plan would be achieved. After he repeated the question for the fourth time, one of the English managers said, "You are obviously driving at something with your repeated question about our commitment. I know what the word *commitment* means, but I am not sure I understand what you mean when you use that term in the context you are using it." Before he could respond, another English manager spoke up. "Actually it's quite simple and analogous to 'ham and eggs.'" Noting that his analogy had brought a quizzical look to everyone's face, he then went on to say, "In the case of ham and eggs the chicken is involved but the pig is committed. Isn't that the way you are using the word *commitment* in your question to us?" The president responded quickly, "That is a perfect analogy. It reflects exactly what I mean."

2. Achieve planned results that have been approved by management.
3. Then, and only then, start to plan for longer-term growth and development.

Every manager typically has more things to do than he or she can possibly get done. Slotting tasks under these priorities is the only way to put "first things first."

Ground Rule 5

Every manager must keep the surprises out of the operation. Most business surprises are a reflection of not knowing or anticipating what is going on, and this gap simply cannot be tolerated in today's dynamic business environment. To avoid surprises, a manager must be active, not reactive. An active manager seeks to make things happen rather than getting caught off base and then scrambling to salvage a situation that could have been avoided if he or she had stayed on top of the operation. Active managers never drift into decisions or actions or permit them to be taken by default. They know what is going on and what they are doing at all times.

To be an active manager, a person must know the details of the operation. The greatest threat to the business is past success that tends to breed complacency. For this reason, active managers continually ask hard, probing questions even when the business is doing well. They also cut across or through organization lines to get the information they need. In doing this they must be careful not to interfere with lines of authority or the decision-making process. However, they communicate freely and openly with everyone in the organization and encourage everyone to communicate with them. They know this is the only way they will really know what is going on. Any manager who tries to get by without knowing the details of the operation is bound to be superficial and can only be reactive because he or she doesn't know enough to take any kind of action until a crisis develops. There is no way this kind of manager can succeed. One crisis will lead to another, and the whole operation will ultimately drift out of control.

Ground Rule 6

No individual manager should ever seek or accept the credit for good results. Good results flow from a successful team effort, and the whole team deserves the credit. Conversely, however, every manager must shoulder the responsibility when the organization fails to perform. Poor results occur when the manager has not done a good job of planning, staffing, organizing, and following up, which we have stressed are inescapable core responsibilities.

Now let's look at some basic ground rules that affect organization and staffing.

ORGANIZATION AND STAFFING

Ground Rule 1

It is essential to recognize that it is the quality and capabilities of people, not the genius of the structure, that makes any organization work or fail. Blindly following organization concepts or principles simply because they are theoretically correct or because they have proved successful elsewhere is a sure route to wasted talents and efforts and inadequate results. Capable people who are fair minded and dedicated can make almost any organization structure work. Conversely, self-centered, politically motivated people or marginal performers will not be effective under any arrangement. There is nothing more useless or damaging to morale and results than shuffling the same names among different boxes and titles if the people involved do not have the necessary skills or personal attributes. It accomplishes nothing, and everyone in the organization generally knows it. Even more damaging, it deludes management into thinking it has taken positive action when in fact it has not really faced up to the problems.

This does not mean that organization changes should never be made. Of course, they are necessary to better utilize talents, streamline the decision-making process, achieve better planning and control, reduce costs, and so on. But the effective managers ensure that they do not fall into the common trap of tinkering with the organization as a means of escaping or putting off fundamental personnel problems that are difficult or uncomfortable to face.

Ground Rule 2

The management pyramid in any organization narrows quickly and limits the opportunities available to test and nurture fresh talent. This means that a sufficient number of lower-level management positions must be preserved as a proving ground to test and provide experience for high-potential individuals who appear to have capacity for growth. Turnover should not be considered a problem in these positions unless it is excessively high or too low. Clogging all the lower rungs on the management ladder with men or women who are not going any further undermines the whole organization. It creates a pool of mediocrity that is the logical source for meeting organization needs. More important, it causes good people to become frustrated because they are blocked from upward movement. Unless this frustration is relieved, they will ultimately leave because they are not given an opportunity to take on added responsibility in a time frame that is reasonable to them.

Ground Rule 3

Every manager should have a backup person who is potentially better qualified for the job than he or she is. If a manager concludes that he or she does not have anyone in the organization who has the necessary potential, he or she must give top priority to bringing in someone who does. This does not mean that the staff should automatically be enlarged. In most cases, it means that one or two individuals within the organization who do not have the necessary qualifications or potential should be replaced by someone of this caliber. Ensuring this kind of backup is crucial. No manager has a right to feel he or she has done a good job if a logical successor is not clearly visible or if a succession plan is not clear.

Ground Rule 4

Everyone in the organization should always know what is expected of him or her, how his or her assignment fits into the whole, and how his or her performance will be measured. This means that each individual should have a set of specific results that he or she agrees to accomplish within a certain time frame so that there is no confusion about what he or she is supposed to do. To be meaningful, these objectives should be defined in measurable terms so that there can be no misunderstanding or argument about what was accomplished and what was not. Accomplishment of these objectives should then serve as the standard of performance to determine how well the individual performs.

The organization's whole system of rewards and penalties should reinforce this management by objective (MBO) concept. Payoff should always be for achieving planned results and not for effort alone. In other words, those who achieve results should receive significant recognition and reward; those who fall short must expect more limited rewards.

Ground Rule 5

As many individuals advance in age, they reach a point where their job responsibilities tend to move beyond their energy level or capabilities. This is a natural development and should be expected. Unless someone figures out a way to halt or reverse our life process, it will happen to most of us. Senior management and the organization have an obligation to men and women who have served loyally and now encounter this situation. They should be treated fairly and be given assignments where they have an opportunity to make a continuing contribution. But if they can no longer pull their own weight on mainstream assignments, they must be moved aside. It is not fair to the organization to allow them to continue as weak links, and it certainly is not fair to the incumbents who must struggle to keep up.

Conversely, advancing age alone should not be regarded as a reason for excluding anyone from consideration for added responsibility. There is nothing more wasteful than pushing an experienced man or woman to the sidelines simply because the calendar has advanced, when he or she still has the energy and capability to succeed.

Ground Rule 6

Managers must always be alert for misfits who are almost certain to creep into the organization, no matter how carefully people are screened or evaluated, and move quickly and decisively to weed them out. We have used the term "misfits" purposely, because these people often represent a destructive force in the organization. They should not be confused with individuals who depart from the norm to create healthy organizational improvements. Rather, they are the "rotten apples" in the barrel that destroy the whole. Three types of misfits are especially damaging to any organization:

1. Anyone who does not have the integrity or intellectual honesty necessary to command absolute trust.
2. "Politicians" who always have their fingers in the air to see which way the wind blows and are more interested in making the right move than in doing or saying what is right.
3. Organization bullies who are bastards to their subordinates and sycophants to their superiors.

Not moving quickly on anyone who fits any of these descriptions detracts from the manager's credibility. Most people in the organization know who the "misfits" are and think less of the manager's capability or integrity if he or she permits them to remain.

Ground Rule 7

Although widely used in many organizations, most committees and committee assignments are a complete waste of time. They may be an ideal vehicle for government and other bureaucratic organizations that are most interested in the appearance of getting something done and in syndicating the risk on tough decisions and issues. However, no committee ever made a decision, accepted a commitment, or developed a program for which it could really be held accountable. And committee members almost inevitably find a way to avoid criticism of their specific role by pointing to what other committee members did or said.

For these reasons, a committee may be an appropriate vehicle for brainstorming sessions to spark new ideas, to ensure cross-functional coordination on major projects, or where an oversight function is required and it is unfair to assign the responsibility to an individual (such as an audit committee of a board). However, in the mainstream of business management, where accountability for actions and decisions is essential, committees should play a very limited role.

These are the ground rules to keep in mind as organization and staffing considerations are weighed. Now let's look at some ground rules to ensure a continuing stream of talent for the organization.

PEOPLE DEVELOPMENT

Ground Rule 1

A primary task of every manager is to create an attractive work environment for the people in the organization so they can perform, develop, and fulfill their aspirations. This doesn't mean that the manager should try to make everyone happy or to make all the tasks easier. Rather, the manager seeks to develop a work environment that has these characteristics:

1. Everyone speaks and acts with absolute honesty and integrity at all times. It is not easy to ensure that these principles are always followed, particularly in larger companies where effective communication is often difficult and where the chance for different interpretations of policies and situations is very great. It is management's job to ensure everyone understands that honesty and integrity are full-time principles that cannot be turned on and off to suit one's desires and needs of the moment. Management must make it clear that sticking to these principles comes first, even if it means sacrificing some things (such as new business, added sales, increased earnings) that are obviously to the company's advantage. There is no way management can compromise on these principles and still create and maintain an outstanding work environment.
2. There is open communication up, down, and across the organization. Everyone recognizes both the right and necessity to be open and constructively critical of things that can be improved. No "sacred cows" are tolerated. Superiors are willing to really listen to the other points of view, and are willing to say "I'm wrong" if facts and logic show that this is the case.
3. There is a genuine interest in getting problems out on the table and correcting them, rather than pinpointing blame or scurrying to keep one's "shirttails" clean. Everyone knows his or her individual assignments, but works hard and effectively as a team member. Since team results are the goals, no one tries to be a hero or make a grandstand play.

There is always an air of excitement in the organization that one can sense when he or she is on a winning team, and it is the manager's responsibility to create this excitement. Unless this kind of environment exists, good people will leave and only the mediocre will remain. And any organization staffed with the mediocre is certain to lose.

Ground Rule 2

Managers should recognize that the most frequent and insidious personnel mistake they can make is to live too long with marginal or poor performers. Most managers delude themselves into thinking that they are being fair by allowing these individuals to continue and that somehow time will correct the situation. Nothing could be farther from the truth. Basic personality flaws or skill deficiencies generally do not get corrected with time. It is totally unfair to the individual and a reflection of weak management to reach an agonizing conclusion that someone cannot do the job after he or she has been on it for several years.

As a general rule, it should not take more than six months to a year to determine whether someone can perform on a given assignment. The capable manager is tough-minded in performance evaluations, "ruthless" in decisions on who can perform and who cannot, and then eminently fair and decisive in the way he or she carries these decisions out.

Ground Rule 3

No individual in the organization should ever be damned simply because he or she is "too ambitious," "too aggressive," "too impatient," or "too demanding," as long as he or she is a good thinker and fair and straightforward in his or her dealings and actions. Although people described in these terms are typically cast in an unfavorable light by personnel appraisal systems, they actually represent the kind of people that should be advanced or developed. They may be more difficult to manage, but they will make things happen for the better and enhance the organization's chances for success.

It is those who are too easygoing, too willing to compromise principles to avoid conflict, or more interested in being liked than getting things done who should come under fire. They are the weak links in an organization that makes it impossible to develop a strong team or achieve outstanding results.

Ground Rule 4

Every manager should ensure that all people in the organization know exactly where they stand and what their career outlook is at all times, even if it hurts. This doesn't mean that people should expect to have their career path mapped out for them, or to be promised future promotions if they do this or do that. It does mean, however, that people should know whether they are performing well or poorly in their current assignment and whether they are regarded as having the potential for future growth.

There is nothing kind about glossing over weaknesses an individual could correct if he or she were made aware of them. Nor is there anything kind about allowing someone to think that he or she is doing better than he or she really is or has a greater opportunity in

EVALUATING HONESTLY: IT'S ONLY FAIR

When managers are reluctant to be as frank or honest as they should in their discussions with employees about performance and opportunities for personal growth, situations like the following can easily develop.

The new president of a large electrical products manufacturer decided to travel and work with a half dozen of the company's sales engineers to develop a better understanding of the company's customers and selling requirements. He was particularly impressed with one of the younger sales engineers who had graduated from Lehigh University and had been with the company for three and a half years. This young man had an outstanding academic and extracurricular record, was very personable, and obviously very interested in moving into a sales management position. He told the president that he enjoyed his work with the company very much and that his only disappointment so far was that he had not been given a district manager's position that had opened up. That position had been given to another salesman who had been with the company for about five years. Although disappointed, he was still enthusiastic about his future with the company. He explained, "My regional manager assured me that I would be a very eligible candidate when the next opening occurred."

That evening the president had dinner with the regional manager to discuss the events of the day. Among other things, he complimented the regional manager on the quality of the sales engineers he had met and noted that he was particularly impressed with the young man from Lehigh University. He went on to say how enthused this young man was about the company and the opportunity he saw to become a district manager in the near term. The president was more than a little surprised at the regional manager's response. "Frankly, I don't see him as a near term candidate. He has too much to learn. Moreover, there is some question in my mind whether he is not better off in a career selling position." Since this didn't square with what the sales engineer had said, the president made it a point to get the young salesman together with the regional manager the next morning. During this discussion, it was obvious that the regional manager did not want to tell the sales engineer about his limitations as directly as he had told the president. After the regional manager made several vague comments about the salesman's performance and potential, the president brought the matter to a head by stating in very blunt terms the way he understood the regional manager's position and asked if that was correct. The regional manager responded "yes" and a look of disappointment was apparent on the young sales engineer's face.

The young sales engineer subsequently resigned from the company and later became associated with another major equipment manufacturer where he is now the senior sales officer of the company. While the experience with the regional manager and the president may have been painful for the sales engineer, it helped him on to a career path that was ultimately more successful for him.

the organization than is actually the case. There is no reason to be rude or inconsiderate in explaining where deficiencies exist, but the explanation must be clear and straightforward. Failing to be clear or completely honest can easily hurt someone's chances to become an effective contributor and may even jeopardize that person's career. No manager has the right to do that (see the box).

Ground Rule 5

Finally, every manager must understand that inherited characteristics or background have nothing whatsoever to do with an individual's effectiveness. Managers cannot be influenced or even notice whether an individual is black or white, young or old, Christian or Jewish, male or female, an Ivy Leaguer or someone from the ghetto. Rather, managers must concentrate an evaluation on the things that really count:

1. Who has faced the problems squarely? Who has the guts to tell it like it is? Who does not?
2. Who is an effective contributing team member? Who is not?
3. Who has and can articulate good ideas? Who cannot?
4. Who produces results? Who gets the job done? Who does not?

Managers who concentrate on personal characteristics and do not give sufficient consideration to the things that really count are going to lose. Competition and the whole world will pass them by, led by those who know what it takes to succeed.

SUMMARY

There is nothing new or particularly sophisticated about any of the points covered in this chapter. They have been recognized and followed by good managers for years. They are based directly on common sense, logic, and a sense of fair play, which we believe are the underpinnings of effective management in any situation.

None of these ground rules is hard to accept; the difficulty develops in trying to follow them. Doing so requires managers to dig deeper into problems, to stay on top of more details, to make more difficult decisions, and to take more uncomfortable actions than many people care to do. We don't claim that following these ground rules alone is any guarantee of management or marketing success. A host of other factors weigh heavily in each situation. We do submit, however, that any manager's chances for success are greatly reduced if he or she does not follow these guidelines and that there is virtually no chance of a successful marketing effort if they are not broadly followed throughout the organization.

Name Index

Subject Index